GEOMETRY AND ARCHITECTURE IN ISLAMIC JERUSALEM

A STUDY OF THE ASHRAFIYYA

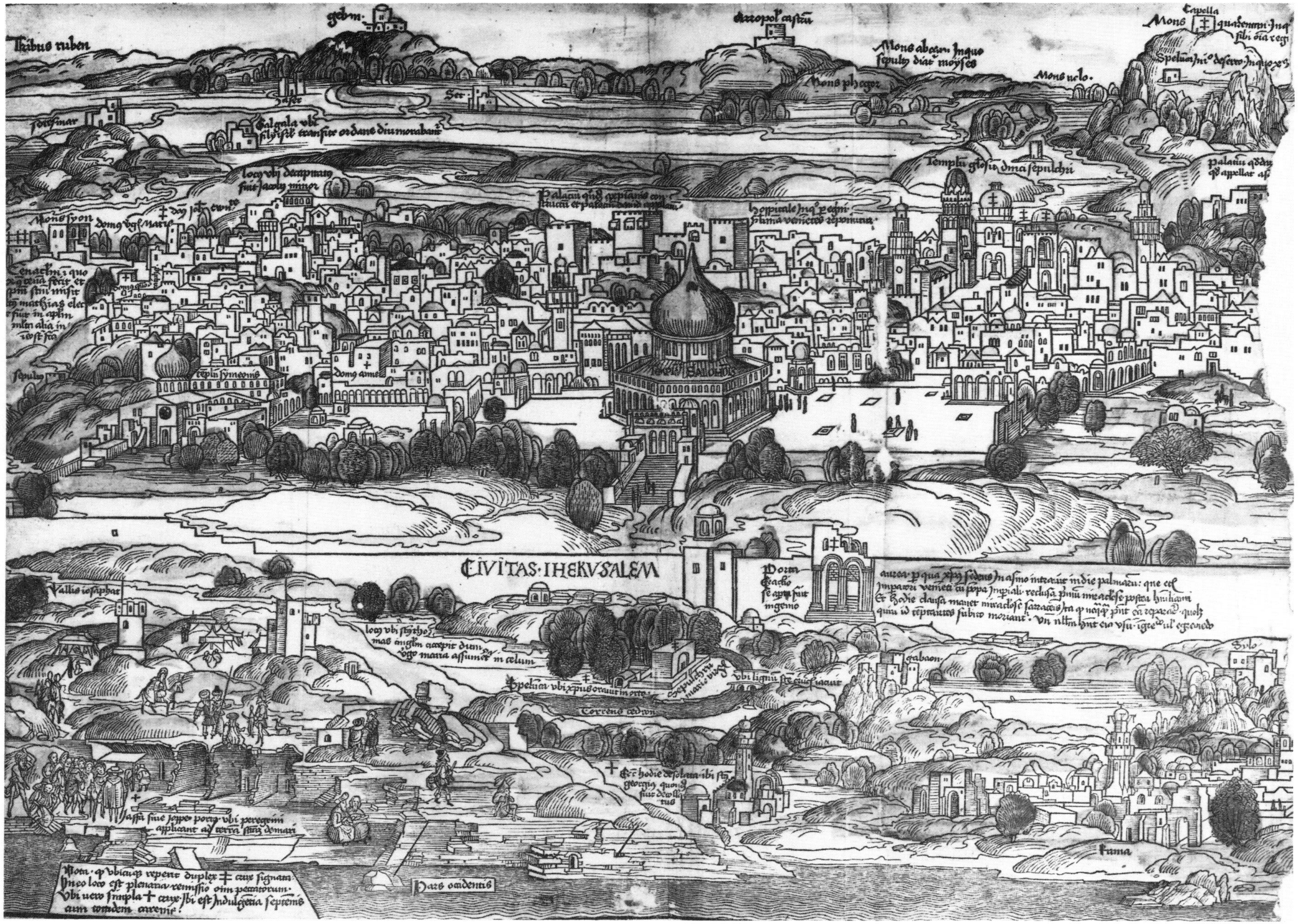

Plate 1 Jerusalem in 1486, from Bernhard of Breydenbach, *Peregrinationes in Terram Sanctam* (Bodleian Library, Oxford)

GEOMETRY AND ARCHITECTURE IN ISLAMIC JERUSALEM
A STUDY OF THE ASHRAFIYYA

ARCHIE G WALLS

SCORPION PUBLISHING LTD
WORLD OF ISLAM FESTIVAL TRUST

First published in 1990 by
Scorpion Publishing Ltd, Victoria House,
Buckhurst Hill, Essex, England

ISBN 0 905906 89 6

Editor: Leonard Harrow
Design: Zena Flax
Typeset in Linotype Plantin
Printed on Huntsman Superwhite Cartridge 115 gsm
Printed and bound in England by Biddles, Guildford.

CONTENTS

NOTE

The spelling of transliterated words and names from the Arabic follows a system based on that used in *Levant*.

Where dates of the Hijra and Christian eras are shown together, the Hijra date comes first.

The bibliographical details of the sources used are given in the notes. There is so little work immediately relevant to this study that no separate bibliography is given. The only work of direct architectural relevance to be added, which can be regarded as of particular use to the study, is Prisse d'Avennes, Achille C. T. E., *L'Art arabe d'après les monuments du Kaire depuis le VIIe siècle jusqu'à la fin du XVIIIe*, 4 vols, Paris, 1877.

ACKNOWLEDGEMENTS

The view of Jerusalem in plate 1 and the detail, plate 16, from Bernhard of Breydenbach, *Peregrinationes in Terram Sanctam*, 1486 (S.Seld.d.9), are reproduced with the permission of the Bodleian Library, Oxford. The publishers acknowledge with gratitude permission to reproduce plate 14 from the Creswell Archive, Ashmolean Library, Oxford. Efforts to locate the copyright owner of plates reproduced here as 12, 17, 18, taken from Tarchi, *L'Architettura e l'Arte Musulmane in Egitto e nella Palestina*, vol. 2, Torino, n.d. (plates 100, 97 bottom, 98 top), and plates 10, 11, 15, reproduced from *The Mosques of Egypt*, vol. II, (plates 125, 127, and 128), published by The Survey of Egypt, Giza, 1949, have been unsuccessful, and anyone with a claim should contact the publishers.

The publishers and author are grateful for the support in the preparation of this publication of Mrs C Hutt, in memory of her late son, the Islamic art historian Antony Hutt, a good and constant friend to both publishers and author.

The author expresses his deepest thanks to his wife, Celia, for her unselfish support in preparing the manuscript. Without her encouragement, diligence and many hours of tedious typing, it would never have reached its final form.

Chapter I
INTRODUCTION

The Physical Setting

Revered by the three monotheistic faiths, Jerusalem has very much the appearance of the oriental city. High fortified walls and towers contain the narrow streets that provide welcome shade from the strong Mediterranean sun. Sometimes winding, and at other times stepped, the streets are frequently spanned by vaults or arches to create numerous sections, each with its individual character. In one section gold and silver jewellery may be sold from small vaulted booths that open directly on to the street; in another textiles may be sold; and not far away, in another section flanked by tall walls with few windows, courtyard houses or whole monastic communities may be found, intermingled with medieval Islamic monuments. **fig. I/1**

However, whichever route one takes after entering the City, one is automatically drawn to the Ḥaram al-Sharīf, a great open rectilinear area in total contrast to the fabric of the rest of the City which is so closely knit. This holy enclosure has for the last thirteen centuries or so been the Third Shrine of Islam, and near its centre and set upon an elevated terrace is the octangular Dome of the Rock, with its splendid dome and colourful exterior. The Ḥaram is a tranquil place set aside from the busy streets. It is imbued with that serenity and peace that comes only to a holy site—the result of the millions of pious pilgrims who have prayed to and contemplated their God.

The views from the upper terrace of the Ḥaram are breathtaking: to the east across the Kedron Valley rises the Mount of Olives, whilst at a greater distance the Hill of Evil Council can be seen to the south. In addition to these natural beauties, within the enclosure there are many objects to delight the eye and set the mind thinking. There are the grand entrances to this area and there are the soaring minarets. There are delightful small buildings built upon the arcades which bound the west and north sides of the area. There are exquisite drinking fountains, and in addition to the many finely carved stone inscriptions there are those composed of brightly coloured tiles or mosaics. All of these features, be they natural or man-made, combine to make the Ḥaram a unique architectural experience. But the greatest of all of these objects are, undeniably, the Dome of the Rock at the centre of the Ḥaram and the Aqṣā Mosque at its southern end; without question these are the two jewels of the Ḥaram.

In the late 15th century, a third jewel was recognised—the Madrasa Ashrafiyya. Unfortunately, in 952/1545[1] an earthquake destroyed 80 percent of the walls belonging to its first floor which, as the main teaching area, contained the majority of the sumptuous decoration. Thus the earthquake left the shell of the teaching area, the grand entrance at ground level and some less important ancillary accommodation, items which can still be inspected.

The Madrasa Ashrafiyya was no ordinary religious school. Firstly, unlike the other madrasas constructed upon the *riwāqs* or arcades, the Ashrafiyya was not restricted by the building line established by the roof edge of the *riwāq*, for it was allowed to break with tradition and extend on to the surface of the Ḥaram, something which has never been repeated.

Secondly, the Ashrafiyya was built by the Circassian Mamlūk sultan, al-Ashraf Sayf al-Dīn Qāytbāy, after whom it is named, and who has been described as the Prince of Builders since his reign was outstanding for the construction of beautiful monuments.

Sultan Qāytbāy

Generally, the Arabic word *mamlūk* refers to white Turkish slaves from the Caucasus or southern Russia. After capture in war or purchase by Arab masters, these slaves were educated, formed into regiments and later, in many cases, manumitted. This practice of recruiting regiments of Turkish slaves began in Baghdad in the second decade of the ninth century, and despite the fact that the *mamlūk* regiments soon controlled the Baghdad caliphate, this practice was adopted by the Fāṭimid caliphate of Egypt which, from 1050 was crippled by the rivalries between the Berber and Turkish guards until 1171 when the Fāṭimids were supplanted by Ṣalāḥ al-Dīn (Saladin) from whom are descended the Ayyūbid sultans.

The Ayyūbids did not learn from their predecessors for they continued the practice of maintaining *mamlūks* with the same inevitable consequences. In 1250 the Mamlūks seized power, made one of their number sultan, and thereby created a military oligarchy that ruled over Egypt, Palestine and Syria up to the Ottoman Conquest of 1517. This oligarchy was composed of two slave dynasties, the Turkish Mamlūks 1250-1382 and the Circassian Mamlūks 1382-1517, and had a total of 48 sultans. But due to the constant rivalries and plotting by the Mamlūk amīrs some of the sultans held the throne for a matter of weeks only, whilst others held on for years, indeed Sultan Qāytbāy reigned from 872/1468 to 901/1496, longer than any other Circassian sultan.

It was an unpleasant period with assassination and treachery taking place under corrupt and illiterate rulers. However, in spite of all of the excesses, their system of law, police, military organization and naval enterprise, their postal service, their irrigation works and engineering operations were far in advance of their time and, rough soldiers though they may have been, they were munificent patrons of art and literature.

Sultan Qāytbāy epitomises these characteristics. He was an excessively severe and unjust individual, as demonstrated by his treatment of the alchemist, 'Alī b. al-Marshūshī, whom he blinded and from whom he cut out the tongue when al-Marshūshī failed to turn dross into gold. But through his patronage architecture and its associated crafts flourished in a way unparalleled for over 150 years. The result was a number of magnificent Muslim monuments which have been unequalled since: indeed, throughout the Middle East poor reproductions of these monuments are being constructed now, if only to satisfy the need to make the odd 'commercialized' gesture towards the tradition of Muslim architecture.

We should not be misled by Qāytbāy appearing as the great patron of architecture: he always had a political motive. Through architecture he was able firstly to publicise and reinforce his own position as sultan, the Lord on Earth, and secondly to enhance still further the image of that position by linking his name with the names of his great predecessors. He made additions to the holy shrines of Islam at Mecca and Medina, and built a new entrance and minaret at the Great Mosque of al-Azhar in Cairo, the largest Muslim university, which was founded in the 10th Century. To those foundations established in Cairo by his predecessors, he added a *sabīl-kuttāb* at the Mosque of Ibn Ṭulūn, and a *minbar* in the Mosque of Faraj b. Barqūq. He initiated and carried out more practical schemes too, such as caravanserais, aqueducts and military establishments, and all these bore his mark in the form of a circular shield divided horizontally into three and containing his names and titles.

The Madrasa Ashrafiyya together with a small *sabīl* lying nearby are seen as his contribution to the Third Shrine of Islam, the Ḥaram al-Sharīf. The Ashrafiyya had a prime location, enhanced by its proximity to the Dome of the Rock, and it is likely that today it would have been as famous as any one of its contemporaries had it not been for the earthquake in 1545.

The Background to the Study

Despite its ruined condition, the Ashrafiyya still retains much of its original beauty, especially in its decorated panels, and it was this which first attracted me and led me in 1971 to begin recording them whilst I was architect to the British School of Archaeology in Jerusalem.[2] As a collection of Mamlūk decorative forms it is unequalled in Jerusalem, and unhappily it was, and still is, threatened with extinction through the ever accelerating effects of modern pollution combined with the heavy winter rains and snows, and the hot sand-bearing summer winds which attack the City.

The rate of this damage can be gauged from photographs taken in the 1920s by Sir Archibald Creswell. The decorative panels are as crisp and clearly defined as any to be found in the interiors of Cairo buildings belonging to the period of Qāytbāy, and it will be remembered that those of the

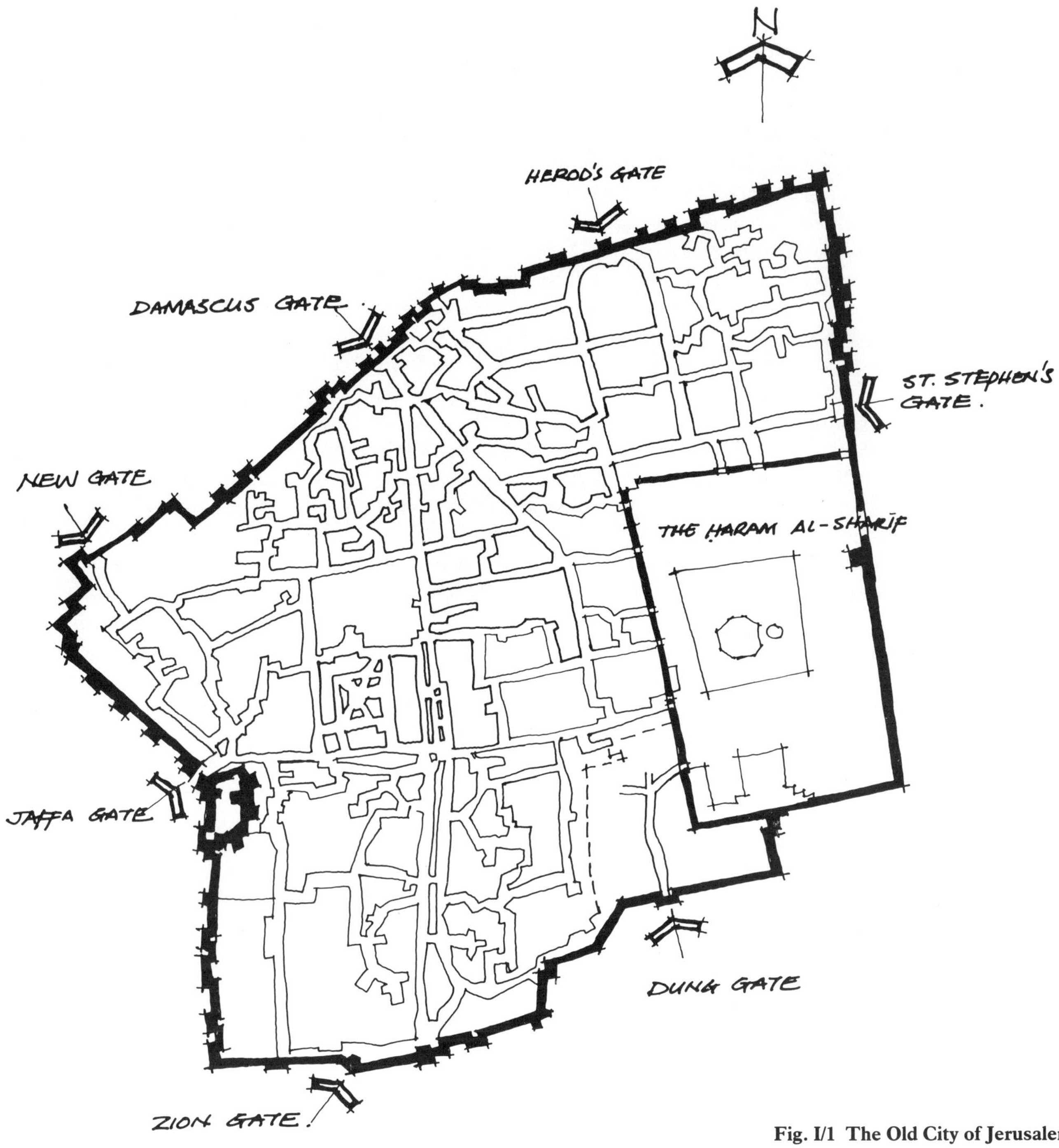

Fig. I/1 The Old City of Jerusalem

Ashrafiyya had lain exposed for 400 years since the earthquake. Creswell took his photographs at distances of 10 metres and more: 50 years later, I was unable to gain the same details with photographs taken only half a metre away and supported by paper squeezes or impressions, tracings or rubbings.

Notwithstanding these hazards of near obliteration, through my studies, I became aware not only of the obvious visual arabesque and geometric vocabularies used in the various decorative compositions, but through the experience of re-drawing them at full size and then reducing each to its simplest format I realised that there existed subtle but obscured inter-relationships linking the different decorative compositions, and that often these links were of a geometric nature.[3]

In the spring of 1975 I left the BSAJ. However, the decoration of the Ashrafiyya had so captured my imagination that in 1977 I spent a year in Cairo cataloguing the designs of the great Mamlūk monuments in that city. During this period I made several visits to Jerusalem to continue and complete the recording of the decorative areas of the Ashrafiyya, and to survey as much of the architecture as was necessary to enable the different decorative elements to be located. A further year was spent studying, comparing and understanding the hidden analogies of the designs found in Cairo before the emphasis of my research switched to the search for the lost architectural form of the Madrasa Ashrafiyya.

This change came about as my knowledge of and feeling for this period of architecture grew. I spent days on end with the monuments themselves, and gradually gained an appreciation of their individual characteristics through the study of their spaces and volumes. At the same time, however, I found similarities and parallels in the design and decoration of monuments erected by members of a recognisable group, such as that formed by a sultan and his chief officers of state, and occasionally I found that a specific design would be repeated in different buildings.

It was, in fact, the repetition by Qāytbāy's craftsmen of certain panels in the Ashrafiyya, which can be seen also in his Mosque built seven years earlier in the Qal'at al-Kabsh quarter of Cairo, that unveiled the particular relationship that these buildings had to each other and lead to my using the Mosque as one of the 'yardsticks' for my reconstruction of the architectural form of the Ashrafiyya. Repetition is only a minor aid, and of far greater importance is the fact that sufficient material evidence exists in areas of the first floor of the Ashrafiyya to enable a theoretical reconstruction to be made.

Some while after the completion of the reconstruction I made the chance discovery that the simple geometric construction of an inscribed hexagon with two of its sides extended so as to form an equilateral triangle seemed to control the relative positions of the external faces of the west and east walls of the Madrasa, the central point of the *ṣaḥn* and intriguingly the centre of the *miḥrāb*.[4] Seven years were to elapse before I had time to look again at the Ashrafiyya to see if that simple geometry could be extended to control the relationships of other architectural details. I must underline the point that it was never my intention to foist some preconceived mathematical theory on to the ruins of the Ashrafiyya and then to try and discover an apparently 'acceptable' reconstruction that could be compressed or stretched in order to fit the mathematics. However, having found a geometry which fits the Ashrafiyya, as a practising architect I am convinced that geometry was used by Qāytbāy's architects to control the architectural design and it was with this in mind that the following drawings and their explanations were made.

Notes

1. This date is discussed by A. G. Walls and D. A. King: 'The Sundial on the West Wall of the Madrasa of Sultan Qāytbāy in Jerusalem', *Art and Archaeological Research Papers* XV, London, 1979.
2. Some idea of the decorative quality can be gained from a few of my drawings reproduced in *Mamlūk Jerusalem*, pub. by the BSAJ and the World of Islam Festival Trust, London, 1987, figs. 63.10, 63.13, the fly leaves and rear cover.
3. Consequent to these and other findings in the architecture of Jerusalem, my researches in Cairo unearthed similar design games devised by 15th century craftsmen. See A. G. Walls 'Symmetry and Asymmetry in a Cairo Minbar', *Art International* XXV/3.4, 1982, pp. 30-40.
4. At this juncture it may be of use to clarify some of the terms that will be used. The word '*madrasa*' means a school; thus when referring to the building as a whole, the Madrasa Ashrafiyya will be used, whereas the term 'Madrasa' will denote the actual cruciform planned school hall on the first floor. The *ṣaḥn* is the central court of the Madrasa around which are disposed the four '*īwāns*' or deep bays where the sheikhs taught. The *miḥrāb* is the niche facing Mecca and so showing the direction of prayer (the *qibla*); in Jerusalem a *miḥrāb* is generally placed in a south wall.

Chapter II
THE SITE

The site of the Ashrafiyya is ideally located, lying between the two most frequented gates into the Ḥaram—the Bāb al-Silsila (Gate of the Chain), and the Bāb al-Qaṭṭānīn (Gate of the Cotton Merchants), and close to the magnificent Dome of the Rock. Although restricted in size, it had the potential to become a visually significant site within the Ḥaram. This point would not have been lost on Qāytbāy for he strove continually to make his mark on the shrines of Islam and the other significant buildings lying within his dominions. **fig. II/1**

Contemporary descriptions record his success. Firstly, there exists the *waqfiyya* (title deeds of a religious endowment) written by al-Shaykh Khitāb b. 'Umar al-Danhāwī.[1] This is 22.5 metres in length and describes the arrangement of the Ashrafiyya when finally completed. Although the *waqfiyya* begins by giving details of the earlier madrasa on the site (herein referred to as the Old Madrasa), it ends with a description of the land and buildings which formed the *waqf* (religious endowment).

Another contemporary written source is a guide to the religious monuments of Jerusalem and Hebron written by al-Qāḍī Mujīr al-Dīn al-'Ulaymī in 901/1496.[2] He includes information on the founders, the dates of the construction and restoration of their buildings, descriptions of the buildings themselves, and in some instances, including that of the Ashrafiyya, the materials used. It was al-'Ulaymī who described the Ashrafiyya as 'The Third Jewel of the Ḥaram', the first and second being the Dome of the Rock and the Aqṣā Mosque. He also records that the lighting of the three buildings followed a specific sequence according to the days of the week, a fact which can be construed as indicating a recognition of the especial significance of the Ashrafiyya within the Ḥaram at that time.

Edward Reuwich of Utrecht also captured these visual qualities in an illustration of Jerusalem (plate 1) published in 1486 just after the completion of the Ashrafiyya.[3] This illustration is most valuable for it confirms the written descriptions of the Ashrafiyya where they mention a loggia at the centre of its east elevation which looks onto the Ḥaram. This feature which formed part of the cruciform planned madrasa is unique in Mamlūk architecture as it broke the architectural traditions associated with this plan form.

To create an image of the original building and its details, it is necessary to return to the site as it was before 886/1481 when a Christian architect and a team of craftsmen first arrived in Jerusalem.[4] They would have found a site with one fundamental draw back: it was too small to contain an existing madrasa (which had already expanded into areas below the *riwāq*), let alone a madrasa such as they intended to build on the scale of those found in Cairo. **fig. II/2**

To the south the site was limited by a minaret, and to the north by the Madrasa 'Uthmāniyya, the distance separating the two being 27.5 metres. The width, being that of the roof of the *riwāq* and the east *īwān* of the Madrasa Baladiyya, measured a mere 14.5 metres.

Their first task, therefore, was to find a solution to the restrictions of the site. They had two options: either to acquire the religious foundations abutting the site, the madrasas of Baladiyya and 'Uthmāniyya, and incorporate their areas into the Ashrafiyya, or, under imperial authority, to impose upon the authorities administering the Ḥaram a design which broke an apparently sacrosanct regulation which had been adhered to by the architects of every building sited along the west and north boundaries. Until now no building had been allowed to extend beyond the cornice of the *riwāq*—in effect, the equivalent of a modern 'building line'.

In the event, the architect chose the latter option, and having established that a standing regulation could be broken, there was nothing physically to prevent a 'platform' extension of the *riwāq* **fig. II/3**

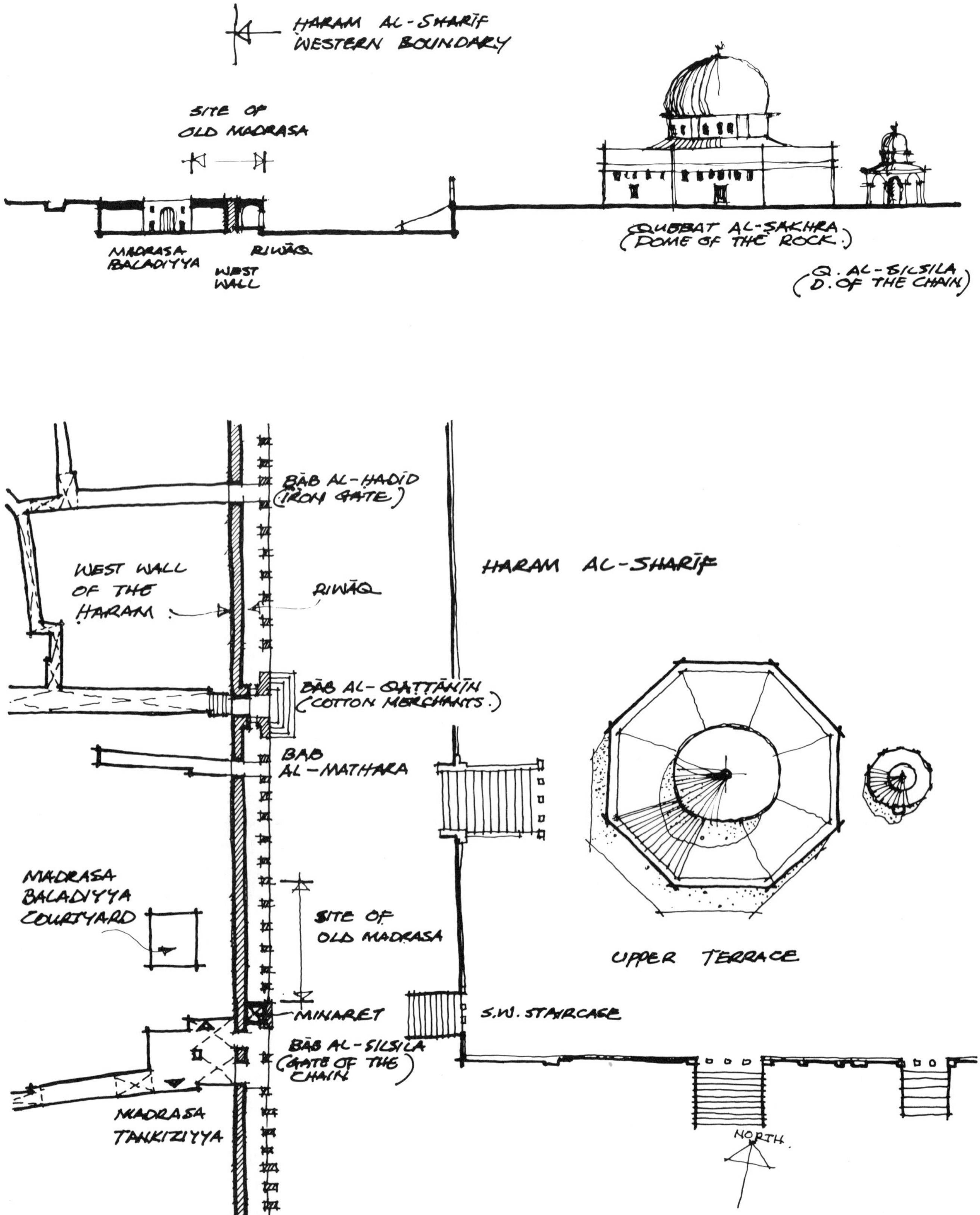

Fig. II/1 The site of the Old Madrasa

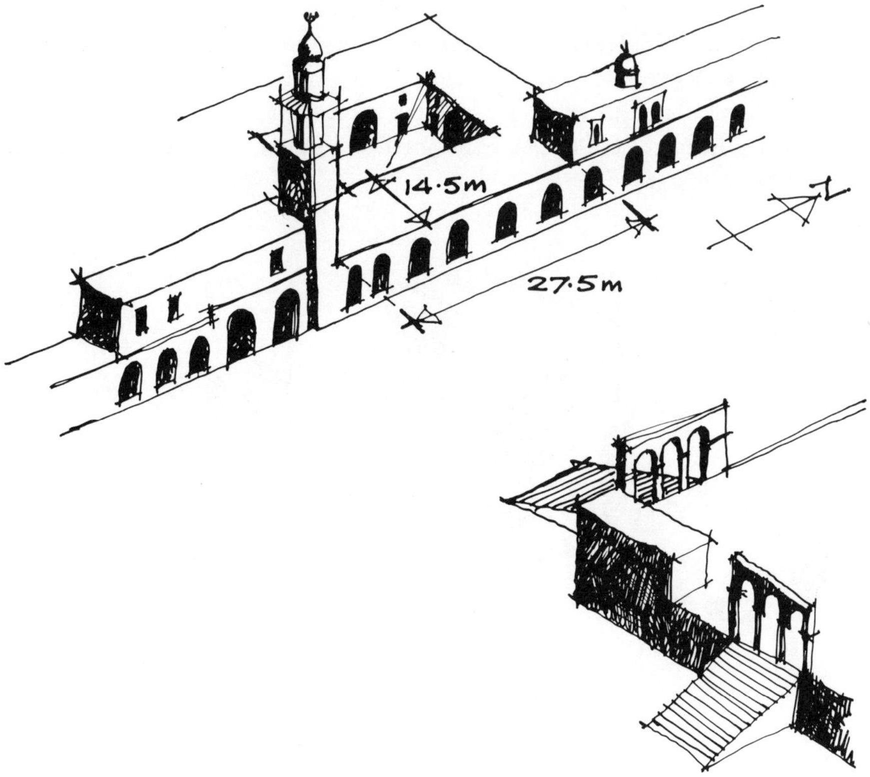

Fig. II/2 The site before 886/1481

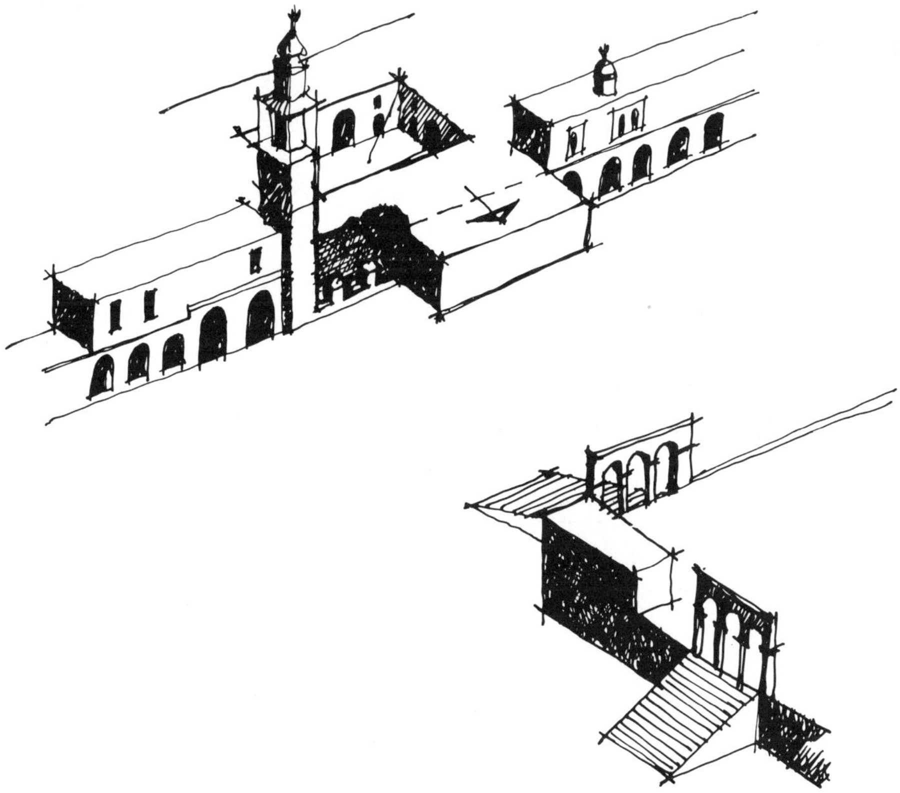

Fig. II/3 The demolition and construction of the platform, 886/1481

roof to the east. Thus they began its construction and at the same time they demolished three arches of the *riwāq* (built 737/1336-37) to clear the site for the dazzling entrance and processional staircase that were to lead to the Madrasa.

fig. II/4 Once the platform had been completed, work could start on the Cairo-sized madrasa, which would not only dwarf the buildings to the north and south, but would also provide strong competition to the adjacent minaret.

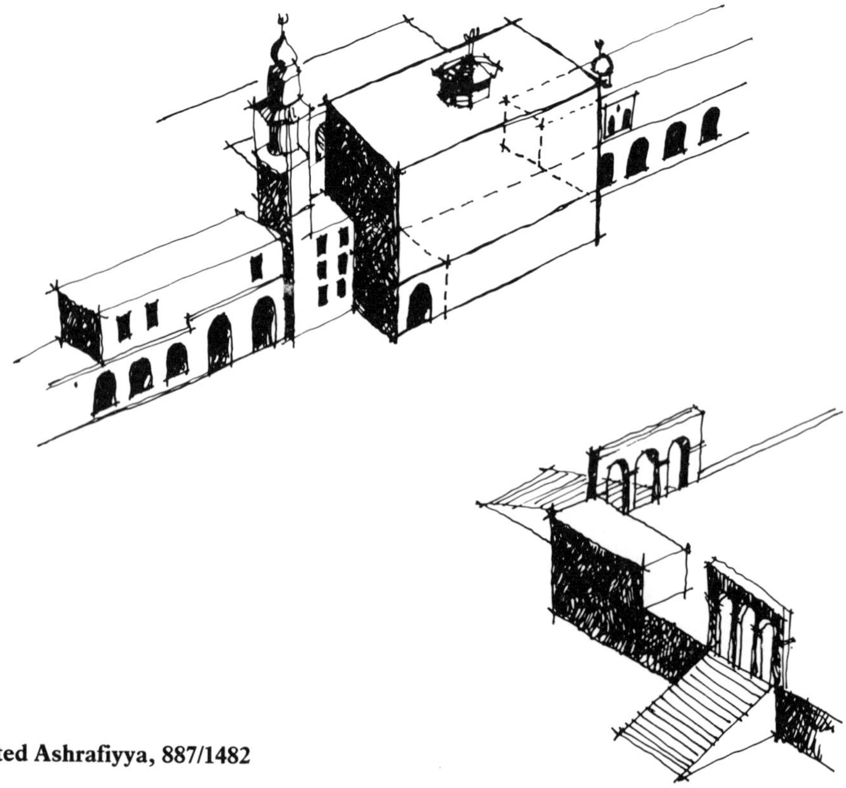

Fig. II/4 The completed Ashrafiyya, 887/1482

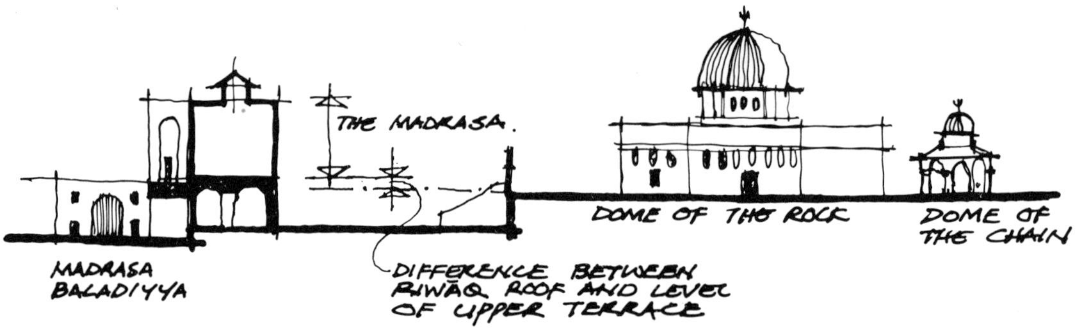

Fig. II/5 Section showing the relationship of the Ashrafiyya and the Dome of the Rock

fig. II/5 In addition to its size, it benefitted from the *riwāq* roof being slightly higher than the upper terrace of the Ḥaram as this provided an uninterrupted view of the Dome of the Rock—a feature the architect and his team understood and one which they were to utilise fully in their design with the
fig. II/6 introduction of the central loggia. We should not forget that the converse view was probably the more important one in the eyes of Sultan Qāytbāy, as from the Dome of the Rock his Madrasa, his major contribution to the Third Shrine, would be seen and displayed in all its splendour.

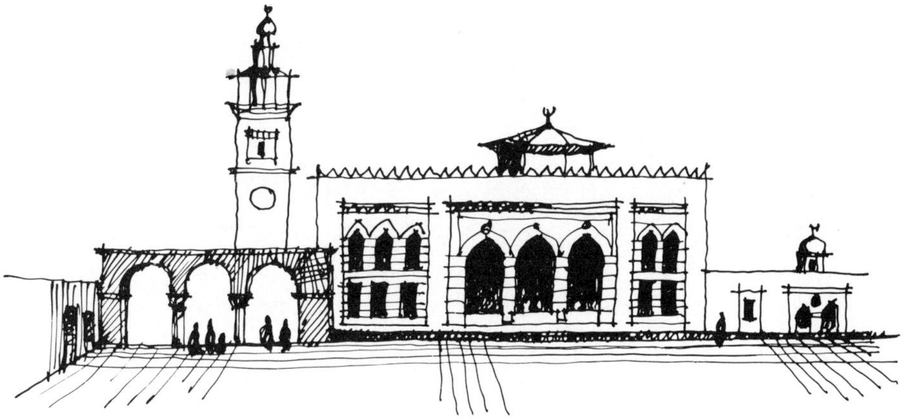

Fig. II/6 The Ashrafiyya seen from outside the south door of the Dome of the Rock

Plate 2 The remains of the Ashrafiyya seen in a montage from the south door of the Dome of the Rock

Plate 3 The Ashrafiyya seen in a montage from the edge of the upper terrace. The structure on the right with the carved stone dome is the Sabıl of Qāytbāy

Fig. II/7 The Ashrafiyya seen from the edge of the upper terrace

However, it is only from the edge of the upper terrace that the complete east elevation of the Ashrafiyya can be seen, for in addition to the Madrasa on the first floor, on the ground floor this elevation includes the *majma'*, or meeting hall, and the main entrance. These two components are significant, not least in providing the structural base on which the Madrasa could be built. They contrast sharply with each other: the facade of the *majma'* is restrained and its decoration gives little idea of what lies behind; whereas the entrance is flamboyant and heralds the architectural qualities to be found inside the Ashrafiyya. **fig. II/7**

Thus the Madrasa of Ashrafiyya had four distinctive architectural attributes: firstly, it broke the age old traditions by extending into the Ḥaram; secondly, the Madrasa was built at a height of 8 metres above the paved surface of the Ḥaram, whereas its forerunners in Cairo had been built on or near ground level; thirdly, by forming a new entrance to the holy enclosure a processional path was introduced between it and the Madrasa; and fourthly, it adapted a well known architectural element, the loggia, for this cruciform-planned Madrasa and its unique site.

Notes

1. I am indebted to Miss Amal Abul-Hajj for providing a translation from Arabic of Ibrāhīm 'Abd al-Laṭīf, 'Wathīqat al-Sulṭān Qāytbāy: al-Madrasa bi-'l-Quds wa-'l-jāmi' bi-Ghazza' (Contract of Sultan Qāytbāy: the Madrasa in Jerusalem and the Mosque in Ghaza), *Silsilat al-Dirāsāt al-wathā'iqiyya*, II (Series of Studies concerning Documents, II), Mu'tammar al-thālith li-'l-āthār fi 'l-bilād al-'arabiyya, (The Third Congress for Archaeology in Arab Countries, Fez, November 1959), pub. Cairo, 1961, pp. 389-444 and 16 pls.
2. Mujīr al-Dīn al-'Ulaymī, *Al-uns al-jalīl bi-ta'rīkh al-Quds wa-'l-khalīl*, written in 901/1496, published Cairo 1866. Translated into French by H. Sauvaire, *Histoire de Jerusalem et d'Hebron: Fragments de la Chronique de Moudjir-ed-Dyn traduits sur le texte Arabe*, Paris 1880.
3. The illustration is in Bernard of Breydenbach, *Peregrinationes in Terram Sanctam*, (1486) after Edward Reuwich of Utrecht.
4. The complexities of the building sequence of the Ashrafiyya are outlined below in Appendix A: A Chronology of the Building of the Ashrafiyya.

Chapter III
THE EXISTING PHYSICAL EVIDENCE

Having considered the site and its limitations, it is now important to look at those parts of the Ashrafiyya which still exist before embarking on the reconstruction of the Madrasa.

Whilst the earthquake in 952/1545 devastated the upper part of the Ashrafiyya, it left much of the ground floor intact, and this dating from 887/1482 provides a good basis on which to reconstruct the design of the Madrasa.[1]

A brief description of the east, north and south elevations, and the ground floor, follows, as well as details of those areas of the Madrasa on the first floor which still remain.

The East Elevation

fig. III/1

The east elevation is the principal one and faces the Ḥaram. The existing wall is nearly 10 metres high and 25 metres long, and within it three groups of architectural features can be identified which relate to the three parts of the Ashrafiyya: the *majma‘*, the meeting hall, the entrance and the Madrasa. At ground level most of the elevation is taken up by the two grilled windows and the doorway of the *majma‘*. Each is surrounded by a moulded frame containing *ablaq*, or polychrome, jambs, with a white lintel and an *ablaq* relieving arch. Arched clerestories appear almost directly above these. In the southern part of the elevation, a large archway with *ablaq* voussoirs gives in to the porch and entrance.[2]

At first floor level there is little evidence of the Madrasa's original elevation, and the jumbled stonework (including some decorated stones) indicates considerable rebuilding of the wallhead after the earthquake of 1545. About the centre of the elevation in the upper six stone courses a pattern emerges of an *ablaq* joggled string course, four courses of an *ablaq* jamb, and two upright red stones, all contained by a simple moulding.

To the right of this area, the continuity of the upper four stone courses is broken by two straight joints, indicating some lost architectural details. In the drawing of the elevation the joints appear to coincide with the north and south walls of the north *īwān*. Between these a pair of windows is set, and this might also have been the case in the east elevation.

The North Elevation

fig. III/2

The north elevation has two distinct parts which are separated by a pier of the *riwāq*. The earliest part is the wall blocking off the *riwāq*, which contains the grilled window set in *ablaq* masonry, surrounded by a simple moulding, and also the four course high rectangular window, belongs to the 885/1480 construction of the old Madrasa.

The second part of the elevation has a maximum height of 13.5 metres, and a width of nearly 7 metres. Its main features are a doorway set within *ablaq* masonry with a moulded border and an arched window above.

Two vertical straight joints exist in the upper part of this wall. Above the right hand one and set back from the wall face is the remains of an *ablaq* window jamb. The masonry that now separates these two joints is not original, but must date from Ottoman rebuilding undertaken some time after the earthquake of 952/1545. Included in this rebuilding are three well decorated stones, possibly taken from the debris of the earthquake.

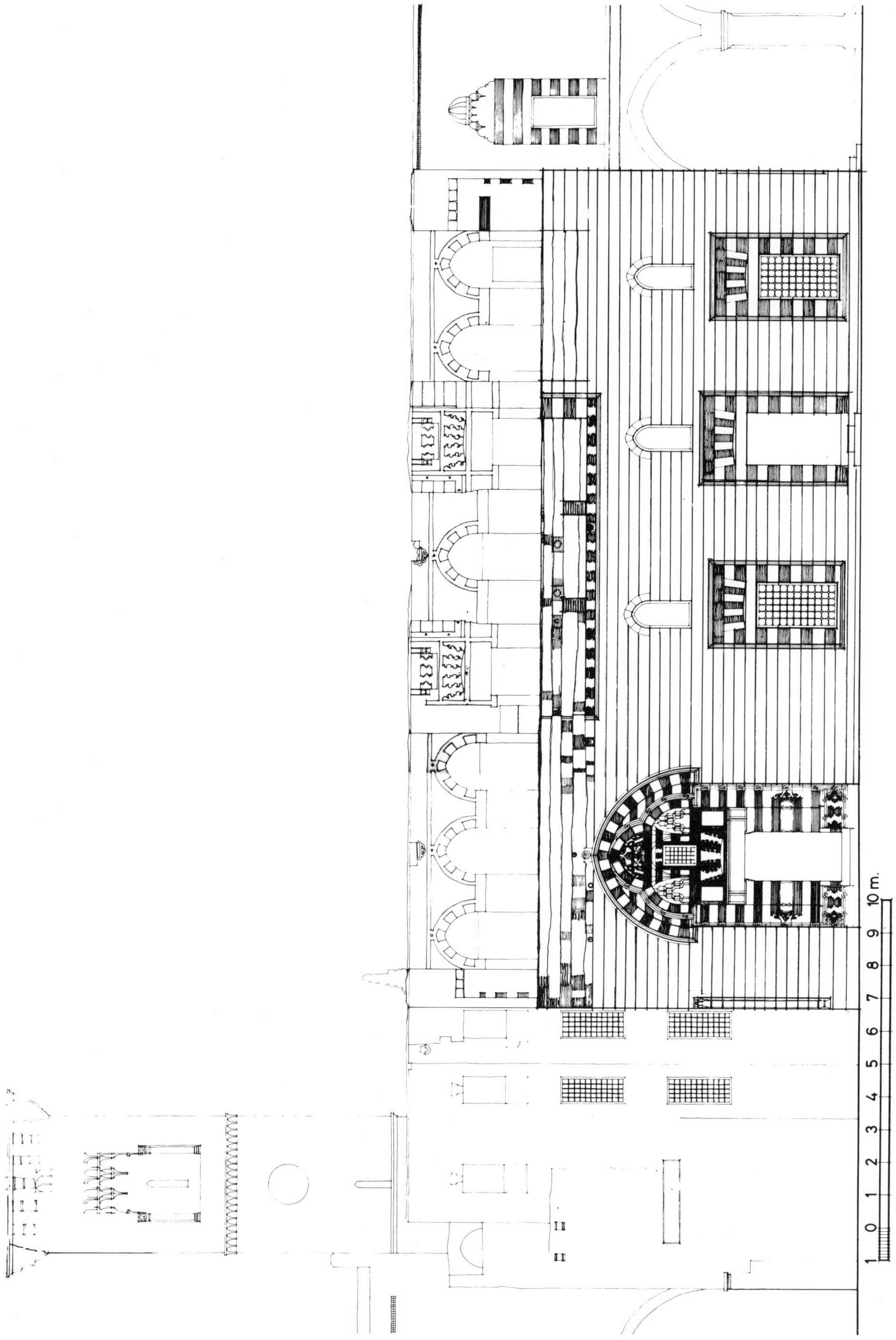

Fig. III/1 The east elevation

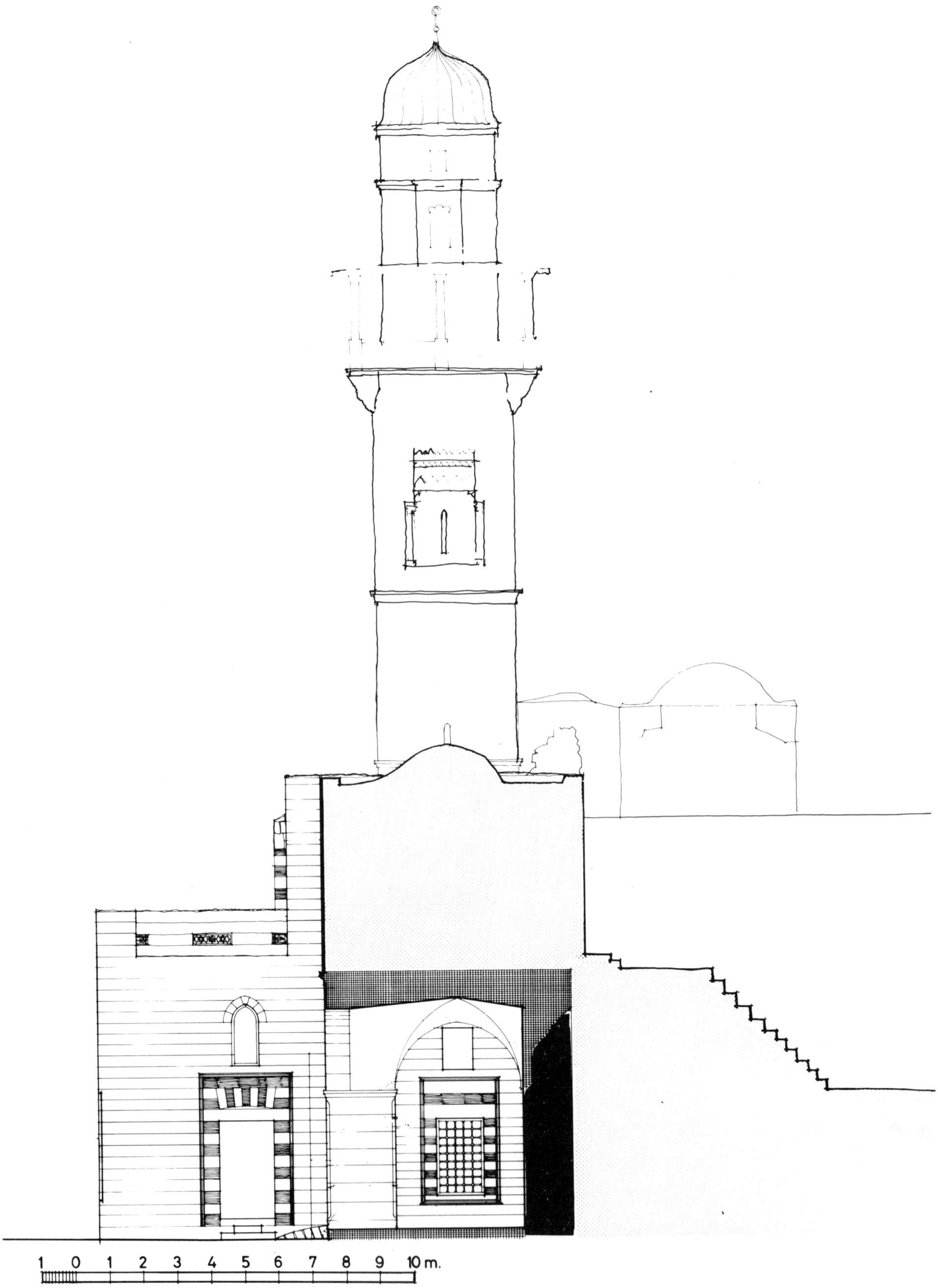

Fig. III/2 The north elevation

The South Elevation

The south elevation stands at a height of about 14 metres, and forms the external part of the south wall of the Madrasa. It is dominated by a large arch which frames the porch and is similar to that in the east elevation, although it has a slightly greater span. **fig. III/3**

Like those of the east and north elevation, the upper courses of this elevation were rebuilt after the earthquake. One straight joint can be seen and above it, set back, with an *ablaq* window jamb, a combination similar to that found in the north elevation.

The Wall between the Ashrafiyya and the Bāb al-Silsila

The variety of stones and styles of cutting and dressing indicates the considerable age of this wall and the many changes it has undergone. **fig. III/4**

The area nearest the porch is three storeys high and has tall rectangular grilled windows. It certainly belongs to the Ashrafiyya since the masonry courses are compatible. However, some stones at the foot of the wall may represent the remains of one of the piers of the *riwāq* demolished in 886/1481. Another area of stones defined by a straight joint once formed the base of the minaret, and this area contains a long two line inscription commemorating the restoration of the minaret under Malik Nāṣir Muḥammad in 730/1329-30 by the Amīr Tankiz. This is interesting because although the minaret is definitely one of the minarets of the Ḥaram, it was associated through this inscription with the Madrasa Tankiziyya, whose entrance is just outside the Bāb al-Silsila, but whose upper areas joined the minaret.

We know from historic documents that formerly other inscriptions had also been placed in this wall: imperial decrees from Sultans Jaqmaq 853/1449 and Qāytbāy 881/1476, though these have since been removed.[3]

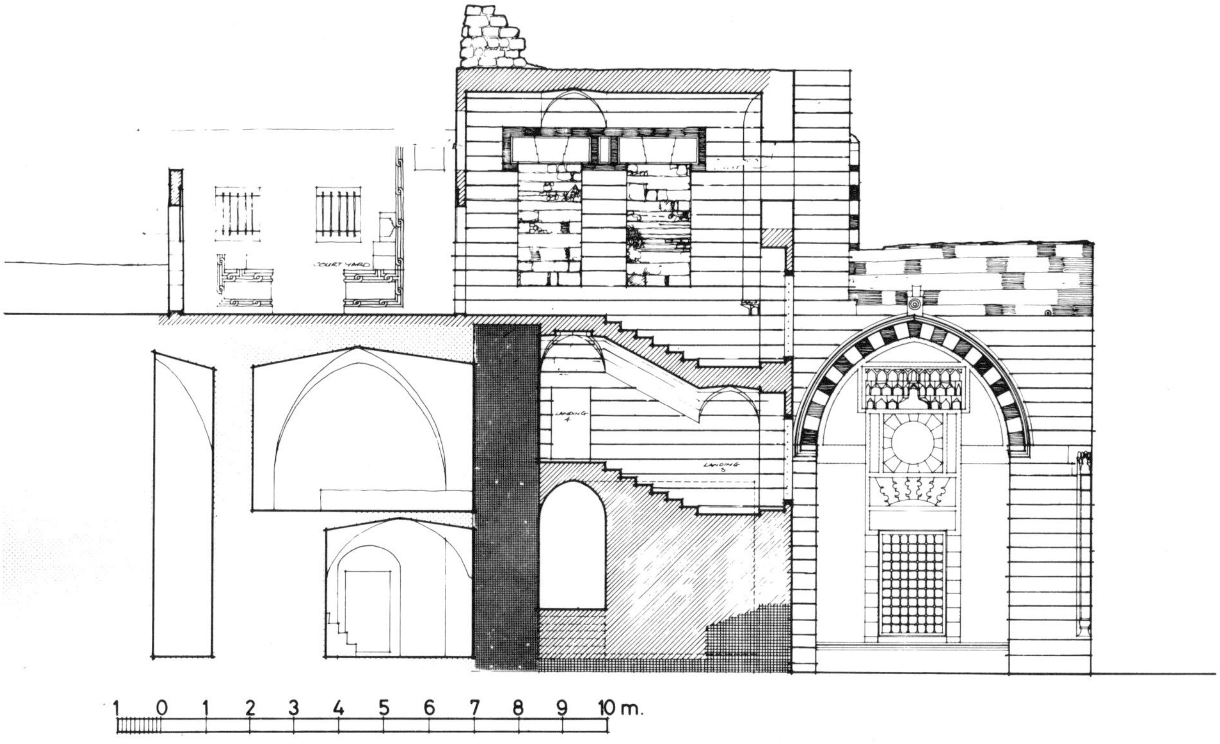

Fig. III/3 The south elevation

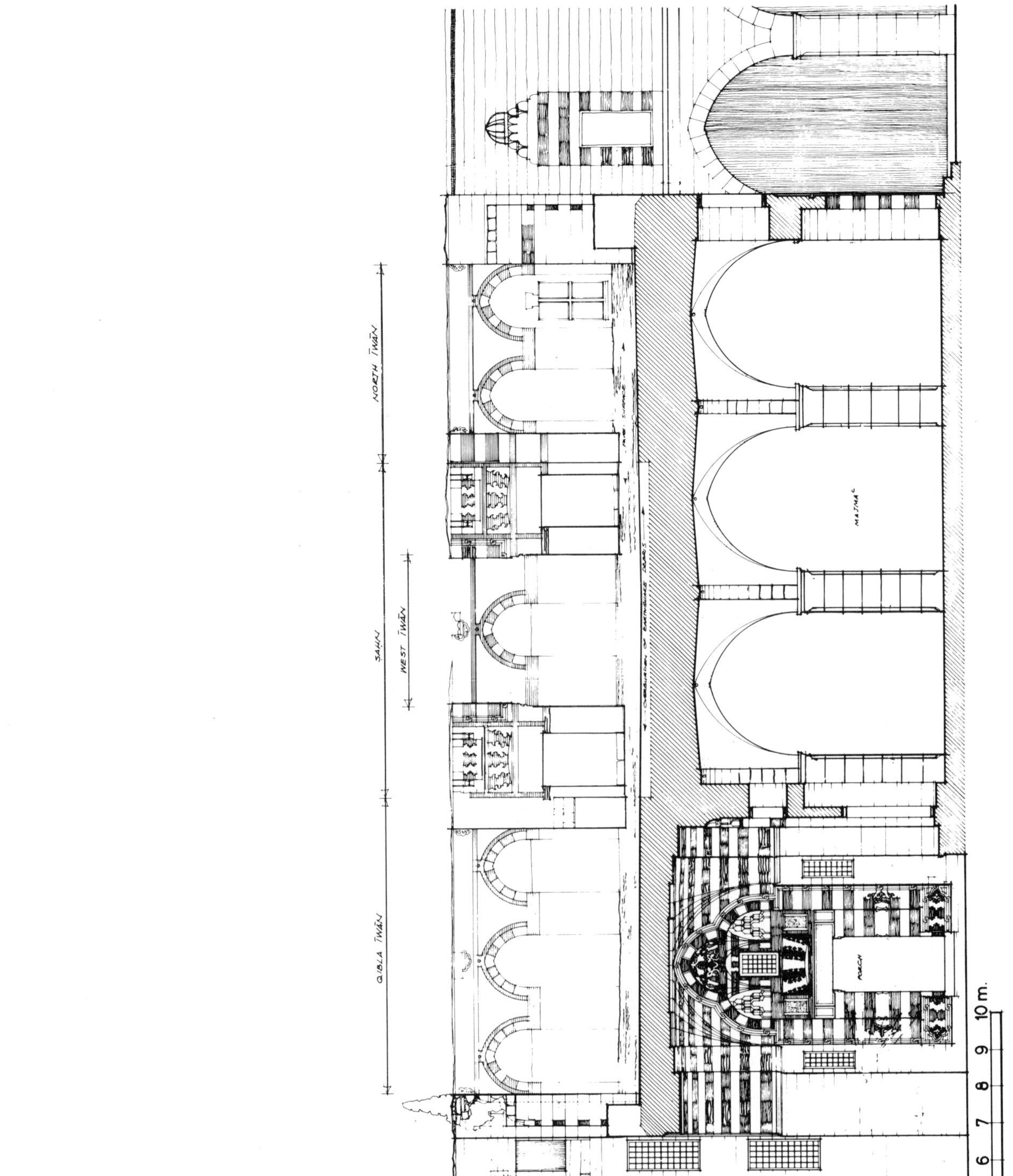

Fig. III/4 The wall between the Ashrafiyya and the Bāb al-Silsila

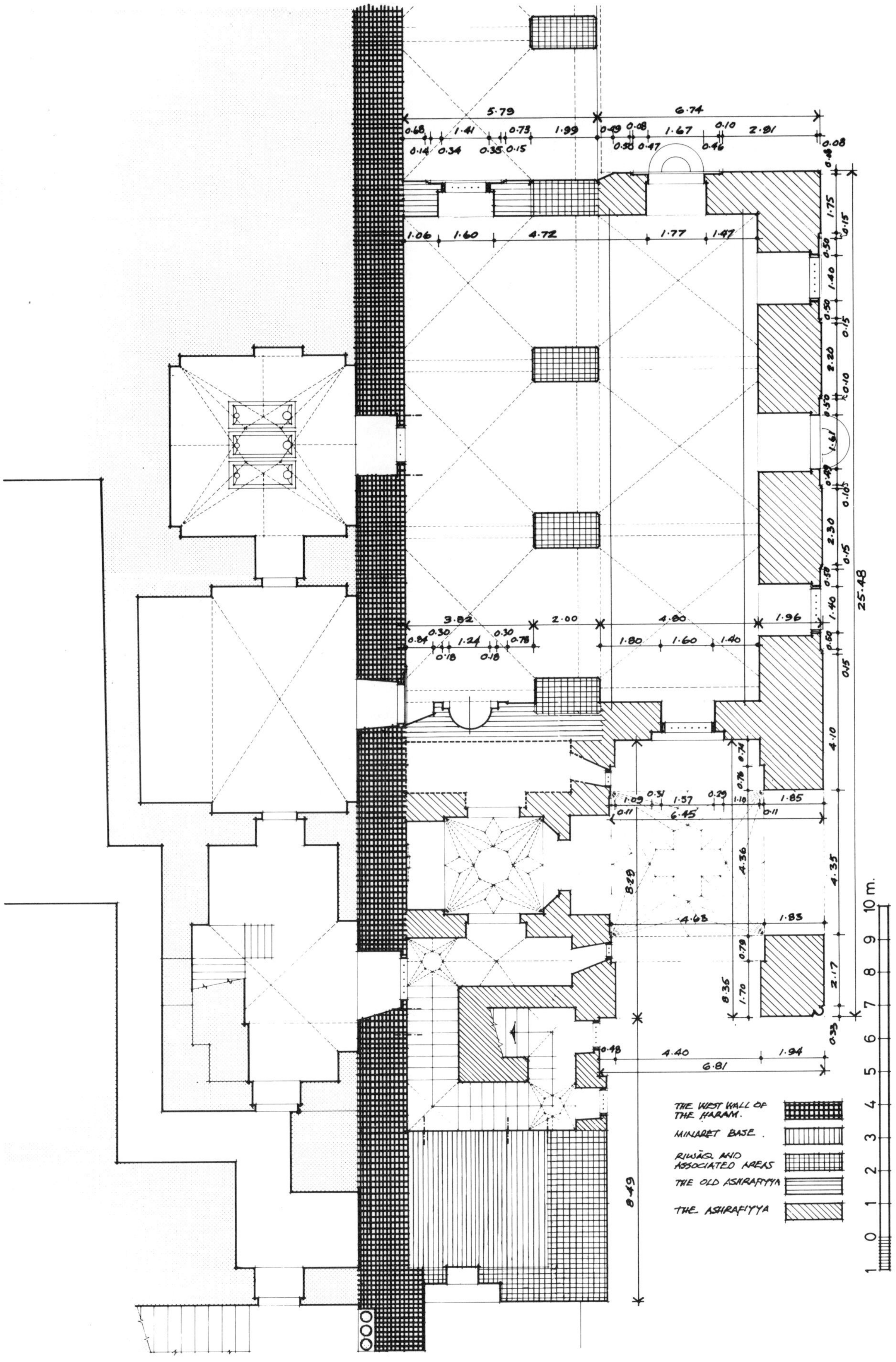

Fig. III/5 The ground floor

The minaret was used by the chronicler al-ʿUlaymī to define the southern boundary of the site of the Ashrafiyya. Also in view of the fact that the Old Madrasa was built on the *riwāq* by Sultan Khushqadam, it is intriguing to find over a window above Bāb al-Silsila the shield of that sultan inscribed on a marble or white stone.[4] Although it has been suggested that this might be a re-sited part of Khushqadam's decree of 870/1465, the architectural detailing provides evidence to the contrary. The northern half of the window in which the shield is placed still retains some *ablaq* masonry and *muqarnaṣ* (stalactite) decoration which is definitely Mamlūk, whereas the southern half looks like an Ottoman rebuild.

The significance of this shield, however, is that it raises the question of whether or not the predecessor of the Ashrafiyya, the Old Madrasa of Khushqadam, extended further south of the minaret than had previously been thought. If this were the case, the Ashrafiyya might also have done so and extended into the areas which now form part of the Madrasa Tankiziyya. Unfortunately this question can only be answered by a thorough survey of the Tankiziyya, a task which is presently impossible as the madrasa has been occupied by the Israeli army since shortly after the 1967 war.

fig. III/5

The Ground Floor: the Majmaʿ *and the Entrance to the Old Madrasa*

Although forming part of the overall structure of the Ashrafiyya, the *majmaʿ* acts as an independent unit within it, and has its own entrances. It is a vaulted room divided by a line of four piers within chamfered corners, the fourth of which is buried in the north wall. Since these piers are identical to those of the *riwāq* immediately to the north, it is possible to establish the extent of the earlier *majmaʿ* built in 885/1480. The builders simply blocked up the openings between the four piers, and linked the northern and southern piers to the west wall of the Ḥaram. These two links are all that remain of the *majmaʿ*; the northern link contains the window with a clerestory above it, previously remarked on in the description of the north elevation, and the southern link has a *miḥrāb* with an identical clerestory above it, though this second clerestory was blocked up in 887/1482 during the construction of the final Ashrafiyya. (**fig. III/6**, **fig. III/7**, **fig. III/8**)

Although the workmanship of the two linking walls is very different to that used in the construction of the final Ashrafiyya, the most significant indication of their belonging to the 885/1480 building is the similarity of the *miḥrāb* to that of the nearby Madrasa al-Muzhiriyya in the Ṭarīq Bāb al-Ḥadīd (the Street of the Iron Gate) which was built in the same year by Abū Bakr b. Muzhir the Superintendent of the Chancery of Sultan Qāytbāy, who would certainly have had access to the same craftsmen.[5]

fig. III/6 In the west wall and adjacent to the *miḥrāb* there is a window which originally allowed a person standing in the Ḥaram to look into the east *īwān* of the Madrasa Baladiyya. Then with the construction of the earlier *majmaʿ* it was converted into a doorway, as at the time the entrance to the Old Madrasa and the minaret was shared with the Madrasa Baladiyya; and indeed, although now the entrance serves only the Baladiyya, it still bears an inscription recording the construction of the Old Madrasa in 875/1470.[6] Following the construction of the Ashrafiyya and the existing *majmaʿ* the doorway was no longer necessary and it reverted to being a window.

The evidence suggests that by 870/1465, when Sultan Khushqadam founded the Old Madrasa, a dividing wall had been constructed across the east side of the *ṣaḥn* of the Baladiyya causing it to lose its east *īwān* and its flanking rooms to the Old Madrasa. In the room to the north of the east *īwān*, three tombs lie side by side,[7] and before the construction of the Old Madrasa the existing window looked out onto the Ḥaram. A window in the room to the south of the east *īwān* had a similar view, and it is from this room that a stair gave access to the minaret and to the Old Madrasa sited on the roof of the *riwāq*. It is worth noting that each of these openings in the west wall have *ablaq* jambs providing further proof that they were once open to the Ḥaram. (**fig. III/9**)

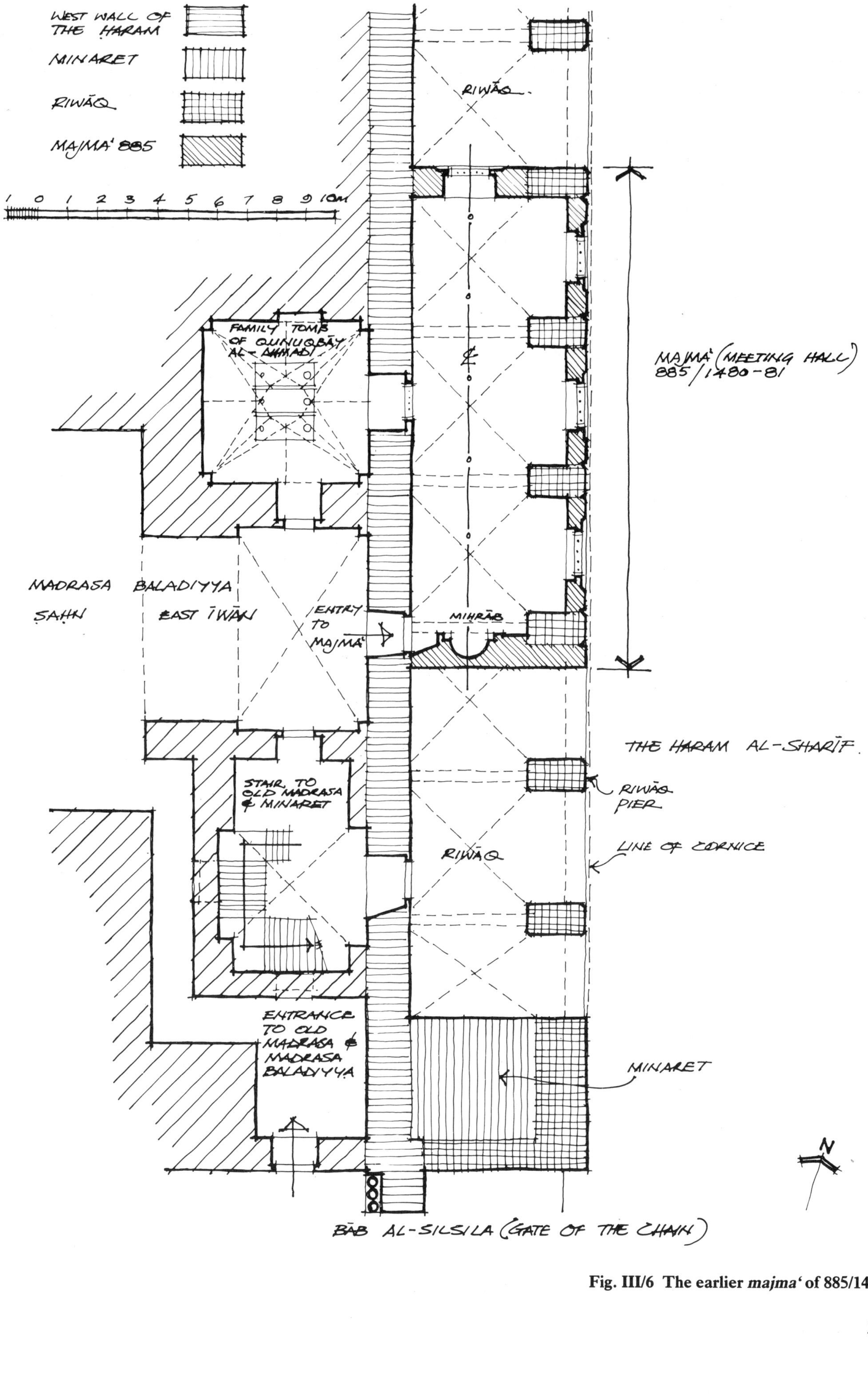
WEST WALL OF THE HARAM
MINARET
RIWĀQ
MAJMA' 885
1 0 1 2 3 4 5 6 7 8 9 10M
RIWĀQ
FAMILY TOMB OF QUNUQBĀY AL-AHMADI
MAJMA' (MEETING HALL) 885/1480-81
MADRASA BALADIYYA
SAHN
EAST ĪWĀN
ENTRY TO MAJMA'
MIHRĀB
THE HARAM AL-SHARĪF
RIWĀQ PIER
STAIR TO OLD MADRASA & MINARET
RIWĀQ
LINE OF CORNICE
ENTRANCE TO OLD MADRASA & MADRASA BALADIYYA
MINARET
N
BĀB AL-SILSILA (GATE OF THE CHAIN)

Fig. III/6 The earlier *majma'* of 885/1480

The Processional Way

fig. III/4
fig. III/15

The porch is open to the Ḥaram on its east and south sides. On its north side it has a large grilled window surrounded with fine decoration and a bench seat, and its west side contains a beautiful recessed portal. Spanning the porch is a fan vault constructed in *ablaq* stone courses rising to large decorated panels at the zenith.

fig. III/13

The decoration of the vestibule is restrained in comparison with that of the porch. In the flanking walls arched doorways with *ablaq* voussoirs can be seen, and a plain stone fan vault rises up to decorated panels at its zenith.

fig. III/10

At the rear of the vestibule stands the ancient west wall of the Ḥaram with a bench running across it. This wall still displays one of the springings that belonged to the three southern arches of the *riwāq* demolished in 886/1481.

fig. III/11 and III/8

The barrel vaulted passageway starting at the southern doorway of the vestibule continues up the grand staircase and along a further passageway on the first floor which leads out into a courtyard. The barrel vault is punctuated by fan vaults with decorated centres. The first occurs just before the beginning of the stair and the others over three of the quarter landings. Grilled windows in the stairway look out onto the Dome of the Rock and the Ḥaram. Internally these windows have arched heads complementing the vaulting, but from the outside they appear as taller rectangular openings.

The combinations of fan vaults and barrel vaults seem to give an architectural identity to these areas and one senses that they were designed very much as a processional way linking the Ḥaram with the Madrasa on the upper level.

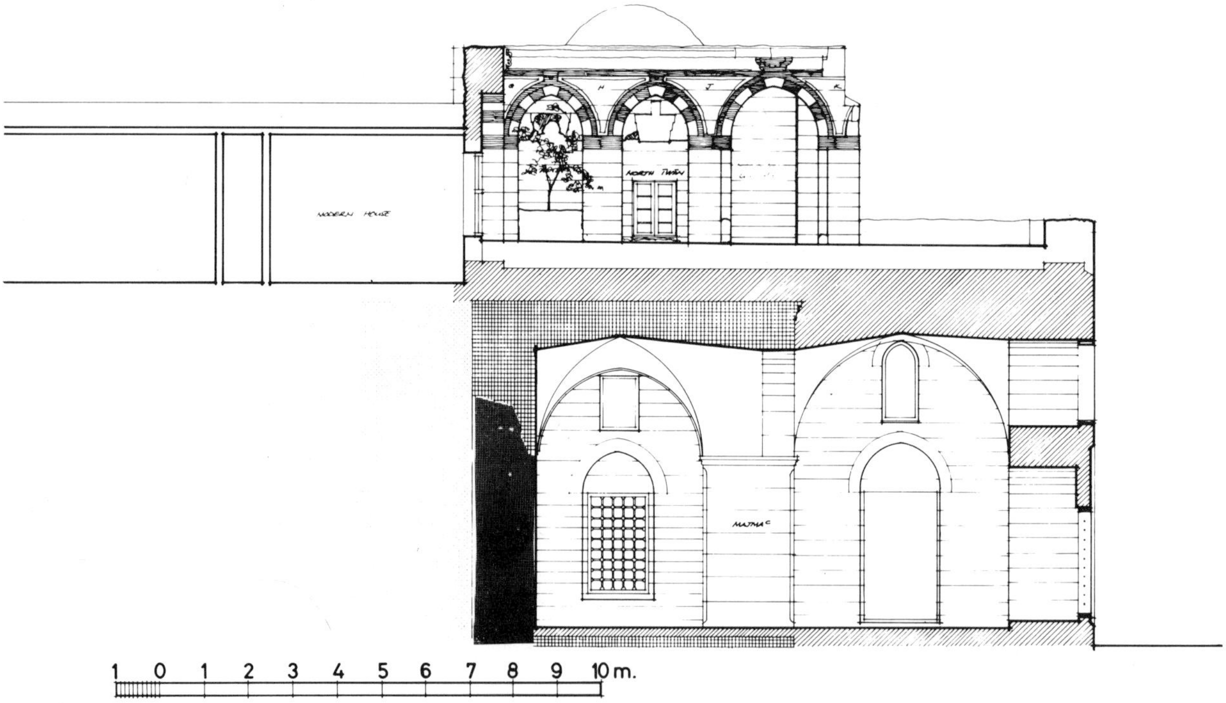

Fig. III/7 The north wall of the *majma‘* and the Madrasa

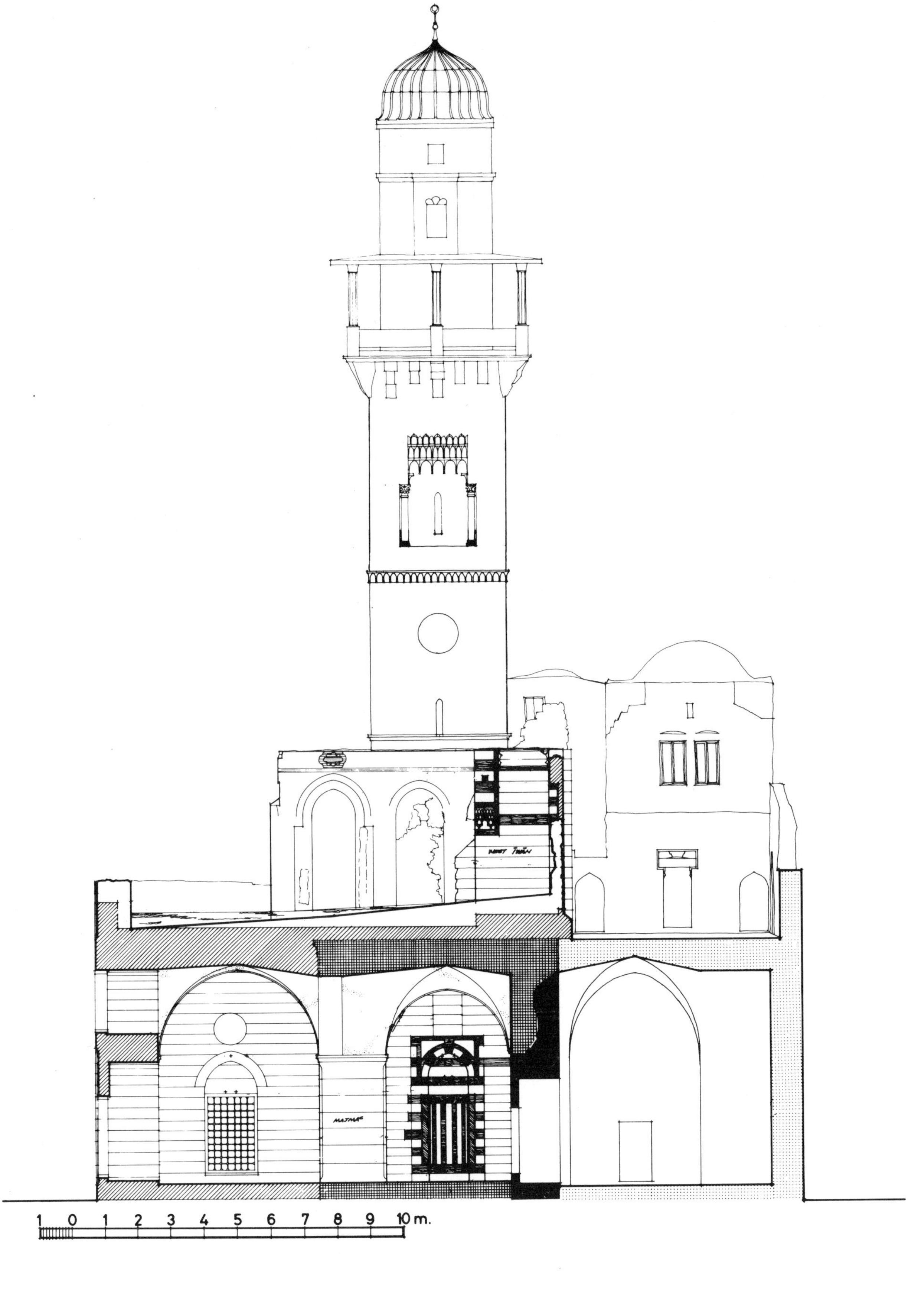

Fig. III/8 The south wall of the *majma'* and the west *īwān*

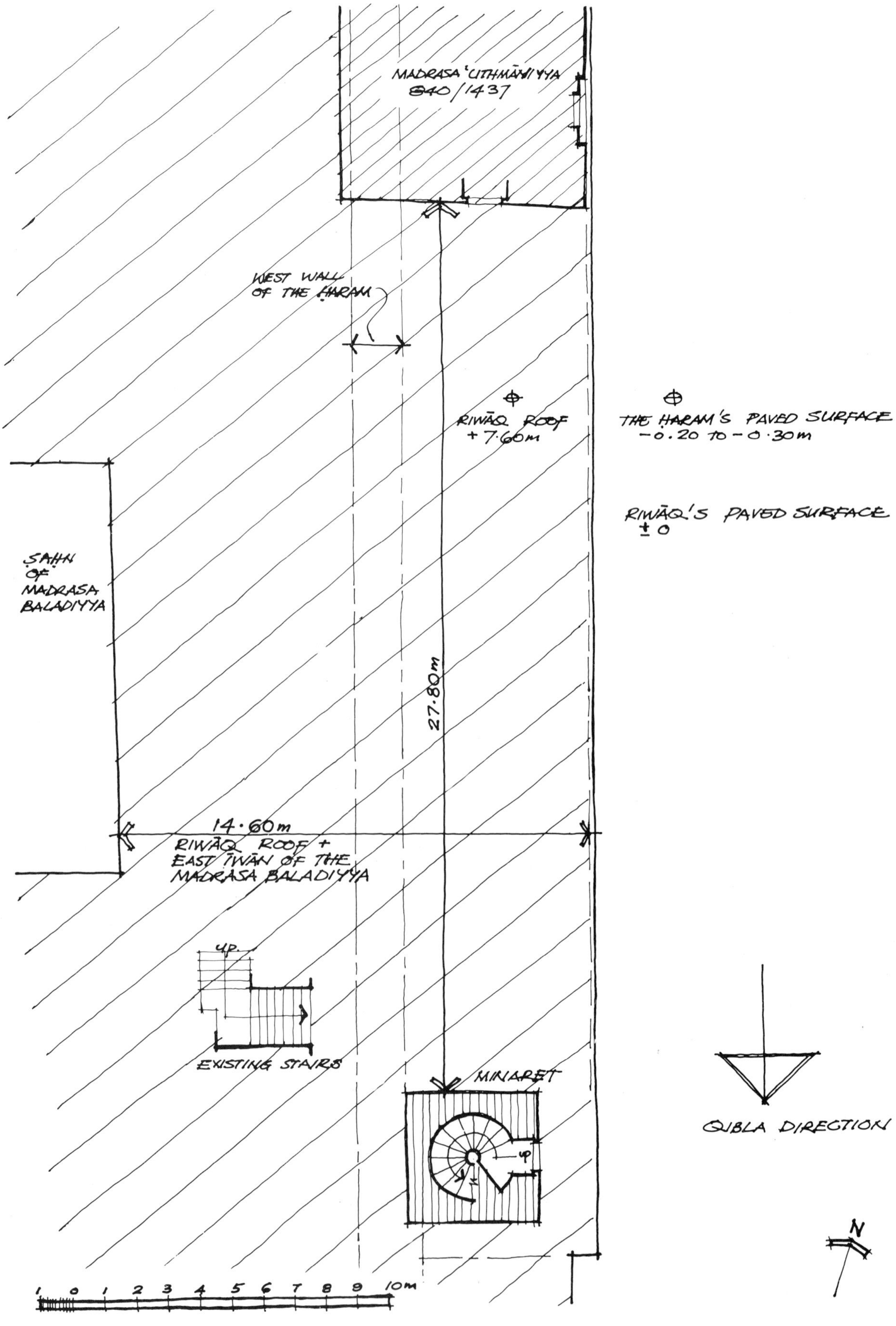

Fig. III/9 The site of the Old Madrasa on top of the *riwāq*

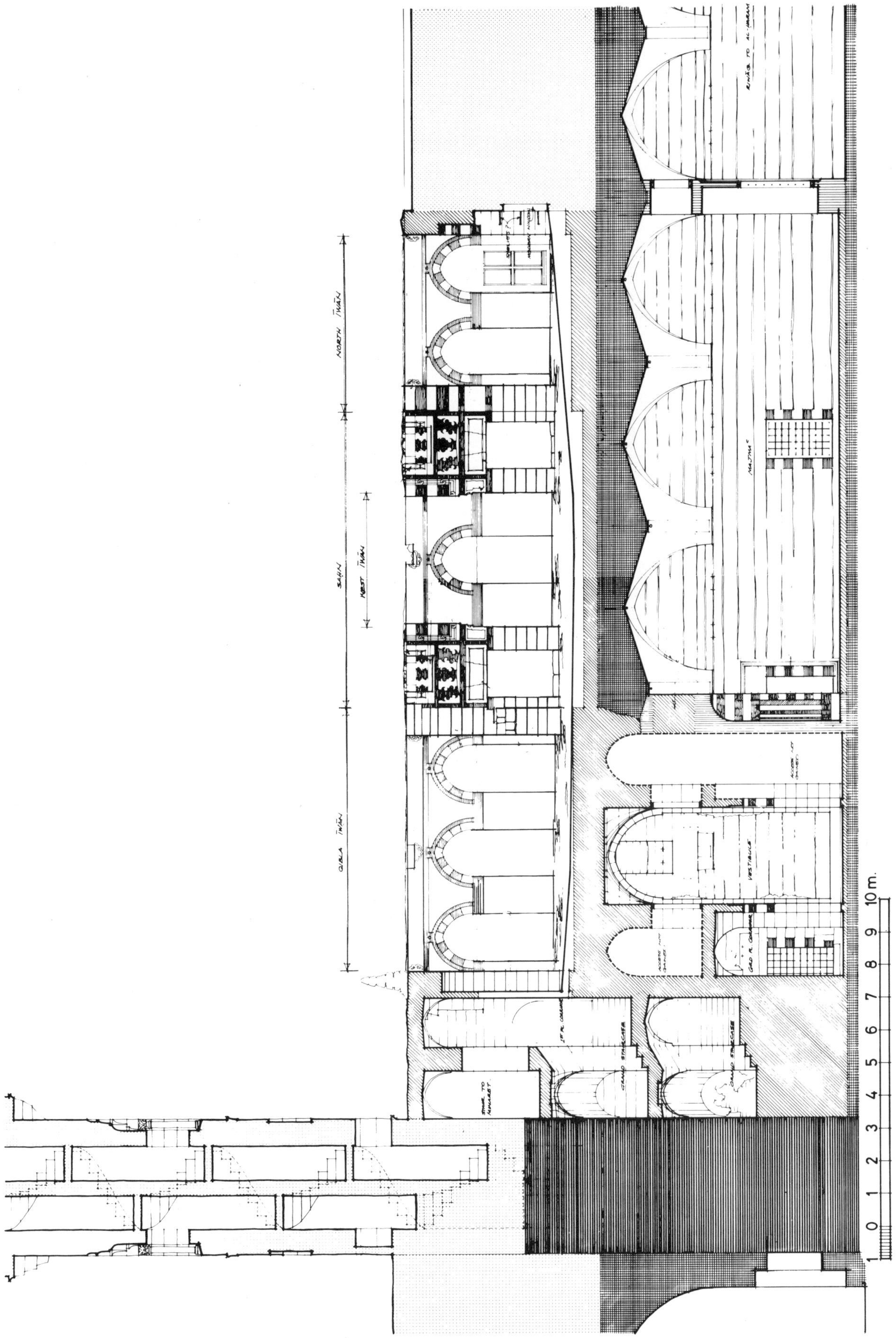

Fig. III/10 The north-south section taken through the *miḥrāb* of the *majma'*

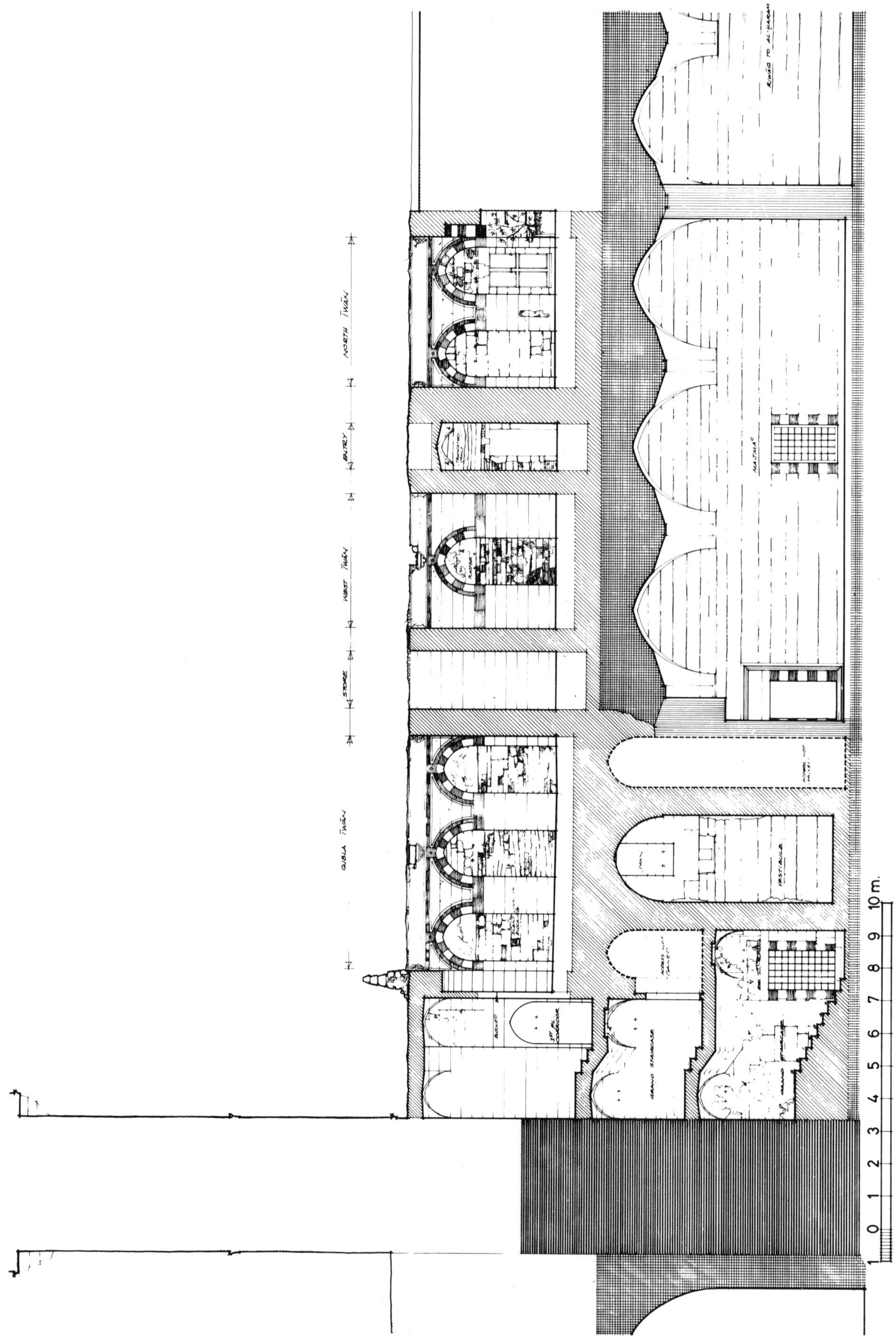

Fig. III/11 The north-south section taken along the west wall of the Ḥaram

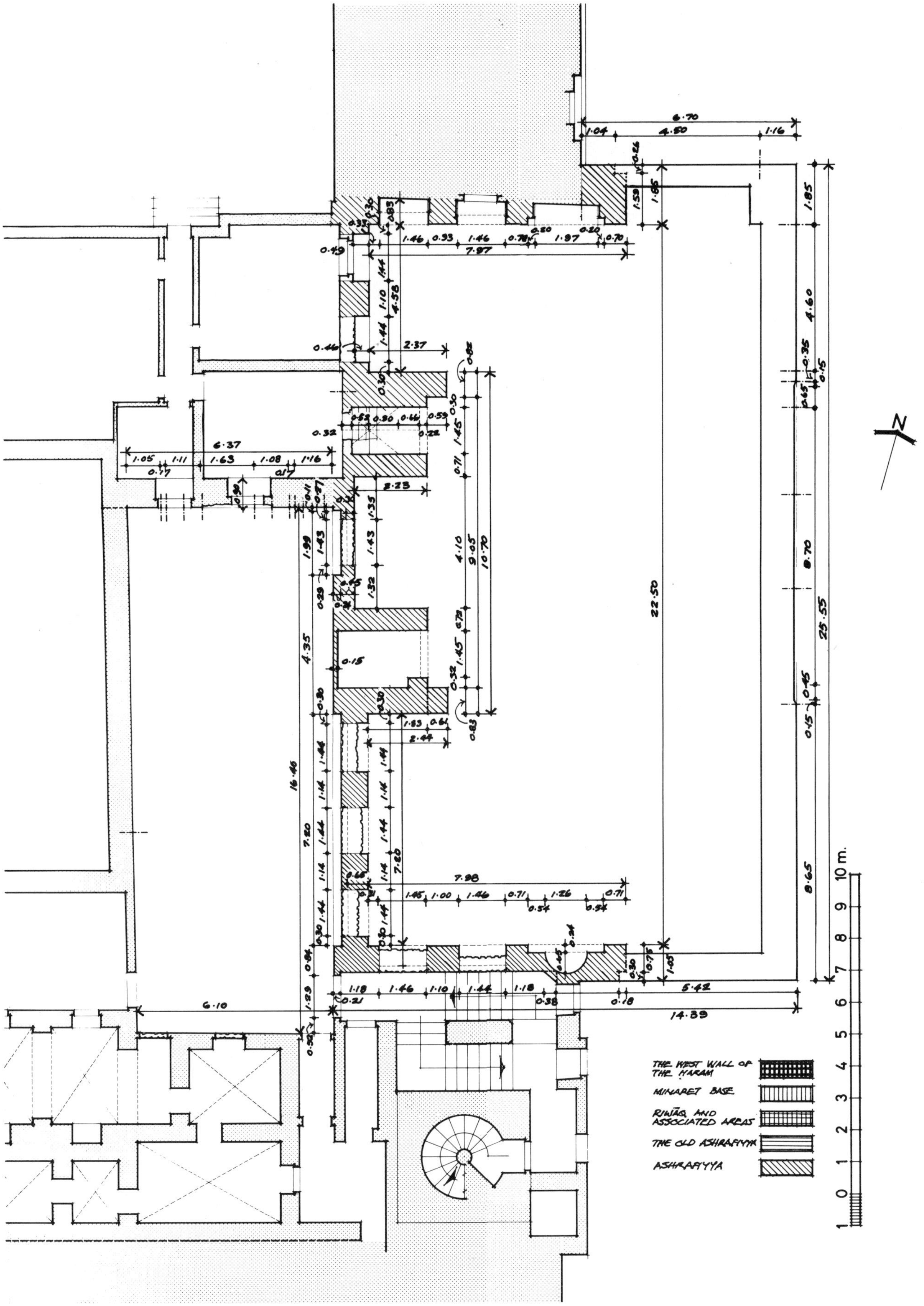

Fig. III/12 The first floor

fig. III/12

The First Floor: the Courtyard

fig. III/3

The main details of the barrel vaulted passageway have already been described, but additional points require to the mentioned. In the north wall of the passageway on the first floor there are two grilled windows with decorated lintels which before they were blocked up opened into the *qibla īwān* of the Madrasa. On the south side of the passage there are two further openings; through the eastern one the stair continues upwards to the entrance of the minaret, and the other, a doorway, leads to ancillary accommodation. At its western end the passageway is closed by an arched doorway, beyond which is the rectangular courtyard that used to lead to the recessed portal of the Madrasa.

fig. III/14

The exterior of this arched doorway, and that of a similar doorway opposite it in the south west corner of the courtyard, have *ablaq* voussoirs. The latter leads onto the roof of the Madrasa Baladiyya, where the ancillary accommodation of the Ashrafiyya was situated including cells for the sixty sufis mentioned by al-'Ulaymī.[8]

fig. III/13

Along the south wall of the courtyard only the lower stone courses (up to a height of 2.5 metres) and the three door openings are original, the upper courses are undoubtedly Ottoman. Of the three doorways, the central one has a rectangular opening which is now blocked up, with an *ablaq* relieving arch over a lintel, both being set in a moulded frame. The side openings have arches adorned by joggled keystones. Above the arched doorway of the passage and above the simpler arched openings in the south wall there is evidence of rectangular windows, openings that lit the internal corridors.

fig. III/14

The eastern side of the courtyard is defined by the west wall of the Madrasa which was reduced to its present height by the earthquake of 1545. However, we are fortunate in that Archibald Creswell took photographs shortly before the earthquake of 1346/1927, for they show that this earthquake further damaged the wall. Nevertheless three blocked up windows can still be seen set back in a recess, and another smaller recess holds a further blocked window. These recesses provide ample evidence of the expertise of the craftsmen who constructed the Ashrafiyya and their attention to detail, attributes which play an important role in this architectural reconstruction.

fig. III/15

Despite the north wall of the courtyard forming part of a modern house, a fact which slightly hampers our investigation, there are still to be seen fragments of the recessed portal that led into the Madrasa. Again we are indebted to Creswell for his photographs as they will be invaluable when the time comes for us to interpret these fragments.

The Madrasa

fig. III/12

Entered through the modern house, the Madrasa is a windswept area of almost 25 by 14 metres now used as an extension to the house, with clothes lines, a rabbit hutch and a dovecot. However, for contrast, there are spectacular views of the Ḥaram with the Mount of Olives in the background and, on clear days, the Judean desert to the south east. We do not need to stretch our imaginations to reconstruct the views seen by the Mamlūks when looking out from the Madrasa, for they are still here, a breathtaking panorama.

fig. III/13, III/10 and III/7

The area is contained by what remains of the walls of the Madrasa, two thirds of the south wall, the full length of the west wall, two thirds of the north walls, completed by low parapets. The south, north and west walls now stand at a height of 5 metres where they end in carved inscriptions. The south wall contains the arched *miḥrāb*, and the west and north walls *ablaq* window openings and recesses.

Attached at right angles to the west wall run four walls which help define the original divisions of the Madrasa. To the south the *qibla īwān* is defined by the remains of the wall which originally

fig. III/16

abutted one of two great arches which existed within the Madrasa. To the north the north *īwān* is similarly defined by an abutment of the second great arch, but here the decorated springing and a number of the arch voussoirs remain. Originally the *ṣaḥn* or central court of the Madrasa extended between these two great arches. The other two walls form the west *īwān* and along with the abutments they also define the entrance to the Madrasa and a store room perhaps intended to house copies of the Qur'ān.

Fig. III/13 The entrance porch, vestibule and *qibla* wall

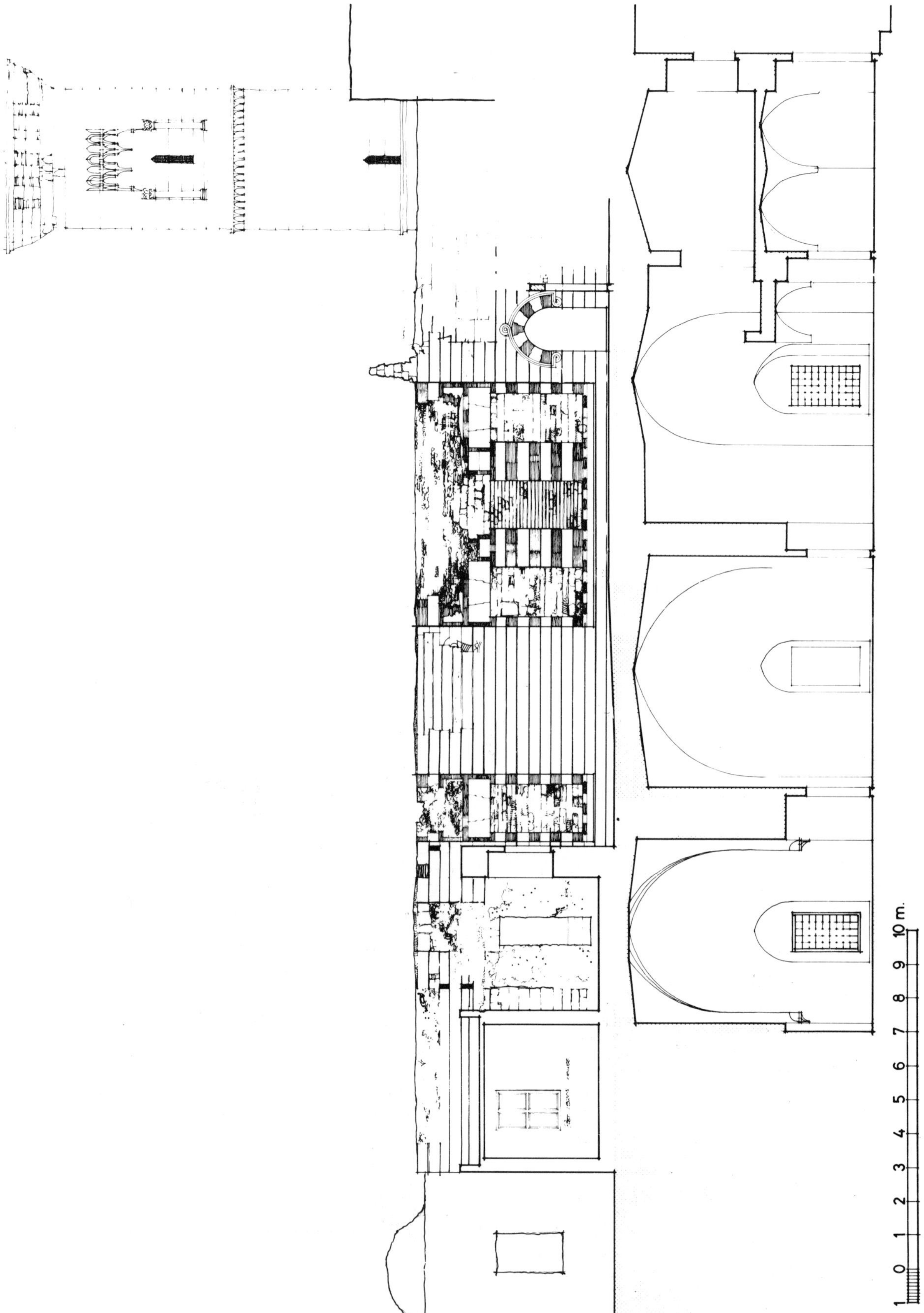

Fig. III/14 The exterior of the west wall of the Madrasa

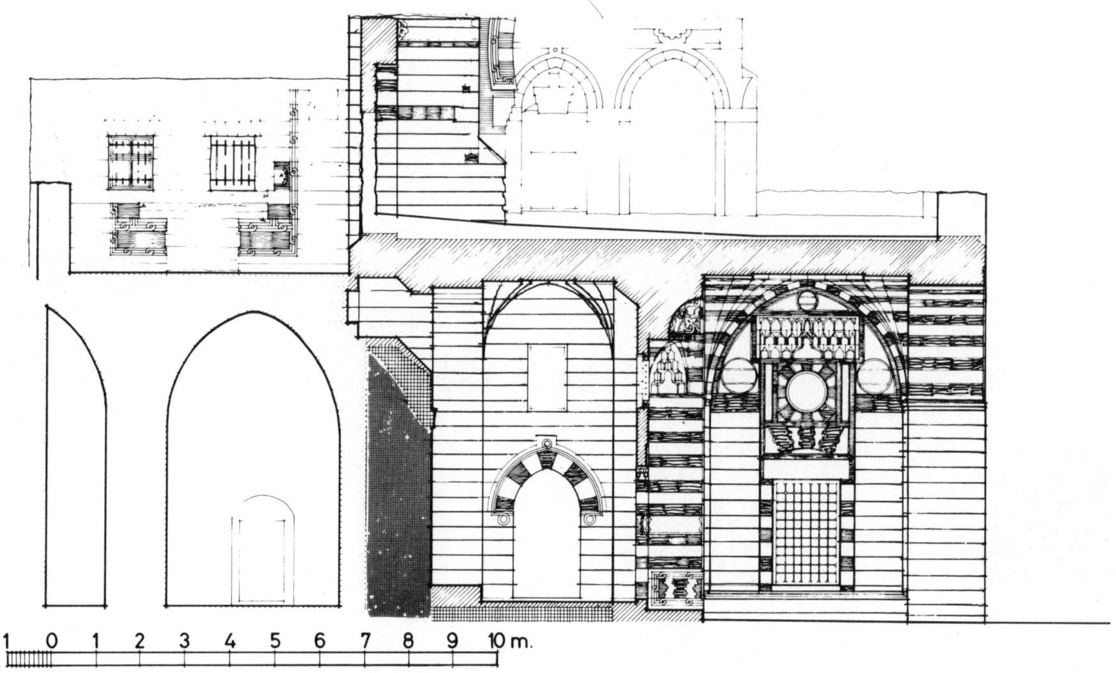

Fig. III/15 The entrance porch, vestibule and north wall of the courtyard

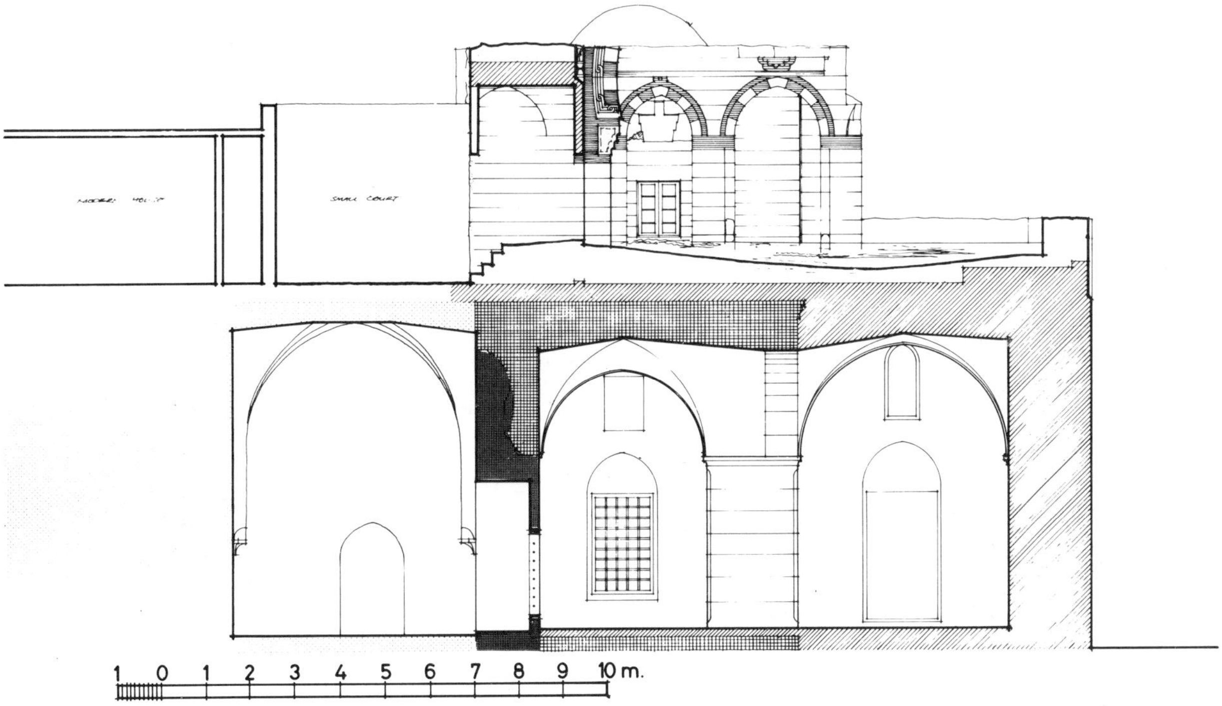

Fig. III/16 The entry from the modern house to the Madrasa

Plate 4 The arched *miḥrāb* in the south wall of the Madrasa

Plate 5 The remains of the south west corner of the *ṣaḥn*, with the *qibla īwān* on the left and the west *īwān* on the right

Plate 6 The remains of the great arch that spanned the north side of the *ṣaḥn*

Plate 7 The south bracket to the side arch seen from the *ṣaḥn*

Plate 8 The north bracket to the side arch seen from mid-span

This arrangement means that the Madrasa falls into the category of 'cruciform' mosques and madrasas, where each of the four *īwāns* or side halls is reserved for the teaching of one of the rites of Islam.

fig. III/10 In those wall areas that formed part of the *ṣaḥn*, *ablaq* work is found in profusion: there are the surrounds to the decorated lintels of the two door openings, and the joggled *ablaq* relieving arches above these lintels: higher still there are joggled *ablaq* string courses, and on each side of the west *īwān* above the level of the lintels *ablaq* stones are found which are similar to the remaining voussoirs of the great arch.

fig. III/12 One less obvious, but nevertheless significant feature, should be referred to, if only to indicate how the restrictions imposed by the size of the site were overcome: the thickness of the north wall of the Ashrafiyya varies. Its western half has a thickness of about 70 to 80 centimetres and is built up against the wall of the Madrasa 'Uthmāniyya, whereas the truncated eastern half of the wall is an extra metre thick. Assuming that we are dealing with an orthodox method of construction, our first conclusion must be that, when completed, the north wall would have been seen to have a uniform thickness throughout its length, and for this to have occurred the upper portions of the western half of the wall had therefore to be partly founded on the wall of the 'Uthmāniyya. Our second conclusion follows directly from the first: the design of the Ashrafiyya was so regular and precise that it required the north wall to go beyond the site boundary and extend onto the site occupied by the 'Uthmāniyya.

Notes

1. An earlier detailed study and reconstruction of the Ashrafiyya was published by Shlomo Tamari in Hebrew in the *Bar-Ilan Departmental Researches* I, 1973, and later in English in *Atti della Accademia Nazionale de Lincei*, Serie VIII, Vol. XIX under the title of 'Al-Ashrafiyya: An Imperial Madrasa in Jerusalem'. Tamari's restoration is reviewed in Appendix B. Most recently the Ashrafiyya has been described in *Mamlūk Jerusalem*, pp. 589-605 and includes new and additional historical material researched by D. S. Richards.
2. This entrance and the fan vaulting associated with it is discussed by W. Harvey, 'Saracenic Vaulting', *Architectural Review*, London, Nov. 1911, pp. 241-245; he includes a well-drawn plan and perspective of the entrance porch. Later the perspective was reproduced by Briggs, M., *Muhammadan Architecture*, Oxford, 1924 (reprinted New York, 1974); see also *Mamlūk Jerusalem*, pl. 63.7.
3. Commentaries on the imperial decrees are given by van Berchem, *CIA 'Ḥaram'*, pp. 141-156, nos. 182-186; see also Walls and Abul-Hajj, *Arabic Inscriptions in Jerusalem*.
4. This inscribed stone is illustrated in *Mamlūk Jerusalem*, pl. 63.1.
5. The *miḥrāb* in the Muzhiriyya is illustrated in *Mamlūk Jerusalem*, pl. 62.6.
6. See van Berchem, *CIA 'Ville'*, pl. 358, inscription no. 105.
7. Two out of the three tombs carry inscriptions. See Walls and Abul-Hajj, *Arabic Inscriptions in Jerusalem*, inscription nos. XLIII and XLIV, both dated to 797/1395.
8. Descriptions of their ancillary areas are given by Tamari, op. cit., and in *Mamlūk Jerusalem*, pp. 598-599.

Chapter IV
THE PLAN OF THE MADRASA

Before the geometries referred to in Chapter I come into play, the basic outline of the completed Madrasa has to be established. As described by al-'Ulaymī, the overall plan was cruciform in shape and indeed we have seen that the existing remains give some support to this. Nevertheless, to arrive at a fuller plan the main axes of symmetry must be identified and considered in relation to those original features which still exist. **fig. IV/1**

Upon doing so a cruciform plan is arrived at which is similar to those published by van Berchem, and more recently by Tamari: the *ṣaḥn* and the *qibla*, the west and the north *īwāns* are complete, the only unclear area is the east *īwān* described by al-'Ulaymī as a loggia. This therefore could never have mirrored the plan of the west *īwān*, and neither van Berchem nor Tamari was able to provide a satisfactory or practical solution to this problem of the appearance of the loggia. **fig. IV/2**

Having now an idea of the basic form of the Madrasa, the question of a geometry underlying its design can be broached. We must first accept that the construction of a platform in order to solve the problem of the severe restrictions of the site is fundamental to our search. Therefore the dimensions of the platform would be no more and no less than those required by the design approved by Sultan Qāytbāy. Thus we must look at the width of a site to see if it can generate a geometry which can control the design.[1] As a start, plan dimensions that have a simple arithmetic relationship to the width (such as 1:2) must be found, and they may then allow a simple geometric network to be created.

The overall width of the Madrasa, taken from the exterior face of its west wall to the eastern edge of the platform, is 14.39 metres, a length which will be referred to as the Basic Unit of Generation (BUG). A ½ BUG will therefore equal 7.20m—a ratio of 2:1.

On measuring the existing plan it is discovered that the depth of the *qibla īwān* is 7.20m excluding its great arch, and so is equal to the ½ BUG. Also the depth of the north *īwān*, including its great arch and the width of the north wall is 7.25m (an insignificant discrepancy in a building which has been wrecked by an earthquake). Perhaps it is stating the obvious to observe that the north-south axis of the Madrasa joins the midpoint of the *miḥrāb* and the midpoint of a large arched recess in the north wall. Thus it lies at a distance of 7.20m (½ BUG) from the exterior of the west wall and from the eastern edge of the platform. These relationships viewed as a whole at least hint at an underlying proportional system. **fig. IV/3**

The Fundamental Geometry

Looking at the overall plan of the Madrasa with its central *ṣaḥn*, the most logical starting point for any controlling geometry must be the centre of the *ṣaḥn* (point S). It is here that the two main axes cross, and, as is the case in cruciform-planned *madāris*, it was the visual centre.

If a circle is drawn with centre point S and a radius equal to ½ BUG, its circumference is tangential to the west wall and to the edge of the platform. If a hexagon (with points numbered 1 to 6) is then constructed within this circle, and if the two sides formed by the lines joining points 2-3 and 5-4 are extended, they cut the north-south axis at the centre of the *miḥrāb* (point M). Point M also coincides with the point where the north-south axis coincides with the inner face of the south wall of the Madrasa. The two lines 5-M and 2-M, together with the 'base' line 5-2 (the west-east axis) form an equilateral triangle with sides measuring 1 BUG, the simplest and strongest of geometric figures. Surely this cannot be an unplanned coincidence. The Mamlūks were experts in the field of geometry. They knew and easily recognised such things; therefore is it not highly significant that this triangle with 1 BUG-long sides brings together in a geometrical relationship the outer faces of the walls of the

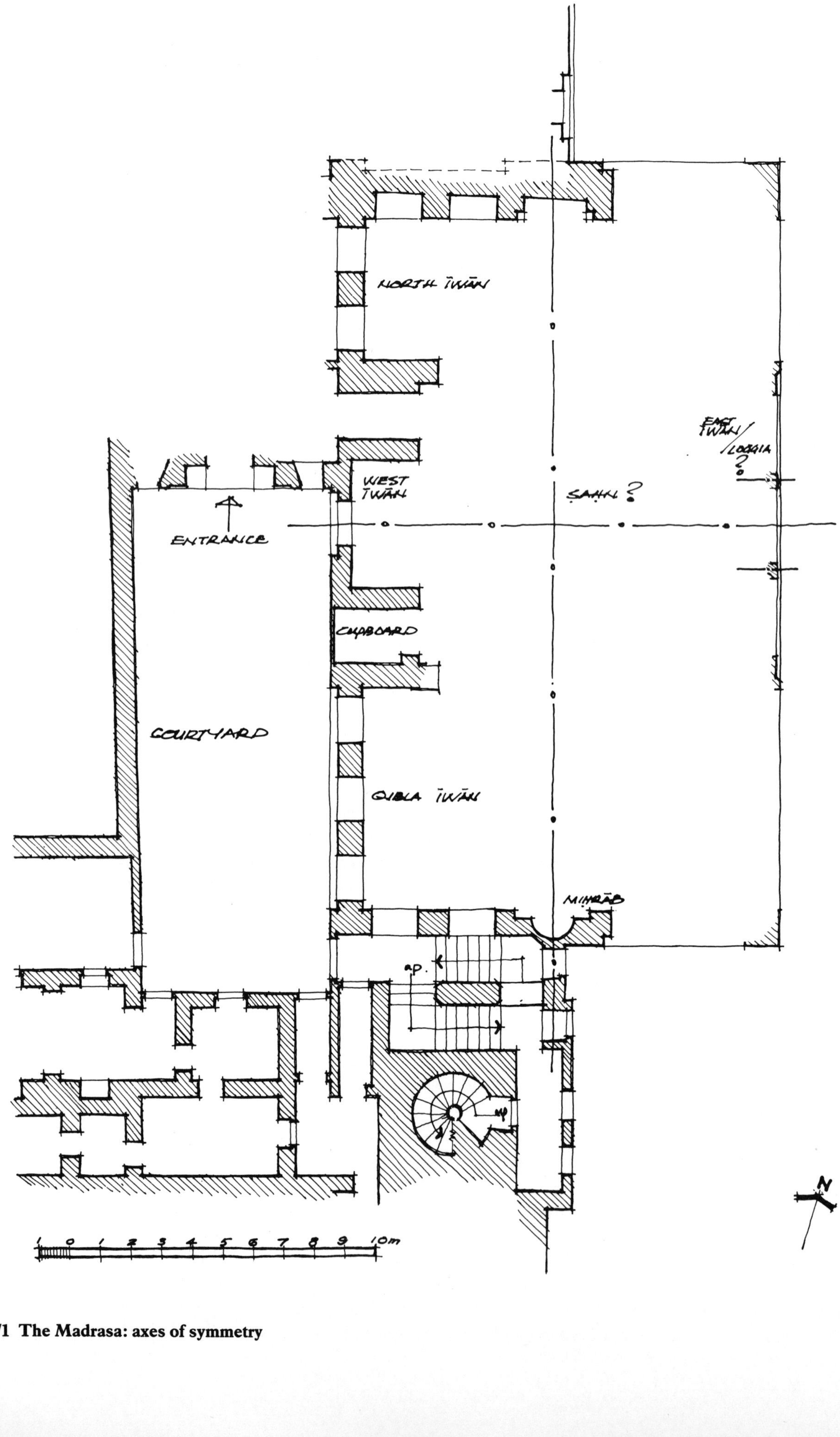

Fig. IV/1 The Madrasa: axes of symmetry

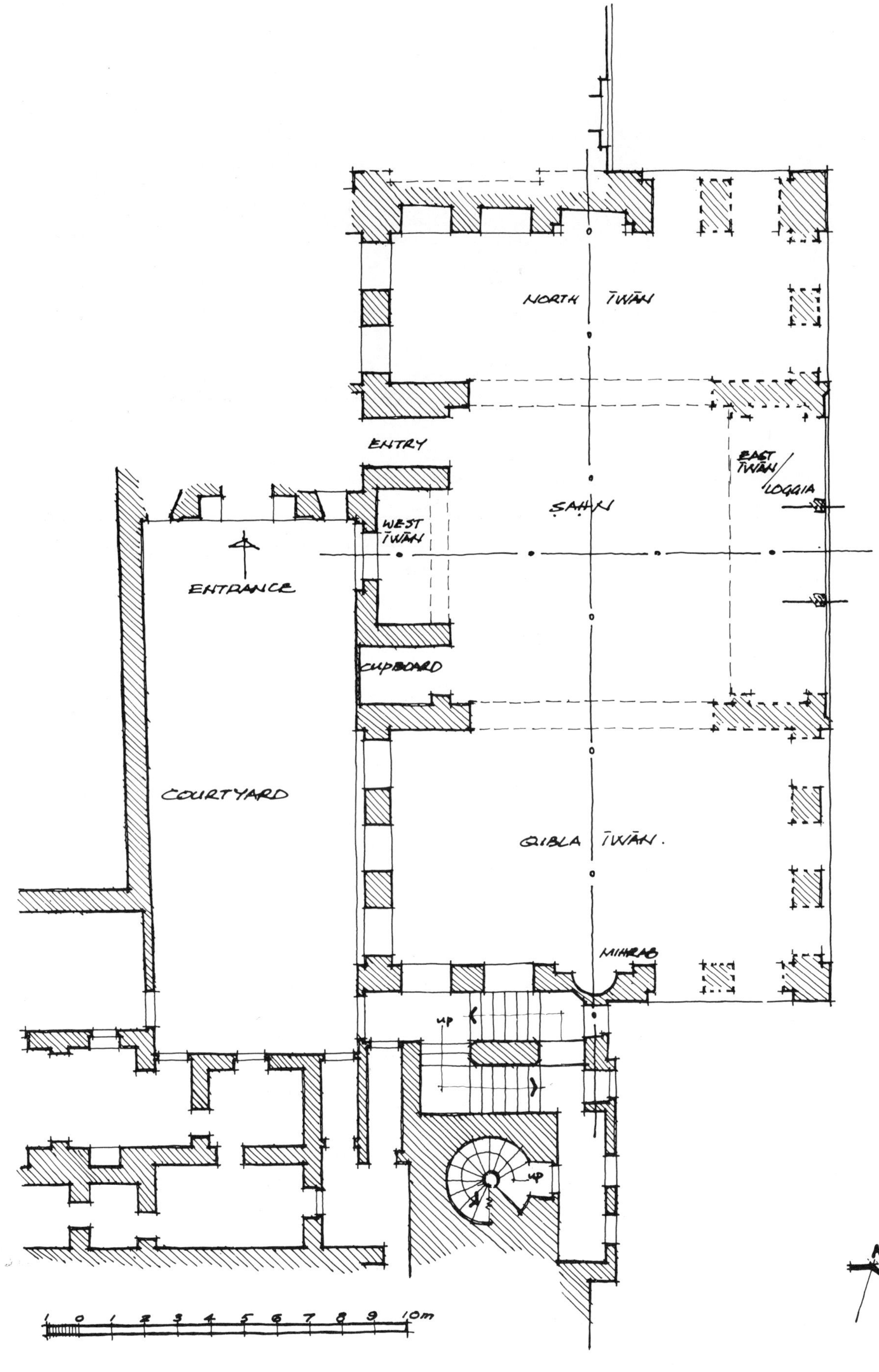

Fig. IV/2 The Madrasa: a symmetrical plan

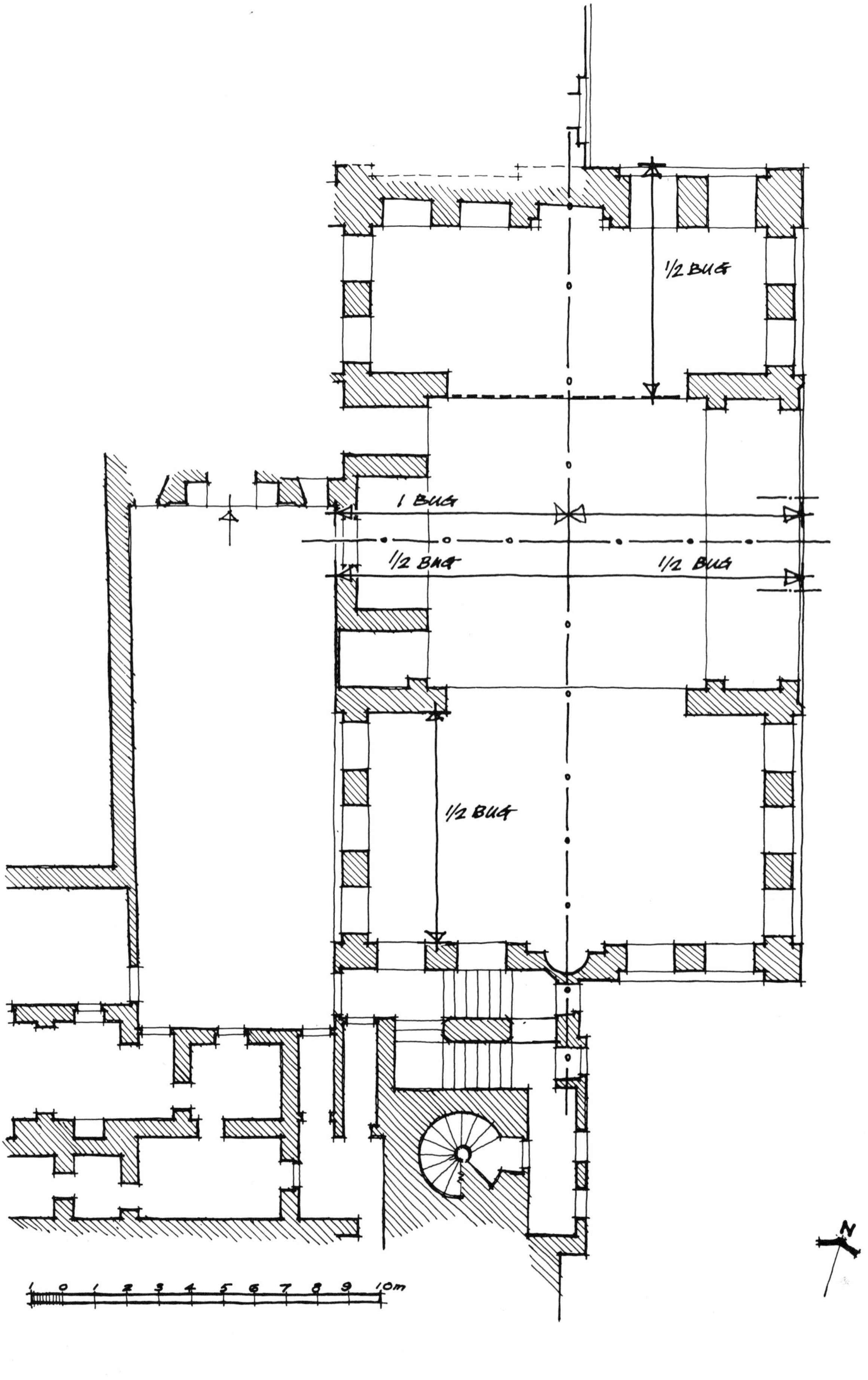

Fig. IV/3 The Madrasa: some ½ BUG relationships

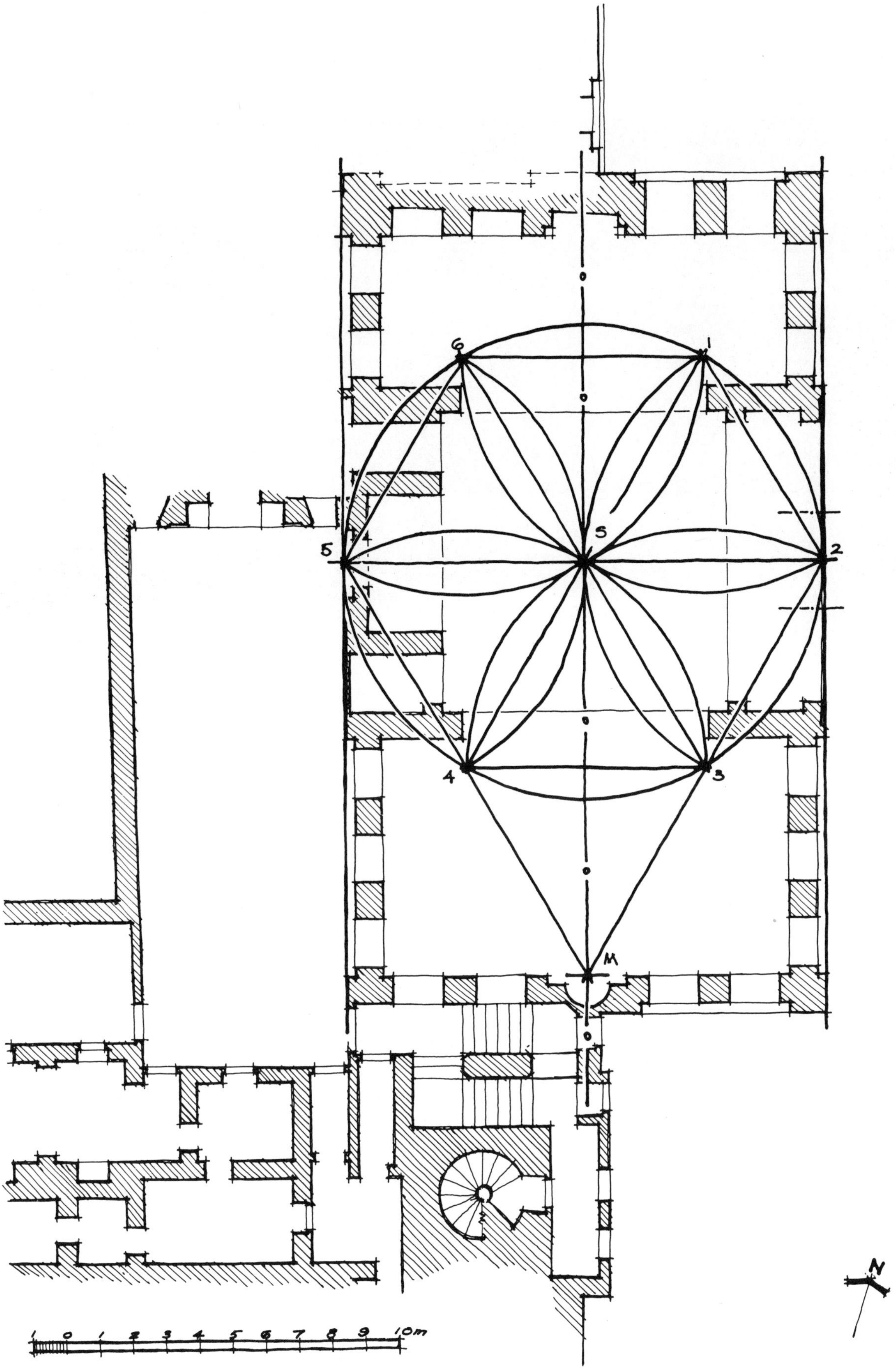

Fig. IV/4 The Madrasa: the fundamental geometry

Plate 9 The north wall of the Madrasa with the pseudo-gateway. The modern window opening lights one of the rooms of the Madrasa 'Uthmāniyya

Madrasa, the visual centre, the centre of the *ṣaḥn* and the centre of the *miḥrāb*, with its vital position in any Islamic place of prayer indicating the direction of Mecca?

These few discoveries give an insight into the ideas of the architect, and confirm his use of geometry in the design of the Madrasa. This geometric figure of the 1 BUG diameter circle and its inscribed hexagon will be referred to as the fundamental geometry as it is from this that all future geometries will be developed.

fig. IV/5

In theory we have been able to find the position of the fundamental geometry using the external faces of the east and west walls of the Madrasa, but from a practical standpoint it has not been fixed for it does not relate to any of the original physical features of the site. An external anchor point is required which restricts the position of the geometry along its east-west axis, and which will remain unchanged as a survey point for the builders. Just such a point is the western edge of the site which can be joined to the fundamental geometry by drawing a circle centred on point 5 and with a ½ BUG radius. When this construction is looked at as a whole, the way in which the size of the platform was determined becomes clear: the width of the site is 1½ BUG and is subdivided into three strips each with a width of ½ BUG.

The Primary Geometries

Having established and fixed the centre of the fundamental geometry it can now be extended to generate primary geometries which will establish the predominant features along the north-south axis: the walls forming the *ṣaḥn*, the *qibla īwān*, the north *īwān*, the minaret in the south and the Madrasa 'Uthmāniyya in the north.

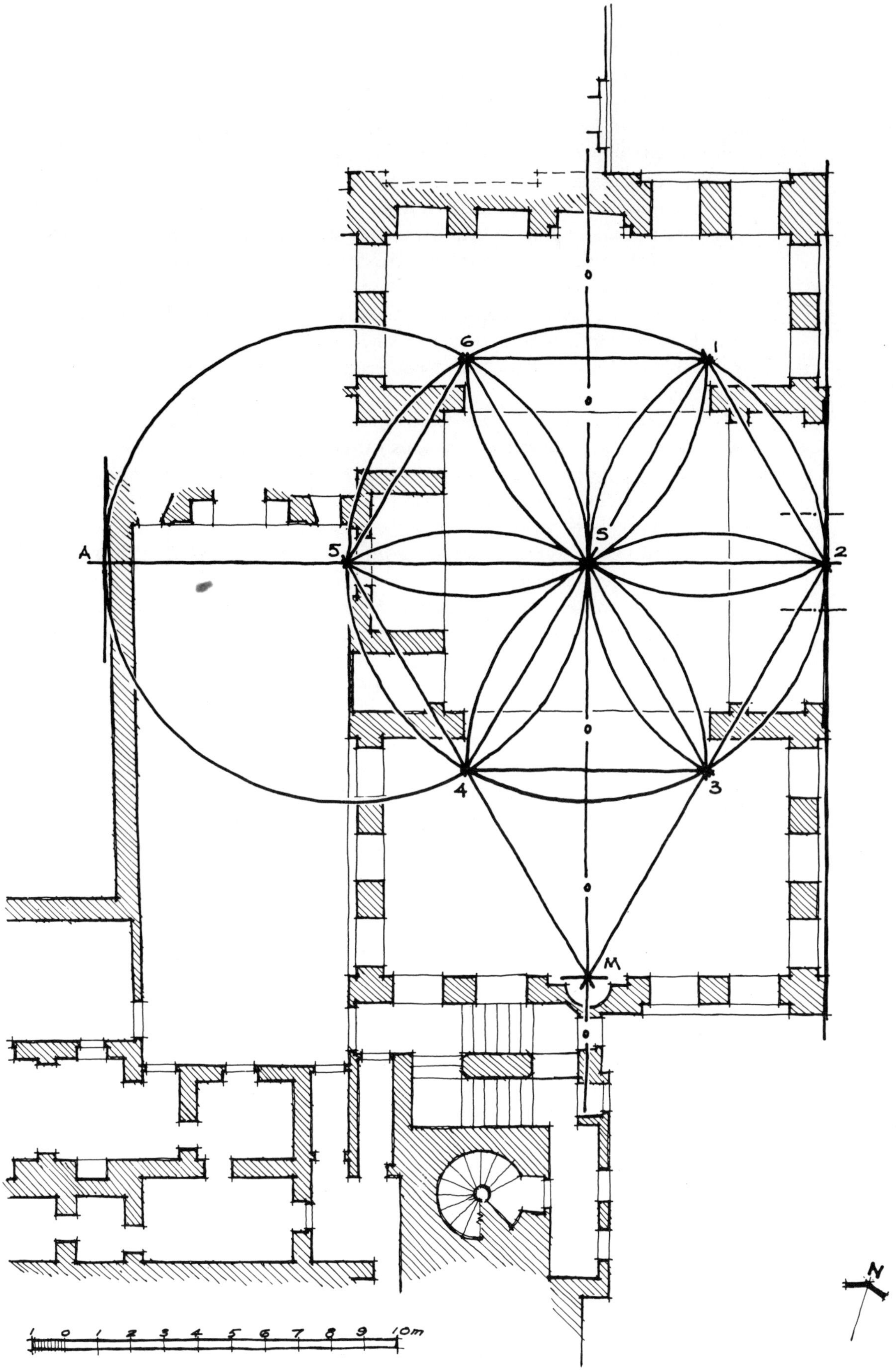

Fig. IV/5 The Madrasa: anchoring the fundamental geometry

fig. IV/6

To establish the dimensions of the *ṣaḥn* a second hexagon (points 7 to 12) is added to the fundamental geometry. By joining four of the points of intersection of these two hexagons, a square can then be constructed running parallel to the west-east axis. The north side of the square runs along the southern face of the great arch in the north wall of the *ṣaḥn*, and the south side of the square runs along the northern face of the great arch in the south wall of the *ṣaḥn*. The west and east sides of the square coincide with the centre lines of the west and east walls of the *ṣaḥn*.

The span of the great arches can now be established, and by eye they appear to be equal to the length of one side of the fundamental hexagon (½ BUG). To confirm this, when two lines are drawn from points 1-3 and 4-6, they touch the eastern and western abutments of the arches. The apparent discrepancy in the diagram can be accounted for by the projecting imposts on each side of the arches.

fig. IV/8

The primary geometry is extended to the *qibla īwān* when a ½ BUG radius semi-circle centred at the mid-point of the line 3-4 is drawn. It will be seen from the plan that the southern or *qibla* wall is thinner in its western half than its eastern half, the eastern being an external wall. It will also be seen that the semicircle is tangential to the southern face of the western half and the rear of the external recess in the eastern half.

The depth of the *qibla īwān* is the next item to be defined. Remembering that the internal or northern face of the *qibla* wall has previously been fixed by point M, the depth of the *īwān* is found by constructing a square on the internal face of the *qibla* wall with sides measuring ½ BUG. The two sides running parallel to the north-south axis pass through points 3 and 4 of the fundamental geometry and the fourth side with point Q_1, the midpoint of the north wall of this *īwān*. Point Q lying on the north-south axis must also be the centre of the *qibla īwān*. This ½ BUG square, apart from locating significant points in the *qibla īwān*, also relates to the square of the *ṣaḥn*, as the distance separating them equals the width of the intrados of the great arch. If a circle centred on Q is then drawn tangentially to line 3-4, a square can be inscribed within it whose sides are equal to the width of the *miḥrāb* panel.

fig. IV/9

The north *īwān* has next to be considered. When from point 7 a circle is drawn which is tangential to point N, and describes a square, the following relationships are created. Firstly, the circle is tangential to the north wall. Secondly, as the south side of the inscribed square coincides with the line of the south wall of the *īwān*, the depth of the north *īwān* is determined. Thirdly, the sides of the inscribed square are equal to the width of the area surrounding the pseudo-gateway.

A semicircle with a ½ BUG radius is then drawn from point N, lying at the centre of the north wall of the *ṣaḥn*. The point at which this semicircle cuts the north-south axis coincides with the external face of the north wall of the north *īwān*. Therefore the distance between point N and this point of intersection equals ½ BUG.

fig. IV/10

The main lines of the west *īwān* are defined by three equal circles. The first of those is the circle centred on point 5 of the fundamental geometry and whose circumference is tangential to the west side of the square of the *ṣaḥn*. Having the same radius as the first, the second and third circles are centred on the corners of the square of the *ṣaḥn*. The points where their circumferences cut the square of the *ṣaḥn* determine the span of the arch to the west *īwān*. The apparent discrepancy between the actual masonry abutments and the geometries is accounted for by the projecting imposts.

If squares are inscribed within the second and third circles, the outer faces of the side walls of the *īwān* are defined by the south side of the northern square and the north side of the southern square. The depth of the *īwān* is found by joining the western sides of these inscribed squares.

fig. IV/11

In the same way that an anchor was required to restrain the geometries on the east-west axis, another anchor is required to prevent the primary geometry from pushing the north wall of the Ashrafiyya further over the roof of the Madrasa 'Uthmāniyya. As before, an external anchor has to be found which will not be removed during the building works and to which the builders can refer, and the likely choice would be the minaret. Indeed it was used by al-'Ulaymī to define the southern boundary of the site.

However, any such anchorage has to be connected to some definite point of the Madrasa, and since the *miḥrāb* was located through the fundamental geometry this would be the logical point from which to begin. So if from point M a semicircle is drawn such that its circumference is tangential to the northern wall of the minaret, it is found that the distance between the *miḥrāb* and minaret is equal to half the length of the sides of the square of the *ṣaḥn*.

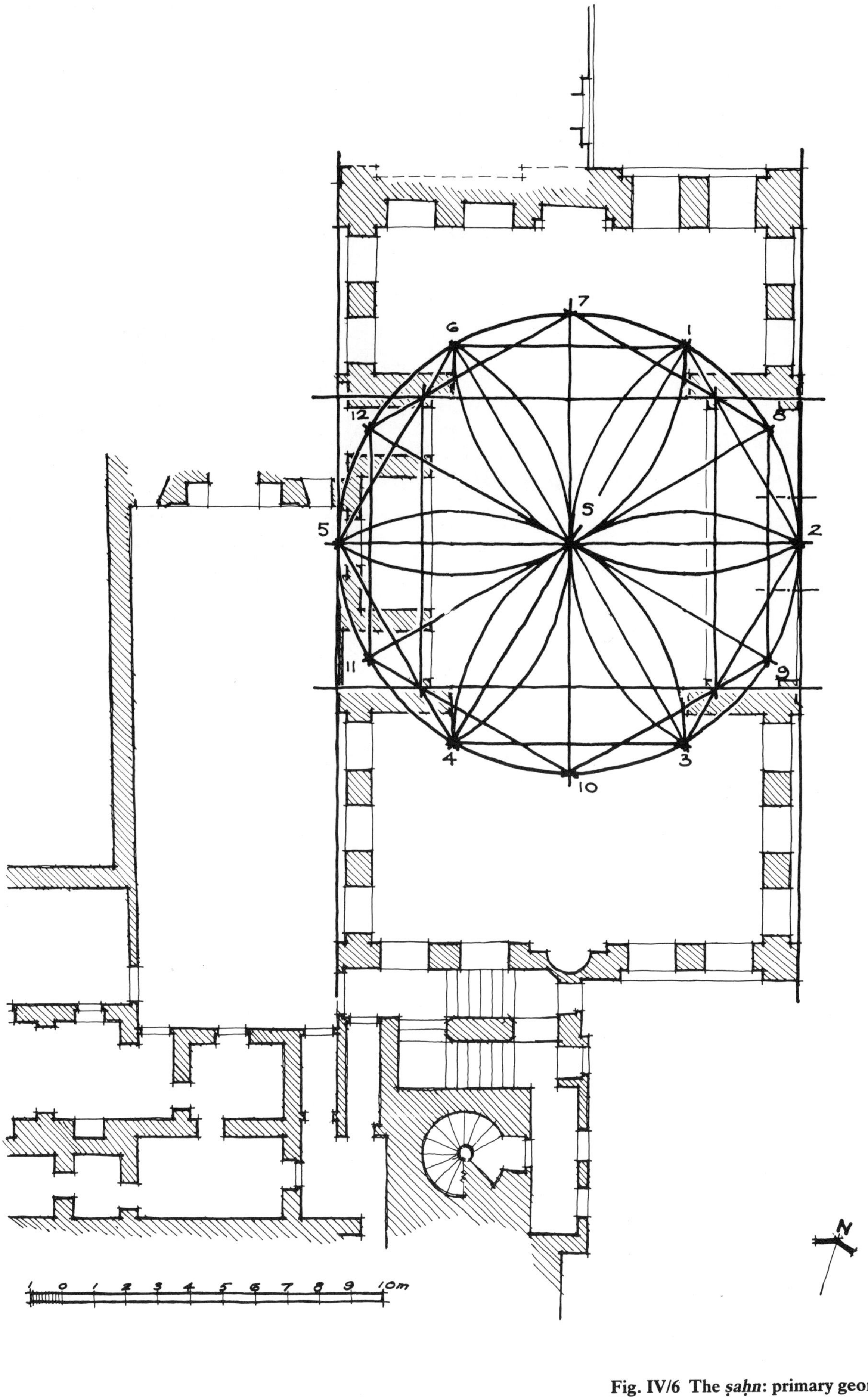

Fig. IV/6 The *ṣaḥn*: primary geometry

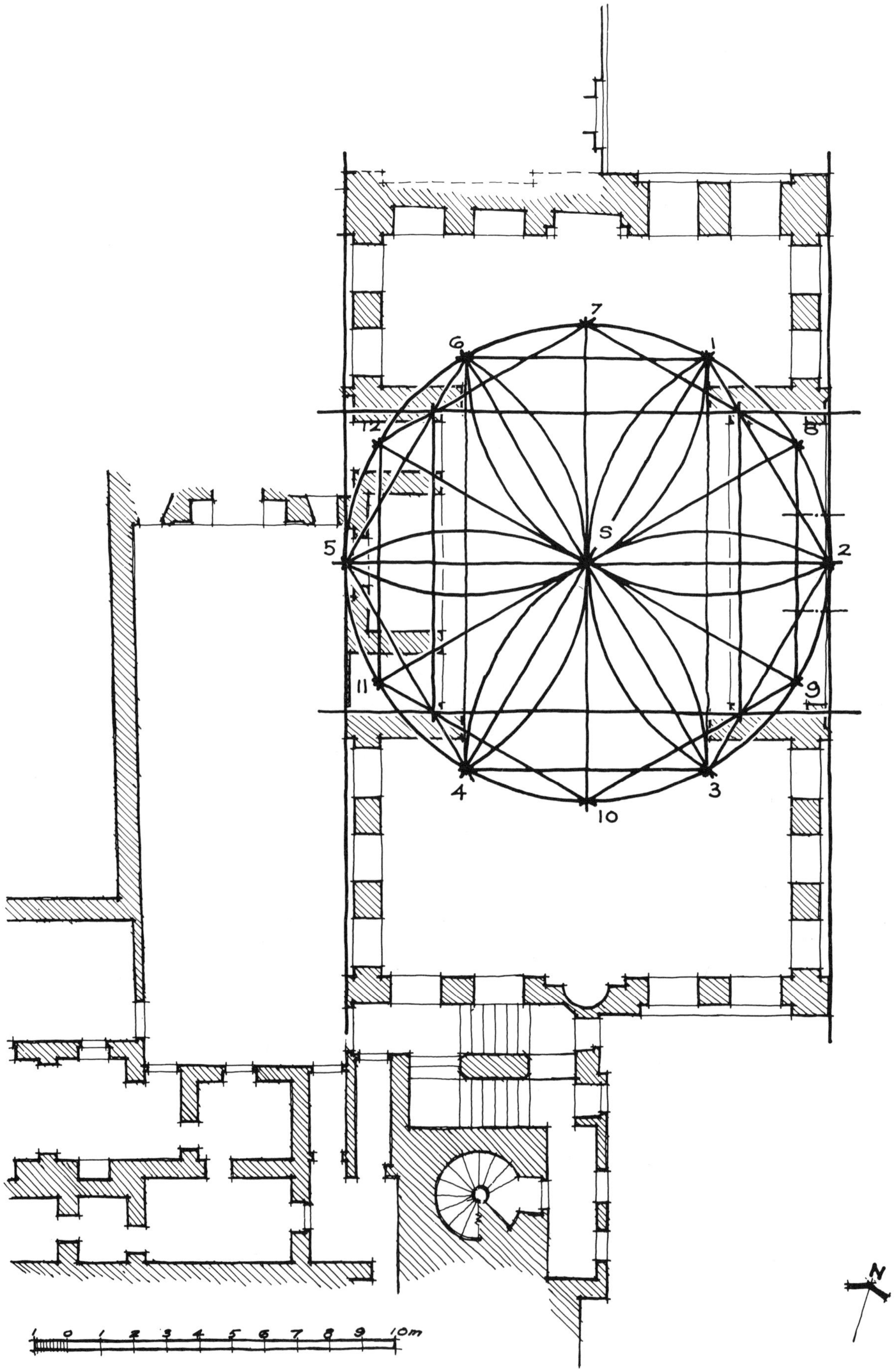

Fig. IV/7 The *ṣaḥn*: the span of the great arches

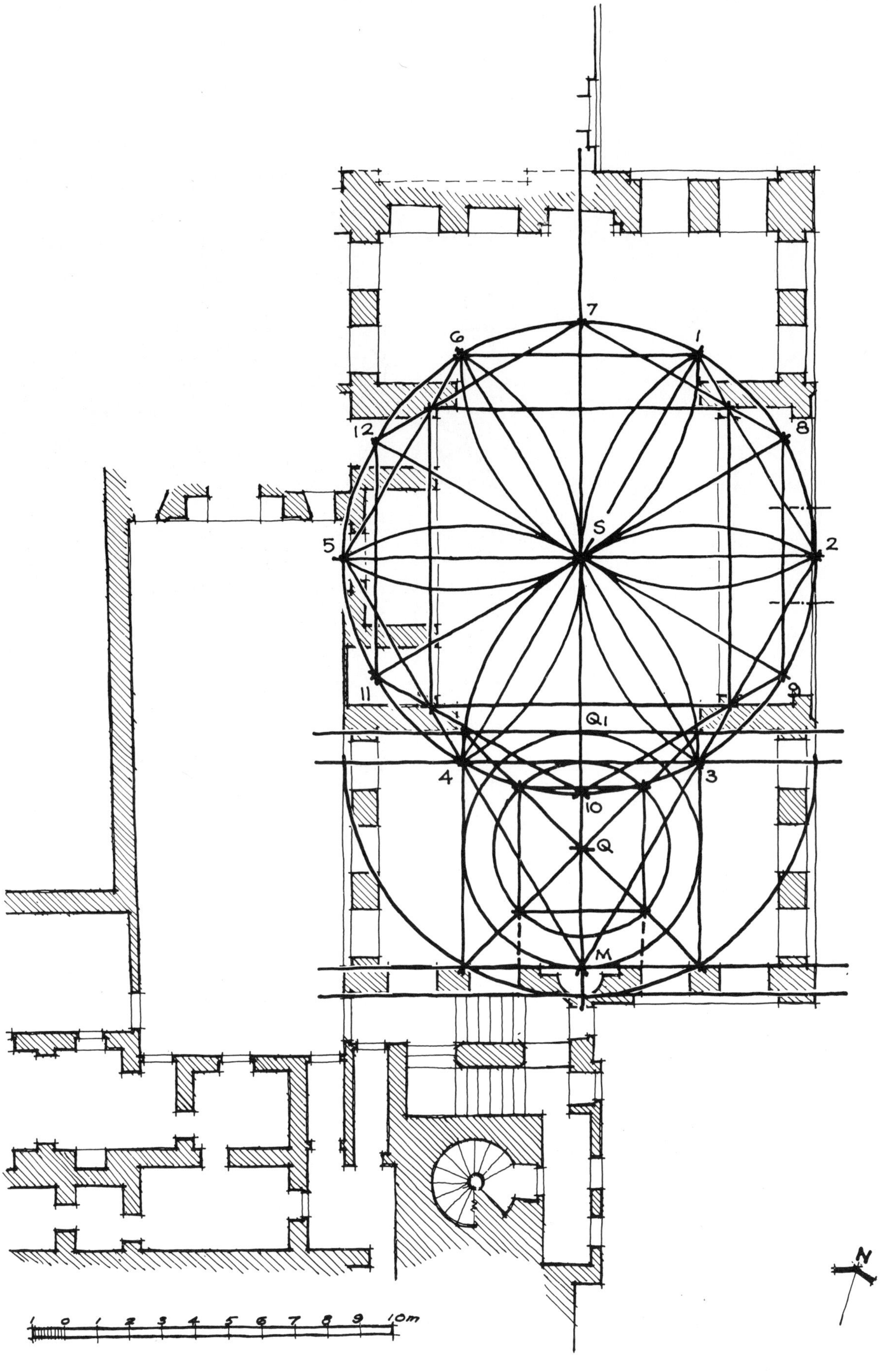

Fig. IV/8 The *qibla īwān*: primary geometry

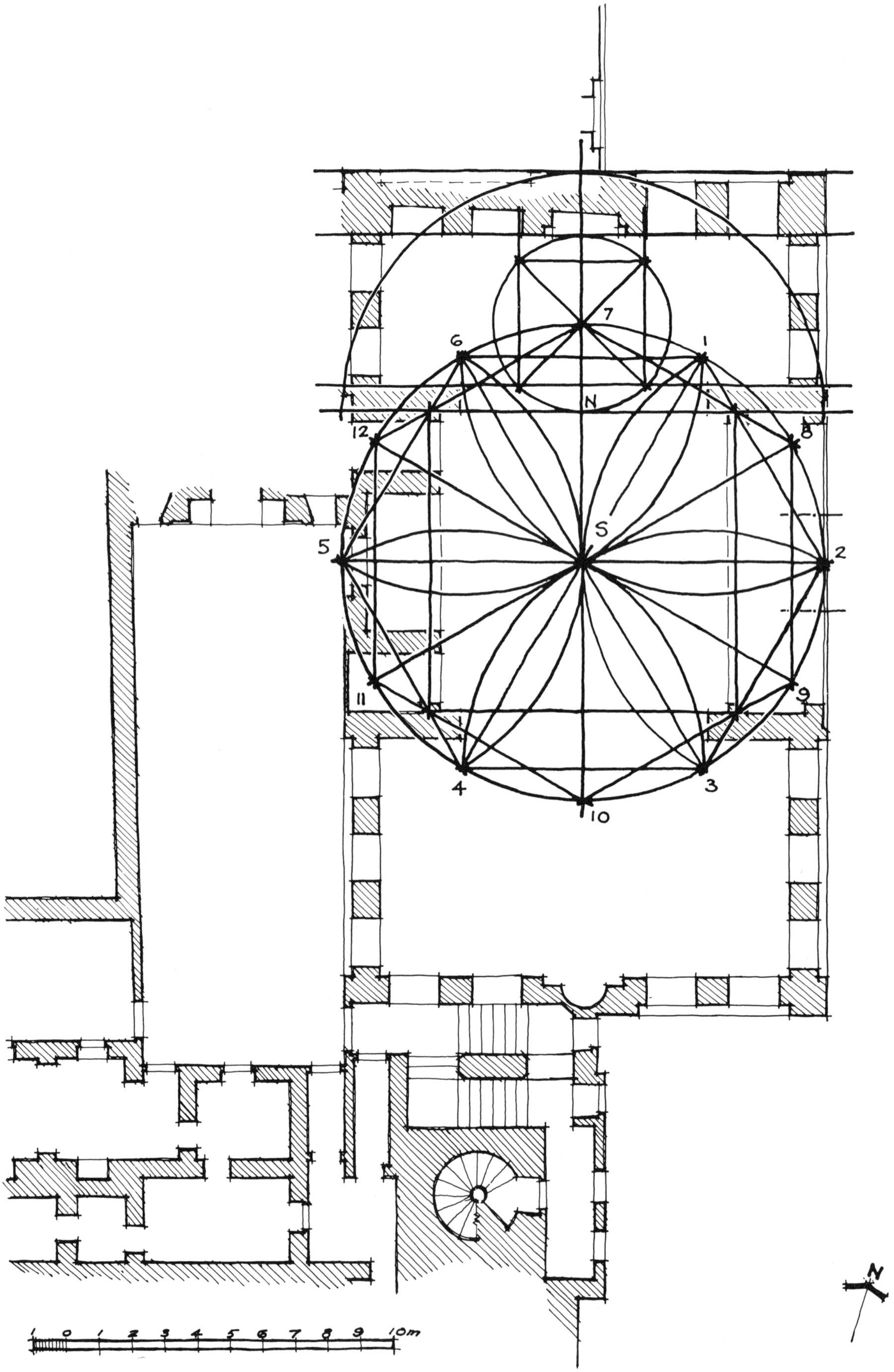

Fig. IV/9 The north *īwān*: primary geometry

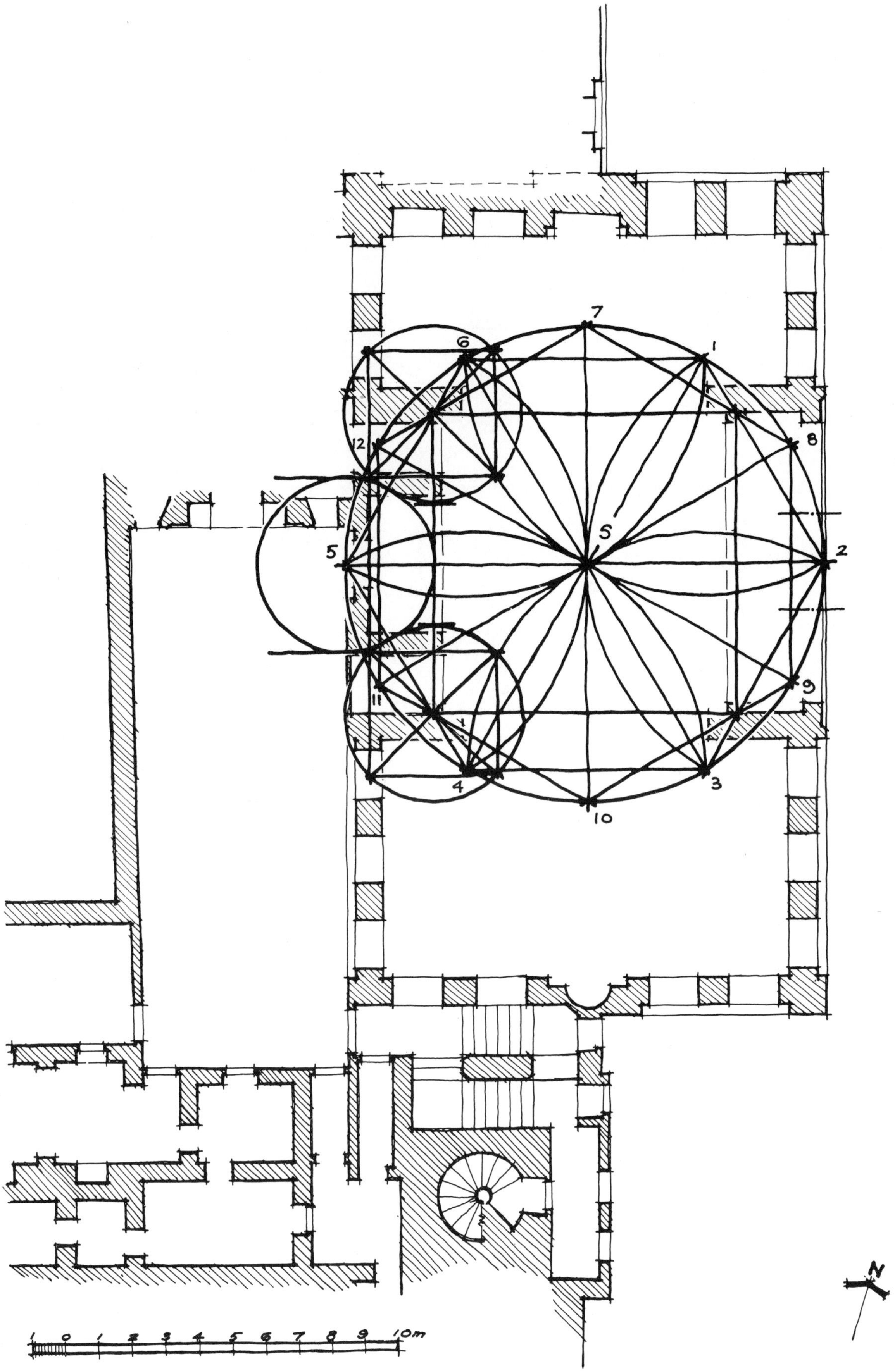

Fig. IV/10 The west *īwān*: primary geometry

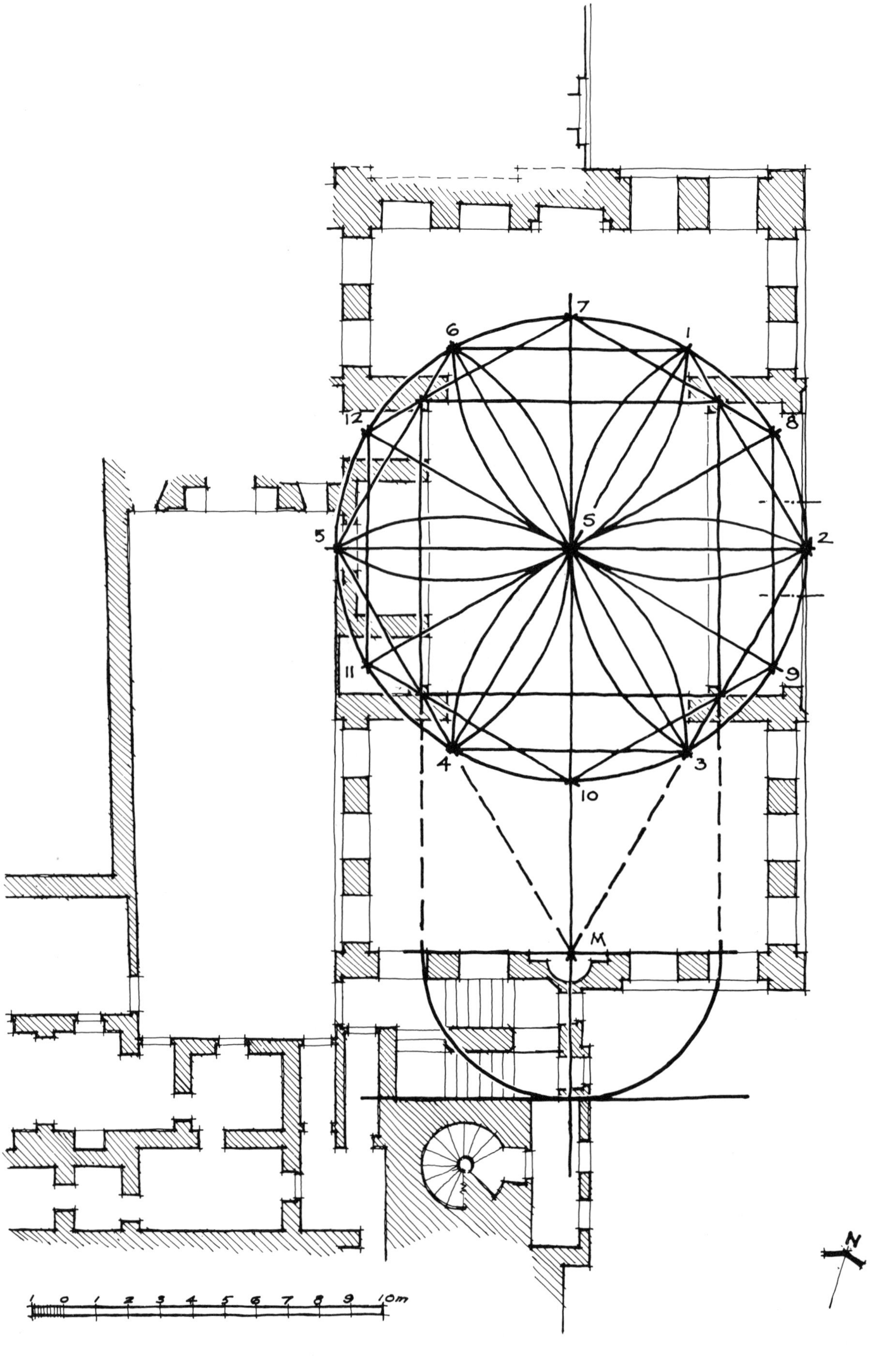

Fig. IV/11 The Madrasa: anchoring the primary geometry

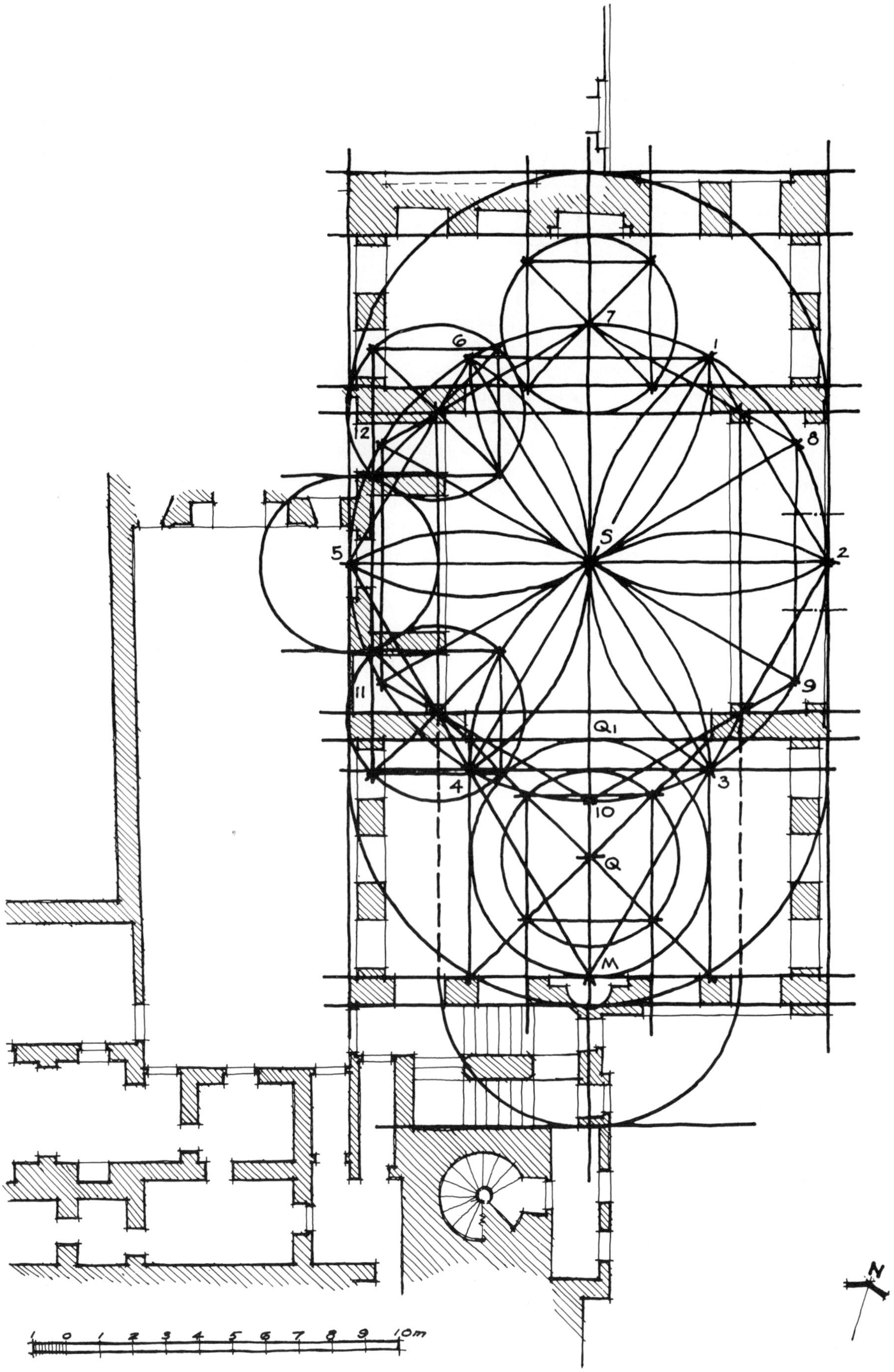

Fig. IV/12 The Madrasa: the primary geometries combined

fig. IV/12 When combined together the primary geometries almost complete the external casing of the Madrasa, and also they define most of the walls and their widths. However, when combined many confusing images arise despite the fact that individually the primary geometries can be easily traced to their generator, the double hexagon of the fundamental geometry.

The new relationships which appear may in fact lead to a deeper understanding of the architect's intentions. For example, the figure of a circle and inscribed square which provides the width of the *miḥrāb* panel in the *qibla īwān* is repeated in the north *īwān* to provide the width of the pseudo-gateway panel. In the west *īwān* the identical figure of a circle and inscribed square is repeated twice.

Some Detailed Geometries

fig. IV/13 To recap, a fundamental geometry composed of a single inscribed hexagon has been established, and this hexagon has been doubled to form the 12-pointed star which generated the primary geometries. If, however, it is doubled yet again, a 24-pointed star is produced which can generate still more geometries—the detailed geometries.

The existing architectural evidence shows the *ṣaḥn* to be rectangular. If the hexagon is developed to produce the 24-pointed star, the corners of the *ṣaḥn* can be located where the lines 18-13, 20-21, 5-16 and 23-24 cut the square of the *ṣaḥn* which was found in the primary geometry.

fig. IV/14 The detailed geometries also define the depth of the external window recesses in the west and east elevations, through producing in both directions the lines joining points 24 to 18 and 21 to 15. It should, however, be noted that since there is no recess in the west wall of the north *īwān*, line 24-18 coincides with its outer face.

fig. IV/15 The thickness of the main walls is the next matter to be considered. Having established through the primary geometry the thickness of the western portion of the *qibla* wall, and in view of the fact that it has no external recess, this can be used as the basic thickness. By adding this basic thickness to the previously established external window recesses, the full thickness of the walls forming the *qibla* and north *īwāns* are determined. Furthermore, the thickness of the north and south walls of the *ṣaḥn* are seen to be equal to the basic thickness.

The north wall of the north *īwān* follows a different pattern. Where its lower stone courses abut the skewed wall of the Madrasa 'Uthmāniyya, the maximum thickness equals the basic thickness. For the remainder of the wall its thickness, including the external recess, is equal to twice the basic thickness.

fig. IV/16 No further geometries are required to establish the main lines of the plan of the Madrasa. Future geometries will either reconfirm a relationship discovered previously by a different geometrical route, or they will add to the main form. As an example of a 'reconfirming' geometry, the lines joining points 20 to 16 and points 23 to 13 when extended in both directions define the panel widths of the *miḥrāb* and the pseudo-gateway found earlier through the primary geometries.

fig. IV/17 The additional details which could be of most use at this stage are the triple windows along the side walls of the *qibla īwān*, for having once discovered the geometry underlying their dimensions, the windows in the west and the north *īwāns* should follow automatically since they have the same opening width. With this purpose in mind another inspection of the primary geometry of the *qibla īwān* reveals an interesting and obvious relationship which was simply not noticed when the *miḥrāb* panel was being considered. The inscribed square centred on Q which defines the *miḥrāb* panel also defines the combined widths of the central window and its flanking masonry in the side walls. For reasons of clarity, figure IV/17 illustrates this construction in the eastern half of the *qibla īwān*.

The next discovery is more obscure and concerns the relationships of the hexagon centred on point W and constructed between the large square with sides equal to the span of the great arch and the side walls of the *īwān*. The side 6-5 precisely positions and dimensions the central window opening which in fact measures 1.44 m wide, or exactly $^1/_{10}$ BUG. It follows, therefore, that the radius of the circle equals $^1/_{10}$ BUG and its diameter is $^1/_5$ BUG. Notice also that the position of the rear of the external window recess can be reconfirmed at the intersections of the lines radiating from centre W at an angle of 60° to the west-east axis and the lines of the north and south walls.

The next step is to develop this geometry so that it controls the flanking windows of the side walls

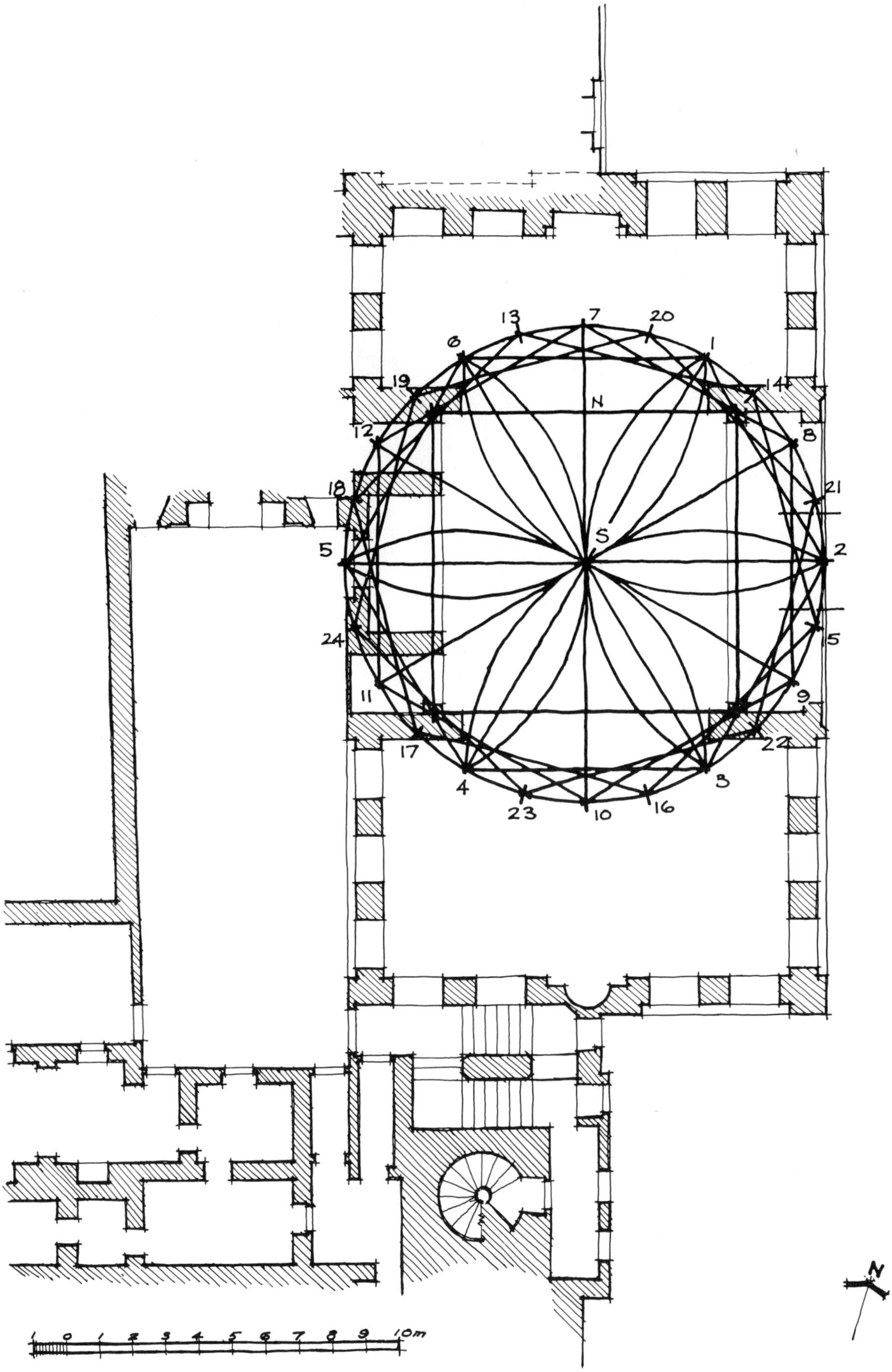

Fig. IV/13 The *ṣaḥn*: its rectangular plan

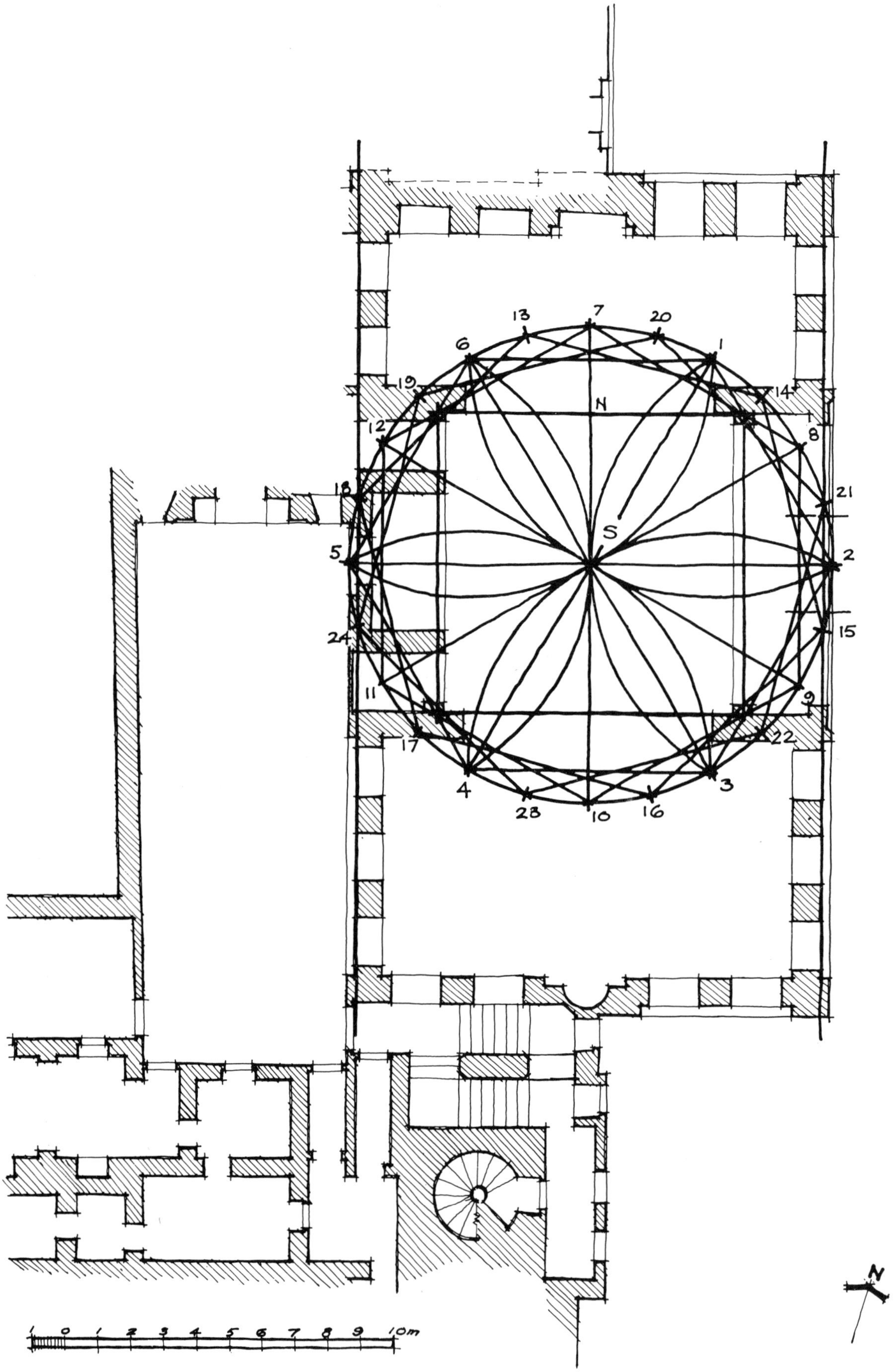

Fig. IV/14 Depth of window recesses

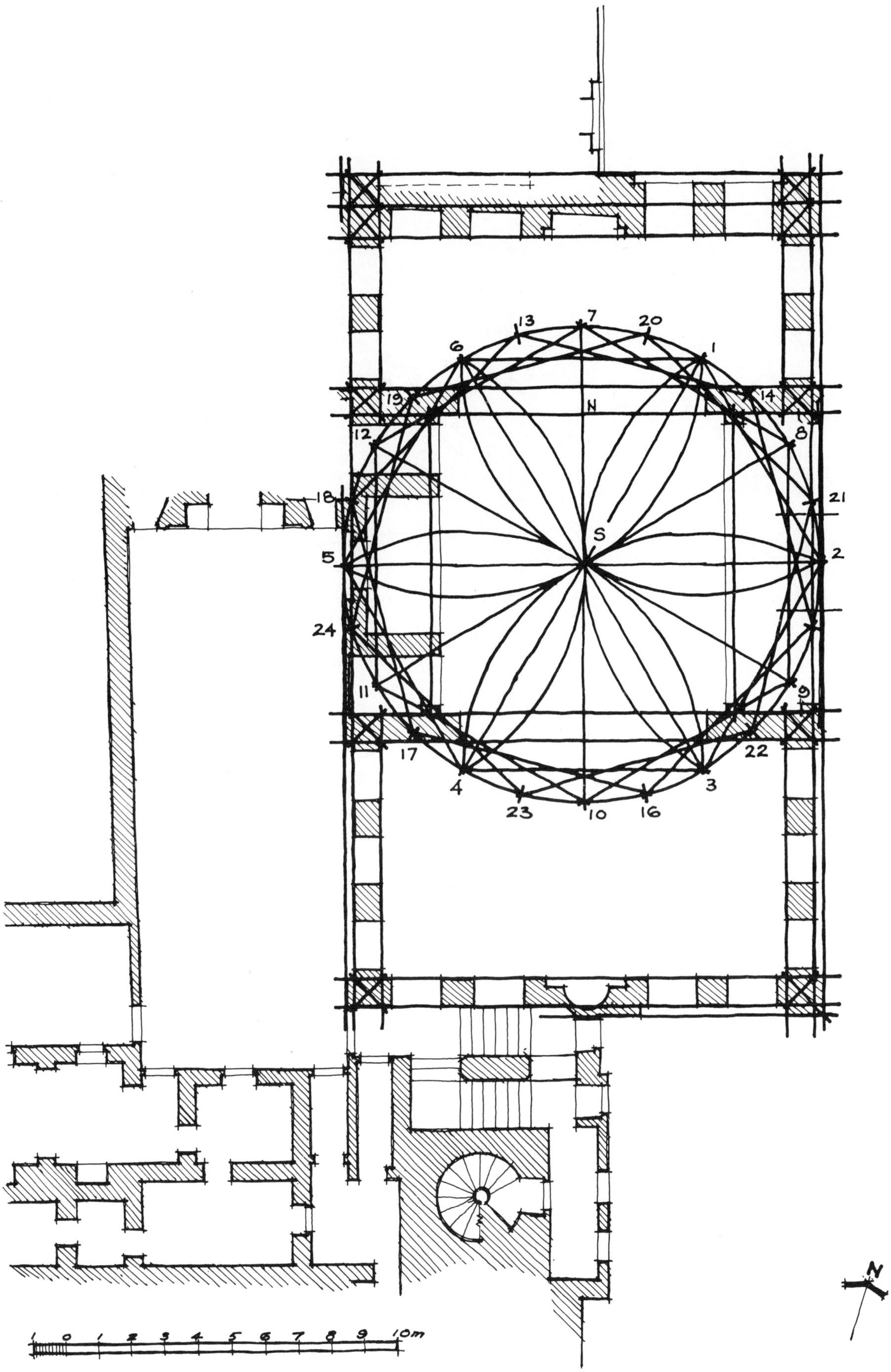

Fig. IV/15 Wall thicknesses standardized

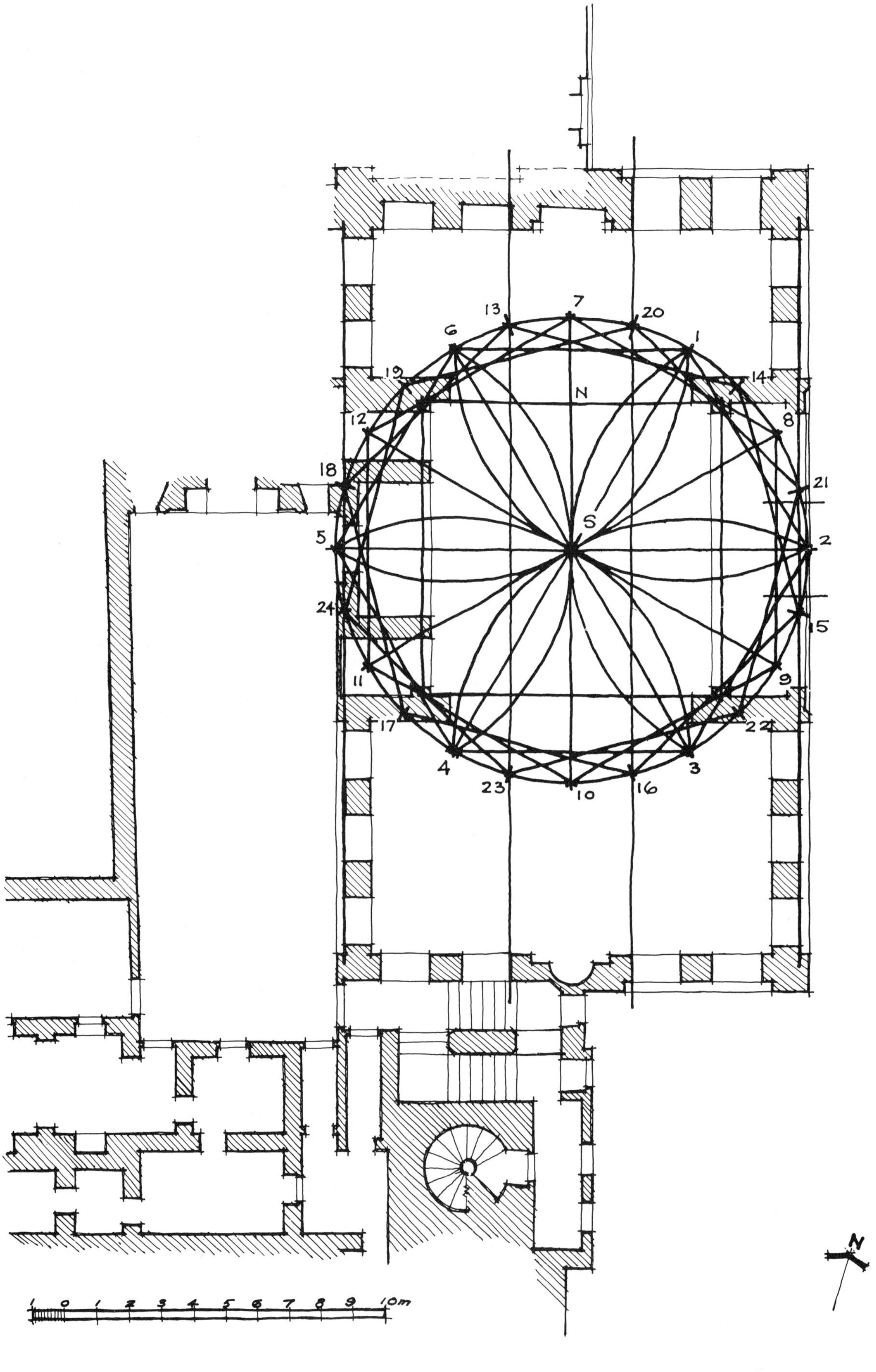

Fig. IV/16 The *miḥrāb* and the pseudo-gateway

(see the construction illustrated in the western half of the *qibla īwān*). Here the inscribed hexagon (1-6) centred on W_1 is the equivalent to that centred on W in the eastern half, and likewise side 5-6 defines the position and 1/10 BUG width of the central window. In order to expand upon this geometry and enable it to control the flanking windows, a second hexagon (7-12) must be added. Its sides 7-8 and 10-11 both lie at right angles to the north-south axis and they can be used to construct two further hexagons—the centre of the one to the north on W_2, and the other to the south is centred on W_3. It is obvious as a consequence of the foregoing that construction points W_1, W_2 and W_3 do have a geometrical relationship, but what is interesting is that the relationships consist of equilateral triangles based on diagonal 12-9, and therefore the sides of these equilateral triangles measure 1/5 BUG. To arrive at the positions of the flanking windows, second hexagons must be constructed centred on W_2 and W_3. As their orientation matches that of hexagon 1-6 centred on W_1, their sides, which correspond to side 5-6 of the hexagon centred on W_1, will each establish the position of a window opening. The positions of the north and south walls of the *qibla īwān* are reinforced when (dotted) lines are drawn from points W_2 and W_3 at an angle of 45°. Where they cross their respective circumferences they coincide with the north and south walls.

Rotation of the Geometry

So far the geometries have been used horizontally to locate the plan features of the Madrasa, but these same geometries can be rotated from the horizontal to the vertical plane to position elevational features. This discovery is crucial as it provides an invaluable insight into the thinking of the Christian architect and thus it has an essential role to play in the search for the physical form of the Ashrafiyya. **fig. IV/18**

The discovery was made as I completed the geometries controlling the plan positions of the windows in the *qibla īwān*. I realised that years before I had uncovered the same geometries whilst contemplating the exterior of the west wall of the *qibla īwān*. We have just seen in plan that the widths and positions of the three windows of this wall are generated by three inscribed double hexagons W_1, W_2 and W_3. Imagine that in each figure the side 5-6 is a large 'piano hinge' lying along the windowsills, and that it allows the geometry to be swung into a vertical position. The figures W_1, W_2 and W_3 are now seen against the existing external elevation. In addition to the 'hinged' sides 5-6 coinciding with the sills, and providing the opening widths, point 9 is level with the soffits of the lintels. Taken together they define the three window openings.

Seeing the geometries in elevation raises the question of their possible relationship to the stone courses. This would be logical in view of their influence on other aspects of the design. To this end, notice that the diagonal 1-4 coincides with a course height, as do sides 5-6 and 2-3, and the distance separating both 5-6 from 1-4 and 1-4 and 2-3 is four courses. On this evidence the BUG is linked to the heights of the stone courses, most of which are 0.31m high, although a few can be found with various heights up to a maximum of 0.34m. The link can be confirmed by calculation also: given the 1/10 BUG radius circle is 1.44m, the length of the line joining points 6 and 2 is found: tan 60° × line 2-3; $\sqrt{3} \times 1.44 = 2.49$m, divide by the number of courses 8 and the average course height equals 0.31m.

Initially few of the existing dimensions of the Madrasa appeared to be linked to the fundamental geometry. However, with the development of the primary geometry, the essential plan dimensions were established through the BUG, and the series of detailed geometries in the *qibla īwān* established the fact that the geometries can be rotated and that the heights of the stone courses are also based on the BUG.

Note

1. The possibility that the width of the site might control the design of the Madrasa Ashrafiyya is not unique in Mamlūk architecture, nor is it unique in Jerusalem, for it has been shown that the width of the site of Kīlāniyya generates the principal elevation. See Walls, A. G., 'The Mausoleum of the Amīr Kīlanī, Jerusalem', *Levant* VII, London, 1975, fig. 21, and for a step-by-step explanation given in strip cartoon form, see Walls, A. G., 'A Gap Site Problem', *Al-Muhandis al-Urdunī* ('Jordan Engineer') XIV/24, Amman, 1981, pp. 64-67.

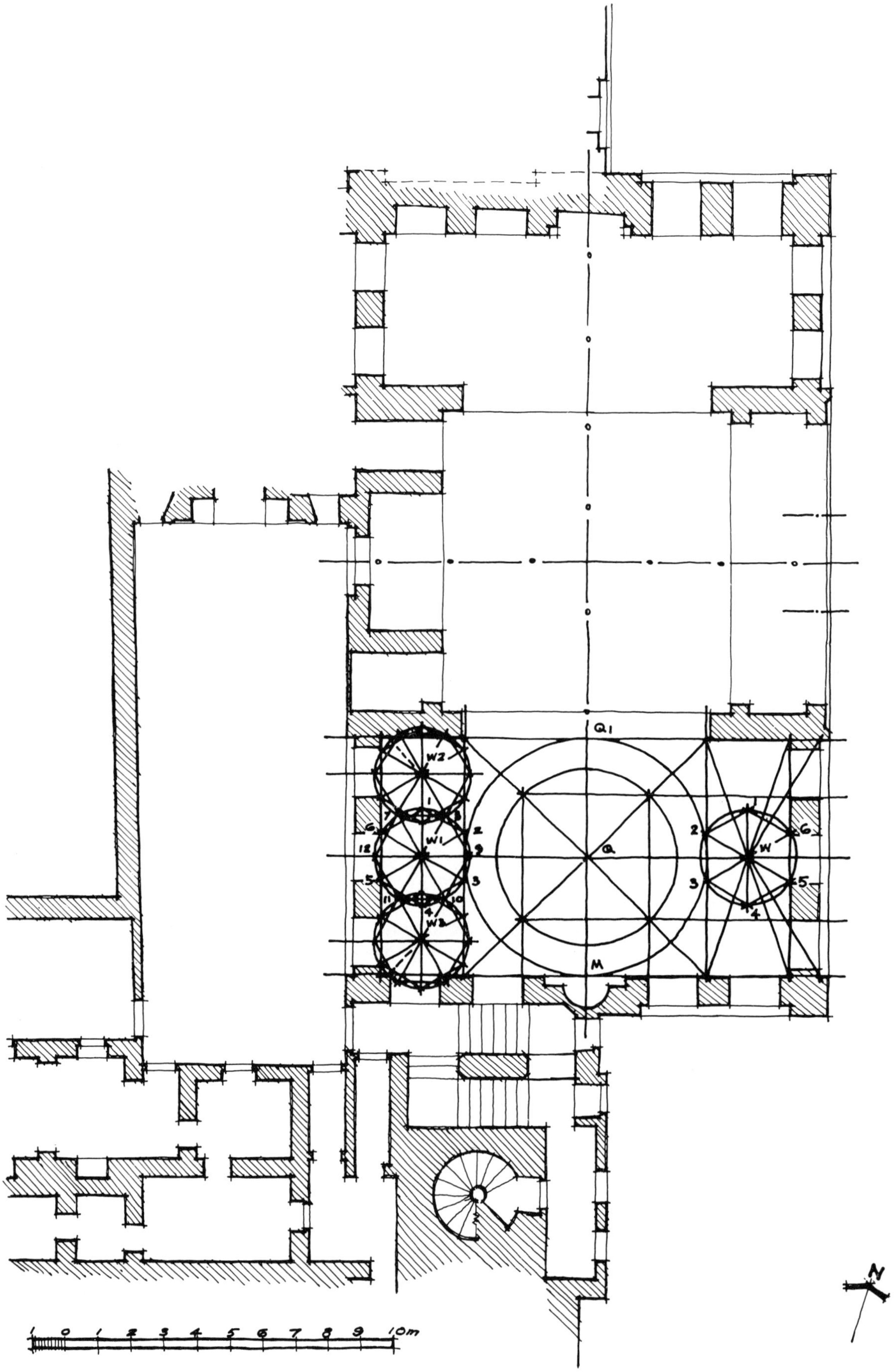

Fig. IV/17 The *qibla īwān*: some detailed geometries

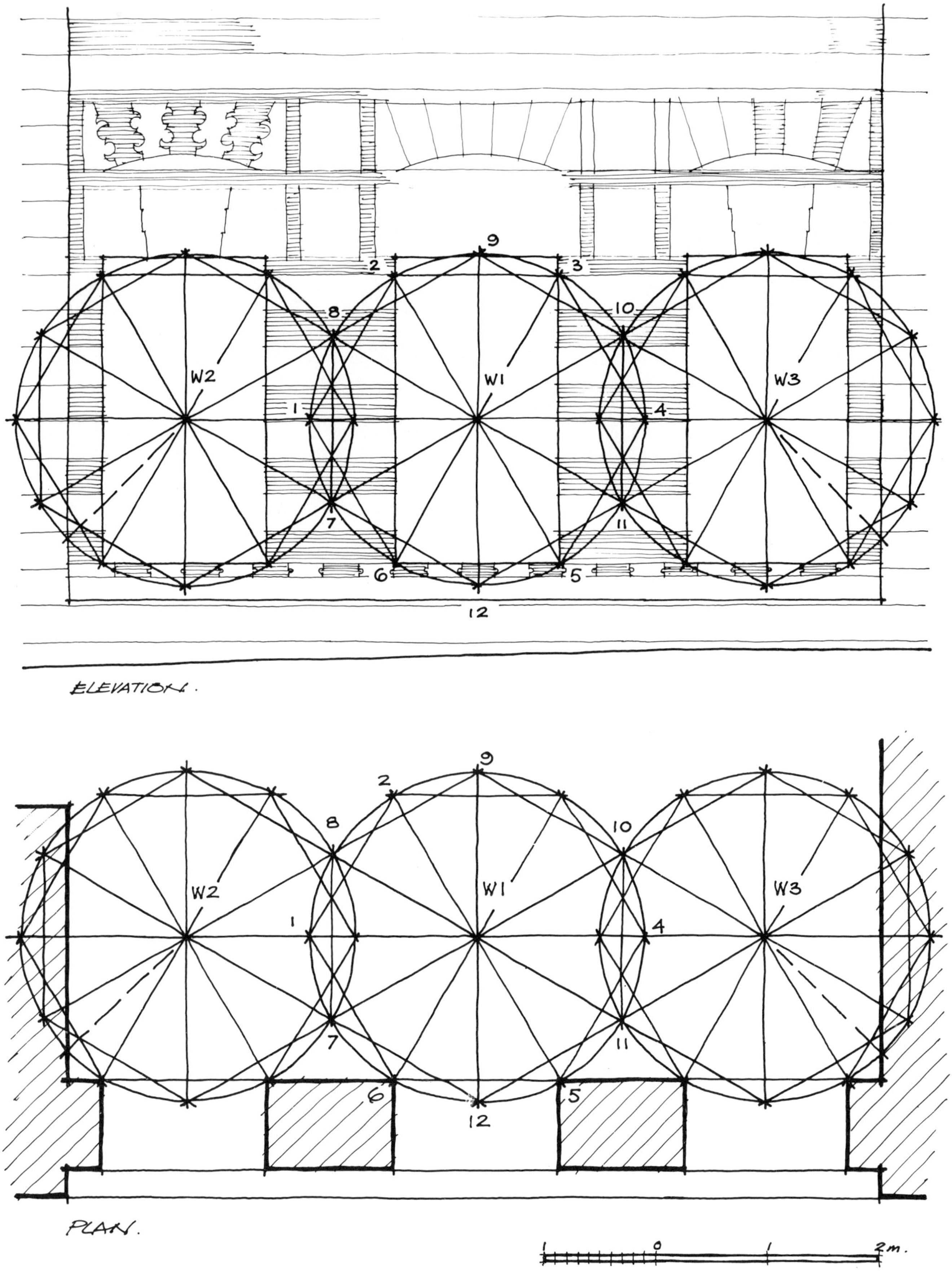

Fig. IV/18 West wall of the *qibla īwān*: the geometry rotated from the horizontal plane to the vertical

Chapter V
STONE COURSES

Having touched upon the subject of stone course heights, when considering the *qibla īwān* and observing that they had an importance, it would be useful to look at stone courses in a wider context by comparing those of the Ashrafiyya to those in other buildings of Sultan Qāytbāy. For if it were possible to establish consistent relationships in the numbers of stone courses used in their various architectural elements, then this evidence would be valuable and could act as a basis for the reconstruction of the Ashrafiyya.

Three of the Cairo monuments of Sultan Qāytbāy have been chosen as comparative examples: his Mosque and Mausoleum 887-79/1472-74, the Mosque in Qal'at al-Kabsh 880/1475 and his Mosque on the island of Rawḍa 886-896/1481-90. In the tables which follow, commonly found architectural features are broken down into their elementary parts and the number of stone courses in each of those parts is given.

In the tables accompanying the figures, a half course indicates that the horizontal compartmentation is included. Other signs are as follows:

+ the element is now incomplete, but originally it would have had more stone courses
- the element either never existed or it has disappeared
? the element is extant but it is presently concealed from view

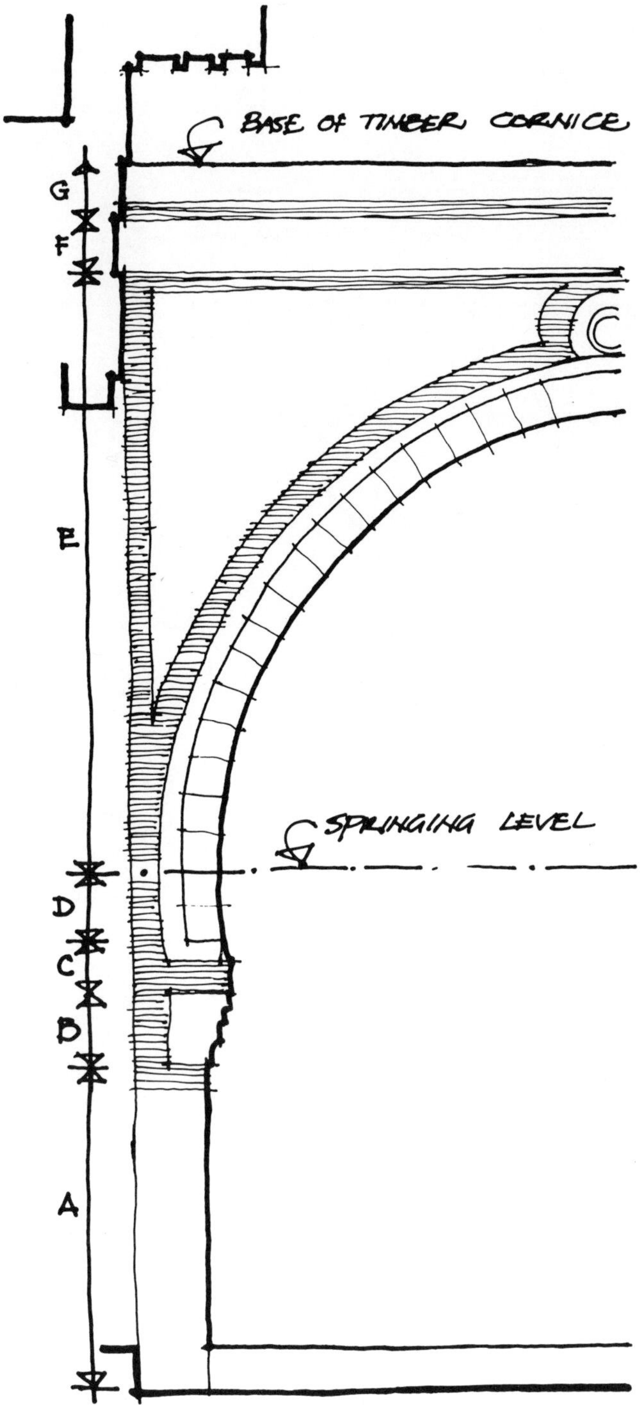

Fig. V/1 *Ṣaḥn*: the great arch

Ṣaḥn: Great Arch

	A	B	C	D	E	F	G	total
Mosque and Mausoleum	9	3	1	3½	16½	2	1½	36½
Qal'at al-Kabsh	8½	3½	1	5	14½	2	1½	36
Rawḍa	7½	2	0	3	17	2	0	31½
Ashrafiyya	+6½	2	1½	2	+2	-	-	+14

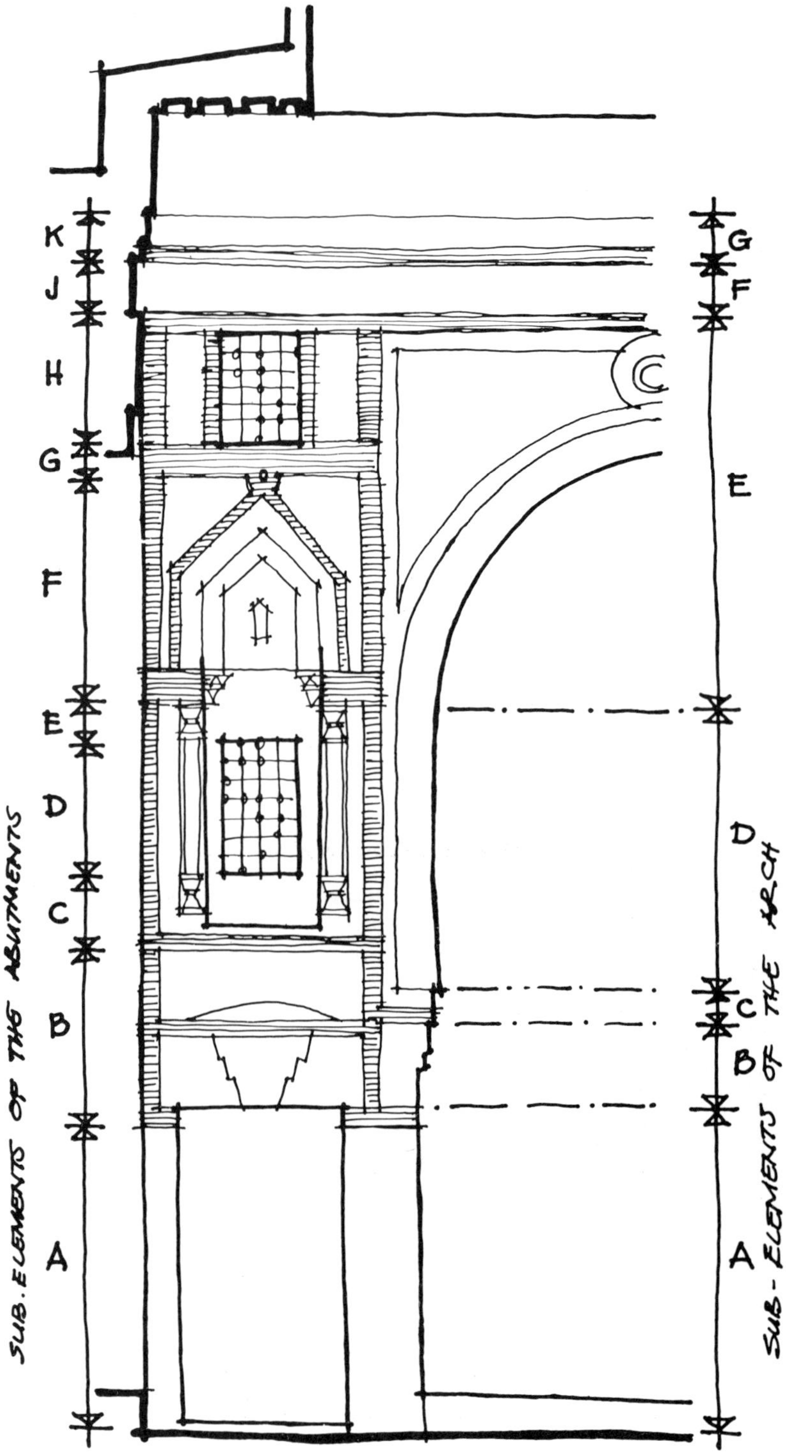

Fig. V/2 *Ṣaḥn*: the side wall

Ṣaḥn: the Side Wall
The Abutments

	A	B	C	D	E	F	G	H	J	K	total
Mosque and Mausoleum	8½	5	2½	4	1	6½	0	5½	2	1½	36½
Qal'at al-Kabsh	7½	4½	2	4	1	6	2	5½	2	1½	36
Rawḍa	7½	5½	2	6	2	6½	0	0	2	0	31½
Ashrafiyya	+6	5	2	+1	-	-	-	-	-	-	+14

The Arch

	A	B	C	D	E	F	G	total
Mosque and Mausoleum	8½	3	1½	10	10	2	1½	36½
Qal'at al-Kabsh	8½	3½	2	8	8½	2	1½	34
Rawḍa	7½	2	0	10	10½	2	0	32
Ashrafiyya	+6½	2	1½	+4	-	-	-	+14

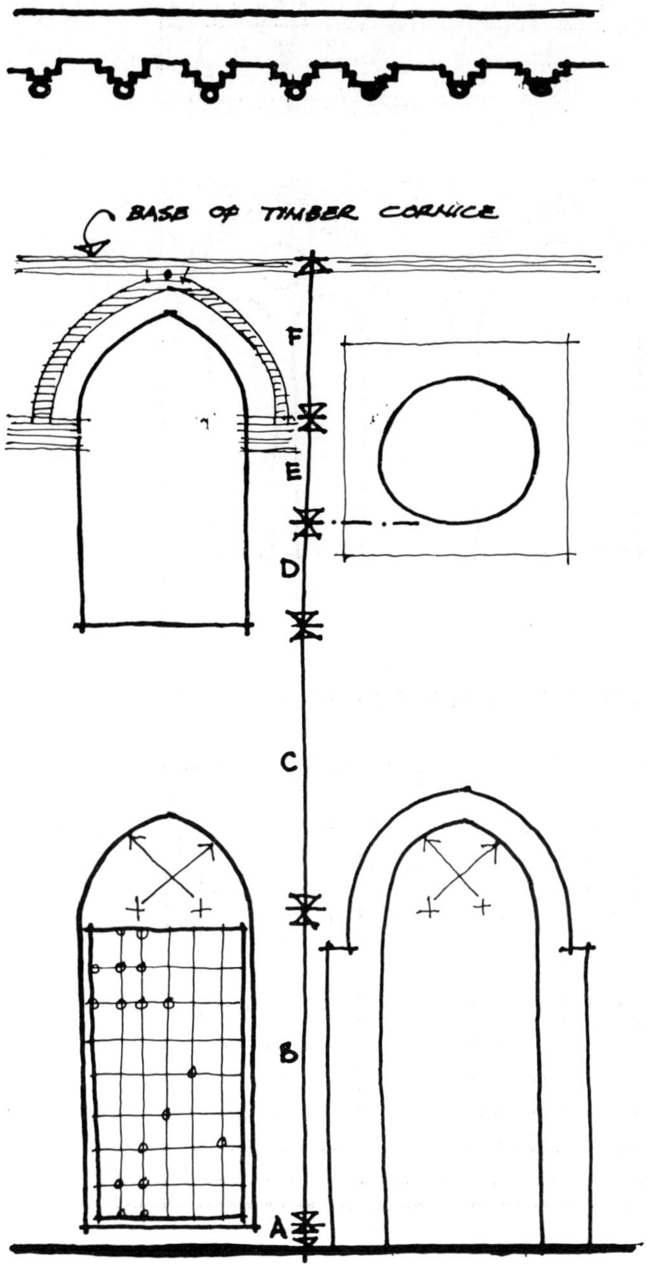

Fig. V/3 The *qibla* wall

The *Qibla Wall*

	A	B	C	D	E	F	total
Mosque and Mausoleum	2	8	9	3	3	4½	29½
Qal'at al-Kabsh	1½	9	9	4	2	4	29½
Rawḍa	1½	8	7	6	0	5½	28
Ashrafiyya	?	9	+6½	-	-	-	+15½

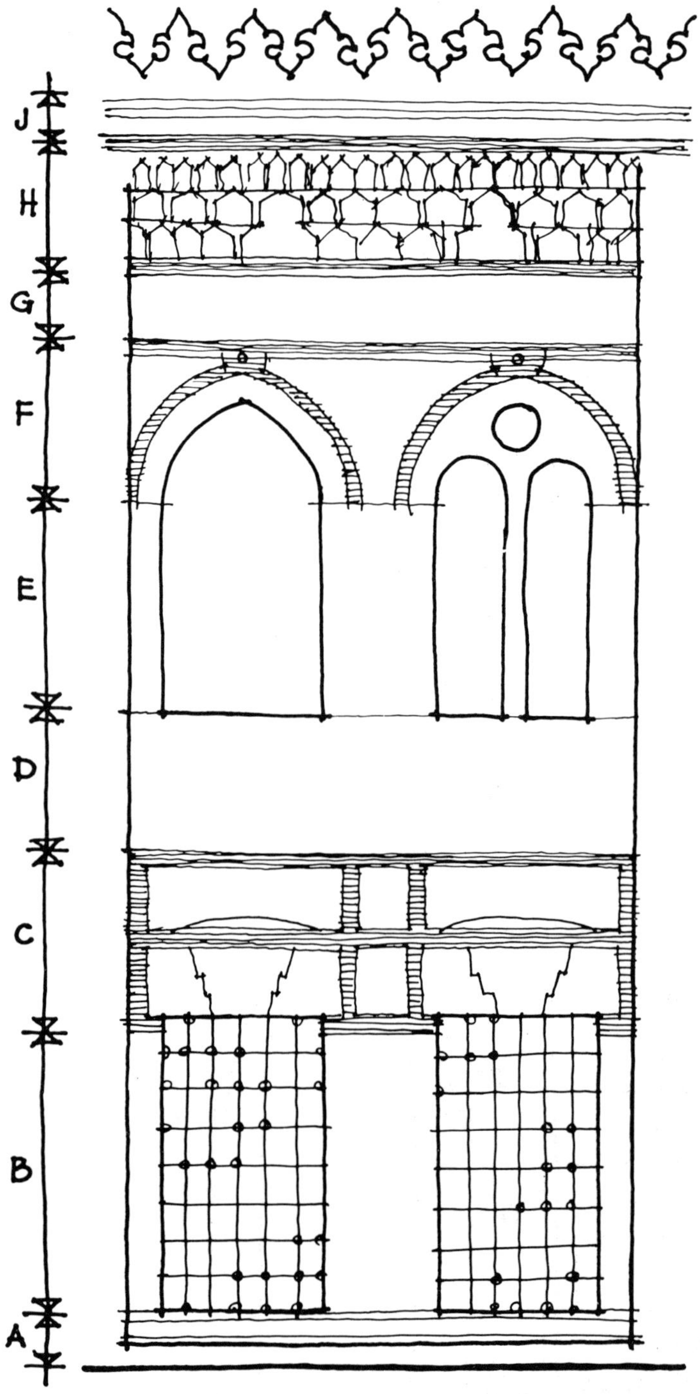

Fig. V/4 *Īwān*: characteristic external fenestration

Īwān: Characteristic External Fenestration

	A	B	C	D	E	F	G	H	J	total
Mosque and Mausoleum	2	8	5	4	6	4½	2	4	1	36½
Qal'at al-Kabsh	2	8	5	6	5	5	2	3½	1	37½
Rawḍa	-	+3	5½	4½	4	4½	2	3½	1	+30*
Ashrafiyya	1	8	5	+2	-	-	-	-	-	+16

*The present ground level obscures a minimum of 7 stone courses and if they were to be included this total would be 37.

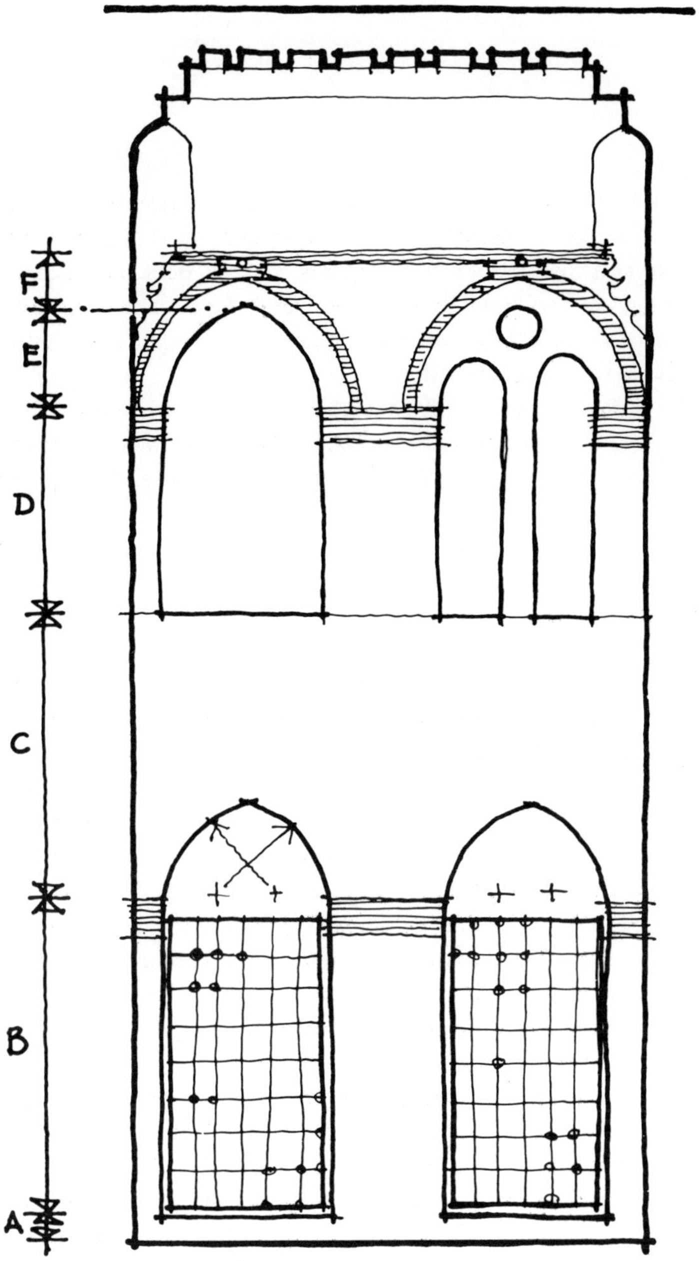

Fig. V/5 *Īwān*: characteristic internal fenestration

Īwān: Characteristic Internal Fenestration

	A	B	C	D	E	F	total
Mosque and Mausoleum							29*
Qal'at al-Kabsh	1½	9	10	5	1	5	31½
Rawḍa	-	-	-	-	-	-	28†
Ashrafiyya	?	+9	+6½	-	-	-	+14½

* This arrangement has: a door 9 courses high; lintel and relieving arch 5 courses; 1 course of stonework; a rectangular window 4 courses; 4 courses stonework and a window 6 courses high placed hard against the cornice, making a total of 29 courses.
†There are no openings in the walls of the side *īwāns*.

Chapter VI THE ṢAḤN

fig. VI/1 and 2

In a Mamlūk cruciform mosque or madrasa, the internal features with the most impact are the great arches and the smaller side arches of the *ṣaḥn*. Consequently it is impossible for their design not to influence the design and position of other elements. Indeed, once these secondary elements have been arranged about the great and small arches, the overall form of the building is nigh on established. Therefore the reconstruction of the destroyed arches in the *ṣaḥn* of the Ashrafiyya is essential before other aspects of the Madrasa are considered.

In view of the close relationships discovered between the Ashrafiyya and the three other buildings of Sultan Qāytbāy in Cairo, frequent comparisons will be made to these buildings—not only in relation to numbers of stone courses, but also in verifying proportions and confirming the likelihood of the presence of one detail rather than another.

The Great Arches

Of the great arches of the Cairo monuments those of the Mosque and Mausoleum are closest to the lost arches of the Ashrafiyya in the richness of their ornamentation. But more importantly the widths of their *ṣaḥns* are similar: in the Mosque and Mausoleum it is 8.61m, and in the Ashrafiyya the reconstructed west-east width of the *ṣaḥn* is 8.54m, a difference of $^1/_{200}$ BUG.

In view of these similarities, a study of the proportions underlying the design of the great horseshoe arches in the Mosque and Mausoleum must be made, as this will provide a solid foundation upon which to base the reconstruction of the great arches of the Ashrafiyya.

fig. VI/3

In the Mosque and Mausoleum the distance separating the abutments and the distance between the floor of the *īwān* and the underside of the linked archivolt are in a ratio of 2:1. This is expressed by the congruent squares 1-4 and 3-6 enclosing the similar circles O_1 and O_2. The height to the archivolt (1-2) is three quarters of the height between the floor of the *īwān* and the springing line (1-8), as shown by the column of three circles.

The mid-point of this line 1-8 coincides with the underside of the compartmentation below the impost, and from this mid-point O_3 an arc can be drawn from the vertical axis of the arch at point 3 to intersect the springing line (8-7) at R_1. Similarly point R_2 is found from the mid-point of line 5-7. Points R_1 and R_2 become the centres for the great arch, and each lies at a distance of $^1/_{10}$ of the arch span from the midpoint of line 8-7. Thus they are $^1/_5$ of the span apart, and as such it seems that they conform to a proportional standard used in most Mamlūk arches. On the vertical axis midway between the underside of the archivolt (2-6) and the springing line (8-7) a circle centred on O_4 can be drawn which is nearly tangential to the circles centred at O_1 and O_2. In addition, it nearly passes through the centre of the lowest circle of the column of circles on line 1-2, as well as passing through the zenith of the arch (Z).

fig. VI/4

Assuming that the reconstruction of the great arches of the Ashrafiyya is to rely on proportions similar to those used in the Mosque and Mausoleum, the first step is to use the distance between the abutments along with the 2:1 ratio to see if they coincide with any point of significance. Fortunately, of the four original abutments of the great arches, much of the north-west abutment still exists for without this it would be impossible to reconstruct the great arches with any confidence. Its presence not only allows the span of the arch to be determined, but it provides further essential details: the exact dimensions and relationships of the decorated imposts, the compartmentation, the moulded and linked archivolt, the *ablaq* voussoirs and the springing line.

However, since the floor level of the *ṣaḥn* (like that of the *īwāns*) is not visible, being overlaid with

Plate 10 Cairo, Mosque and Mausoleum of Qāytbāy: the *qibla iwān* with the central *miḥrāb* and *minbar* to its right seen from the *ṣaḥn*. (*Survey of Egypt*, pl. 125)

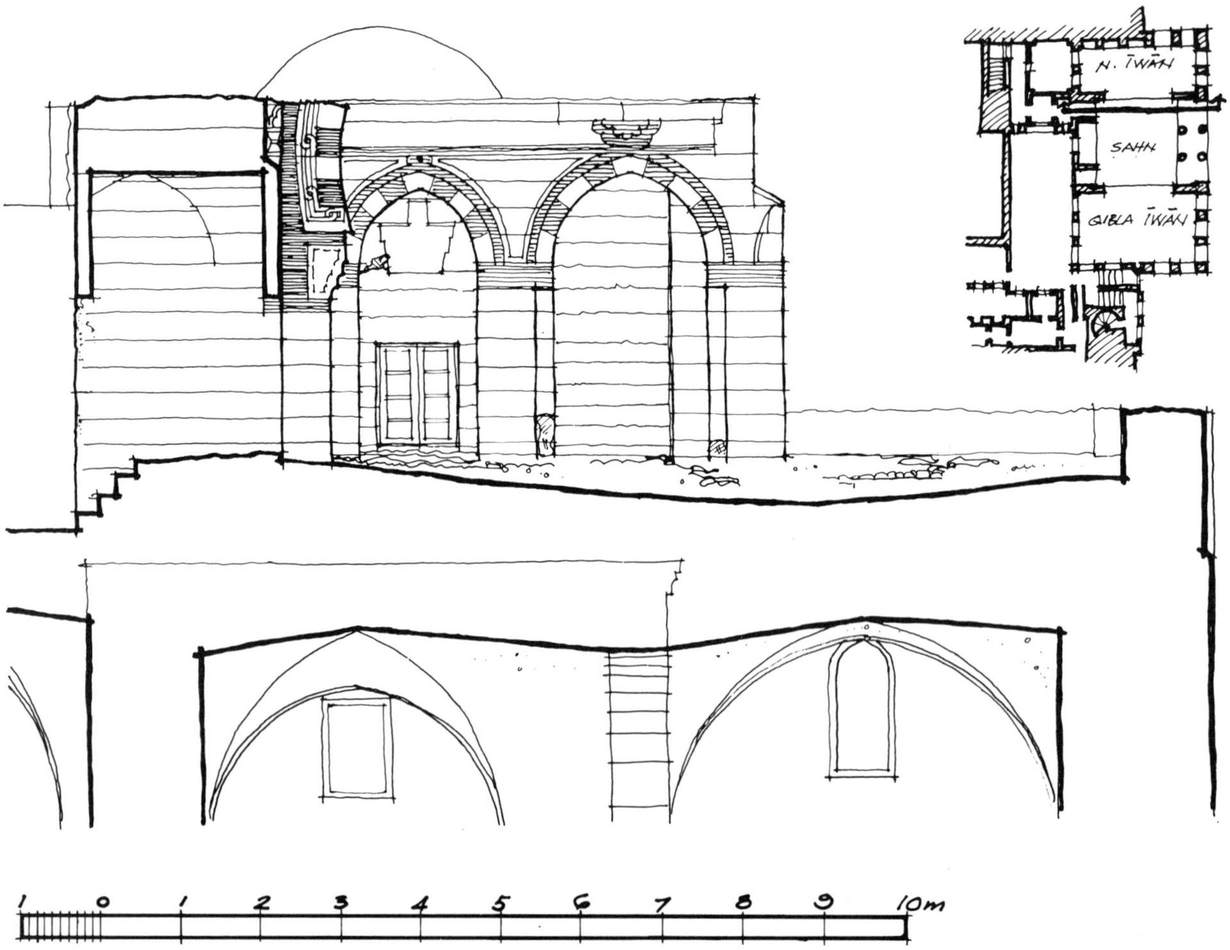

Fig. VI/1 *Ṣaḥn*, the great arch: existing features of the north west abutment

debris from the earthquake, the original heights from the floor to the impost and other details of the abutment can only be estimated. To do this it must be assumed that the architect followed contemporary practice and that the floor level of the *īwāns* was slightly below the level of the window sills. This being the case, and using line 1-5 to represent the floor level of the *īwān*, two squares can be constructed to provide the necessary 2:1 ratio. The result of this is that the top of the squares, line 2-6, does not only coincide with a stone course, but one of significance: it is the top of the archivolt.

In the drawing the congruent squares 1-4 and 3-6 enclose the similar circles O_1 and O_2. The height to the springing line (8-7) is known, and in view of the results of the study of the Mosque and Mausoleum, it can be assumed that R_1 and R_2 are separated by the standard distance of $^1/_5$ of the span. This assumption is borne out by R_2 as it is the actual centre for the existing voussoirs, and therefore when arcs are drawn from R_1 and R_2 they provide the outline of this horseshoe arch with its zenith (Z).

In the great arches of the Mosque and Mausoleum the proportional study concluded with a circle centred at O_4. Its circumference was tangential to those of the circles O_1 and O_2, and passed through the centre of the lowest circle on line 1-2 and the zenith (Z) of the arched opening. In the Ashrafiyya a similar circle drawn from a centre O_4, placed slightly below the midway point between lines 2-6 and 8-7, is likewise tangential to the circles O_1 and O_2, and although here it only passes near the centre of the lowest circle on line 1-2, it does pass through point Z.

A satisfactory outline for the great arch has now been found, but this has been achieved in isolation and without reference to the geometries previously discovered in the Madrasa. It is therefore necessary for the arch to be tied into these geometries, especially if some more of the detailed geometries can be transposed from the horizontal to the vertical plane.

fig. VI/5 In order to make such a transposition a point must be found in the vertical plane which will equate

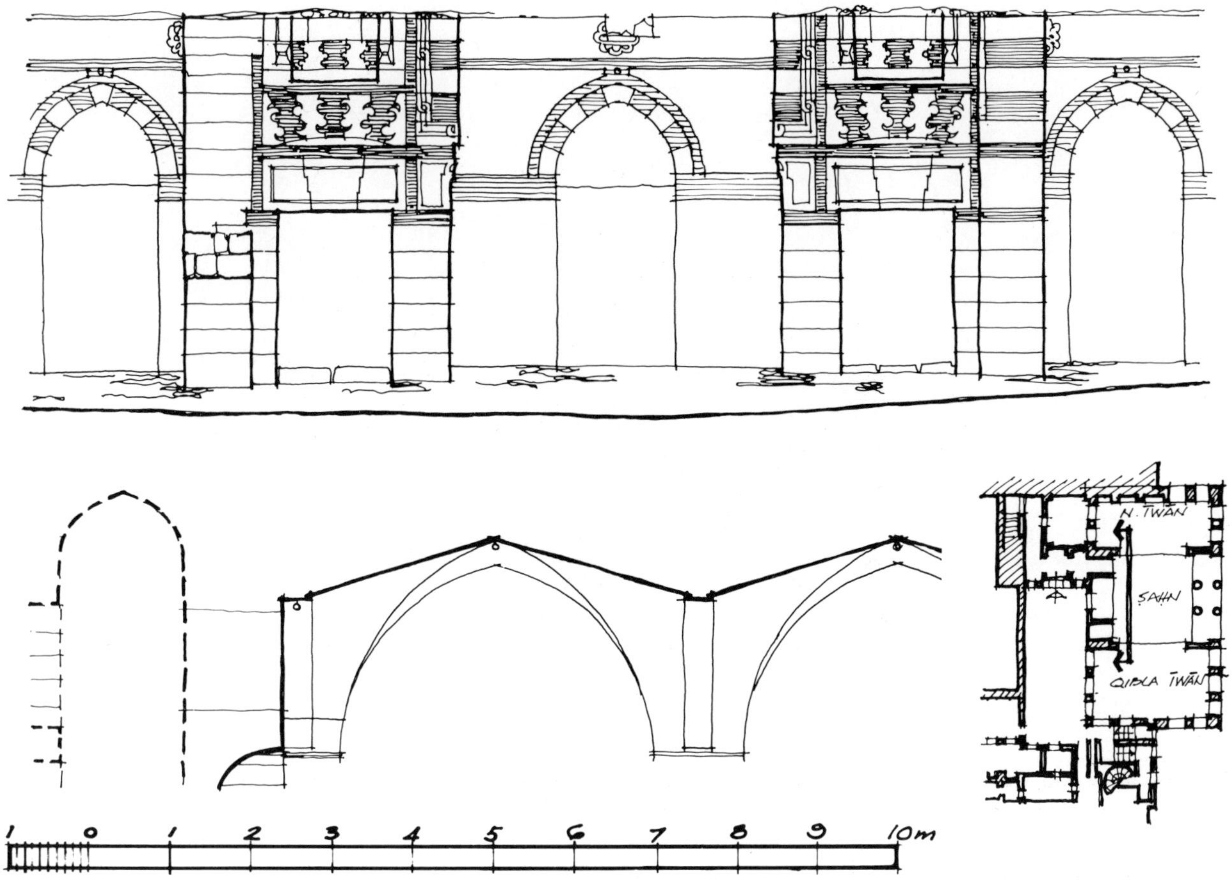

Fig. VI/2 *Ṣaḥn*, the side wall: existing features

to point S, the centre of the plan of the *ṣaḥn* and the point from which all the horizontal geometries were generated. It would be logical for.this point to be located midway between the zenith of the arch (Z) and the floor level of either the *ṣaḥn* or of the *īwān*. Neither floor level is known exactly, but since that of the *īwān* has already been estimated, at this stage it can be taken as the level from which to locate point S in the vertical plane.

Having located point S midway between the floor of the *īwān* (F) and the zenith (Z), the horizontal geometries of the *ṣaḥn* can be superimposed in sequence. The fundamental geometry, consisting of a hexagon described by a circle with a 1 BUG diameter, can be constructed with points 5 and 2 aligned with the exteriors of the west and east walls of the Madrasa. This is followed by the addition of the double hexagon of the primary geometry, the intersections of which produce a square. In the horizontal geometry this square related to the north-south dimension of the *ṣaḥn* and to the centres of the west wall and the restored east wall of the *ṣaḥn*, and this second relationship is reconfirmed in the vertical plane. A further two encouraging, though minor relationships, appear: the base of the square is level with the lower edge of the chamfered sill outside the window of the west *īwān* and it is level with the top of the joggled string course in the east elevation. **fig. VI/6**

When the detailed geometry is added its 24-pointed star and the square of the primary geometry create lines which coincide with the faces of the west and east walls of the *ṣaḥn*, just as they did in the horizontal geometry. Again the detailed geometry defines the rear walls of the external window recesses as they are matched by lines 24-18 and 21-15. **fig. VI/7**

Although these rotated geometries have not themselves joined up with the geometry of the great arch, they have created a framework that allows a connection to be made using the circle centred on S with points F and Z on its circumference. This circle is found to lie tangentially to the west and east **fig. VI/8**

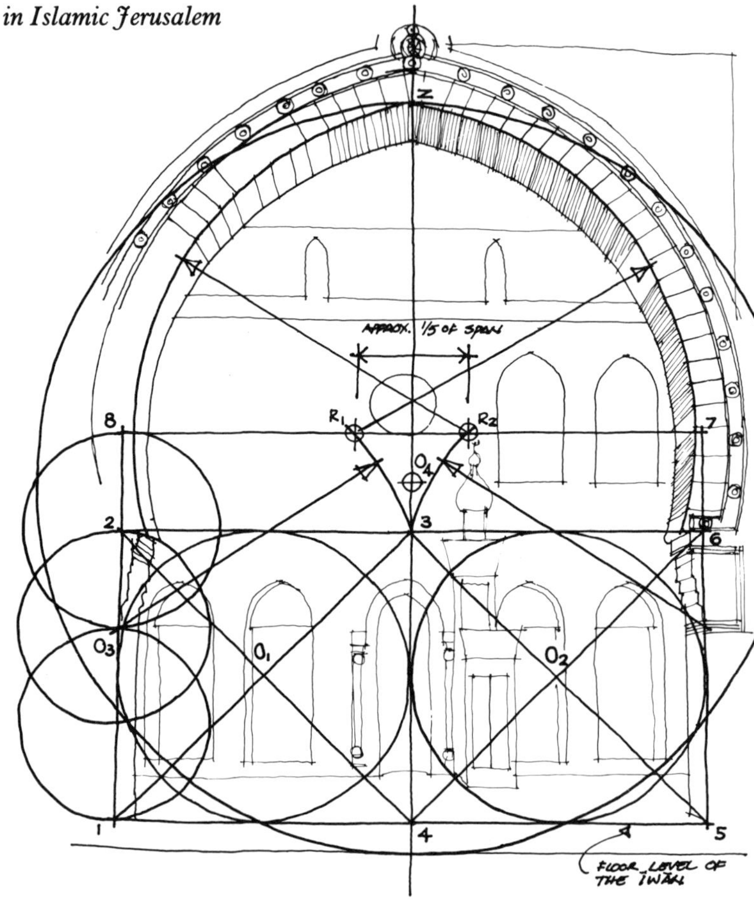

Fig. VI/3 Mosque and Mausoleum of Qāytbāy: proportions underlying the great arches based on pl. 197 in Hautecoeur, Louis and Gaston Wiet, *Les mosquées du Caire*, Paris, 1932

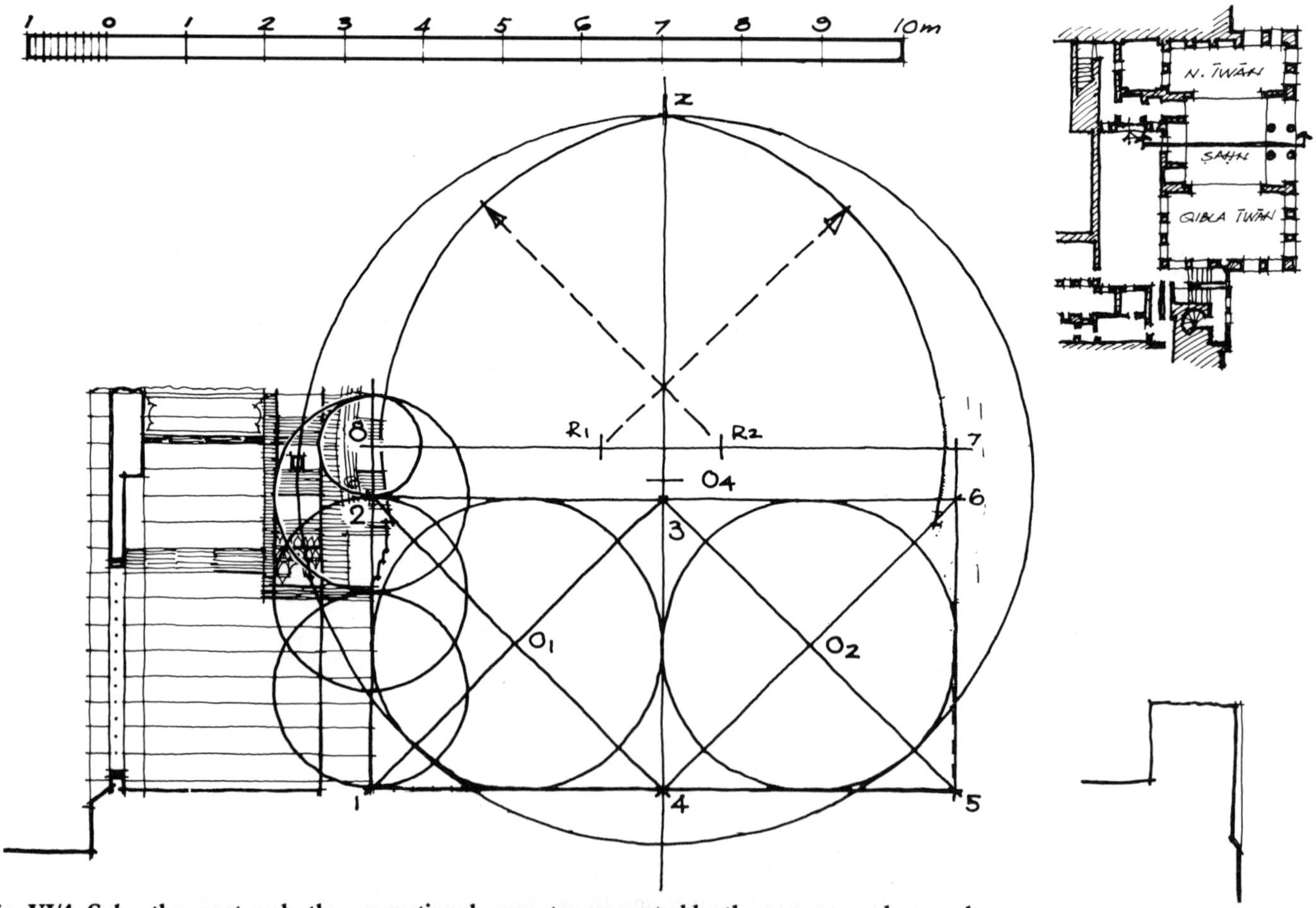

Fig. VI/4 *Ṣaḥn*, the great arch: the proportional geometry suggested by the mosque and mausoleum superimposed on the north west abutment

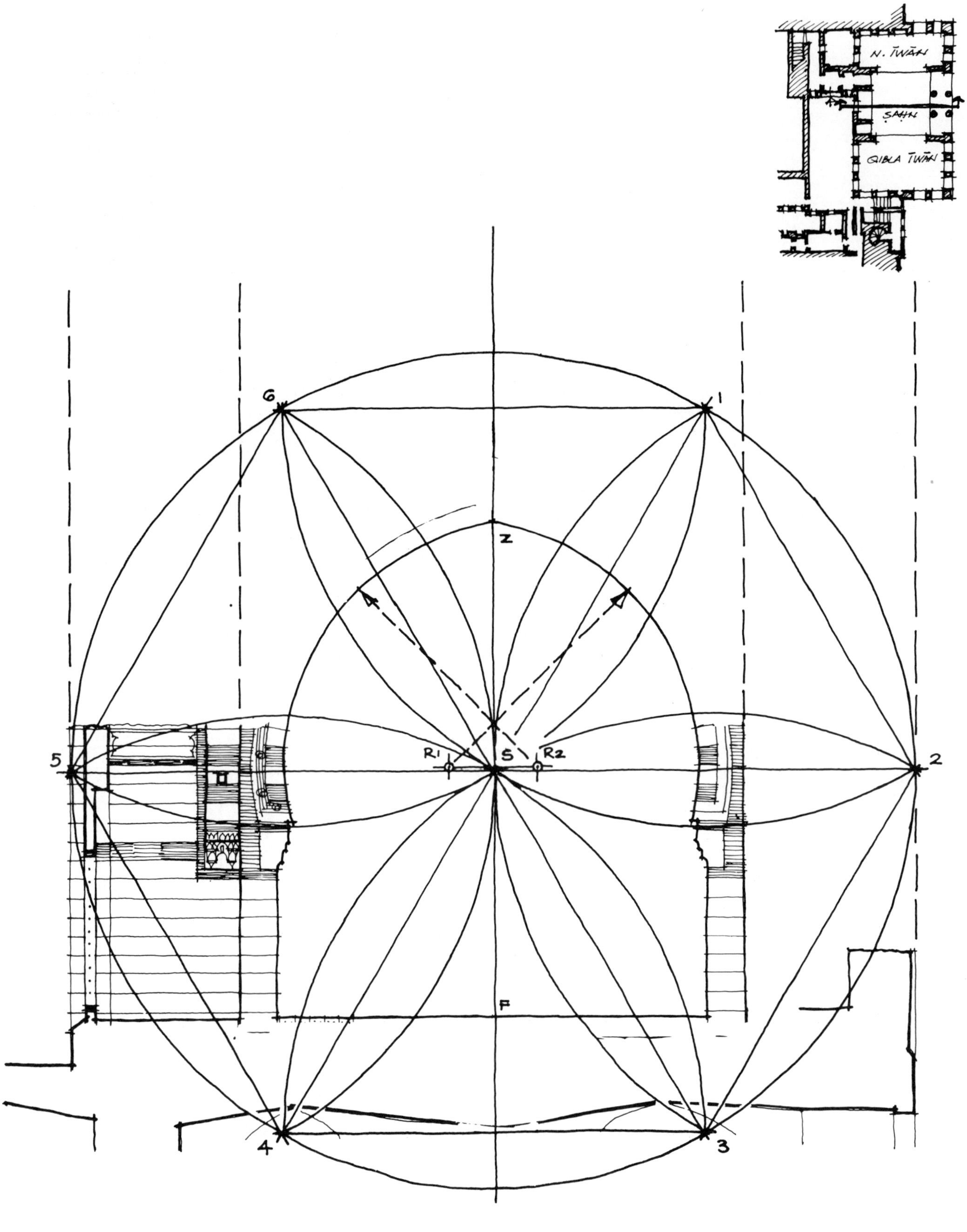

Fig. VI/5 *Ṣaḥn*, the great arch: the fundamental geometry rotated

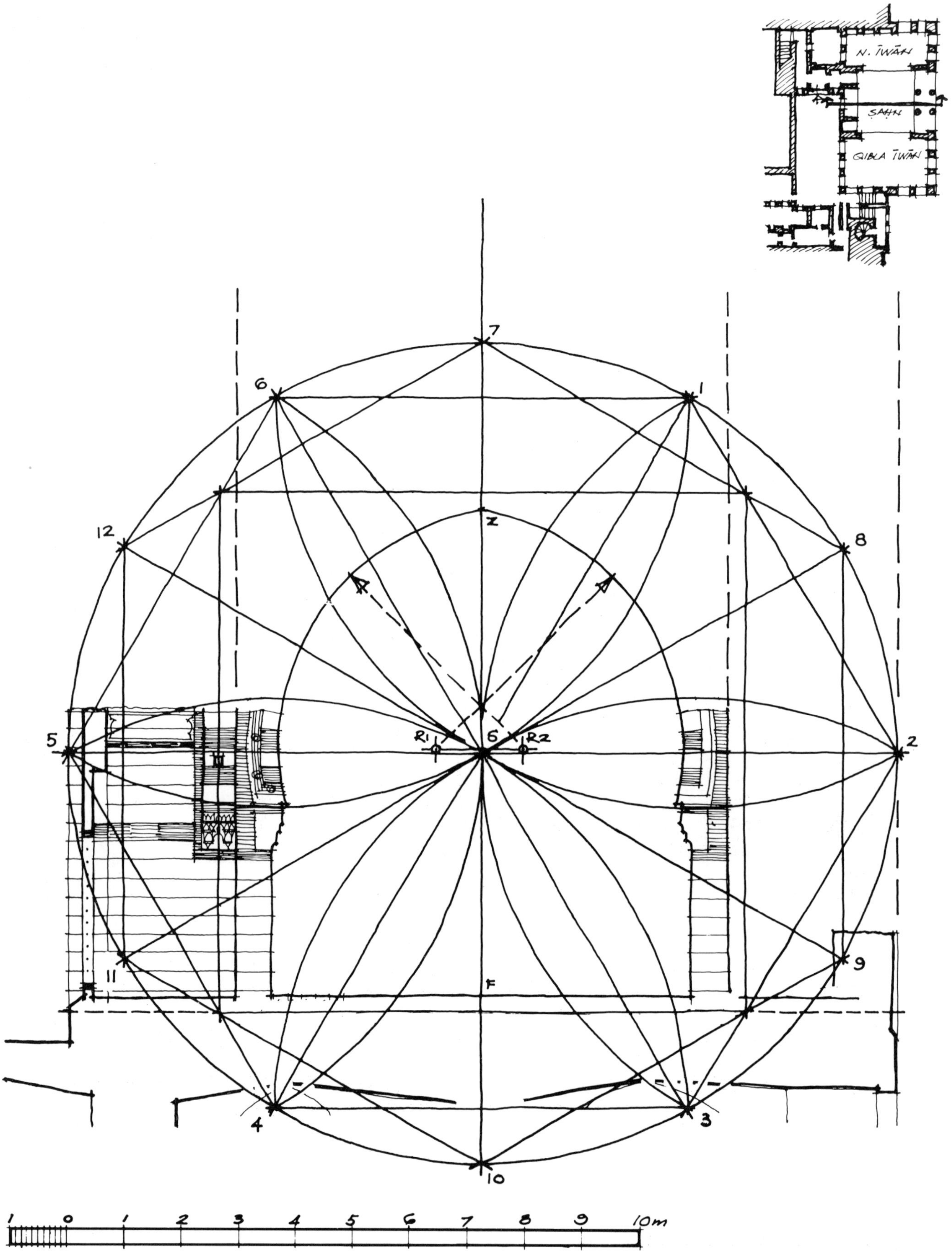

Fig. VI/6 *Ṣaḥn*, the great arch: the primary geometry rotated

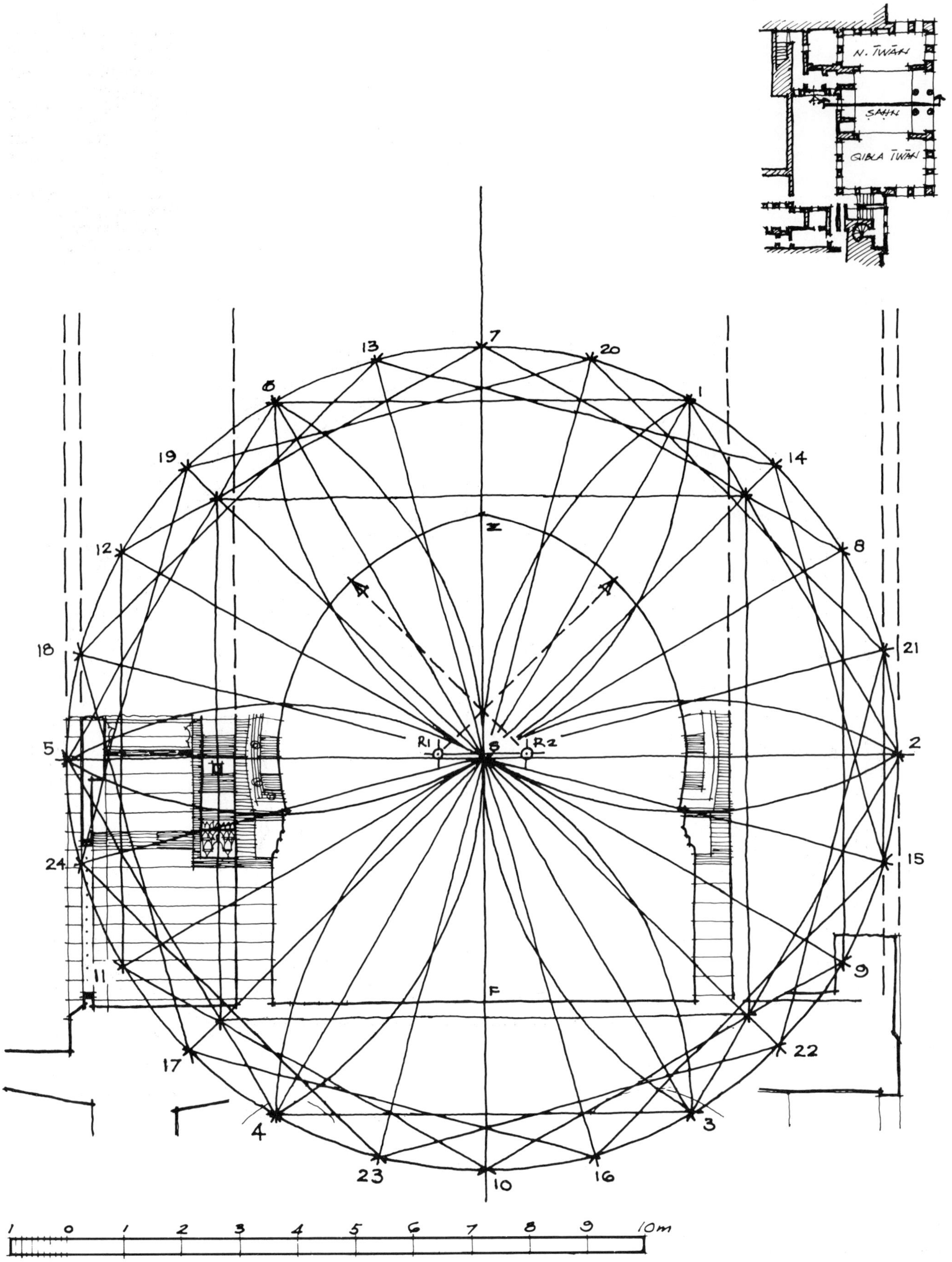

Fig. VI/7 *Ṣaḥn*, the great arch: the detailed geometry rotated

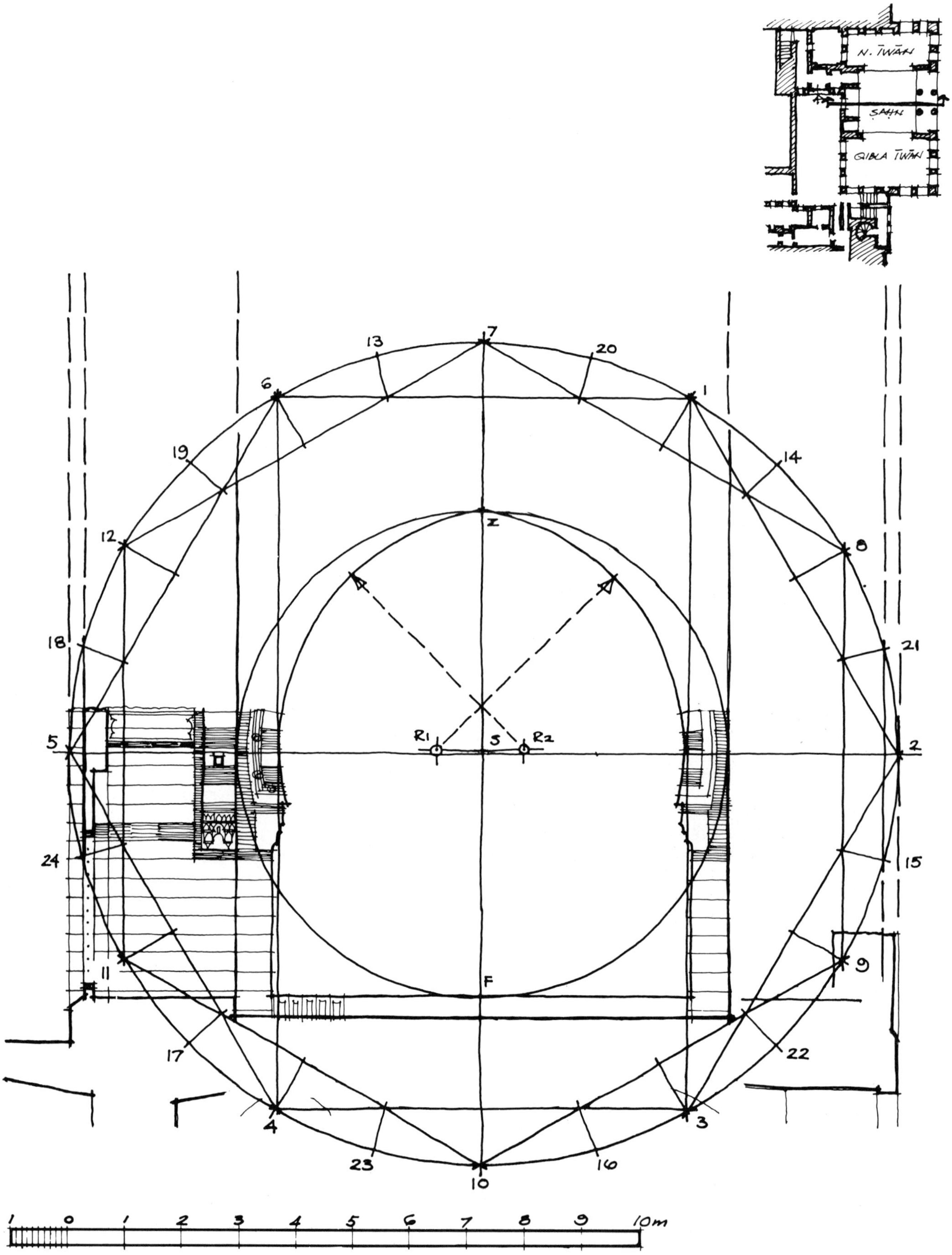

Fig. VI/8 *Ṣaḥn*, the great arch: the detailed geometry simplified and the S-Z circle located

walls of the *ṣaḥn*, and thus proves that the height of the great arch is equal to the west-east width of the *ṣaḥn*. This is a further indication of the relevance of the geometries when they are transposed from one plane to another.

The Side Wall

fig. VI/9

The horizontal geometries when rotated against the side wall of the *ṣaḥn* naturally differ in orientation from those of the great arches by 90°. This is significant for not only does it mean that point N coincides with the face of the north wall of the *ṣaḥn*, to repeat its plan location, but points Z and F are also automatically defined by the detailed geometry without the S-Z radius circle being added, since the height of the side arch must be equal to that of the great arches which have already been found to equal the west-east width of the *ṣaḥn*.

fig. VI/10

However, when the S-Z radius circle is added, it does establish through its circumference the position of the door jambs and the outer engaged columns in the side wall.

fig. VI/11

The zenith of the side arch is known but the level of the springing line, and therefore the radius of its segments, are not known. Nevertheless, it is likely that the arch centres, like those of the great arches, would be separated by $^1/_5$ of the arch span and it follows that the radius of the arch must equal $^3/_5$ of the span. Acting on this assumption the outline of the arch can be completed in the following manner.

Firstly, two parallel lines lying $^1/_5$ of the span apart are drawn vertically either side of the central axis Z-F. An arc with a $^3/_5$ span radius is then drawn from point Z to intersect the parallel lines. The points of intersection become R_1 and R_2 and so the springing line is defined. Finally, from R_1 and R_2 the arch segments can be drawn using the same $^3/_5$ span radius.

It is not known if the moulded archivolt bifurcated as it rose above the springing line, but in any event it would certainly have followed the haunch of the arch and formed a large loop at its zenith.

At this point our analysis of the underlying geometries must cease for a while, because the necessary physical evidence is missing. In a restoration such as this the use of geometry has limitations for it cannot be used creatively in the way the Coptic architect used his geometries to create the design, here their role is to test theories and to provide confirmation. Thus a different analytical method is needed to complete the restoration of the *ṣaḥn*.

We have to begin to rebuild the *ṣaḥn* stone course by stone course. Any assumptions must be tested against the numbers of stone courses recorded in the *ṣaḥns* of the Cairo buildings of Sultan Qāytbāy. Thought will also be given to miscellaneous details which appear in other parts of the Ashrafiyya, or elsewhere, and which may or may not form part of the puzzle of the *ṣaḥn*. At times decisions will be made on aesthetic grounds, and where the way forward is unclear, geometries will again be introduced to assist us.

Although this method will at times appear disjointed and circuitous, the evidence must be gathered and considered in sequence, if we are eventually to achieve our aim—the gradual rebuilding of the *ṣaḥn* from its floor to the top of its lantern. Nor should we forget that coincidence and chance play their part in the restoration of the *ṣaḥn*, for had the earthquake destroyed two more courses in the side wall I doubt whether a convincing solution could ever have been found.

The abutments to the side arch still possess their door openings, the lintels to these openings, the *ablaq* joggled relieving arches above and the two upper courses containing the remains of recesses flanked by engaged columns. Similar recesses with engaged columns can be seen not only in the buildings of Sultan Qāytbāy but in nearly every Mamlūk mosque and madrasa in Cairo, and in most cases they have a grilled window set into them. It can be assumed that this would also have been the case in the Ashrafiyya, although the size and details of the recesses will have to be determined.

fig. V/2

To do this we have to refer back to the comparative table giving the number of stone courses in the abutments of the side walls of the *ṣaḥns*. By comparing the sub-elements given in the table with the existing recess in the Ashrafiyya, it will be seen that this recess has three sub-elements, C, D and E, each sub-element marking some significant point as they ascend the wall. Of immediate concern are the sub-elements C and D: sub-element C exists and is two courses high, one of them being

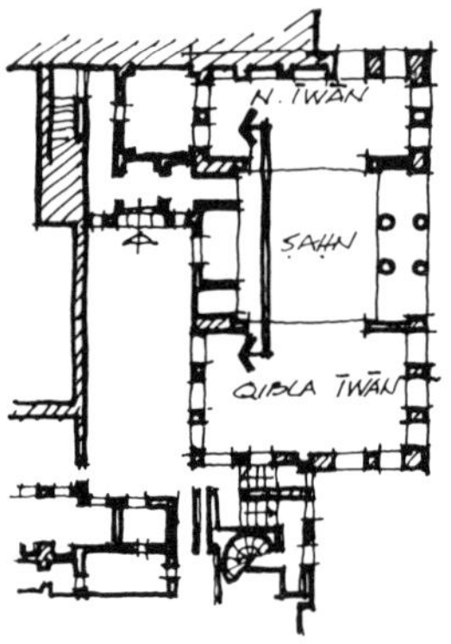

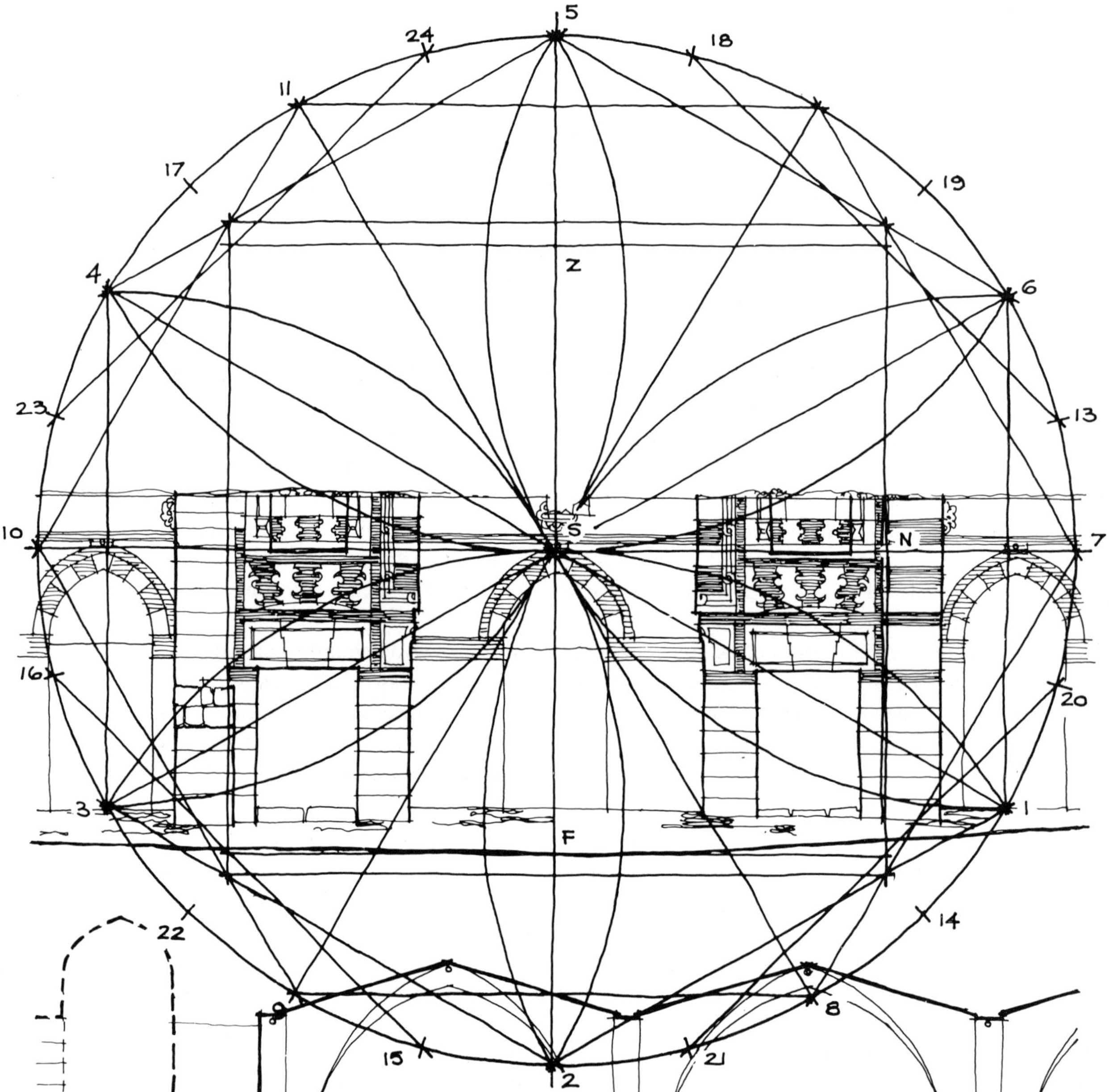

Fig. VI/9 *Ṣaḥn*, the side wall: the horizontal geometries rotated

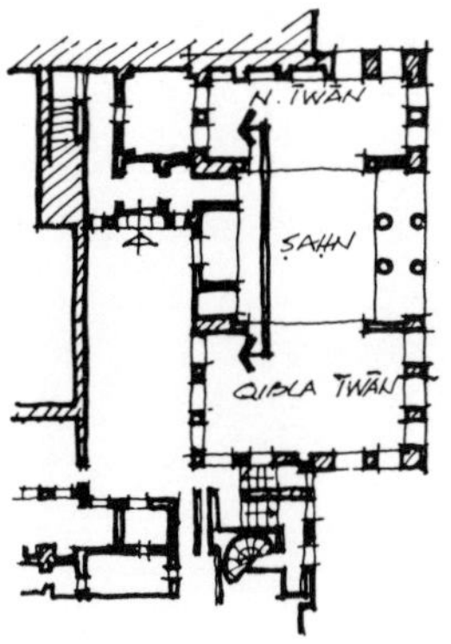

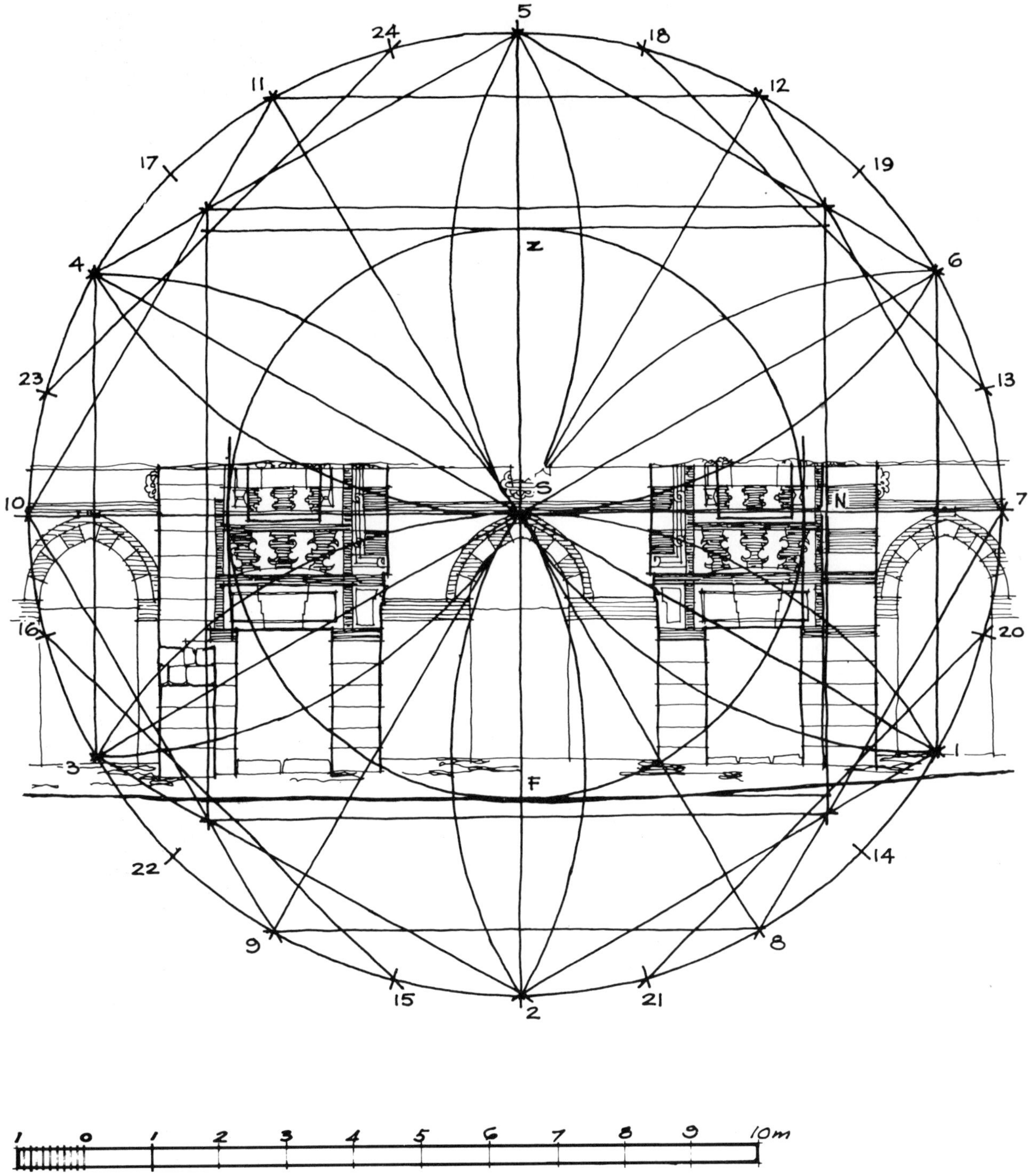

Fig. VI/10 *Ṣaḥn*, the side wall: the S-Z circle

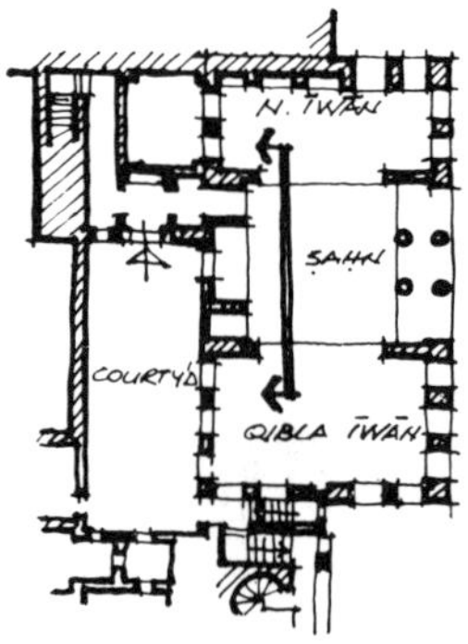

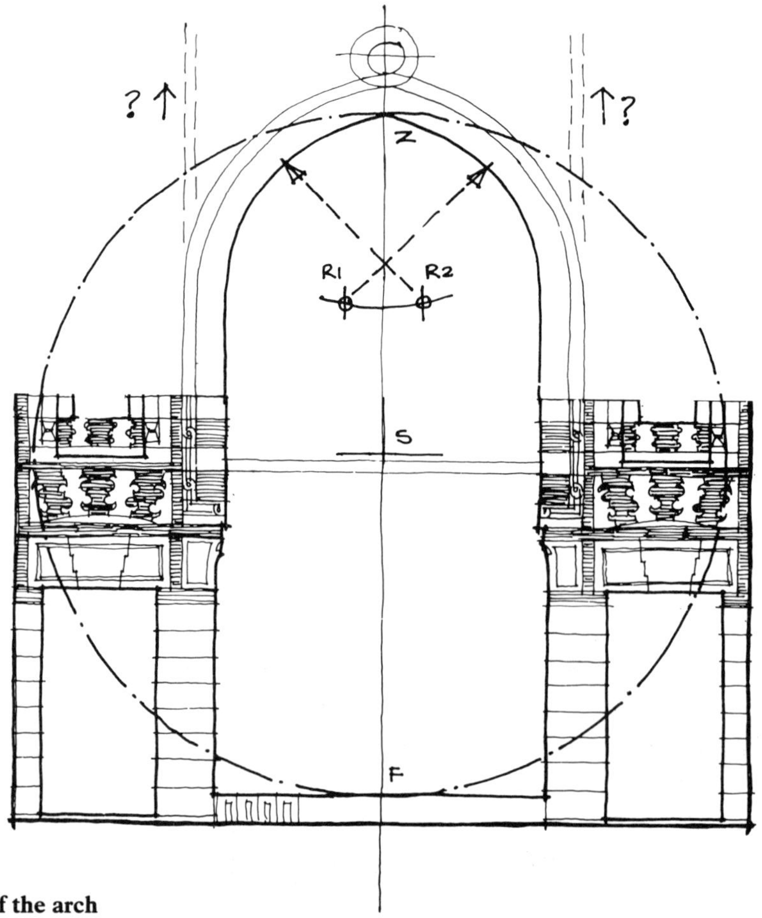

Fig. VI/11 *Ṣaḥn*, the side wall: the form of the arch

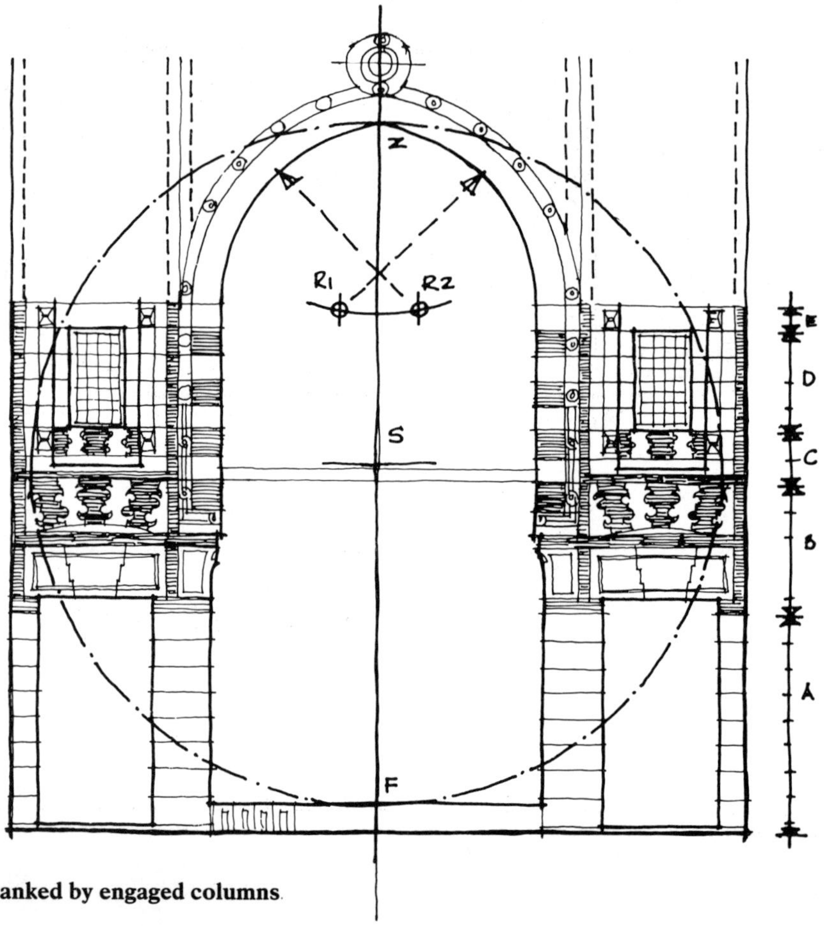

Fig. VI/12 *Ṣaḥn*, the side wall: windows flanked by engaged columns

decorated with a joggled *ablaq* design. Sub-element D corresponds to the height of the window opening and unfortunately in the Ashrafiyya it is incomplete. But despite this and some rebuilding, the existing evidence does allow us to position the sill and jambs of the original window as in Cairo the tops of the column bases coincide with the sill level of the window. Here in both of the recesses the course immediately above the columns bases contains two symmetrically placed vertical joints which were once the window jambs. Incidentally, the width of these window openings is $^{1}/_{20}$ BUG, and equal to half the width of the doors below them.

Even now after centuries of neglect the feeling one gets in the Ashrafiyya is similar to that felt in the Mosque and Mausoleum of Qāytbāy and in his Mosque at Qal'at al-Kabsh, but unlike that found in the Mosque at Rawḍa. Of course these similarities depend largely on the architects of Qāytbāy repeatedly using certain features which were common both in size and in type of decoration. For this reason the height of the window opening (sub-element D) in the Ashrafiyya can be assumed to have been four courses high, as it was so in the other two monuments. Similarly, the lintel block (sub-element E) over the grilled window was probably one course high. **fig. VI/12**

Each of the Cairo models has a keel arch (sub-element F) above the recessed windows, and this appears to have been so in the Ashrafiyya too, for the following reason. Two unusually shaped red stones exist, among the many stones which were re-used when windows and other openings were blocked up after the earthquake. Each stone has at its centre a hollowed out droplet, which restricts its use to the 'blind' loops which occur at the zeniths of the compartmentation surrounding keel arches. However, on their own they cannot provide evidence as to the height of the keel arches and so other clues must be sought.

The one option offered by the archaeological evidence involves a diversion to the sub-elements lying above the keel arch with the hope that they can later be anchored to the sub-elements A-E in such a way as to define a height which will be equivalent to that of the keel arch.

In the upper courses of the north elevation of the Ashrafiyya there are three decorated stones: two are almost square, but the third lying midway between them is a long and thin rectangle. It is remarkable that they survived as part of the rebuilt areas of the Ashrafiyya, and in particular that they survived as an identifiable group, since the earthquake had caused hundreds of other stones to fall and these had subsequently been removed and used in the construction of other buildings in Jerusalem, such as the Khaṣṣakī Sulṭān (959/1552).[1] **fig. VI/13**

Initially these stones seem unimportant; there are no similarly decorated stones in the Ashrafiyya, either in the manner of carving or form of script. For a long time I wondered whether they had come from some other building in Jerusalem. Notwithstanding this hesitant beginning their value as comparative material is, in fact, enormous.

In the Mosque at Qal'at al-Kabsh eight similarly decorated rectangular stones flank the four upper grilled windows in the side walls of the *ṣaḥn* belonging to sub-element H, and it is therefore logical to place this rectangular stone together with three replicas on either side of the two upper grilled windows in the side wall of the *ṣaḥn* of the Ashrafiyya.

This rectangular stone, therefore, assists the restoration by firstly providing an accurate measurement for sub-element H, the height of a window. Secondly, it can be assumed that the width of the vertical compartmentation flanking the door lintel, relieving arch and recessed window below, remains constant throughout its height and that it continued to rise up along the outer edge of the rectangular stone and that compartmentation of equal width separated it from the window. This being the case it allows the width of the window opening to be calculated, and appropriately it is found to equal that of the lower grilled window, $^{1}/_{20}$ BUG. The compartmentation across the top of the window is likely to have maintained the same width, but the dimensions of the blind loops indicate that below the window the compartmentation was thinner. **fig. VI/14**

Returning again to the north elevation, and the pair of badly weathered stones which are inscribed with the same Kufesque, or pseudo-Kufic, script, it is obvious that they have formed part of the same decorative element, but the Ashrafiyya offers no clues. The clue is to be discovered in Qal'at al-Kabsh where the painted timber cornice of the *ṣaḥn* is decorated with a similar Kufesque design. Consequently the use of a Kufesque design in the Ashrafiyya is not impossible. However, the pair of stones still have to be placed within the Ashrafiyya and it is hard to know for certain whether or not they came from the *ṣaḥn*. On balance it can be assumed they did for the following reasons.

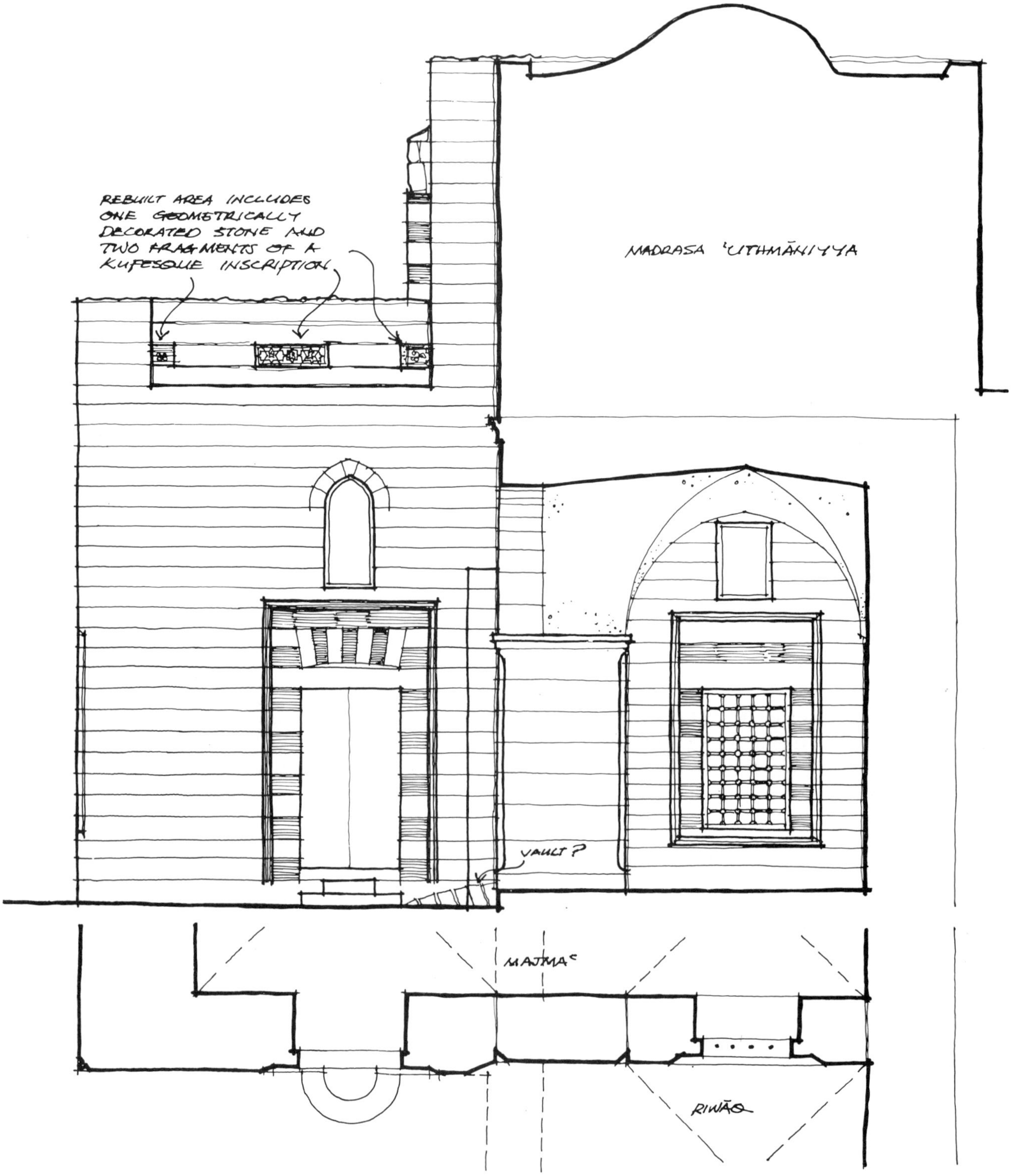

Fig. VI/13 The existing north elevation

Below the cornice painted with the Kufesque design in the *ṣaḥn* of Qalʿat al-Kabsh a grand inscription in *thuluth* script is carved into the upper stone courses, it resembles the grand inscription in *thuluth* script which runs around the existing walls of the *īwāns* of the Ashrafiyya. This similarity, together with the fact that this is the only grand inscription in Qalʿat al-Kabsh, makes it reasonable to assume that the Ashrafiyya would likewise have had only one grand inscription in this script. Yet, as the grand inscriptions of both Qalʿat al-Kabsh and the Mosque and Mausoleum encircle the wallheads of their *ṣaḥn*, it is conceivable that, despite the existence of the grand *thuluth* inscription in its *īwāns*, the Ashrafiyya might also have had a grand inscription encircling the wallhead of its *ṣaḥn*. If so, why not a Kufesque inscription?

Plate 11 Cairo, Qalʿat al-Kabsh, Mosque of Qāytbāy,: the *qibla īwān* seen from the *ṣaḥn*. (*Survey of Egypt*, pl. 127, where it is wrongly identified as the Mosque and Mausoleum of Qāytbāy)

Plate 12 Cairo, Mosque of Qāytbāy, Qal'at al-Kabsh: the *ṣaḥn's* side wall; notice the panels flanking the upper rectangular windows which are repeated in Jerusalem. (Tarchi, *L'Architettura e l'Arte Musulmane in Egitto e nella Palestina*, tav. 100)

Plate 13 Cairo, Mosque of Qāytbāy, Qal'at al-Kabsh: the Kufesque inscription painted on the cornice of the *ṣaḥn*

The three decorated stones found in the upper courses of the north elevation, along with the blind loop, enable the sub-elements H and J of the side wall of the *ṣaḥn* to be recomposed, but we must not forget that the height of the keel arch (sub-element F) has still to be found and once this is done it should anchor the 'floating' sub elements H and J to the lower parts of the wall. The comparative tables provide two possible solutions: 6 courses, as in Qal'at al-Kabsh, or 6½ courses, as in the Mosque and Mausoleum and the Mosque at Rawḍa. A ½ course would make a difference of only fifteen centimetres, but nevertheless a decision must be made, and in order to do so the primary geometry has again to be rotated against the side wall. **fig. VI/15** **fig. VI/16**

Once the primary geometry is in place against the side wall, the floating composition can be moved up and down until it is reconciled to the side wall and the primary geometry. This appears to happen when the top of the floating composition is brought down to the level of the line 11-12. This leaves a space of 6½ courses between the top of sub-element E in the side wall and the bottom of sub-element H in the floating composition. This is where the keel arch (sub-element F) fits, making it equal in height to the same element in the Mosque and Mausoleum and the Mosque at Rawḍa. This arrangement also allows the compartmentation below the Kufesque inscription to run along the top of the archivolt loop of the side arch just as it does in Qal'at al-Kabsh. **fig. VI/17**

This solution should not be seen in isolation because the coursing of the side wall of the *ṣaḥn* continues into the abutments of the great arches. Their respective stone courses must, therefore, be equal in number and continue from one wall into the other. Furthermore, whatever the forms of archivolt and lines of compartmentation, they must resemble those of the Cairo models.

To verify these points a return must be made to the analysis of the great horseshoe arch and its abutments. The position of point S, the height of the arch, and the centres of its segments and archivolt have already been established, as have the sub-elements A to D. A loop of an undefined size can also be added temporarily to complete the archivolt, since such loops occur at the zeniths of the archivolts seen in Cairo. **fig. VI/18**

By applying the primary geometry to the great arches and introducing the wallhead inscription **fig. VI/19**

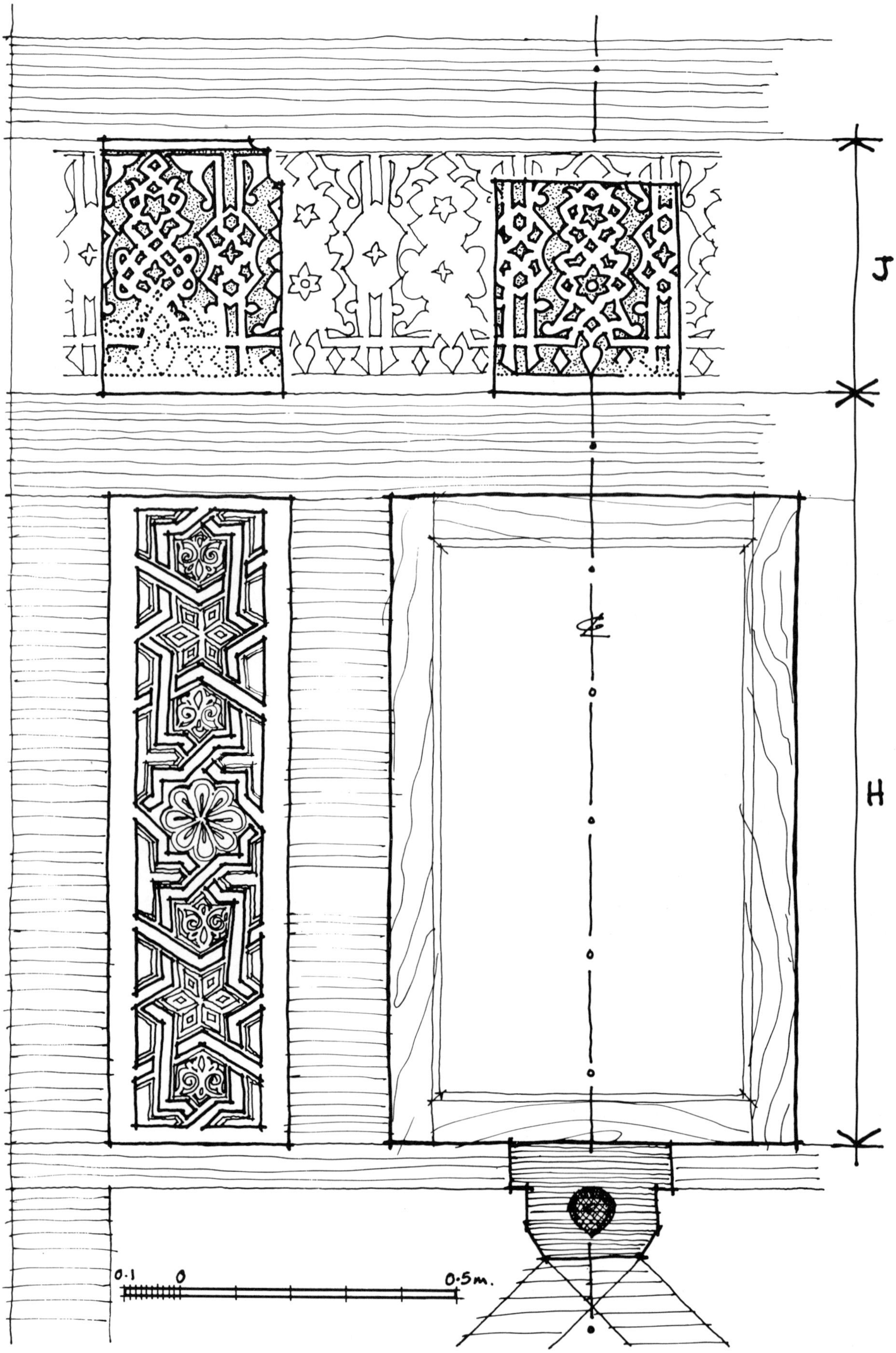

Fig. VI/14 *Ṣaḥn*, the side wall: the upper elements recomposed

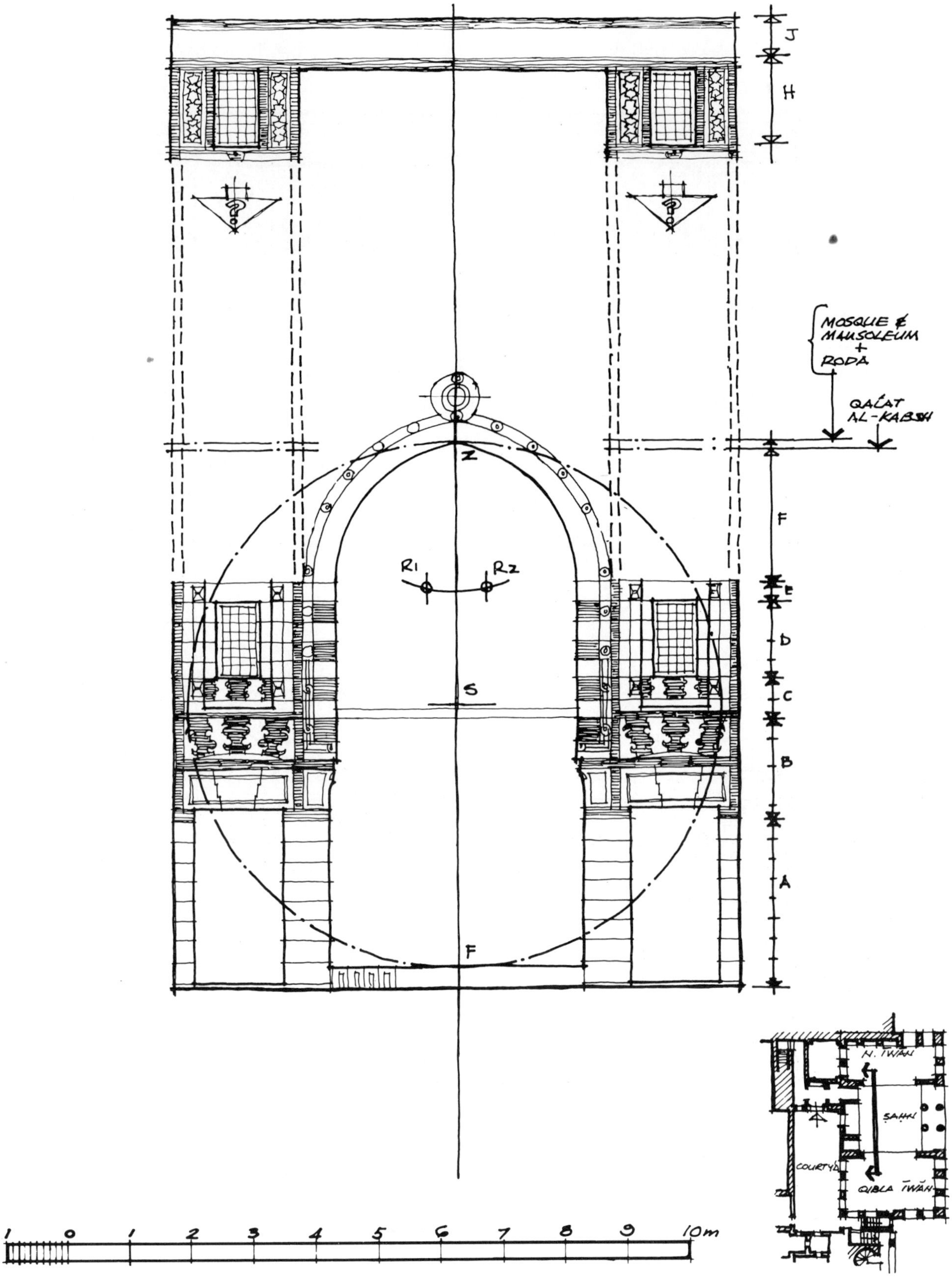

Fig. VI/15 *Ṣaḥn*, the side wall: the 'floating' composition

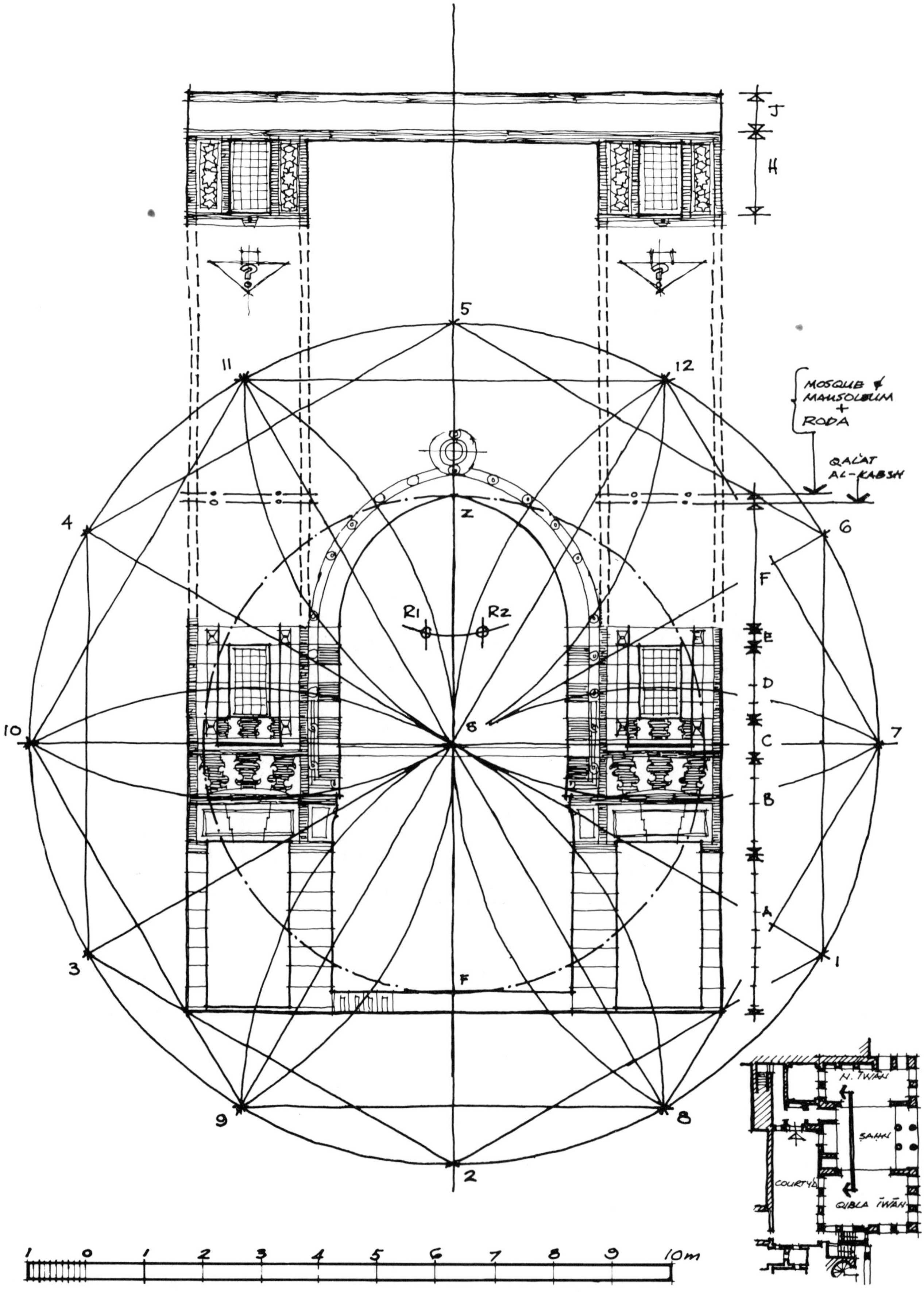

Fig. VI/16 *Ṣaḥn*, the side wall: the primary geometry and the 'floating' composition

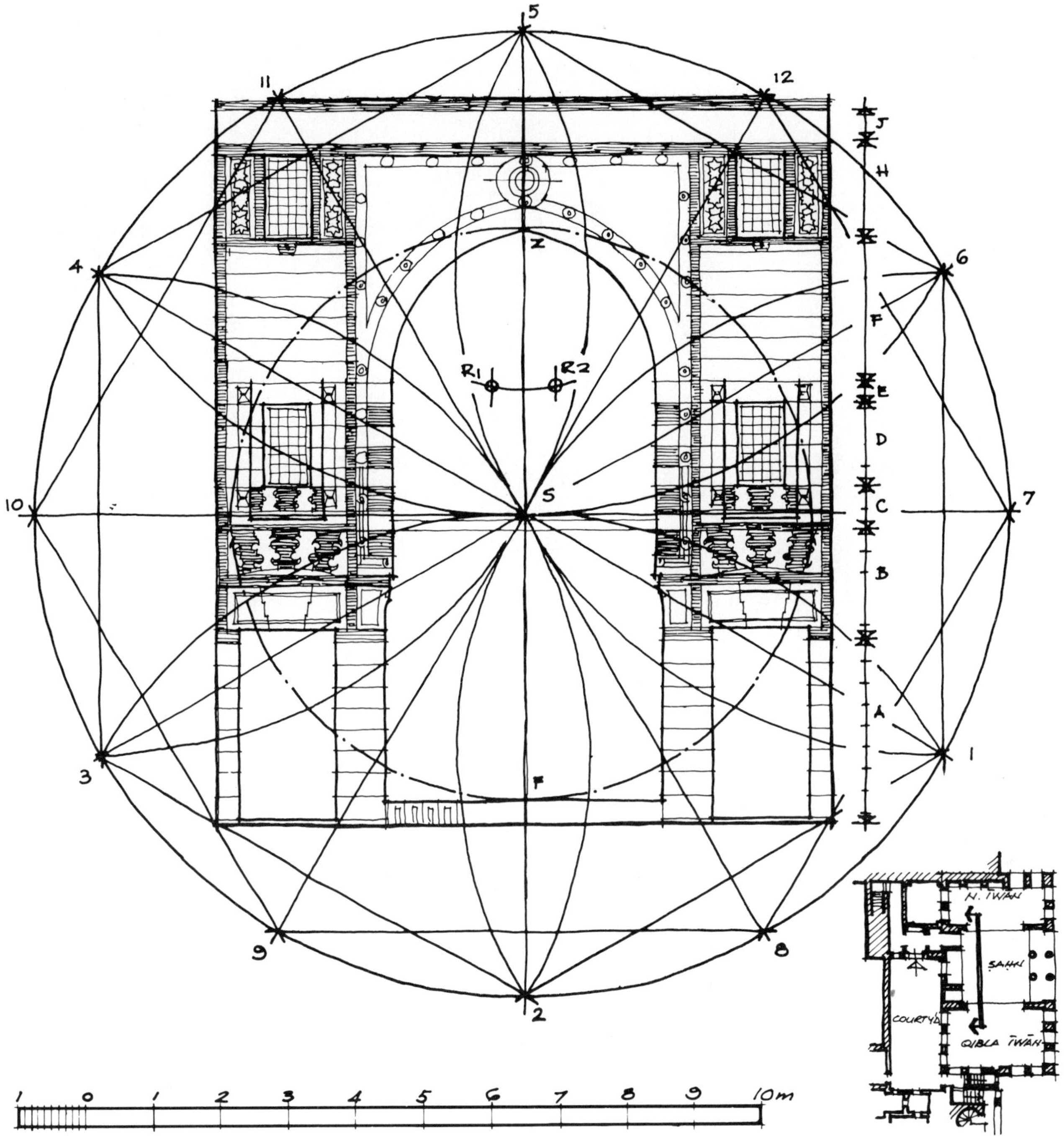

Fig. VI/17 ***Ṣaḥn*****, the side wall: the floating composition anchored by the primary geometry**

(sub-element F) at the level previously established in the side wall, new relationships can be seen and checked, such as the size of the spandrels, the size of the archivolt loop, and the compartmentation to the archivolt. As can be seen from the tables, all are comparable to their contemporaries in Cairo. For **fig. V/1** example, the height from the springing of the great arches to the wallhead inscription (sub-element E) is 17 courses in the Ashrafiyya, the same as in the Mosque at Rawḍa, and differing slightly from the 16½ courses in the Mosque and Mausoleum and the 14½ courses in Qalʿat al-Kabsh.

To develop the theme further, it could be proposed that since in the Ashrafiyya the compartmentation below the inscription runs along the top of the archivolt loop, as it does in the Mosque at Qalʿat al-Kabsh, the spandrels may also reflect those of Qalʿat al-Kabsh with their elaborate decoration and the cartouche of Sultan Qāytbāy.

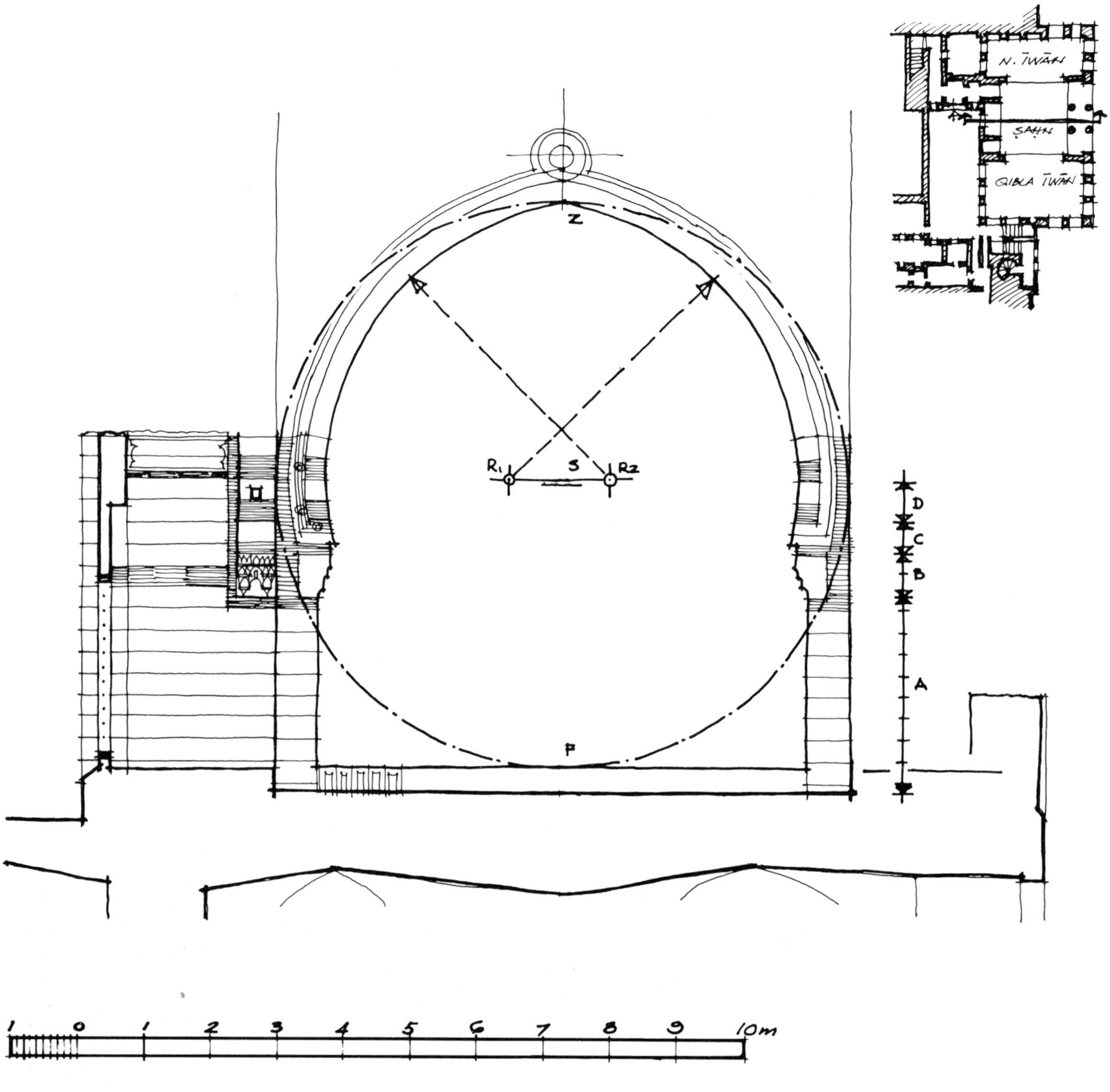

Fig. VI/18 *Ṣaḥn*, the great arch: the S-Z circle

The Lantern

There is considerable evidence that the *ṣaḥn* had a flat roof supporting a central lantern. The chronicler al-'Ulaymī records that all the ceilings in the Madrasa were made of timber and decorated with gold leaf and blue paint, and the architectural remains confirm this. In Jerusalem the use of wood in this manner was unusual since there was a plentiful supply of stone and scarcity of structural timber. Stone vaults with minimal or no wood were the norm, but in this case wood had to be used if the design were to follow the tradition of Cairo.

Interestingly, al-'Ulaymī reports that the ceilings were stable and had been assembled with 'art and nobility'. However, history has proved him wrong as to their stability as they did not withstand the earthquake of 952AH, whereas most of the stone vaults of Jerusalem did.

We must accept, therefore, that above the *ṣaḥn* there was an octagonal lantern, similar in form to

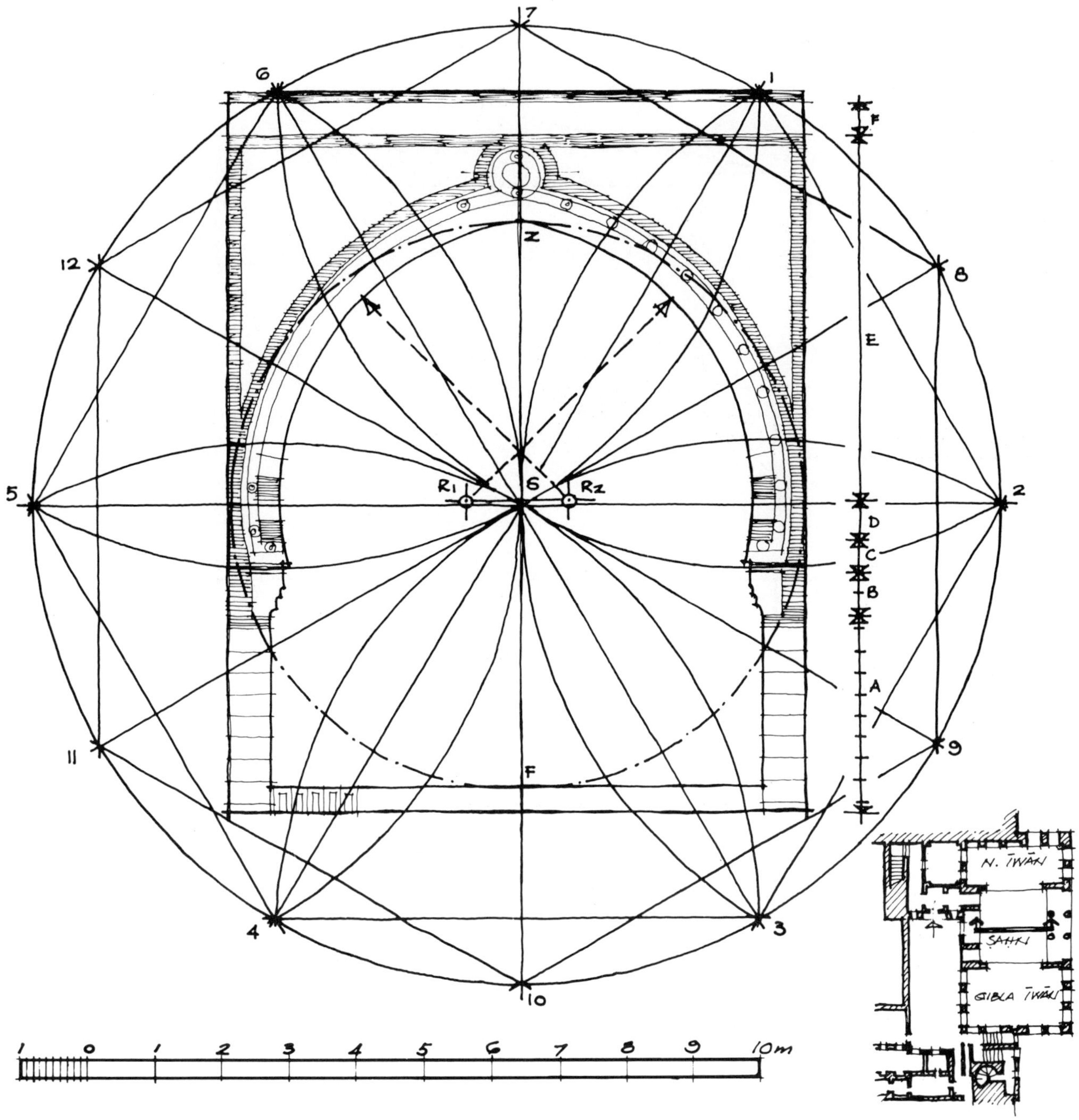

Fig. VI/19 *Ṣaḥn*, the great arch: the primary geometry

its contemporaries in Cairo. Fortunately, while sifting through the archives of the Centre for Islamic and Coptic Documentation in Cairo, an unsigned survey drawing was unearthed. This drawing to a scale of 1:100 was made before the lantern of the Mosque and Mausoleum was restored in about 1897, and in addition to being drawn to scale, a number of measurements are given (although some are slightly obscure since the drawing combines a half section with a quarter plan). However, of particular interest is the measurement of 8.61m for the length of one of the sides of the *ṣaḥn* which varies by only $^1/_{200}$ BUG from the reconstructed west-east dimension of 8.54m in the *ṣaḥn* of the Ashrafiyya. **fig. VI/20**

This unsigned survey drawing can be simplified to show a half section through the octagonal lantern, with the basically square plan of the *ṣaḥn* below. On this plan a geometry centred at point S can be set composed of a circle describing a double square (8-pointed star) with a diameter equal to the width of the *ṣaḥn*. When this is related to the section of the lantern, its essential lines, windows and octagonally planned eaves can all be retraced to their geometric origins. **fig. VI/21**

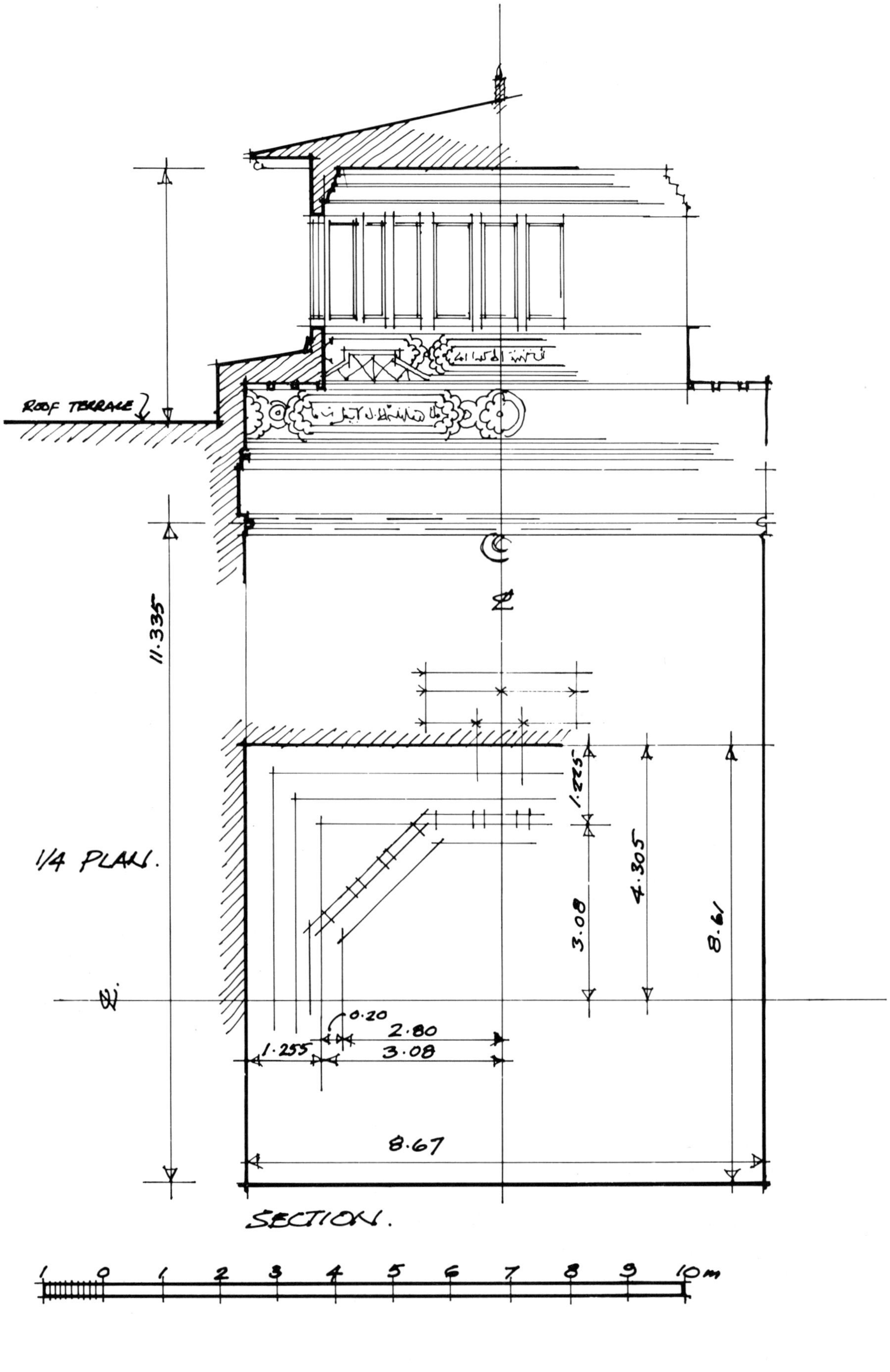

Fig. VI/20 Mosque and Mausoleum: the *ṣaḥn* and lantern after the c. 1897 survey drawing entitled 'Mosquée de Kaitbay du desert: avant projet'.

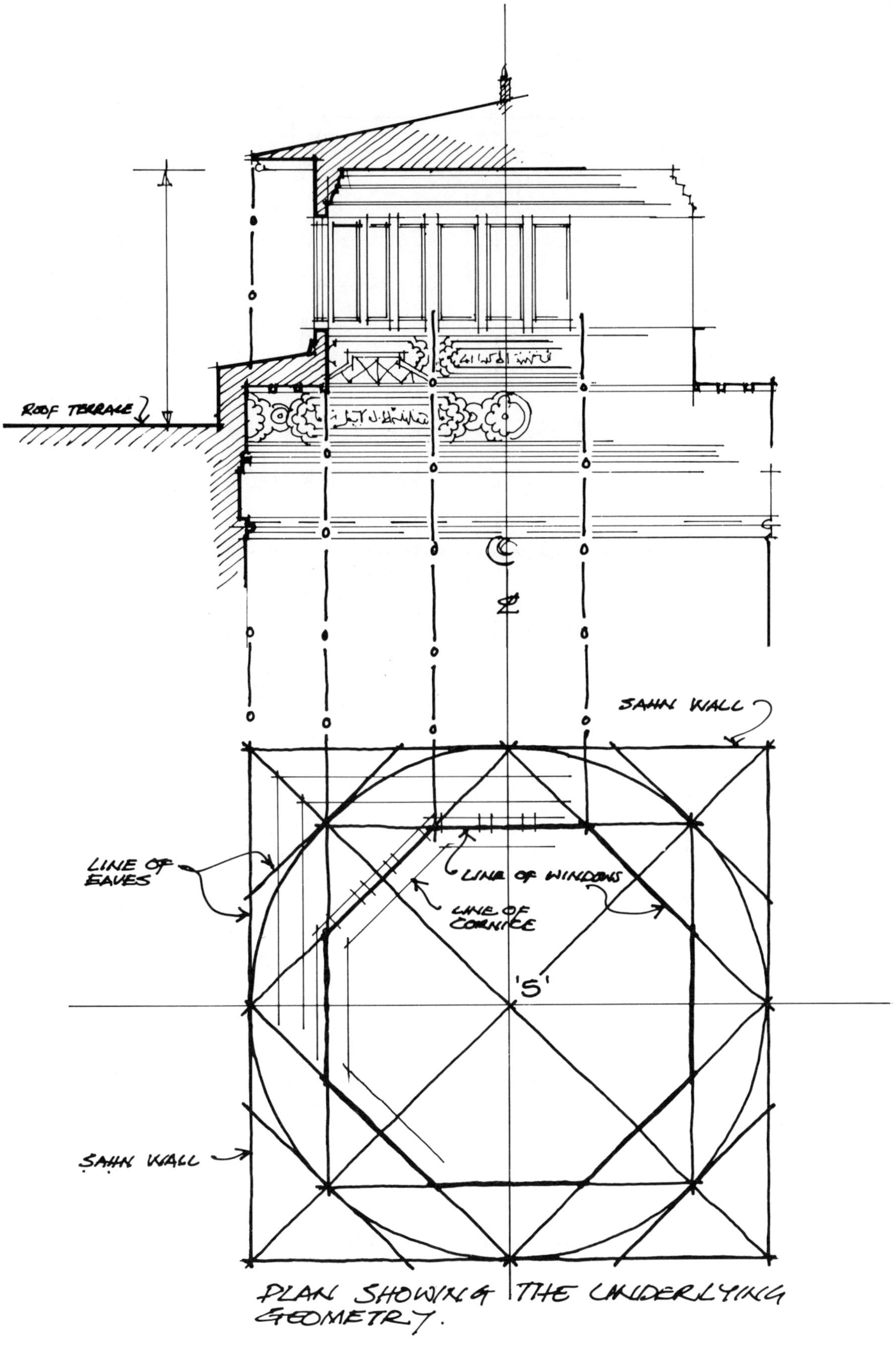

Fig. VI/21 Mosque and Mausoleum: the underlying geometry of the *ṣaḥn* and lantern

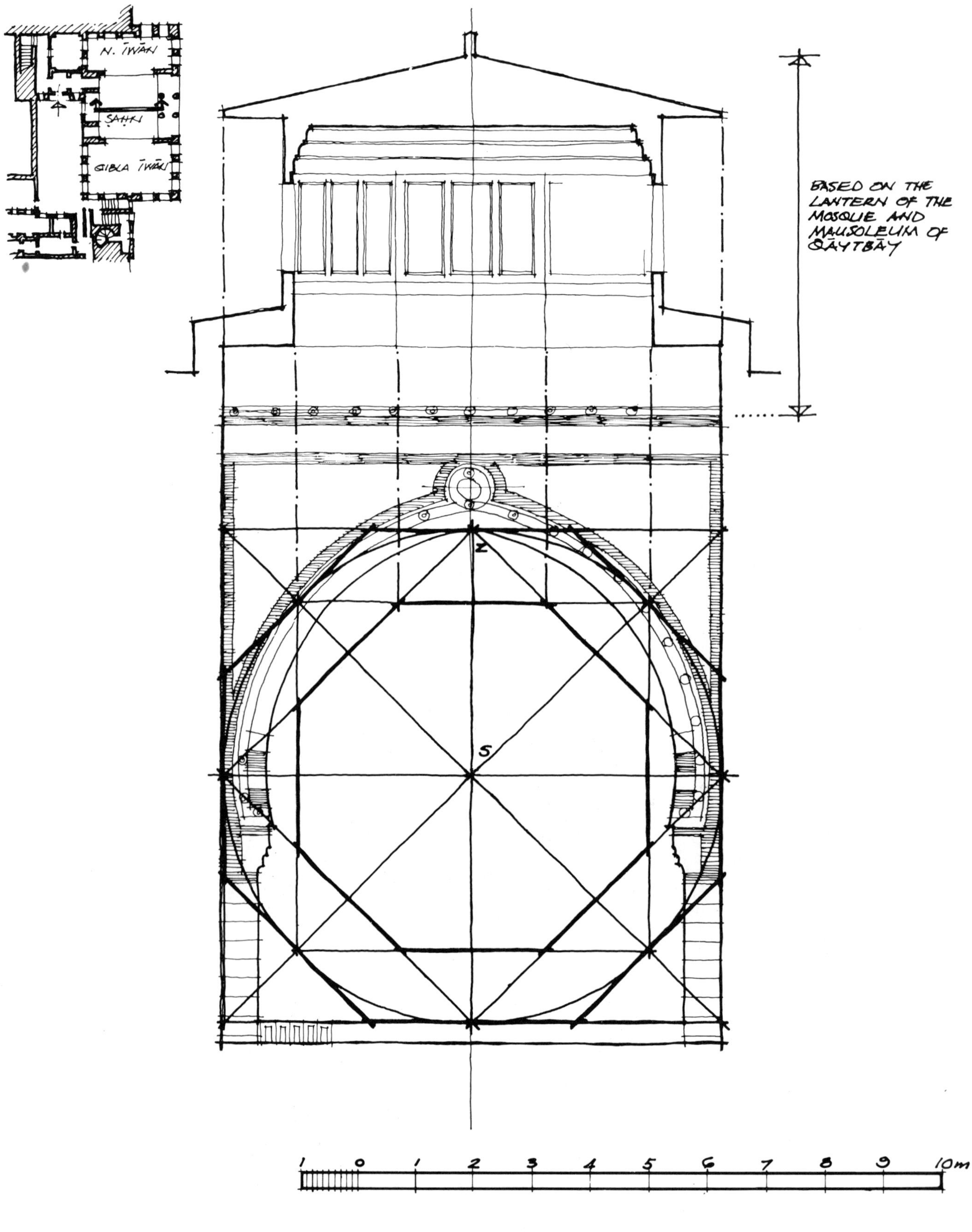

Fig. VI/22 *Ṣaḥn*, the great arch: the underlying geometry of the *ṣaḥn* and lantern

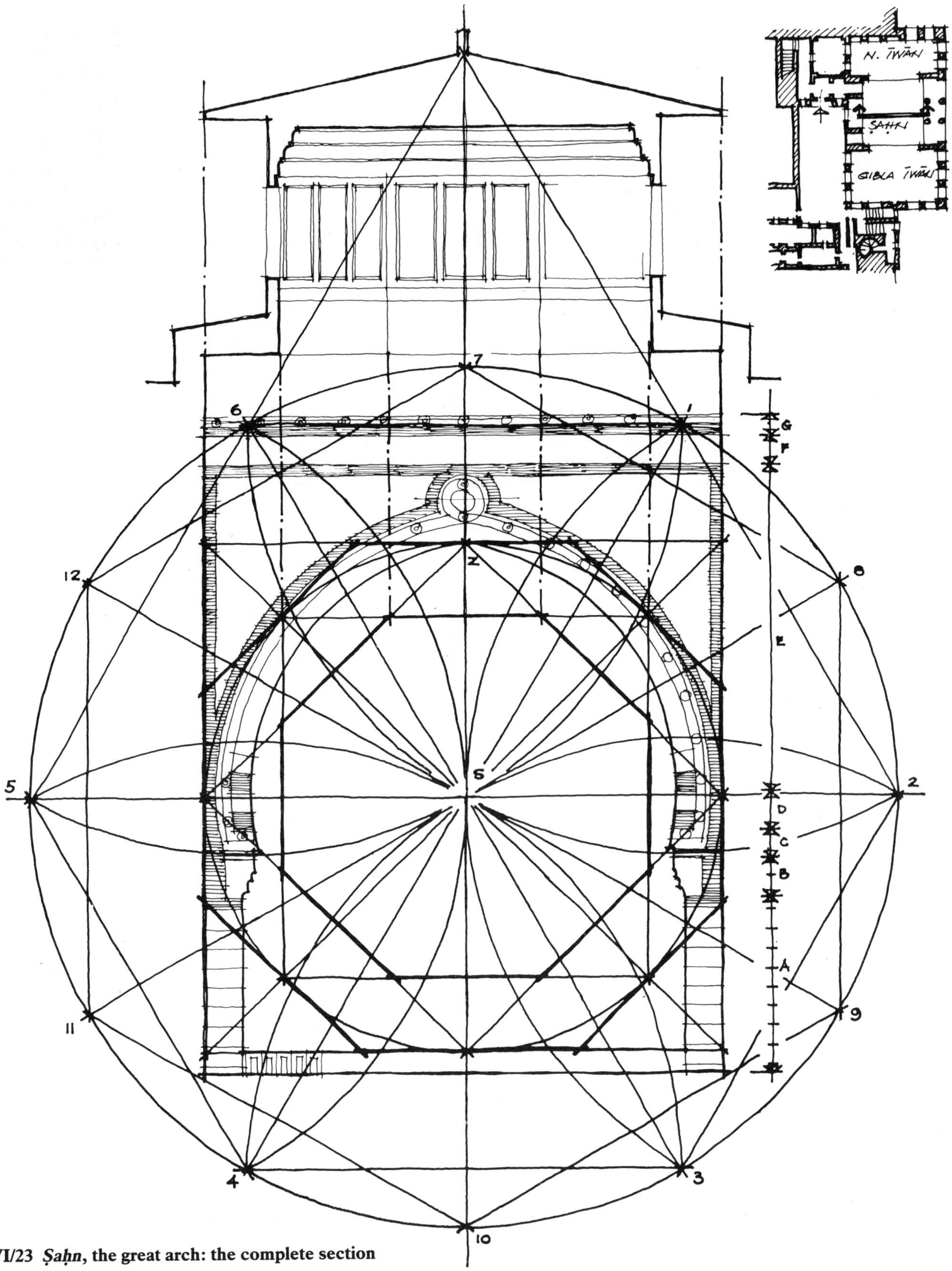

Fig. VI/23 ***Ṣaḥn*****, the great arch: the complete section**

Great Arch to the *Ṣaḥn*	A	B	C	D	E	F	G	total
Mosque and Mausoleum	9	3	1	3½	16½	2	1½	36½
Qal'at al-Kabsh	8½	3½	1	5	14½	2	1½	36
Rawḍa	7½	2	0	3	17	2	0	31½
Ashrafiyya	(9)	2	1½	2	(17)	(1½)	(1)	(34)

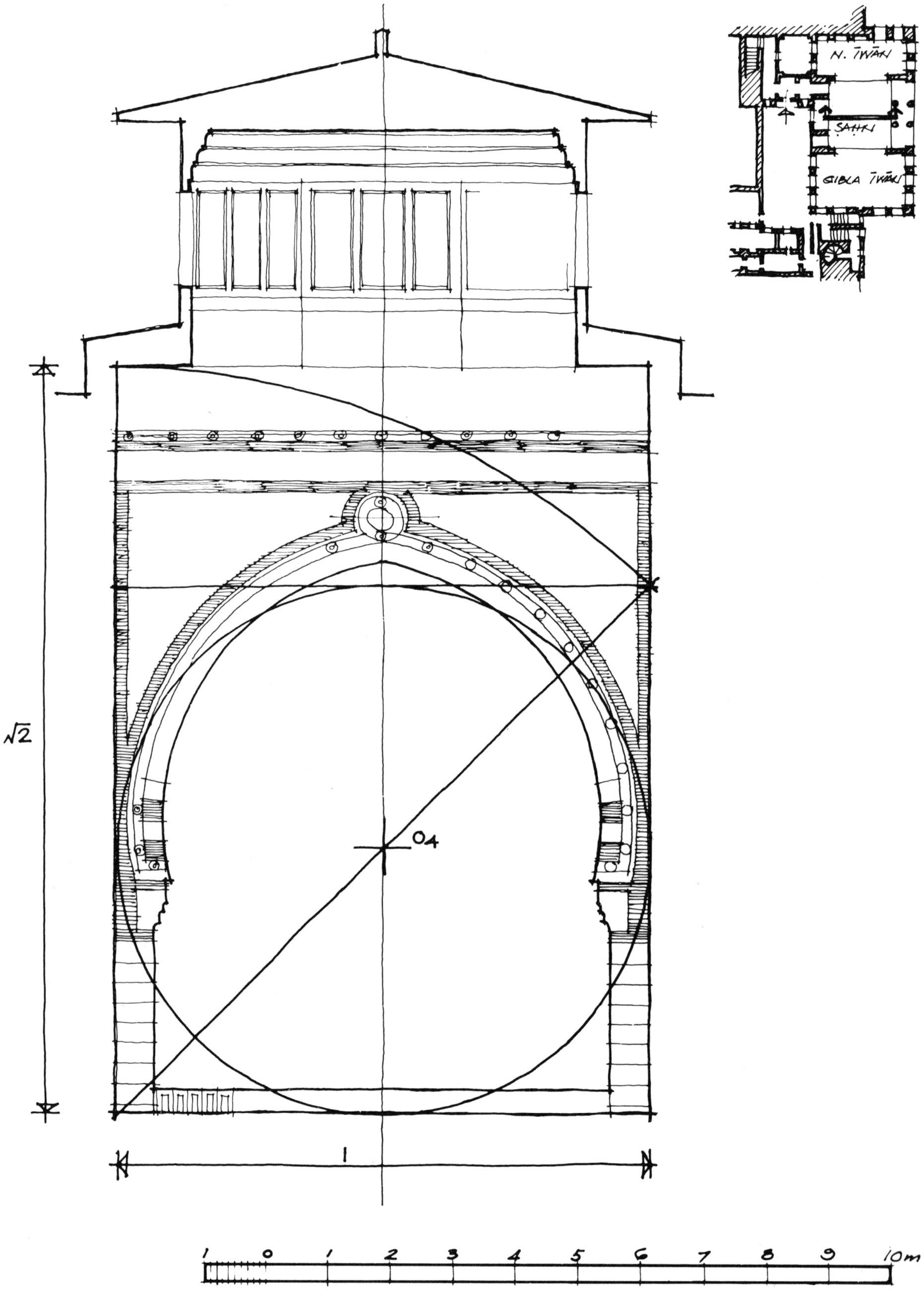

Fig. VI/24 *Ṣaḥn*, the great arch: the root two proportions

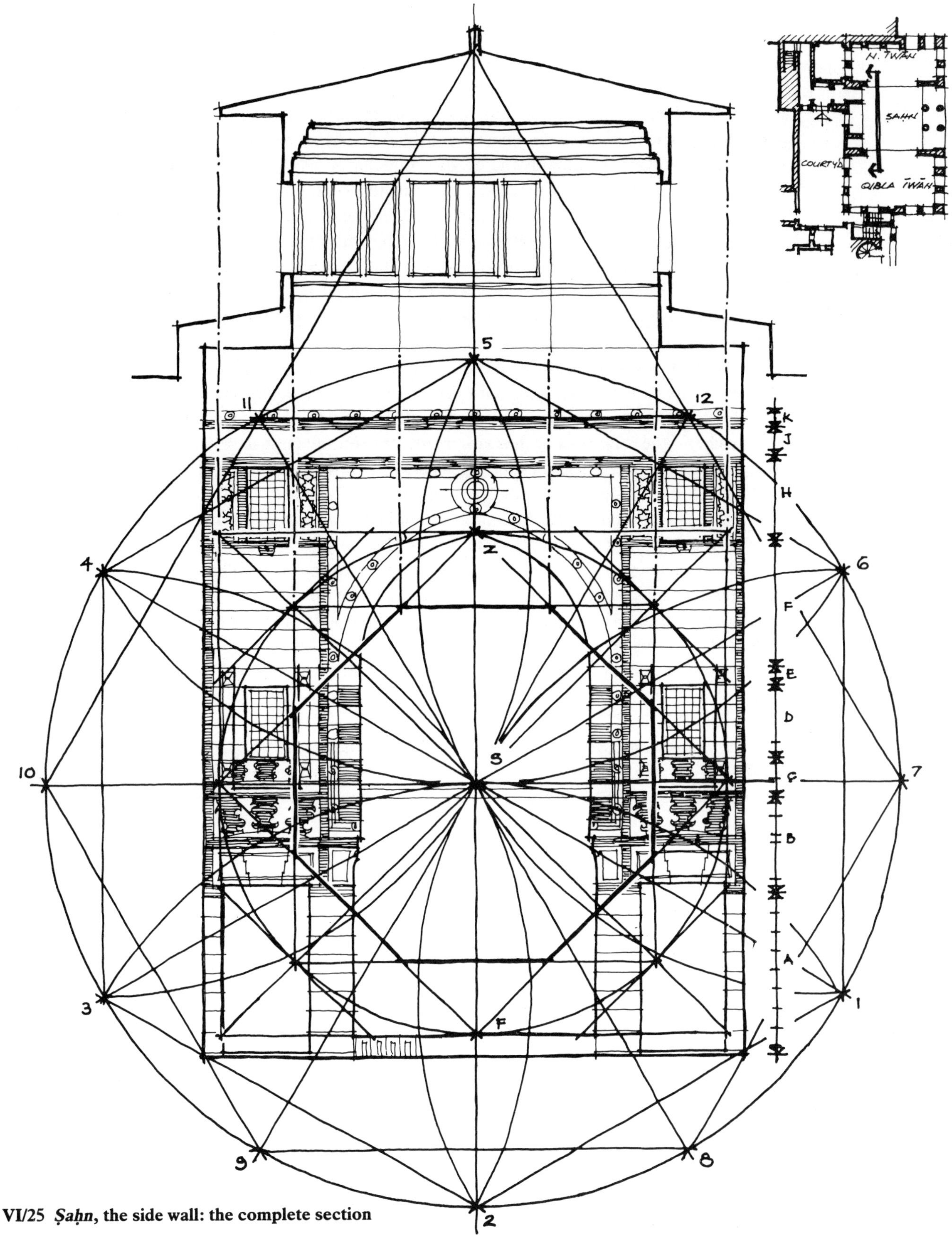

Fig. VI/25 *Ṣaḥn*, the side wall: the complete section

The Abutments

	A	B	C	D	E	F	G	H	J	K	total
Mosque and Mausoleum	8½	5	2½	4	1	6½	0	5½	2	1½	36½
Qal'at al-Kabsh	7½	4½	2	4	1	6	2	5½	2	1½	36
Rawḍa	7½	5½	2	6	2	6½	0	0	2	0	31½
Ashrafiyya	(8½)	5	2	(4)	(1)	(6½)	(0)	(4½)	(1½)	(1)	34

fig. VI/22 This design from the Mosque and Mausoleum can be easily adapted to fit the *ṣaḥn* of the Ashrafiyya. Firstly, since the horizontal and vertical geometries are identical, the circle centred on S with points Z and F on its circumference corresponds to the circle enclosing the double square in the plan of the Mosque and Mausoleum. By adding the double square it must therefore be possible to generate a geometry to fit the dimensions of the Ashrafiyya. Secondly, as the plan dimensions of both *ṣaḥns* are so similar, presumably the heights of the lanterns were too, so the height of the lantern can now be added to the recently reconstructed wall and great arch of the *ṣaḥn*.

fig. VI/23 Although the design of the lantern completes the west-east section across the *ṣaḥn*, it must now be seen whether or not it can be linked back to the primary geometry. Looking at the geometry of the *ṣaḥn* and the lantern together, it becomes clear that the apex of the lantern coincides with the apex of the 1 BUG equilateral triangle based on the diameter 5-2. This relationship is, in fact, a logical extension of the earlier detailed geometries and brings together the various paths followed in the restoration of the *ṣaḥn*. There may also have been some architectural or religious significance for the architect and his team in the fact that the same fundamental geometry defined the *miḥrāb* in plan, and the apex of the lantern in section, but this is a point for theologians to discuss.

fig. VI/24 One final observation can be made about the proportions relating to the sides of the *ṣaḥn* with the great arches. The difference in measurement between the west-east width of the *ṣaḥn* and its height from floor level to the soffit of the ceiling below the lantern is in the proportion $1:\sqrt{2}$ (i.e., equivalent to the diagonal of a square according to Pythagoras' Theorem). This root two proportional system is met continually in Mamlūk architecture. When I first came across its use in a sculpted panel I mistook it for an inaccurate attempt at reproducing the Golden Ratio $(1 + \sqrt{5})2$.[2]

fig. VI/25 The fundamental geometry can also be applied to the side wall of the *ṣaḥn*, where naturally an equilateral triangle again coincides with the apex of the lantern. There is, however, one slight modification in that the width of the ceiling on either side of the octagonal opening of the lantern is increased.

Turning again to the course heights, the *ṣaḥn* from floor level to the underside of the timber cornice has 34 stone courses, a number falling midway between those of the Mosque and Mausoleum (36½), and Rawḍa (31½)., This confirms the validity of the reconstruction. From the variance in the number of stone courses given in the comparative tables, an aesthetic difference could be expected of Rawḍa, and it is in fact the case that the Ashrafiyya is closer in design to the Mosque and Mausoleum and the Mosque at Qal'at al-Kabsh than to its exact contemporary, Rawḍa.

Notes

1. See below, Appendix A, n. 5.
2. A succinct and interesting description of these two proportional systems is given by El-Said, I., and A. Parman, *Geometric Concepts in Islamic Art*, London, 1976, pp. 8-9 and 82-83.

Chapter VII
THE *QIBLA ĪWĀN*

It will be recalled that the fundamental geometry centred on the *ṣaḥn* consisted of a circle with a diameter of 1 BUG, equal to the overall width of the Madrasa. Within the circle a hexagon was inscribed and this generated the equilateral triangle which immediately positioned the *miḥrāb*, as if to emphasize architecturally its religious importance. A further sequence of primary and detailed geometries was subsequently developed which defined the various other features of the first floor plan.

Now as we have been able to unveil the pattern of thought followed by the architect in the design of the walls and arches of the *ṣaḥn*, can we not assume he followed a similar pattern when designing the *qibla īwān*? This being the case then it would be logical to start with the *qibla* wall and then correlate it to the side wall of the *īwān*.

Firstly, the existing features of the *qibla* wall must be defined. It stands at a height of some 14 courses above the present floor level. However, whilst studying the great arches to the *ṣaḥn*, the original floor level of the *qibla īwān* was established, and so the height of the hidden lower portion of the wall can be calculated and added to the 14 visible courses. This makes a total height of 15½ stone courses, and it also establishes for the *qibla* wall the heights of sub-elements A and B, and a part of sub-element C. **fig. VII/1**

From the contemporary descriptions it is known that in the *qibla* wall there was a pair of windows to the east of the *miḥrāb* which balanced the existing pair of blocked up windows to the west. It can be assumed that these windows were largely similar in design, although there is evidence of a minor difference in the level of the voussoirs to the arched recesses. Those of the western windows begin one course above the springing line of the arches, whereas those to the east appear to have begun on the same level as the springing line. In the drawing it can be seen that the zeniths of the arched recesses in the *qibla* wall are lower than those in the side walls, despite the fact that they all have a common springing level and their rectangular window openings are the same size. **fig. VII/2**

One other existing feature in the *qibla* wall is the grand inscription which, to maintain symmetry, would have extended along the full length of the wall. This completes the existing evidence.

In the reconstruction of the *ṣaḥn* the existing evidence was assembled, but before the conjectural evidence was added the fundamental geometry, and subsequently the primary geometry, were rotated into the vertical plane to check that they fitted with the known details. The same steps can now be followed here.

The fundamental geometry is the obvious geometry to choose to rotate against the *qibla* wall. But first the position of the centre Q in the vertical plane must be fixed and if the vertical geometries of the *ṣaḥn* and *qibla* wall are to be immediately correlated then centres Q and S have to be interchangeable. **fig. VII/3**

When the fundamental geometry is rotated against the *qibla* wall, the height of its centre Q is found to be close to the apex of the voussoirs of the upper arch of the *miḥrāb* and to be nearly on a level with the lower edge of the compartmentation below the grand inscription.

By joining points 6-4 and 3-1 two intersections are made along diameter 2-5 separated by ½ BUG, a distance equal to the side of the hexagon and to the radius of the circle. A second circle can then be added using those points of intersection to define the length of its diameter. This circle equates to that in the primary geometry in the plan of the *qibla īwān* with points Q_1 and M on its circumference (see IV/8 above).

Within this last circle a hexagon is constructed with sides equal to ¼ BUG, and by joining the points corresponding to points 6-4 and 3-1 of the fundamental geometry the diameter 2-5 is again intersected twice, the intersections being ¼ BUG apart. **fig. VII/4**

A third circle is then constructed, its diameter defined by these last points of intersection, and this

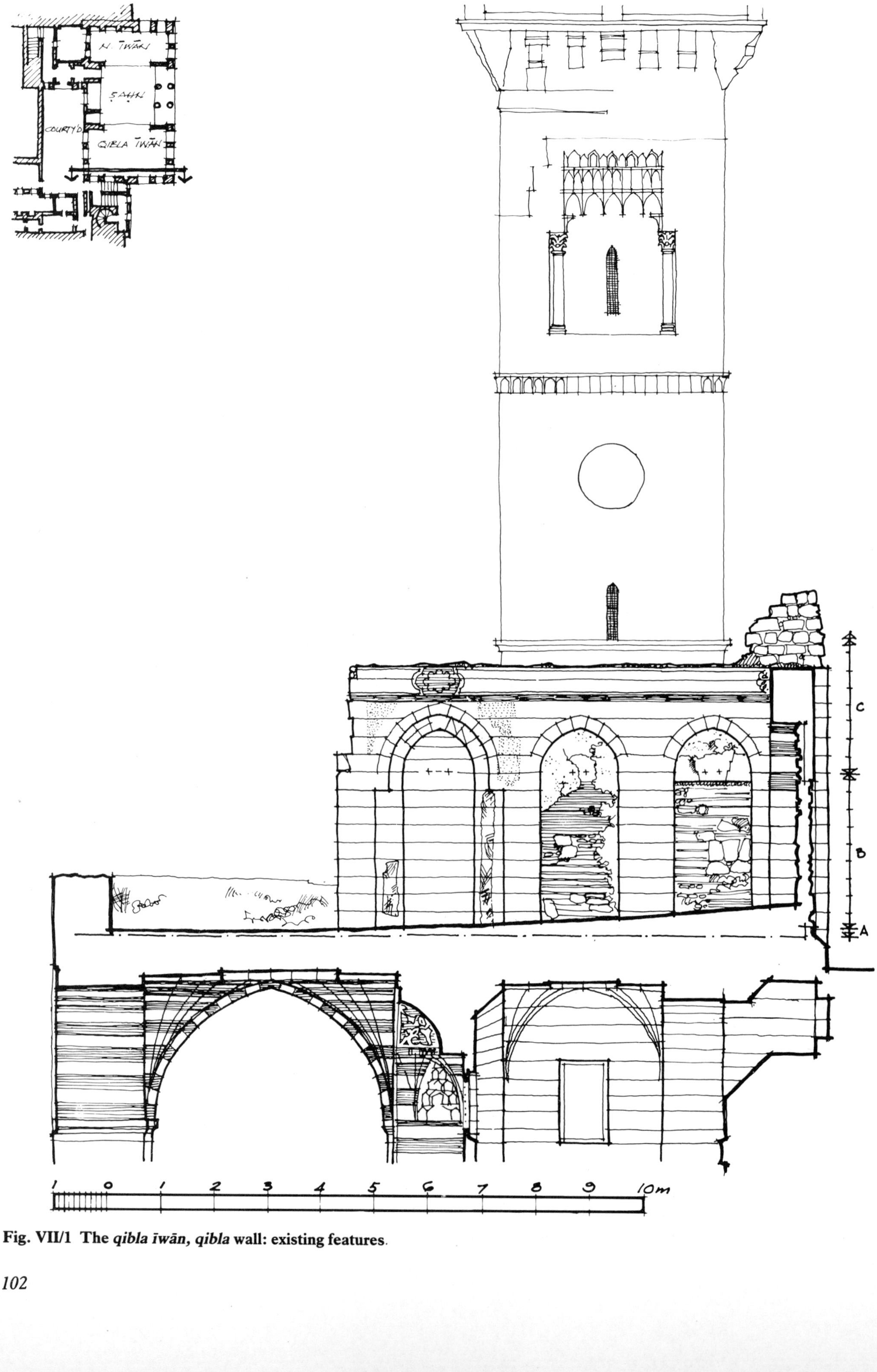

Fig. VII/1 The *qibla īwān, qibla* wall: existing features.

in turn describes a third hexagon with sides equal to 1/8 BUG. Points 3 and 4 of this third hexagon define the span of the upper arch of the *miḥrāb*, and also the point where the intrados ends and the width of the lower part of the recess increases.

A fourth circle can be similarly added to the figure and it could describe a hexagon with sides equal to 1/16 BUG, and this process could continue to generate further circles. However, this fourth circle completes the present sequence of geometries, the construction of which has visually linked the width of the Madrasa, the depth of the *qibla īwān* and the span of the upper arch of the *miḥrāb*, each step being in a ratio of 2:1 to the next.

The width of the *miḥrāb* panel is the one major feature missing from this list of proportionally **fig. VII/5** linked features, but it has already been established by the 24-pointed star centred on the *ṣaḥn*. However, it is reconfirmed here in the rotated geometries by joining point 13 to 23 and point 16 to 20, this produces a theoretical width only three centimetres greater than the actual panel width of 3.70m.

Having reconfirmed the width of the *miḥrāb* panel we still have to find the geometric relationships which control the smaller but equally essential details: the recess and curved niche. If from the fourth circle and its hexagon, the 2:1 proportional sequence were continued, the next step would produce a diameter shorter than the width of the curved niche which would be of little use. Thus another

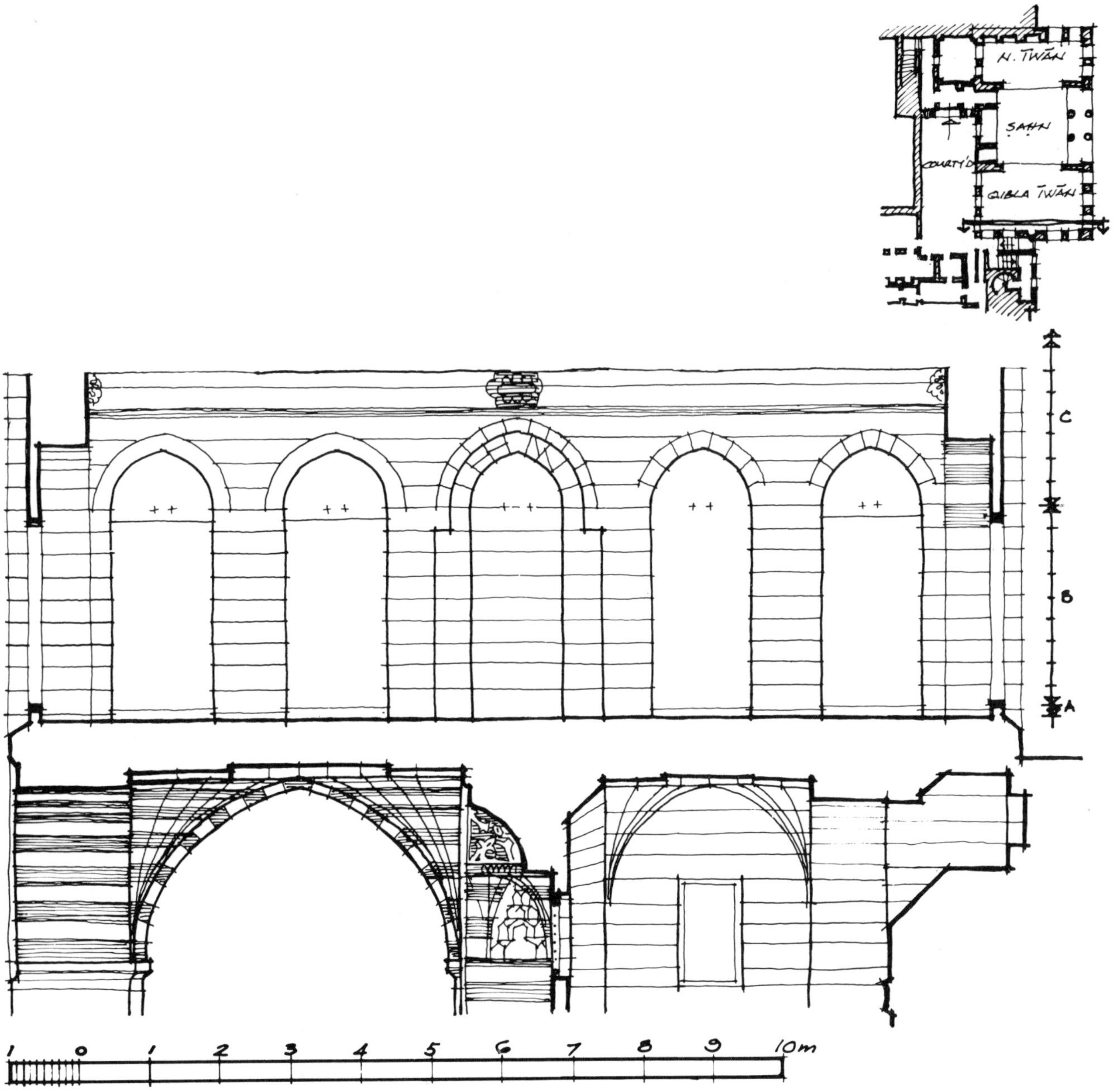

Fig. VII/2 The *qibla īwān, qibla* wall: additions to existing features

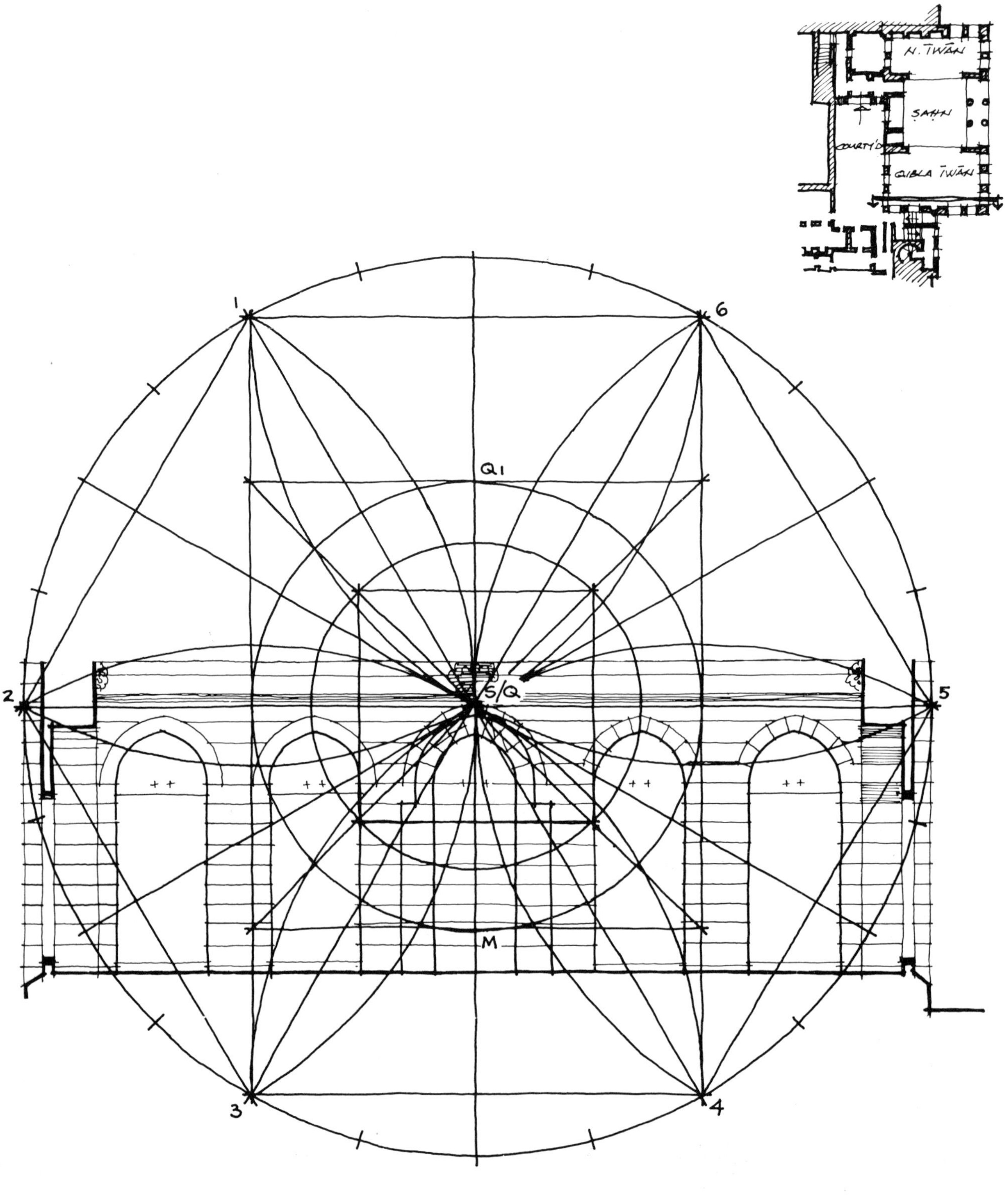

Fig. VII/3 The *qibla īwān, qibla* wall: the rotated fundamental geometry centred on S with the primary geometry on the *qibla īwān* centred on point Q superimposed.

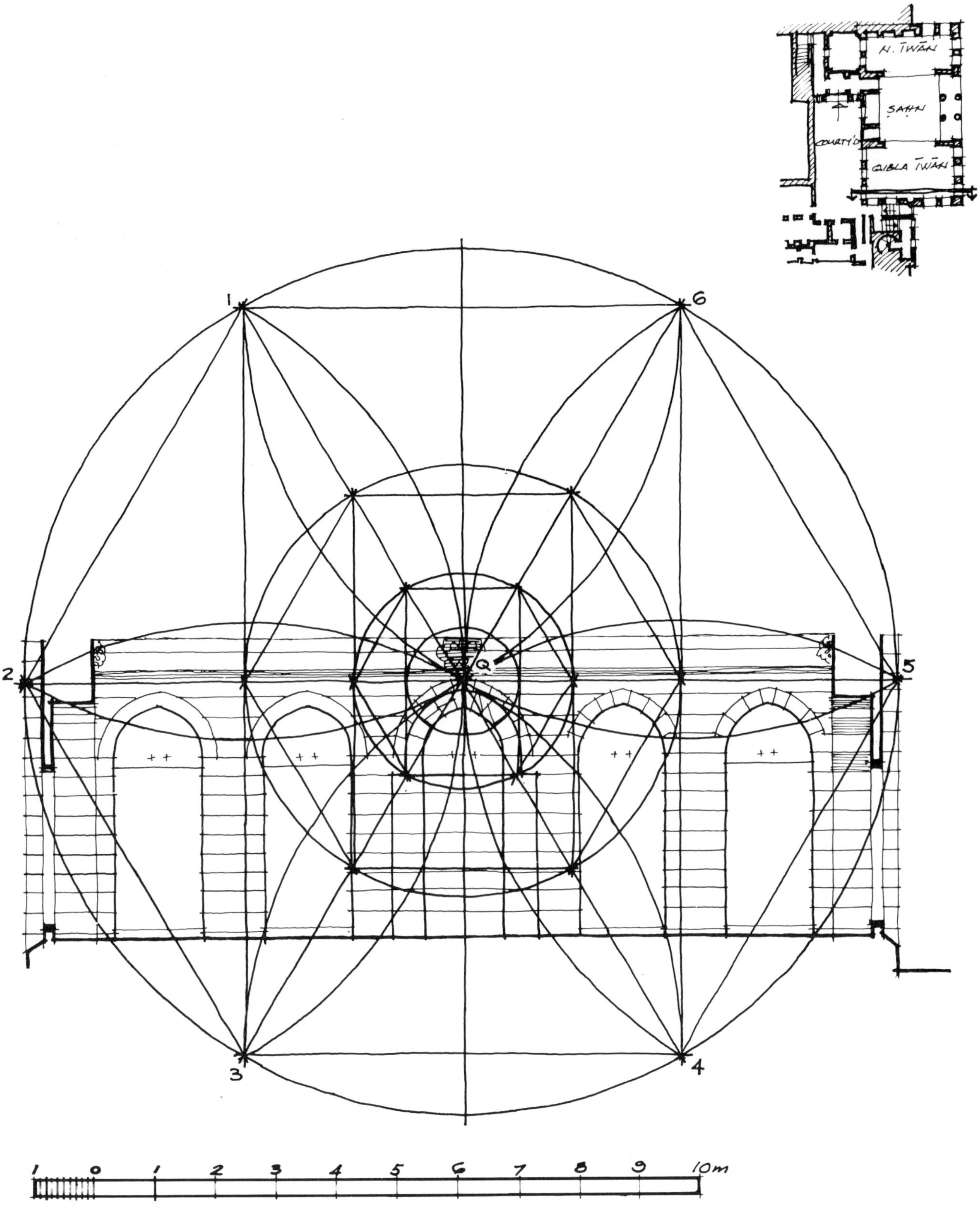

Fig. VIII/4 The *qibla īwān, qibla* wall: the proportional sequence of 2:1

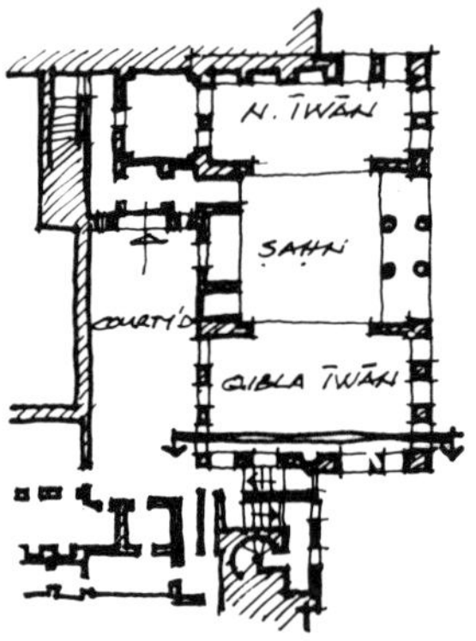

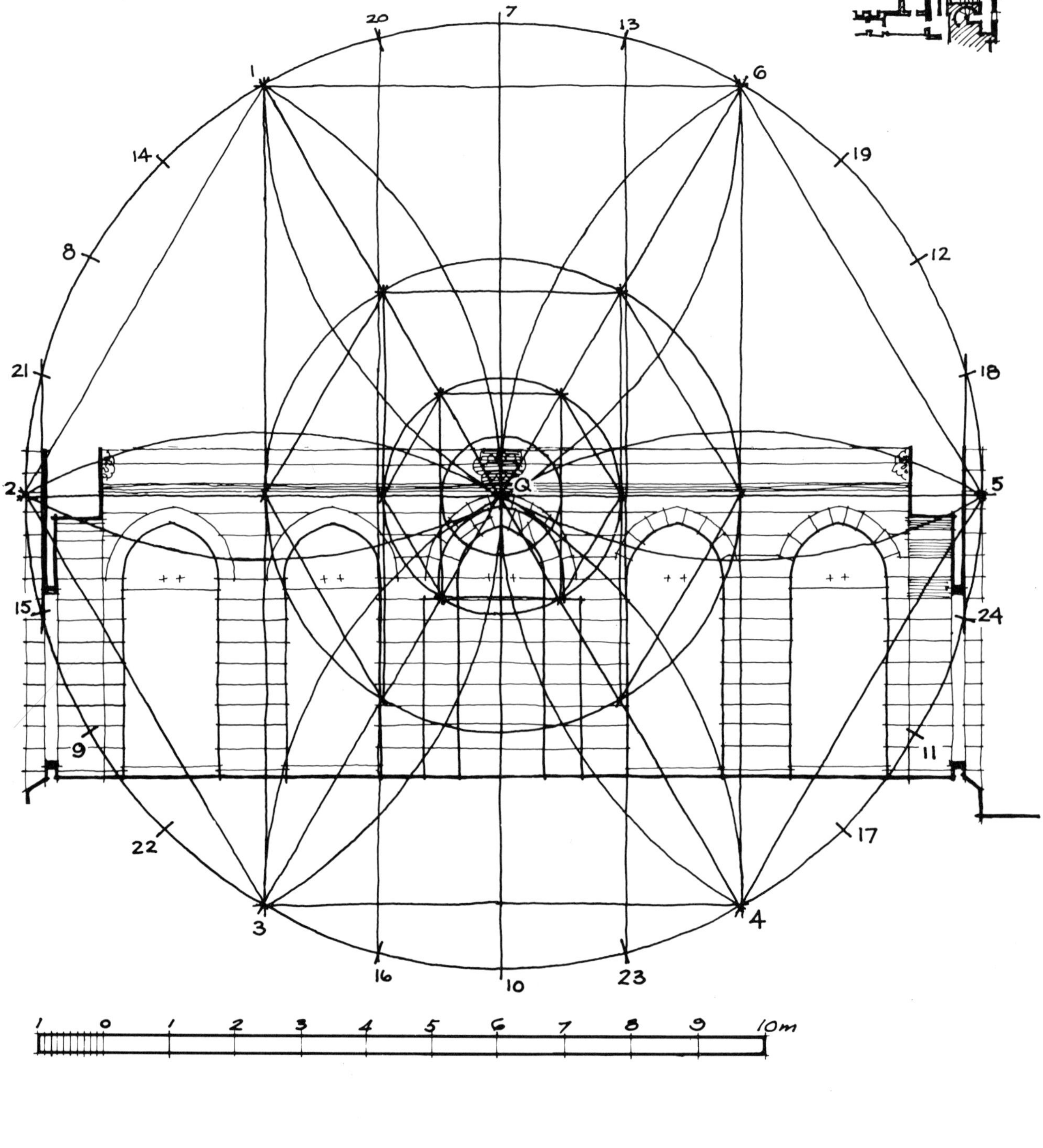

Fig. VII/5 The *qibla īwān*, *qibla* wall: the 24-pointed star (simplified) and the *miḥrāb* panel

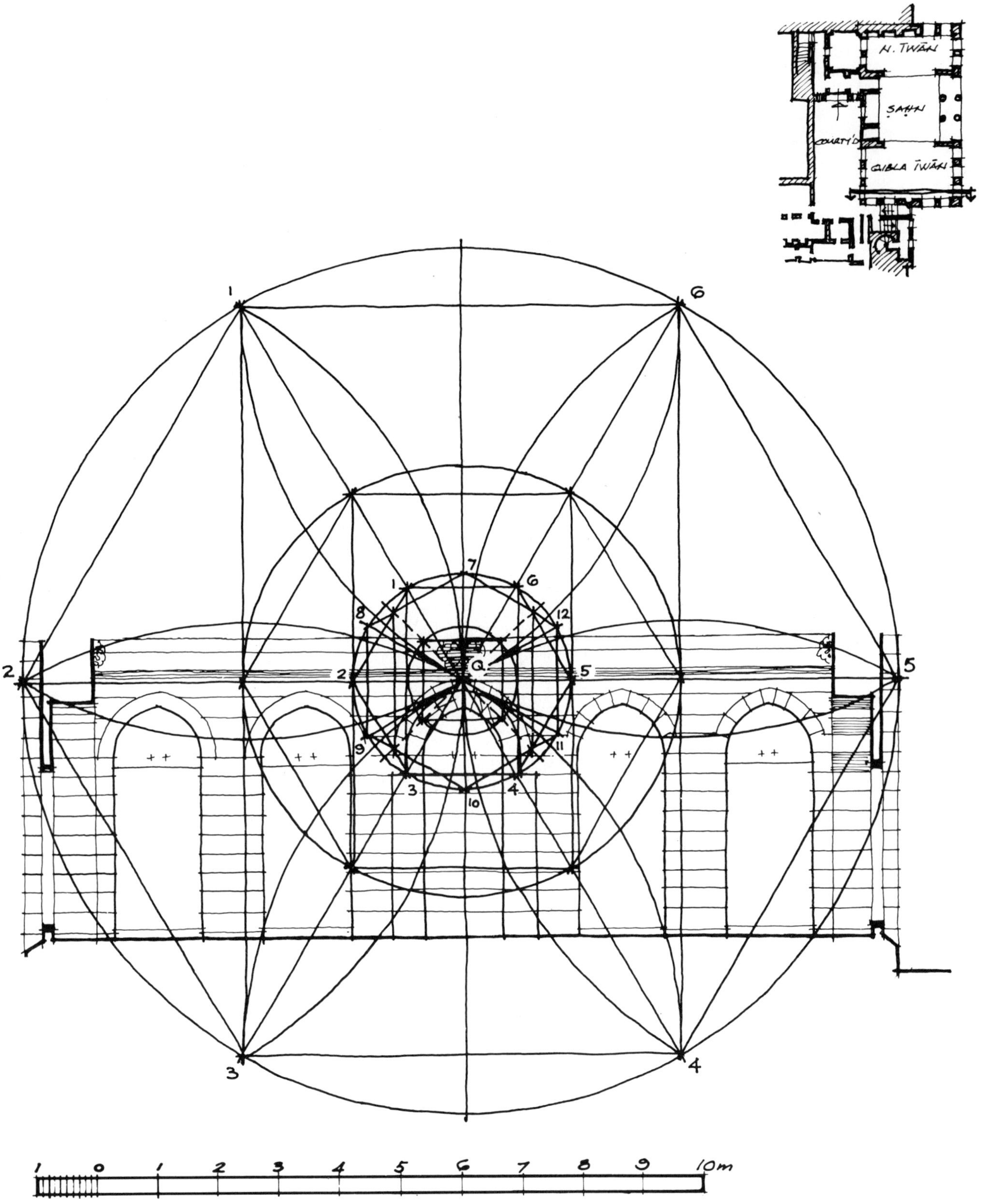

Fig. VII/6 The *qibla īwān, qibla* wall: a double hexagon in the third circle and a square in the fourth

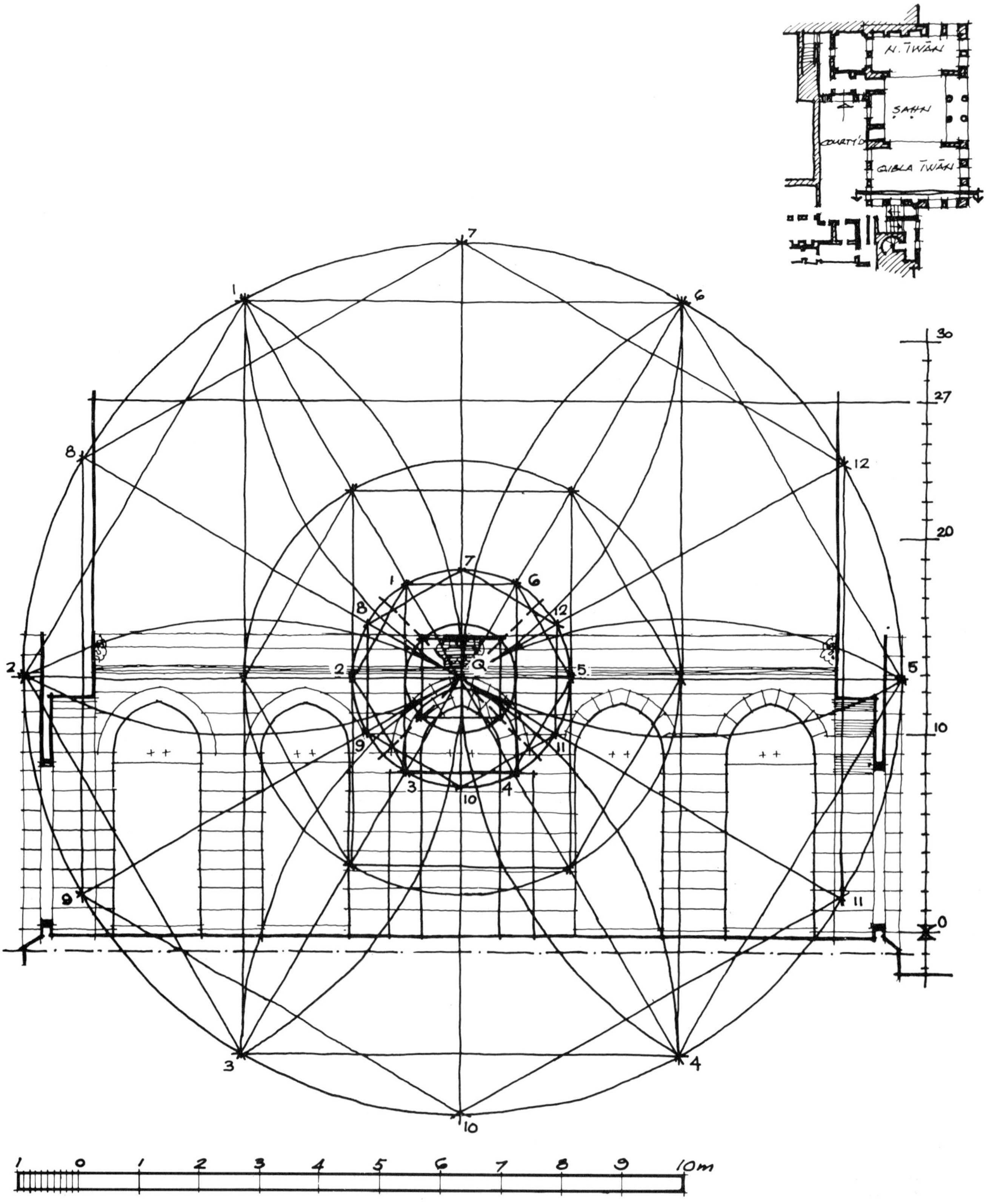

Fig. VII/7 The *qibla īwān*, *qibla* wall: the primary geometry and a scale indicating the stone courses

geometry must be found which can generate more detailed units, and this can be achieved by adding a second inscribed hexagon within the third circle to form a double hexagon (points 1-12). **fig. VII/6**

Immediately this new construction defines the sides of the *miḥrāb* recess where line 5-4 intersects line 11-10 on one side, and where line 10-9 intersects line 3-2 on the other, these points of intersection lie on the 45° axes of the figure. If the points where the 45° axes cut the circumference of the smallest circle are joined, a square is produced. The length of its sides is equal to the width of the niche and the upper side of the square coincides with the top of the grand inscription.

Before further reconstruction of the *qibla īwān* can take place, it is necessary to recall one or two of the rules that apparently governed the designs of the Ashrafiyya's contemporaries. In most cruciform planned mosques and madrasas the *ṣaḥn* is taller than the four surrounding *īwāns*, which are of equal height. A circular window, often set in a square compartment, is usually to be found in the *qibla* wall above the *miḥrāb*, and a deep timber cornice would run above it. The ceiling was generally of timber and, as recorded by al-'Ulaymī, the ceilings of the Ashrafiyya were decorated with gold leaf and blue paint.

Of these features the first to be established here is the height of the *qibla īwān*. By looking at the comparative course tables, it can be seen that the difference in the numbers of stone courses between the *ṣaḥn* and the *qibla īwān* in the Mosque and Mausoleum is 7, and that in Qal'at al-Kabsh it is 6½ courses. A proportionally similar difference should therefore be expected between the 34 stone courses of the *ṣaḥn* of the Ashrafiyya and the *īwāns*. **fig. V/1 and V/3**

In the *qibla īwān*, 17 complete stone courses exist on the exterior of the side wall and in the jambs of its window recess. These can be used to produce a scale against which to measure the 27-odd courses we expect will be required for the reconstruction. **fig. VII/7**

To control the missing upper areas of the *qibla* wall, new geometries are needed. So far the rotated geometries have, with the exception of that relating to the *miḥrāb* panel, ignored the use of a double hexagon. However, it was the doubling-up of the hexagons in the plan of the *ṣaḥn* that transformed the fundamental geometry into the primary geometry thereby increasing the number of geometries which could be generated and used to define features of the *ṣaḥn*. It would therefore seem logical to introduce here the primary geometry with its double hexagon (1-12), in order to increase the number of geometries available to the upper areas of the *qibla* wall.

Having done so, straight away it becomes clear that the lines which were significant in the plan of the *ṣaḥn* are significant here also. The line joining the intersection of lines 5-4 and 11-10, and 10-9 and 3-2, coincides with the level of the stone course immediately below the chamfered sill seen on the exterior of the side wall. The line joining a similar pair of intersections (lines 2-1 and 8-7, and 7-12 and 6-5) is also of importance, since it is on a level with the twenty-seventh division on the scale of stone courses, this being the anticipated height of the *qibla* wall.

Further questions, such as the design of the clerestories, must rely on evidence provided by the side wall of the *īwān*, and apart from a few minor details the results will be applicable to the west and north *īwāns*, but not to the east *īwān* or the loggia, as it had a unique design.

The position of an *īwān* in Mamlūk buildings may often be identified without actually entering the building, for they have certain common characteristics in their fenestration. Externally, the window openings, whether standing alone or in groups, were set back from the wall plane in recesses. These recesses reflect the size of the hidden *īwān* in their dimensions, and they can also provide the details necessary to identify a *qibla īwān*. Usually large rectangular windows with metal grilles were placed just above floor level, and spanned by lintels surmounted by relieving arches. A variable number of stone courses separated these from the clerestory windows, which were either single arched openings, or placed in pairs with a small circular window set above them. **fig. V/4**

Internally the visual impact of such windows is very different. The large rectangular, grilled windows are no longer seen with others in a recess, but appear as individual units framed by deep ingos which rise upwards to form arches. Higher up the wall the arched clerestory windows retain their external shape often with vividly coloured stained glass designs which are never apparent from the exterior. Above these a high timber or stucco cornice is normally present with elaborate pendants at the corners, and finally the *īwān* is covered by a beamed and joisted timber ceiling. **fig. V/5**

These descriptions are more characteristic of the buildings of Mamlūk Cairo than of Mamlūk Jerusalem, but we must bear in mind that the Ashrafiyya was conceived by architects belonging to the

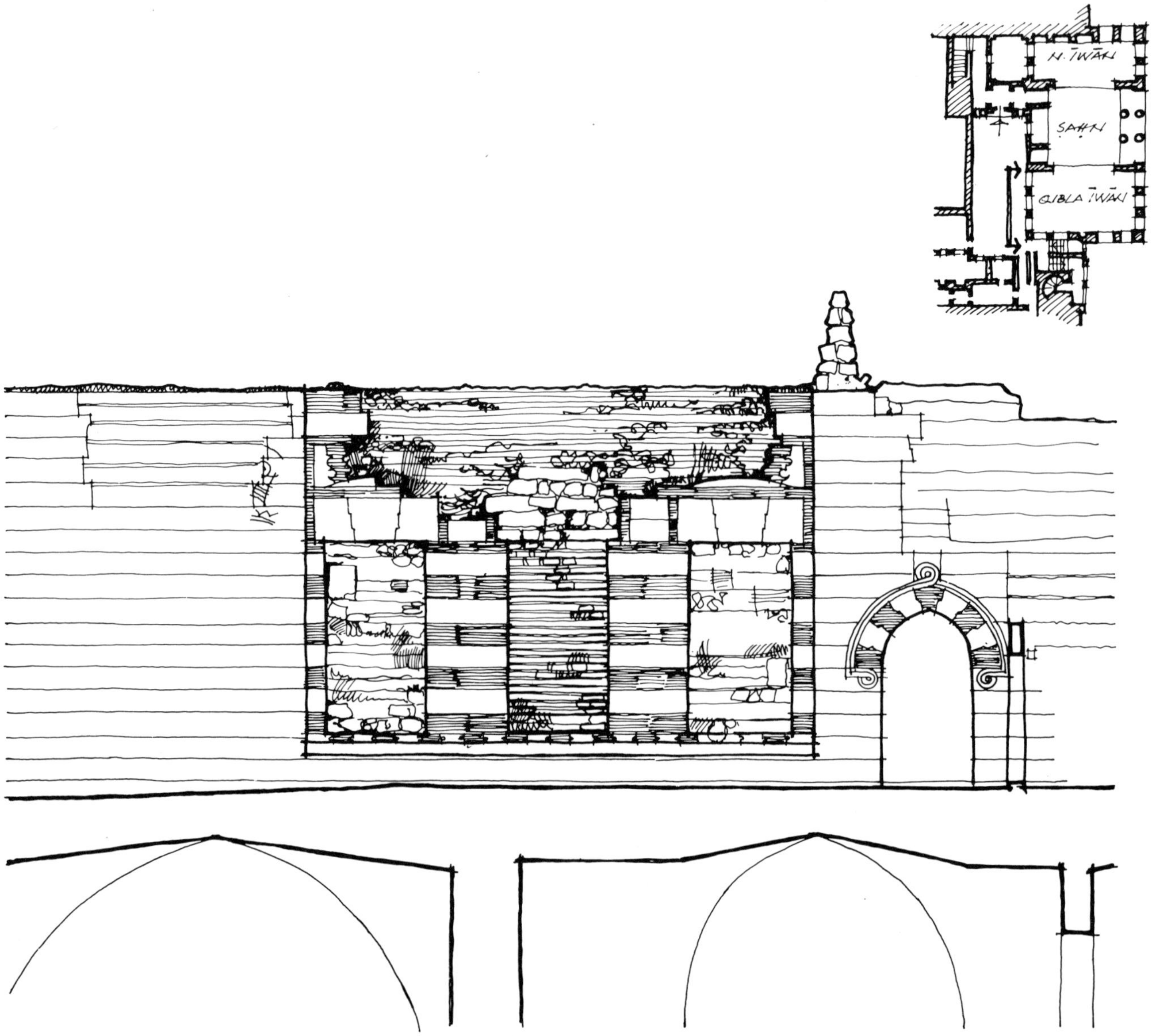

Fig. VII/8 The *qibla īwān*, the exterior of the side wall: the existing features

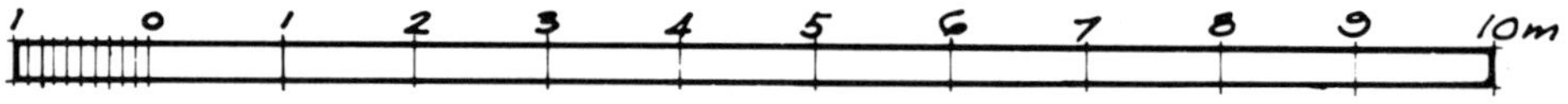

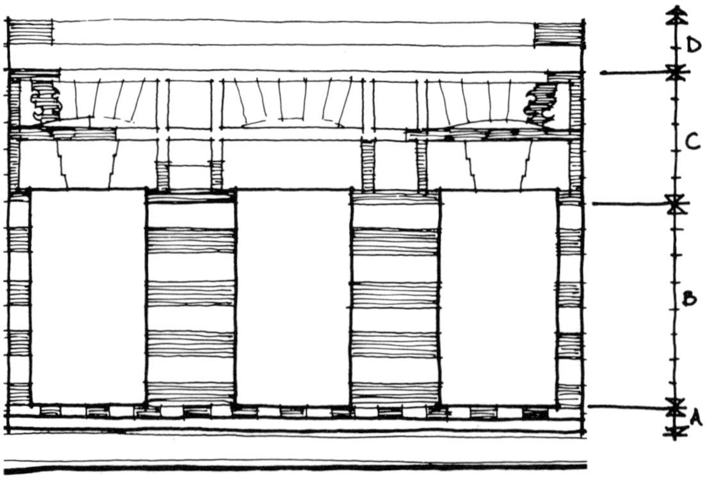

Fig. VII/9 The *qibla īwān*, the exterior of the side wall: additions to the existing features

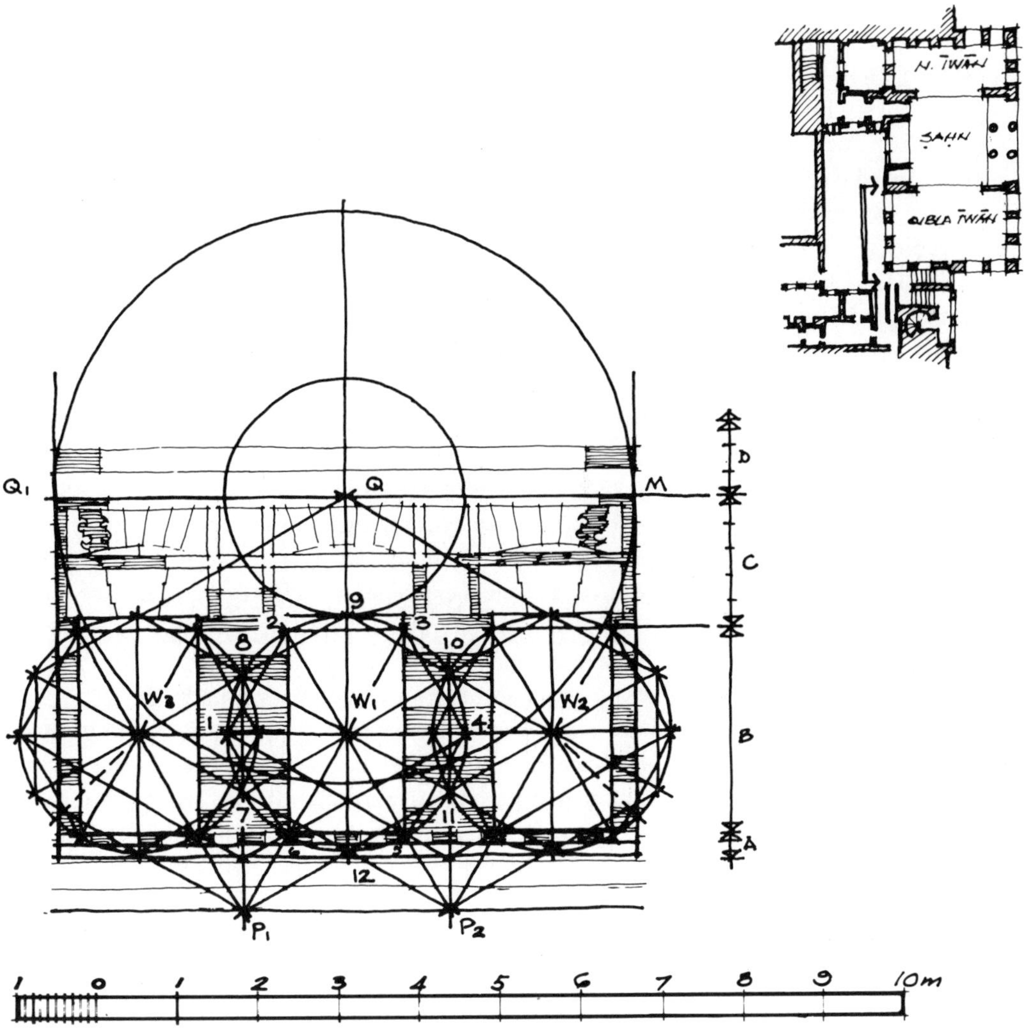

Fig. VII/10 The *qibla īwān*, the exterior of the side wall: the detailed geometries rotated

imperial workshops of Cairo and so the Ashrafiyya can only be seen as a most eminent but distant relative of its Jerusalem contemporaries.

With these general features in mind, we can begin to consider the restoration of the side walls of **fig. VII/8** the *qibla īwān*, where, in spite of the earthquake, some 16 stone courses of the external triple windowed recess still remain. These courses include sub-elements A to C, and two courses of sub- **fig. VII/9** element D. Some details are missing, but there is sufficient evidence to complete the composition of the elements and to form a base for the geometries.

Previously the detailed geometries in plan established the position of the three windows in the **fig. V/10** side wall, and it was these geometries which when rotated to the vertical were discovered to fit the external features of the wall, and so begin the idea of rotation. Now with our deeper understanding when these detailed geometries centred on W_1, W_2 and W_3 are again rotated against the exterior of the side wall, their value can be appreciated more fully. At first the double hexagons, described by 1/10 BUG radius circles set within the window openings, repeat the previous relationships. Line 5-6 coincides with the sill level, lines 6-2 and 3-5 coincide with the jambs, and point 9 with the soffit of the lintel. But with a better awareness of the extent of their influence, additional relationships can be anticipated when the lines of the double hexagons are extended. For example, the 'nose' of the sloping sill is defined by the intersection of the extended lines 4-6 in W_1 and 1-5 in W_3, and the extended lines 4-6 in W_2 and 1-5 in W_1. The level of the pavement across the courtyard varies considerably due in part to the necessity to provide falls for drainage and also partly because the courtyard has aged and weathered. However, as we need to find a general datum from which to work, a good one would be the pavement in front of the portal at the north end of the courtyard. This general level may be located at points P_1 and P_2, the intersections of the extended sides 11-12 of W_1 and 7-11 of W_3, and the extended sides 11-12 of W_2 and 7-11 of W_1.

A third relationship is found when sides 8-9 of W_3 and 10-9 of W_2 are extended. They intersect at a point on the central axis of the recess, which coincides with the level of the course joint running along the top of the compartmentation, containing the lintels and relieving arches, a visually significant level.

It will have been noted that as yet in this investigation of the exterior of the side wall of the *qibla īwān*, the detailed geometries have been considered independently and with no reference to either the rotated fundamental or primary geometries. However, whilst the detailed geometries remain independent they cannot be compared to any of the other vertical geometries, and it is therefore essential that a connection is made if not directly to the fundamental geometry, at least to the primary geometry of the plan of the *qibla īwān* centred on point Q.

Firstly, point Q is known to lie on the central axis of the recess. Secondly, its level is known from the rotated geometry of the *qibla* wall where it nearly coincided with one of the courses in the side wall. It is now apparent that this is the course which runs along the top of the compartmentation containing the lintels and relieving arches. Thus point Q also coincides with the point of intersection of the lines 8-9 of W_3 and 10-9 of W_2, and this makes the sought-after connection between the detailed geometries and the larger fundamental and primary geometries. At the same time it confirms that, at the important visual points, the stone coursing and the geometries work together.

In plan the ¼ BUG radius circle centred on Q had points Q_1 and M on its circumference. When this circle is rotated, points Q_1 and M are found to define the sides of the recess thus giving it a width of ½ BUG. This could have been anticipated for it confirms the ½ BUG relationship discovered earlier through measurement (see IV/3). Yet another geometric relationship can be found by drawing a 1/10

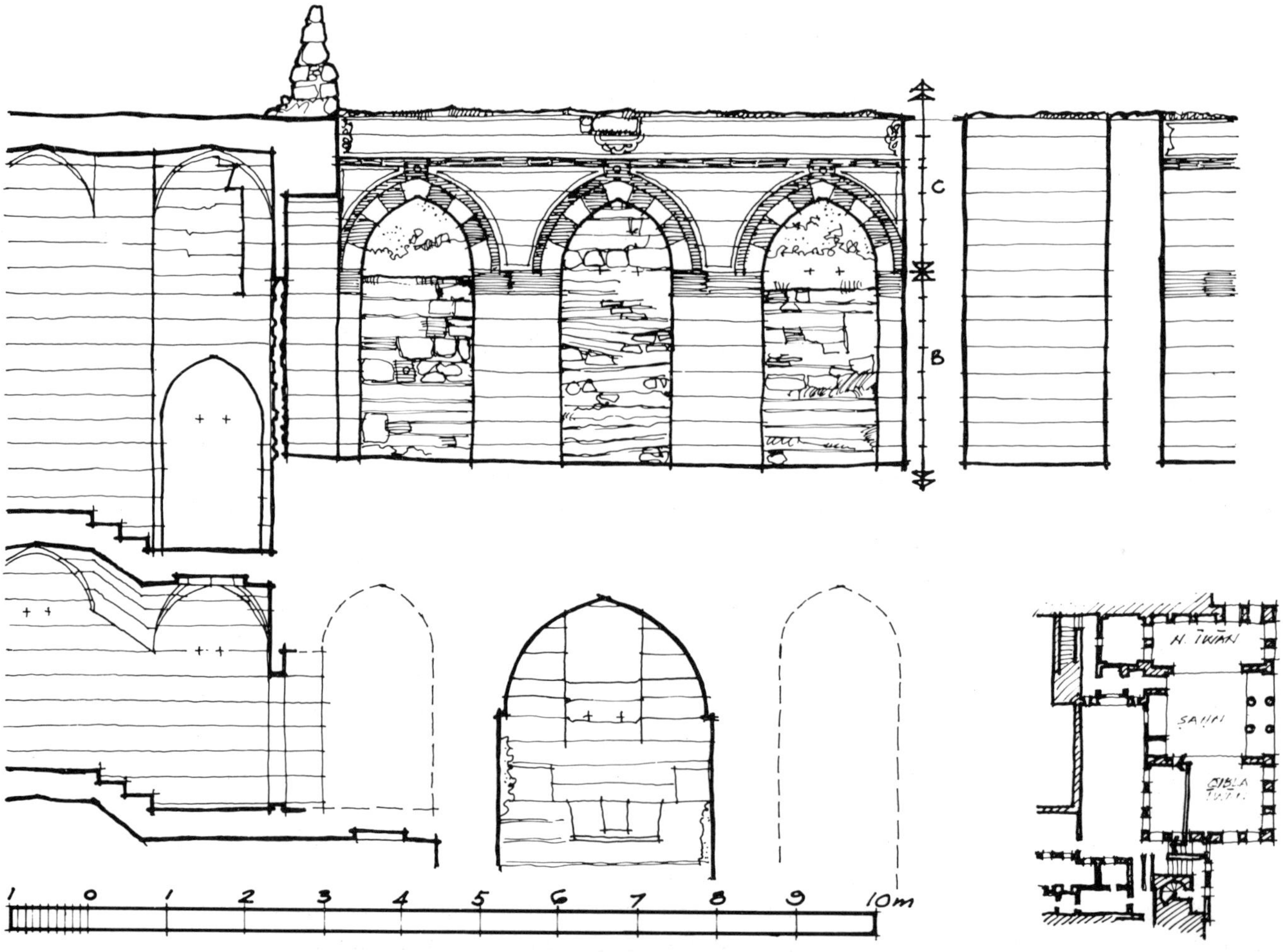

Fig. VII/11 The *qibla īwān*, the interior of the side wall: the existing features

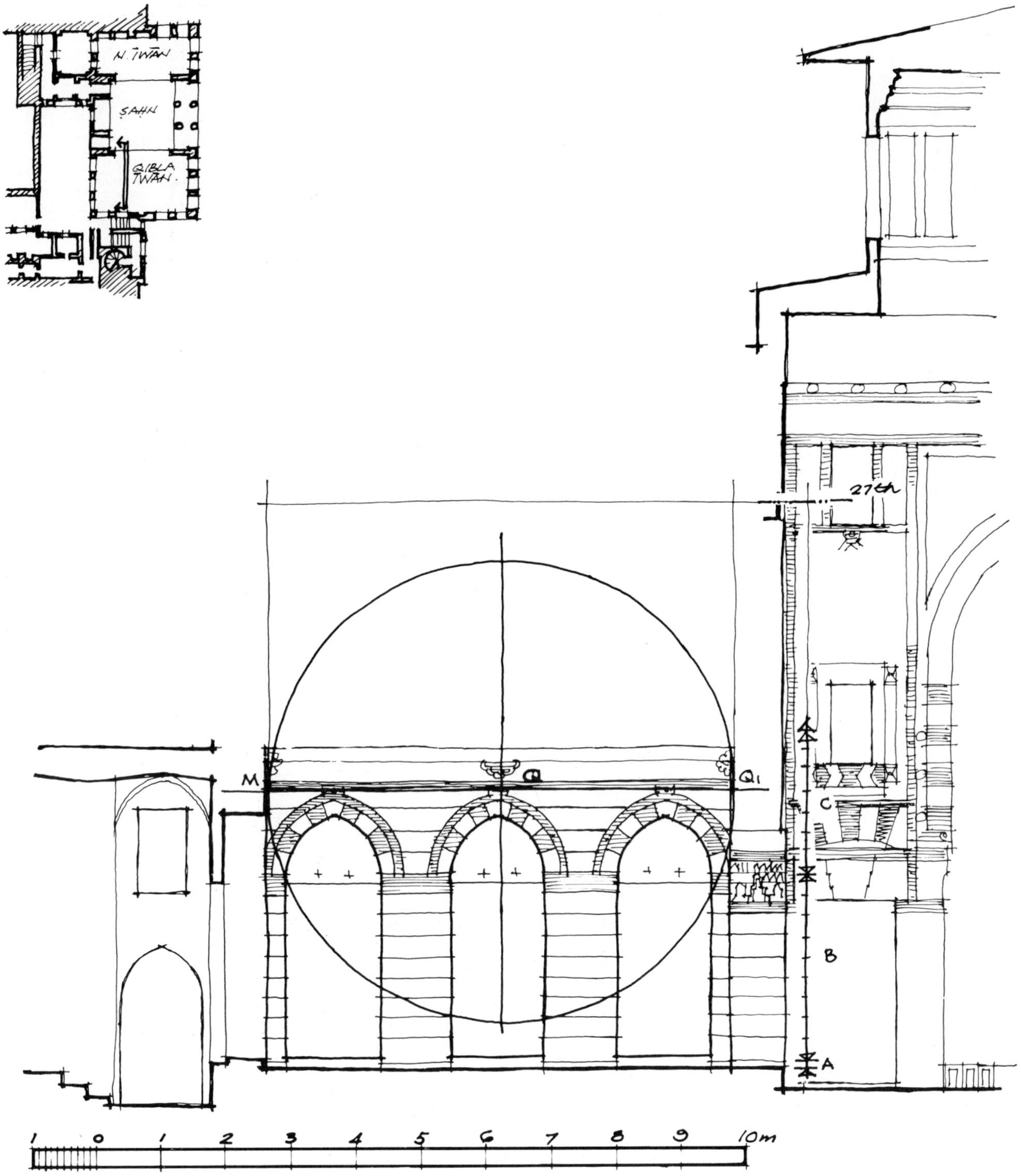

Fig. VII/12 The *qibla īwān*, the interior of the side wall: additions to the existing features and the ½ BUG diameter circle.

BUG radius circle centred on point Q. Its circumference, and that of the 1/10 BUG radius circle centred on W_1, meet at point 9, the point which has already located the level of the soffit of the lintels.

The internal features of the side wall can now be considered using some of these same geometries. **fig. VII/11** After restoring the floor level established previously, the wall is 14½ courses high, exactly the same height as the *qibla* wall, and it contains sub-element A-B and approximately 6 courses of sub-element C. When points Q, Q_1 and M, and the ½ BUG diameter circle are drawn, the level of Q is found to **fig. VII/12** coincide with the silent loops above the arched window recesses, another focal point in the design.

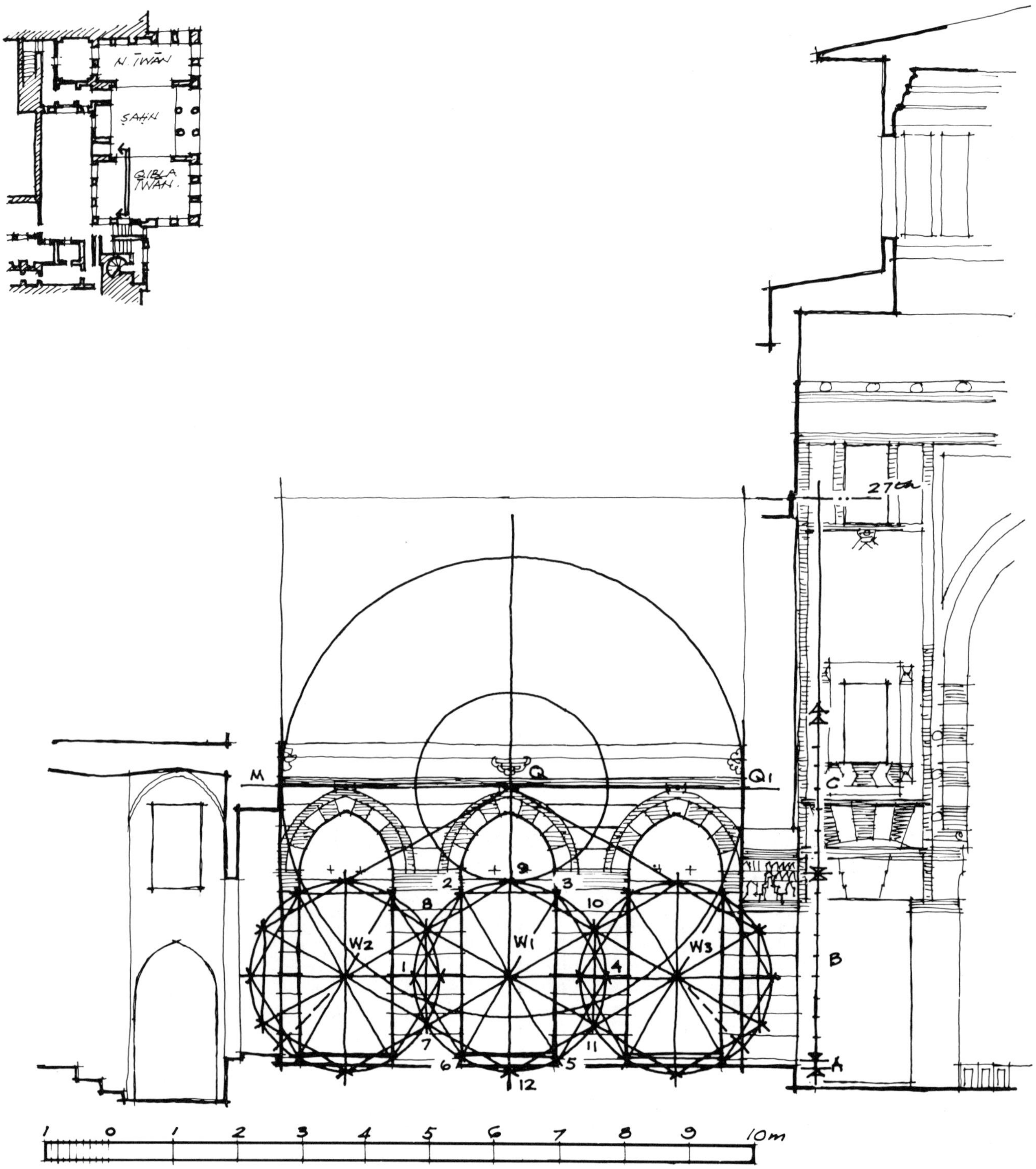

Fig. VII/13 The *qibla īwān*, the interior of the side wall: the detailed geometries rotated

fig. VII/13 The circles centred on points W_1, W_2 and W_3 containing the double hexagons can now be added, and in so doing a new relationship is revealed: the floor level of the *īwān* is at a tangent to the circles.

Having now applied the same geometries to both the existing exterior and interior faces of the side wall of the *qibla īwān*, it is necessary to move on to the restoration of the upper areas and the search for the lost clerestory windows, bearing in mind the estimated inner height of approximately 27 courses.

The grand inscription runs along the top of the existing masonry, and on purely aesthetic grounds the clerestory windows cannot be placed directly thereon without additional masonry separating them. Certainly, as a mimimum, there would be a thin red compartmentation course over the

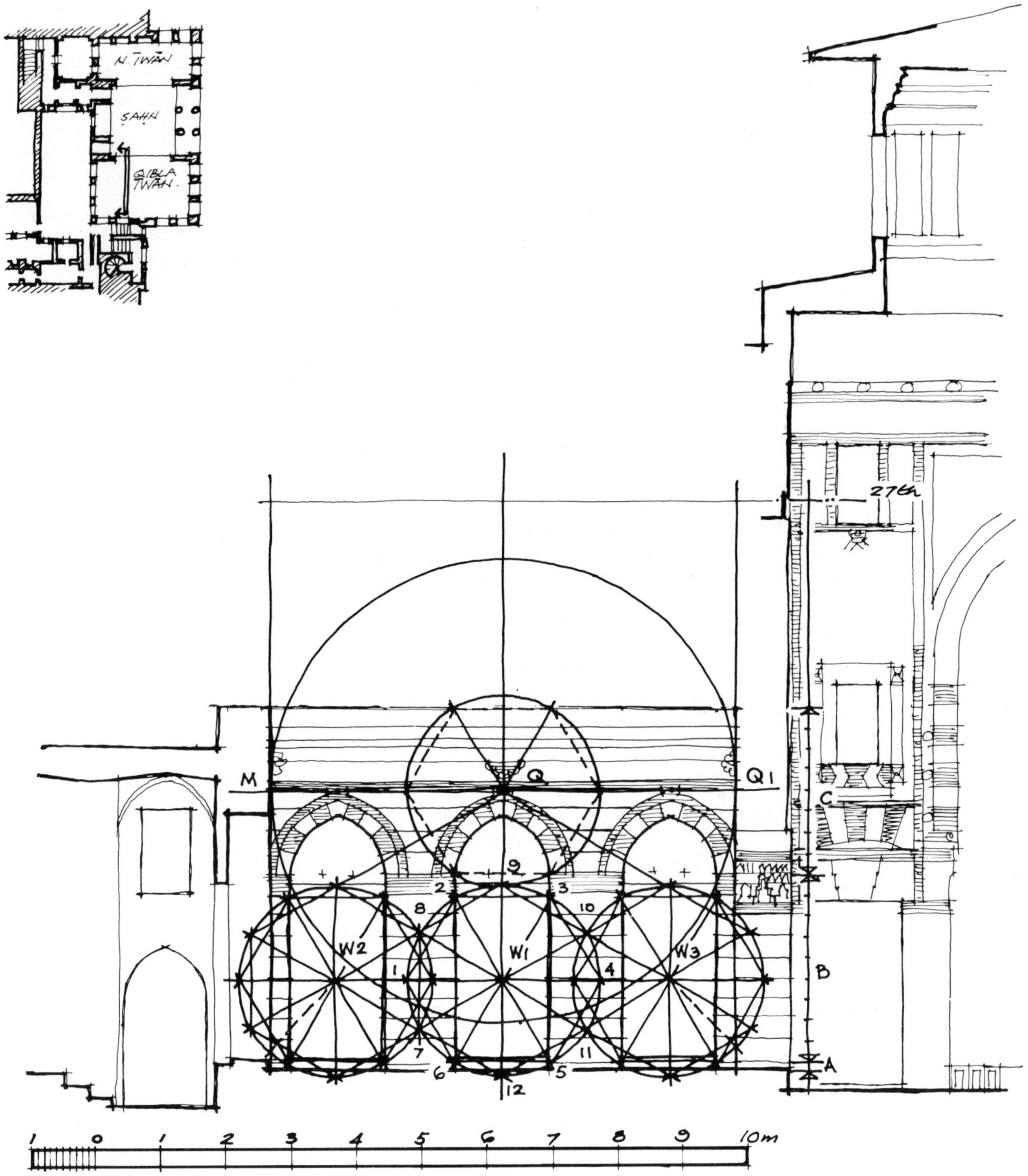

Fig. VII/14 The *qibla īwān*, the interior of the side wall: the height to the top of sub-element C

inscription followed by one full stone course. However, we can be equally certain that to the Mamlūk architect this would insufficient separation; at least one additional course would be required for the division between the two features to be visually acceptable.

To check the viability of this proposal, a layer of compartmentation, plus the masonry required to make it up to one full course, can be added to the top of the inscription, and an additional stone course can be added to this. In visual terms it is acceptable and geometrically it can be confirmed by the hexagon (shown dotted) inscribed within the 1/10 BUG radius circle centred on Q. Its uppermost side coincides with the upper edge of the additional course, which is the level proposed for the sills of the clerestories. **fig. VII/14**

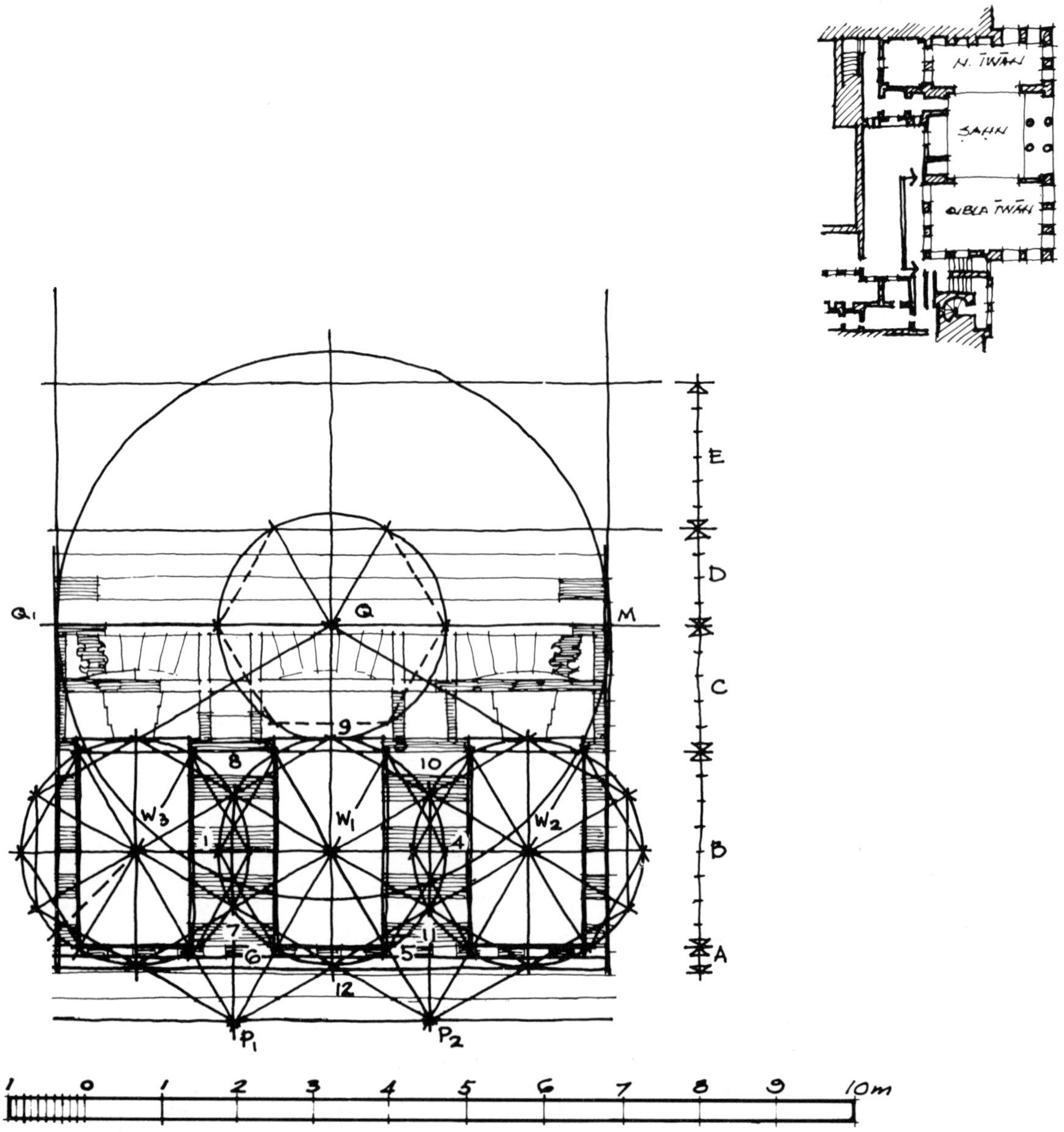

Fig. VII/15 The *qibla īwān*, the exterior of the side wall: the height to the top of sub-element E

fig. VII/15 However, before these ideas are implemented and fitted into the reconstruction, they must be reconfirmed by the aesthetic needs of the external recess. This is done by drawing a hexagon (again drawn dotted) with sides of 1/10 BUG centred on Q and described by the circle with point 9 on its circumference. As well as confirming the exterior sill level, the hexagon acts as a yardstick, since half its height is equal to four stone courses, as can be seen from the drawing of the hexagon 1-6 centred on W_1. Thus, this similar hexagon centred on Q establishes a height of four stone courses for sub-element D, the height from the compartmentation below the lintel blocks to the sills. This also makes it equal in height to sub-element D in the Mosque and Mausoleum. Since the arrangement of the *ablaq* stone courses must continue their existing rhythm, the external sills of the clerestories will consist of red stones.

Earlier the number of stone courses given to each of the sub-elements in the walls and arches of the *ṣaḥn* were found to be closer to those in the Mosque and Mausoleum than those in the Mosques at Qalʿat al-Kabsh and Rawḍa. Nevertheless, despite this similarity being repeated in the elements of the side wall of the *qibla īwān*, it would appear from the drawing published in 1489 by Bernhard of Breydenbach that the clerestories of the Ashrafiyya were single arched openings and not the paired arches with the small circular window of the Mosque and Mausoleum.

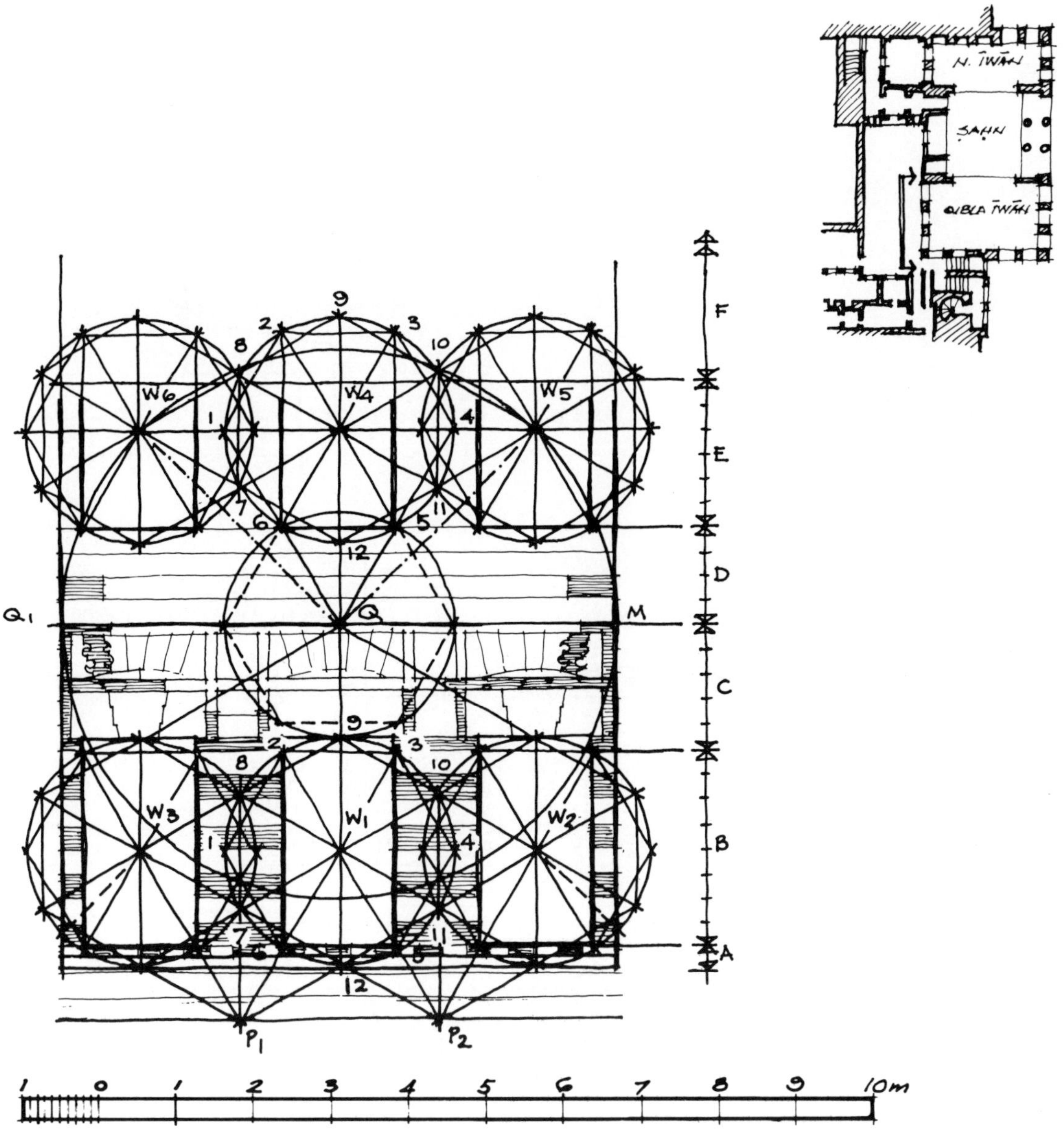

Fig. VII/16 The *qibla īwān*, the exterior of the side wall: the height of sub-element E confirmed

In the external recess in the Mosque and Mausoleum sub-element E, the height from the sill to the springing of the clerestories, is equal to six courses. In the side wall of the *qibla īwān* in the Ashrafiyya a similar number of courses for this element is indicated by the geometries if a circle is drawn with centre W_4, describing a double hexagon (1-12), with the lower side (5-6) common to the upper side of the (dotted) hexagon centred on Q. We know from the similar double hexagon centred on W, that the distance between lines 5-6 and 8-10 must be equal to six stone courses. Therefore, when the top of sub-element E is aligned with line 8-10 its height will be six courses. **fig. VII/16**

Two more clerestories are required to balance the lower rectangular windows, and their centres W_5 and W_6 can be found by repeating the double hexagon constructions which connected W_2 and W_3 to W_1. With the completion of these figures, it is discovered that centres W_5 and W_6 lie on the 45° lines radiating from point Q. These same constructions may be repeated on the interior of the wall where the equivalent sub-element is D. **fig. VII/17**

From the evidence published in 1489 showing single arched clerestories, could they too have been identical in size to the still existing internal arched heads of the lower windows? If this were the case, then internally sub-element E, the height from the springing level to the apex of the clerestory, must be 2½ stone courses. Similarly, the voussoirs of the clerestories should equal the size of the existing **fig. VII/18**

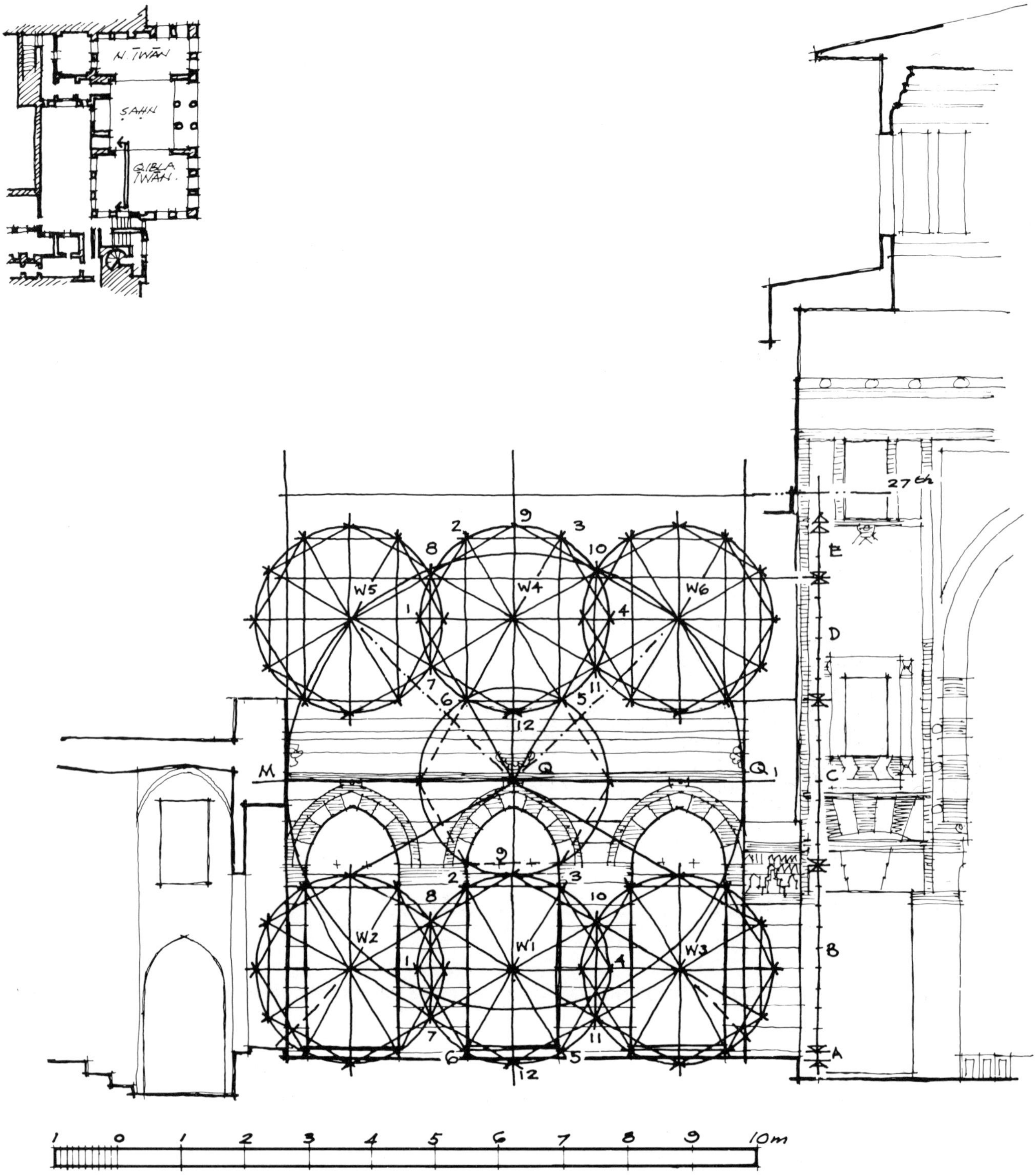

Fig. VII/17 The *qibla īwān*, the interior of the side wall: the height to the top of sub-element D

voussoirs in the lower arches, which can be defined in the geometry centred on W_1 by the intersections of lines 1-2 and 8-9, and 9-10 and 3-4. The clerestory voussoirs are defined by similar intersections in the geometries W_4, W_5 and W_6, and the zeniths of the arched clerestories centred on W_5 and W_6 lie on the lines radiating at 60° from Q. These lines also form the sides 4-5 and 6-1 of the hexagon centred on W_4.

fig. VII/19 The internal sub-element F is measured from the apex of the arched openings to the top of the compartmentation running below the deep timber cornices. This sub-element could be stopped at the level of the twenty-seventh course were it not that the compartmentation requires to sit upon a full

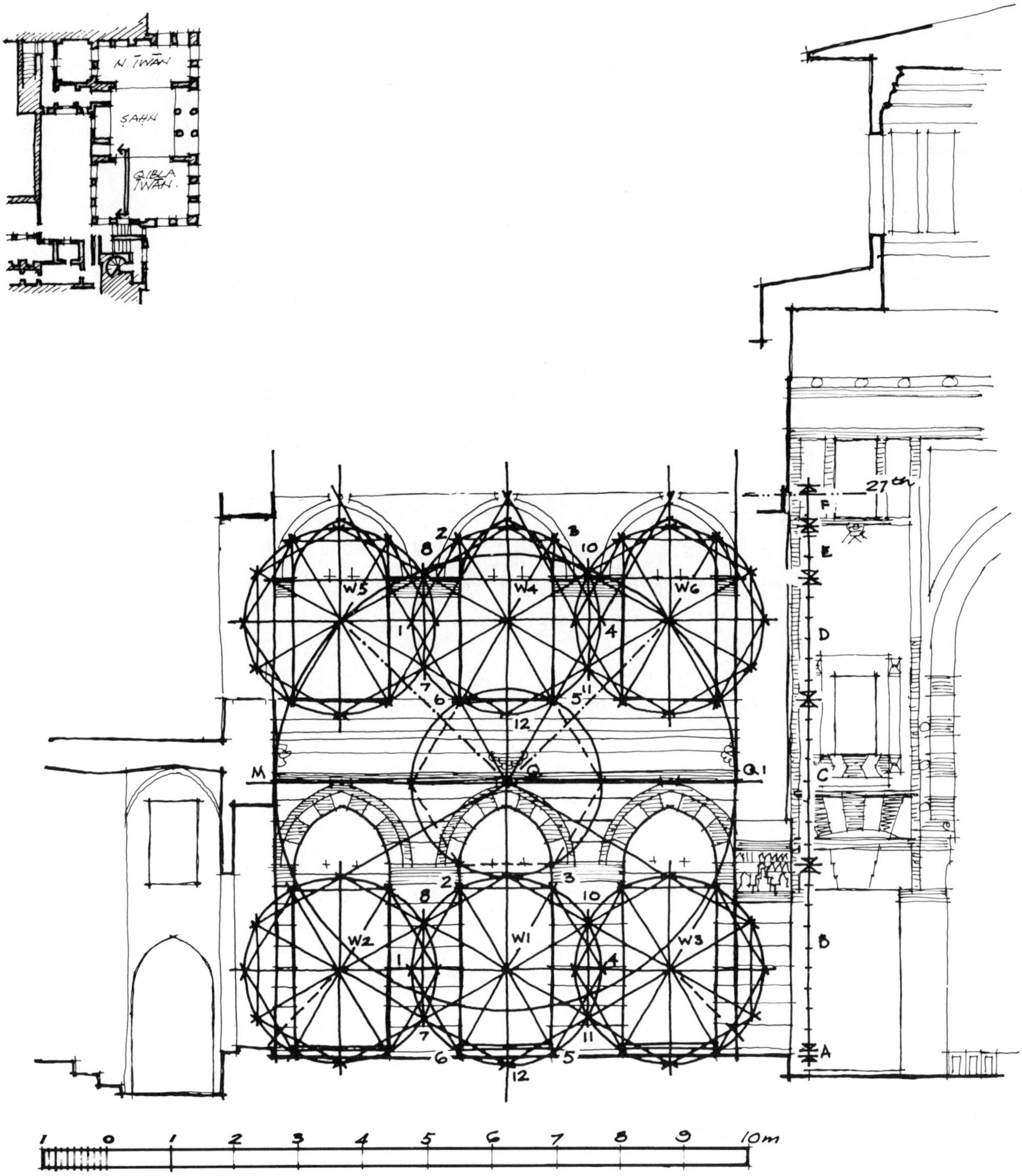

Fig. VII/18 The *qibla īwān*, the interior of the side wall: the height to the top of sub-element E

stone course for aesthetic reasons. Geometrically this is verified by constructing on sides 2-3 of the hexagons W_4, W_5 and W_6, three hexagons, C_1, C_2 and C_3. The lower points of intersection of the sides of the hexagons occur at a distance of about half a course above the twenty-seventh division and define the top of sub-element F. These same intersections can just as easily be traced back to W_5, W_4 and W_6. It is also interesting to note that at its lowest point the circumference of the circle C_1 is tangential to the ½ BUG diameter circle centred on point Q, This relationship reinforces the hope that the present geometries may not be too far from those devised by the architect, despite the odd deviations.[1]

This concludes the study of the sub-elements making up the internal side wall of the *qibla īwān*.

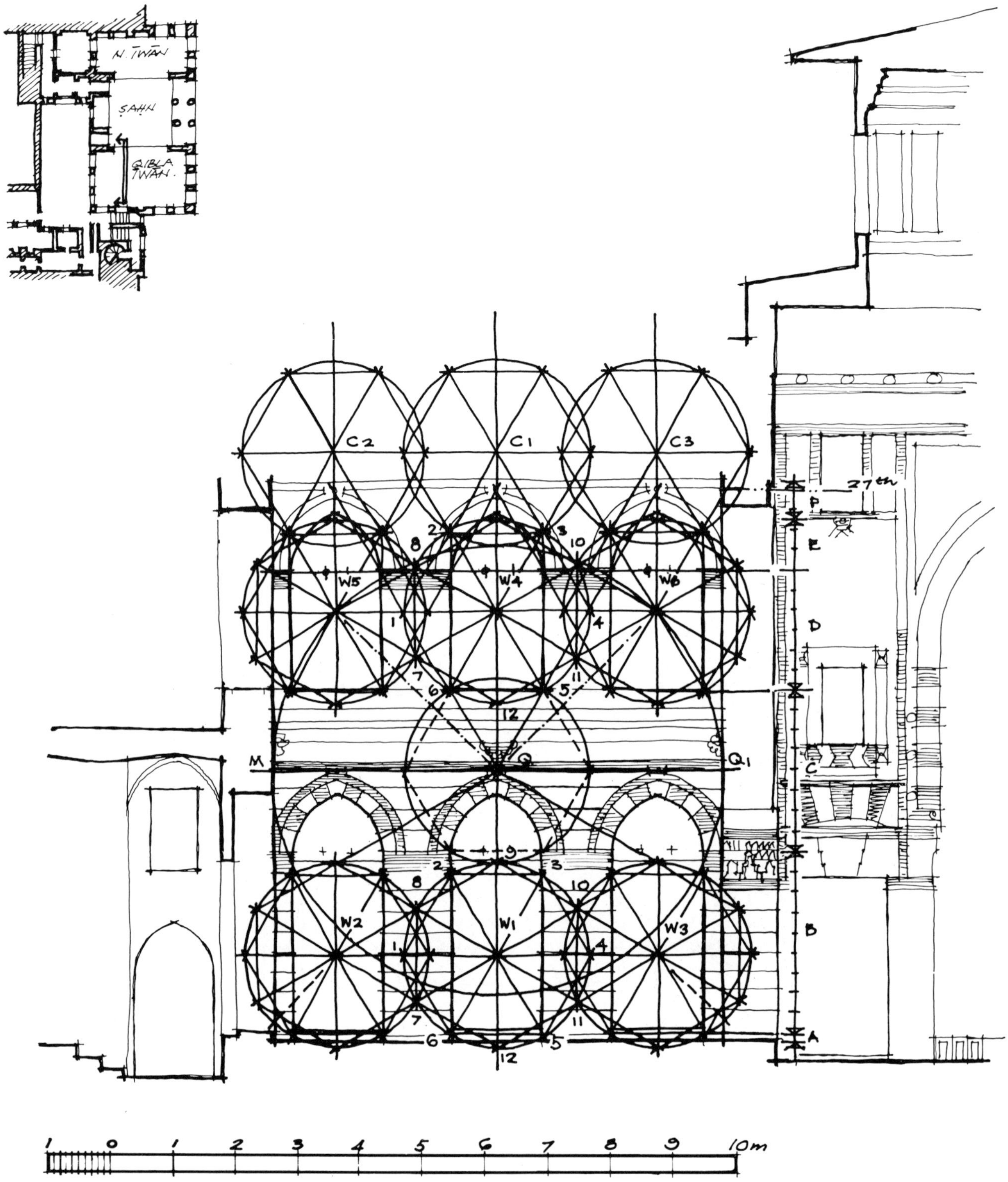

Fig. VII/19 The *qibla īwān*, the interior of the side wall: the height to the underside of the cornice

	A	B	C	D	E	F	total
Mosque and Mausoleum							29*
Qal'at al-Kabsh	1½	9	10	5	1	5	31½
Rawḍa	-	-	-	-	-	-	28*
Ashrafiyya	(½)	(9)	(8)	(6)	(2½)	(2)	(28)

*See table, V/5

and confirms the height from floor level to the underside of the cornice as 28 stone courses, a number akin to those observed in the Cairo monuments.

Externally, the arched heads of the clerestories, which repeat their internal form, and the horizontal compartmentation above them are continued to form sub-element F. It is difficult to assess the number of stone courses which would have made up this sub-element, or subsequently sub-elements G, H and J, but as a guide the number of courses given to these same elements in the Mosque and Mausoleum can be added to the drawings and this may help to generate an appropriate geometry. **fig. VII/20** **fig. VII/21**

The 1/10 BUG radius circle is the most likely key to the problem, as the two previous methods used to extend an existing geometrical framework have both been based on this circle. The first method relied on tangential 1/10 BUG radius circles (for example, those centred on W_1 and Q), and the second involved the construction of a 1/10 BUG radius circle and inscribed hexagon, with one side of the hexagon common to one side of an existing hexagon (for example those centred on Q and W_4). The first method suits our present needs and the circles are therefore added with their circumferences tangential to the estimated top of element J, the cornice. The consequence of this is easily seen. The circumferences of these newly added circles meet the circumferences of W_4, W_5 and W_6. This **fig. VII/22**

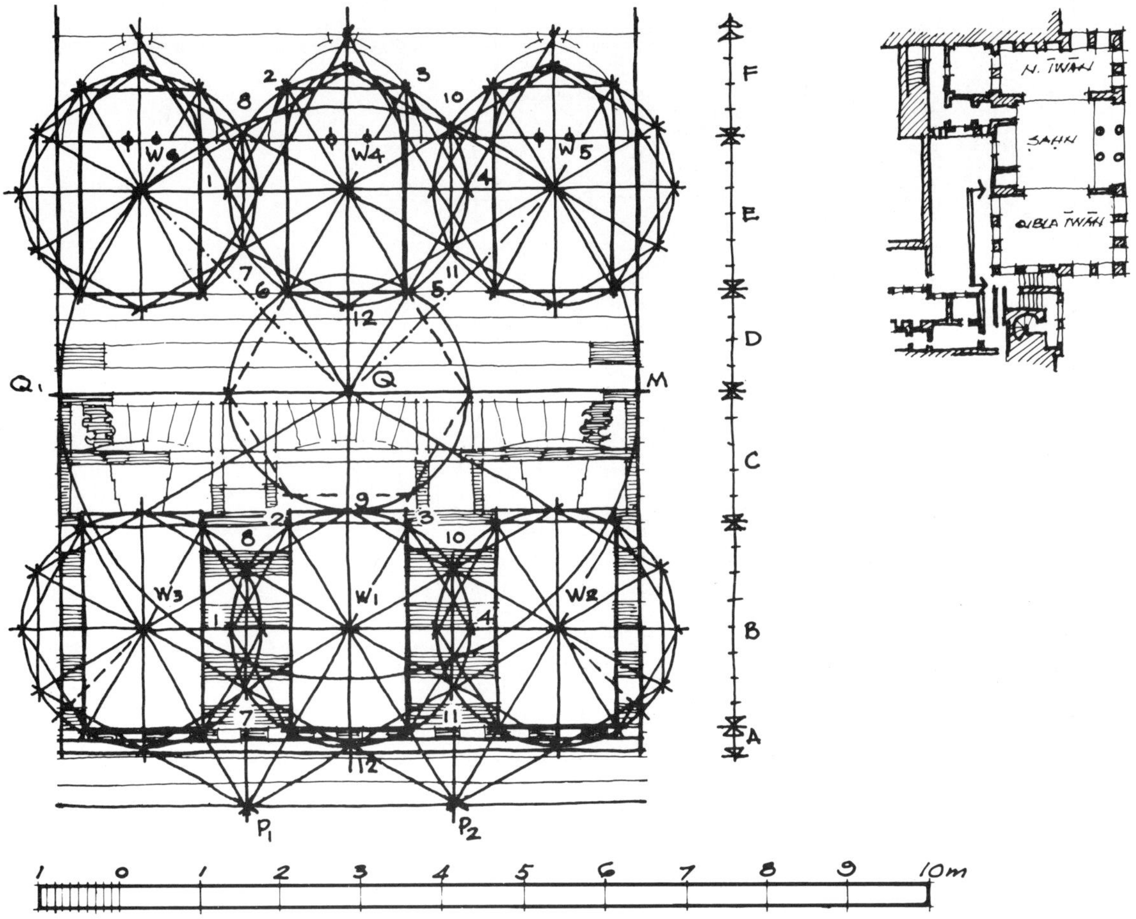

Fig. VII/20 The *qibla īwān*, the exterior of the side wall: the arched heads of the clerestories

relationship gives added weight to the possibility that these elements, E to J, do follow the same pattern of stone courses as their counterparts in the Mosque and Mausoleum. In addition, note that the intersection of the central axis and the top of element J coincides with the upper angle of the equilateral triangle set upon line W_6-W_5. The result of all this is the recessed external windows of the Ashrafiyya have a total height of 35½ stone courses which is one or two courses less than its Cairo relations.

	A	B	C	D	E	F	G	H	J	total
Mosque and Mausoleum	2	8	5	4	6	4½	2	4	1	36½
Qal'at al-Kabsh	2	8	5	6	5	5	2	3½	1	37½
Rawḍa	-	+3	5½	4½	6	4½	2	3½	1	+30
Ashrafiyya	1	8	5	(4)	(6)	(4½)	(2)	(4)	(1)	(35½)

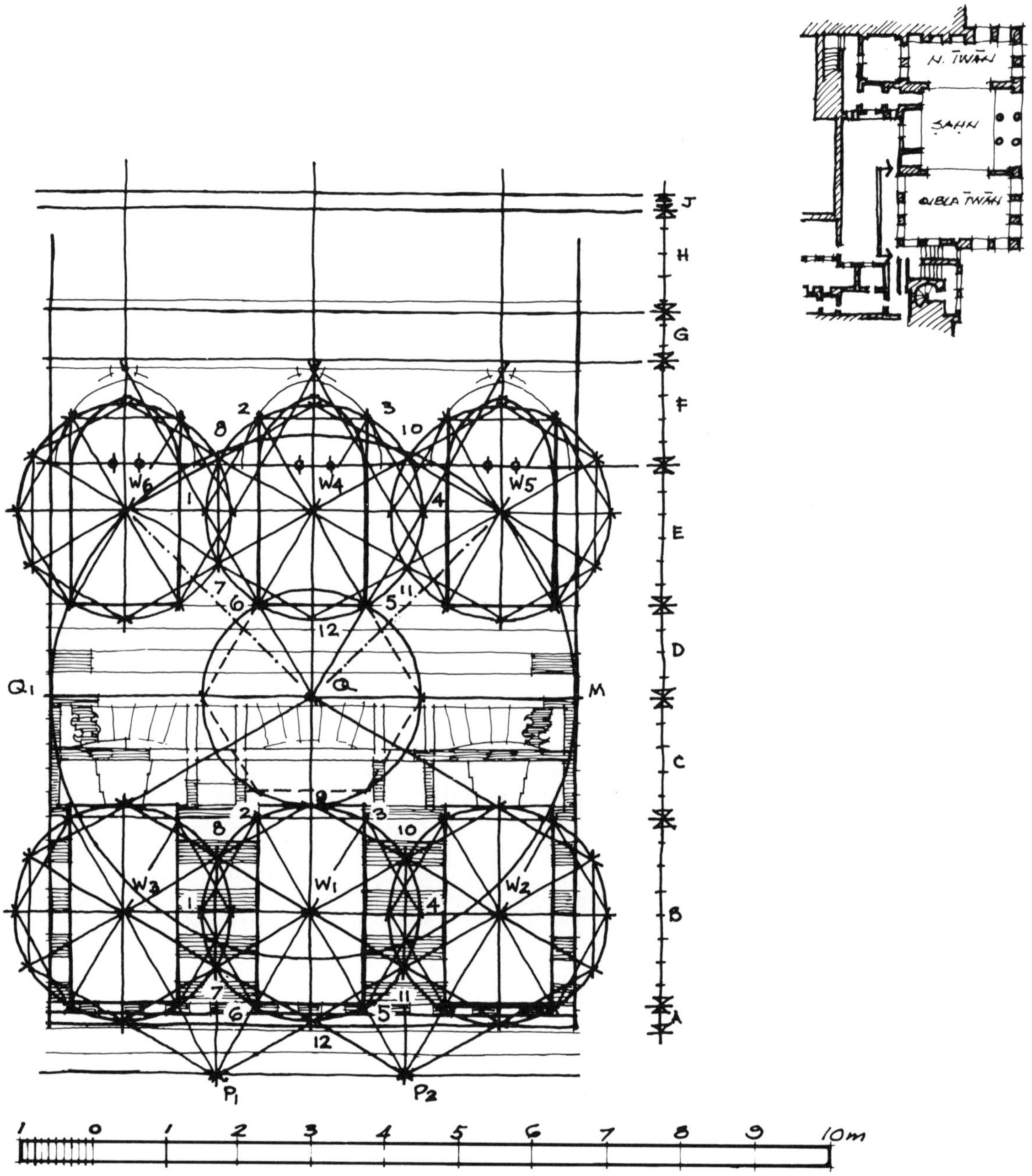

Fig. VII/21 The *qibla īwān*, the exterior of the side wall: the proposed heights for the sub-elements F, G, H, and J following those of the Mosque and Mausoleum.

Having completed both sides of the side wall of the *īwān*, a return can be made to the *qibla* wall. Earlier sub-elements A and B were defined, but sub-element C was left incomplete. The reconstruction followed the symmetries of the existing evidence, and it was proved that most of the features were generated by a 2:1 proportional sequence based on the fundamental geometry. However, no thought was given to the missing details of the wall, other than to propose an approximate height of 27 stone courses.

fig. VII/23 Meanwhile the heights from the grand inscription to the sills of the clerestories and from there

	A	B	C	D	E	F	total
Mosque and Mausoleum	2	8	9	3	3	4½	29½
Qal'at al-Kabsh	1½	9	9	4	2	4	29½
Rawḍa	1½	8	7	6	0	5½	28
Ashrafiyya	(½)	9	(8)	(3)	(3)	(4½)	28

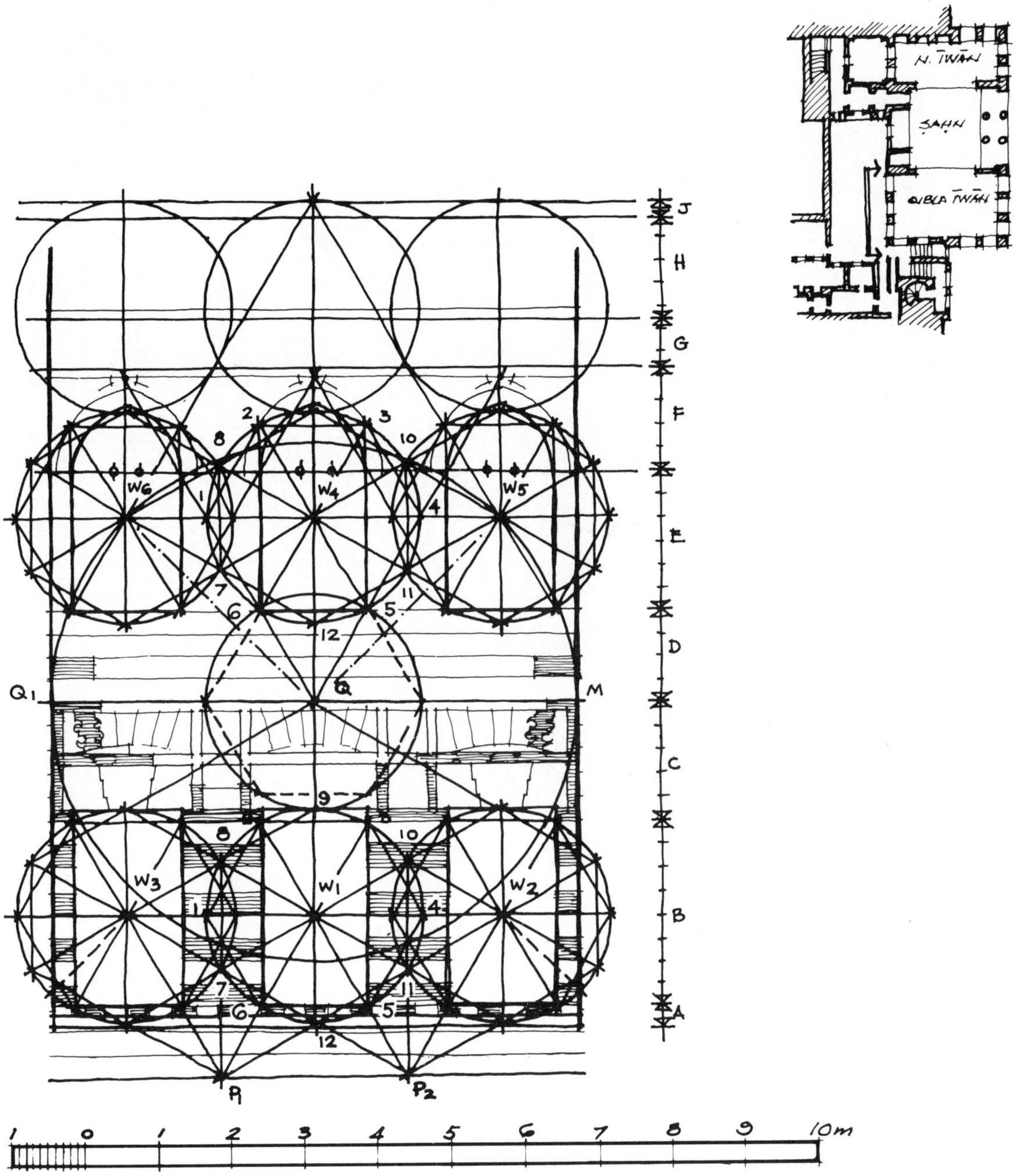

Fig. VII/22 The *qibla īwān*, the exterior of the side wall: the sub-elements completed

to the cornice have been established for the interior of the side wall. This, therefore, enables the clerestory windows of the *qibla* wall to be drawn in, as well as the compartmentation below the cornice. Thus sub-element C can be completed, its top being the sill of the clerestories, as can sub-element F, the height from the springing of the arched clerestories to the cornice. Between these two are the unresolved sub-elements D and E, whose heights are dependent on the size of the circular window, which is a standard feature in the Cairo monuments (plate 14).

The size of this circular window and the square of *ablaq* decoration surrounding it always have a

	A	B	C	D	E	F	G	H	J	total
Mosque and Mausoleum	2	8	5	4	6	4½	2	4	1	36½
Qal'at al-Kabsh	2	8	5	6	5	5	2	3½	1	37½
Rawḍa	-	+3	5½	4½	6	4½	2	3½	1	+30
Ashrafiyya	1	8	5	(4)	(6)	(4½)	(2)	(4)	(1)	(35½)

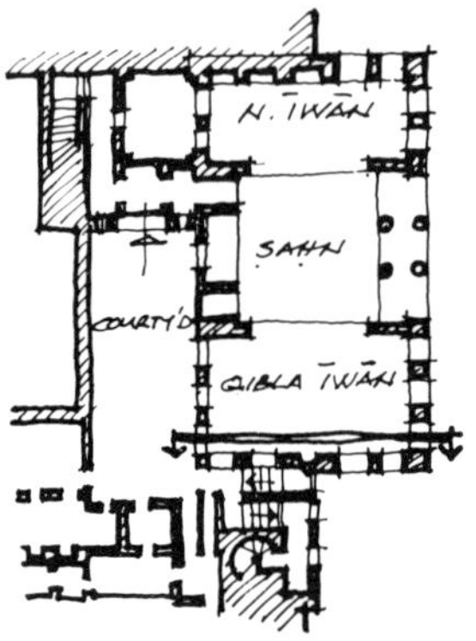

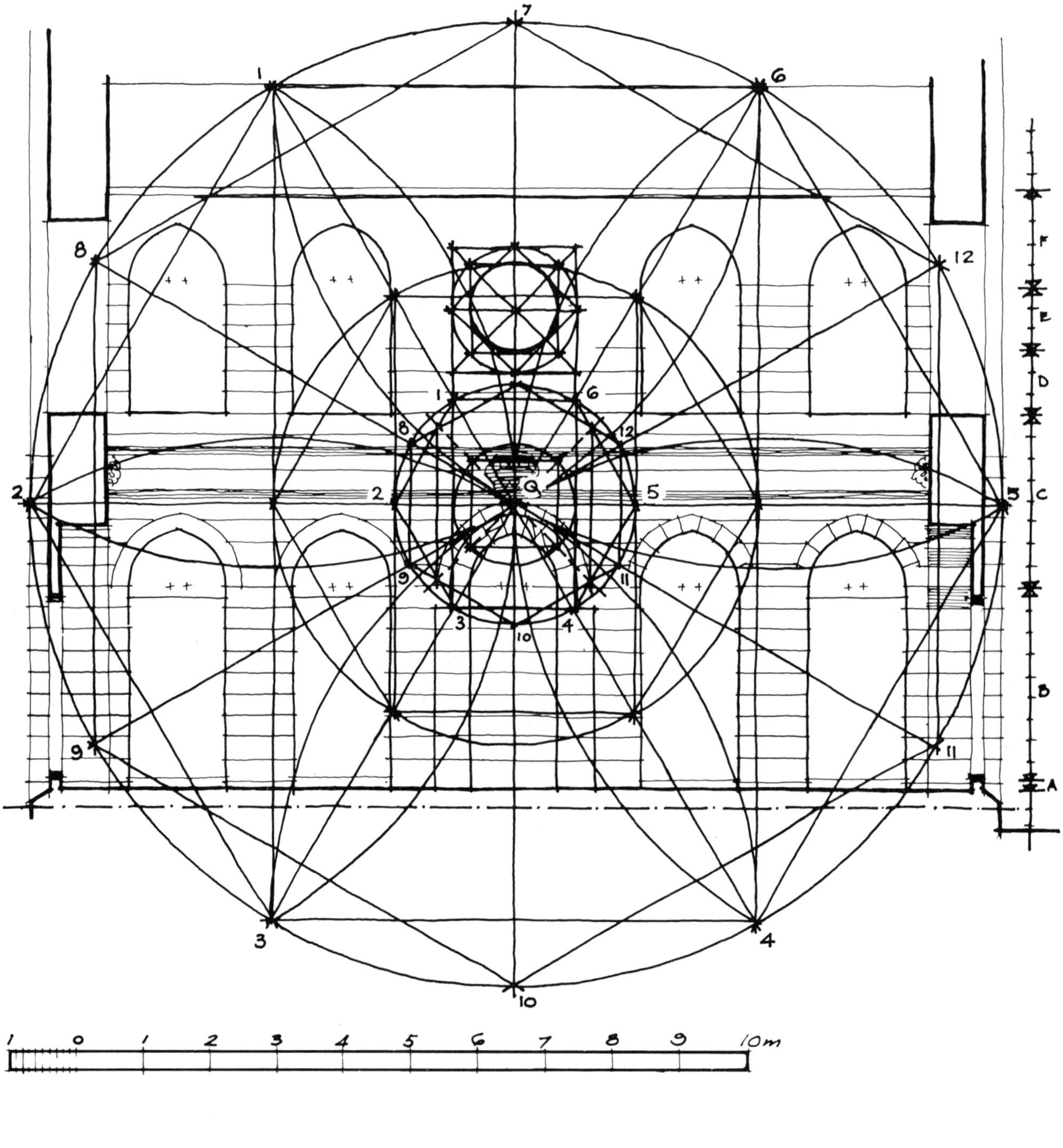

Fig. VII/23 The *qibla īwān*, *qibla* wall: the sub-elements completed

definite visual connection with the *miḥrāb* below. Simply on this visual basis the diameter chosen for the circular opening in the Ashrafiyya is equal to the width of the niche of the *miḥrāb* and the width of the upper arch of the *miḥrāb*. Notwithstanding the reasons behind these choices made with the knowledge that the details of the *miḥrāb* have previously been shown to be controlled by a geometry, these two features, the circular window and square surround, do require to be connected to each other by some geometrical construction. This is begun by inscribing a circle within the surrounding square, which in turn describes a double square or octagonal star which then describes a second circle which is equivalent to the circular opening. In the resultant geometric figure of concentric squares the consecutive parallel sides are related in the proportion of $\sqrt{2}$, and consequently the diameter of the window and the square surround are linked by this portion.

In the Mosque and Mausoleum sub-element D, the height from the clerestory sill to the bottom of the circular opening, is three courses. It may also be so here, but to check this, the above geometric construction should temporarily be thought of as independent of the major geometries. It can therefore be moved up and down the central axis to see if and when it coincides with the rotated geometries in a satisfactory manner. It appears to fit best when the top of the smaller circle representing the opening coincides with the circumference of the ½ BUG diameter circle centred on Q. At this point the bottom of the smaller circle rests on the third course above the sill level of the clerestories and thus the height of sub-element D in the Ashrafiyya matches that of the same element in the Mosque and Mausoleum.

Looking at the fundamental geometries rotated against the *qibla* wall, it would seem possible that the side 1-6 might indicate the level of the ceiling. It would certainly give to the cornice a depth on a par with these in the Cairo models, but for a more convincing identification we shall again work on the geometries of the side wall.

The first step is to extend the internal geometries of the side wall upwards by making sides 3-2 of the inscribed hexagons W_4, W_5 and W_6 common to the three inscribed hexagons centred on C_1, C_2 and C_3. The next step is to add the rotated fundamental geometry centred on Q. This is easily accomplished since the length of the line M-Q_1 is equal to ½ BUG, and using this measurement as the radius the fundamental geometry can be reconstructed centred on Q. Once these additions are completed, the upper sides of the hexagons C_1, C_2 and C_3 can be compared to the level of side 1-6. It is obvious that the two sets of lines do not coincide, but it is possible that each indicates the level of a different component in the timbered ceiling. **fig. VII/24**

For two reasons it is appropriate to end these geometries of the side wall by adding to its exterior the rotated fundamental geometry. Firstly, it enables all of the detailed geometries to be viewed as part of the larger geometry, and secondly, it assists the comparative studies by providing a clear and recognisable basis. **fig. VII/25**

This search for the internal and external characteristics of the *qibla īwān* is now complete. As mentioned before, the characteristics found are common to the west and north *īwāns* also, regardless of the number of windows in each, nor is the presence of a pseudo-gateway in the north *īwān* unhelpful, for it simply reflects the *miḥrāb* in the *qibla īwān*.

Note

1. The description of the geometries and their coincidence with the architectural details (for example, the springing of the clerestory windows) follows the relationships discovered whilst working on drawings at a scale of 1:50. Unfortunately, when these same drawings were reduced in scale in preparation for publication, and their respective goemetries redrawn, variations occurred. Thus there may be a slight repositioning of a centre of a circle, possibly compounded by the centres of second and third circles being fractionally off-centre. These differences are due to the change required in the thickness of the drawn lines at 1:50; the more accurate thin line is legible, whilst at a reduced scale, heavier, and therefore less accurate, lines, are required. I decided to retain the description of the geometries drawn at 1:50, for the above reason, despite the inconsistencies offered by the published drawings.

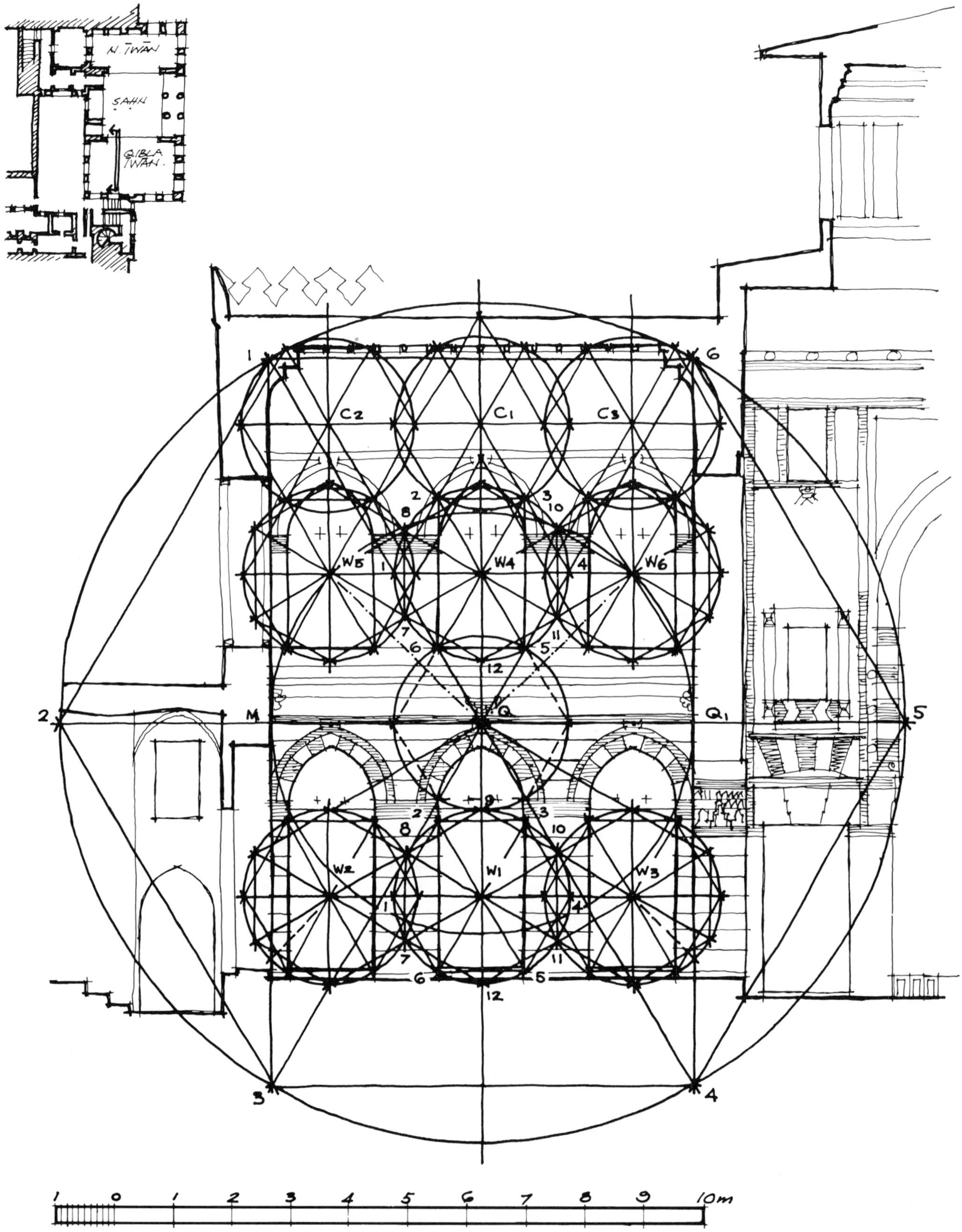

Fig. VII/24 The *qibla īwān*, the interior of the side wall: the fundamental geometry rotated

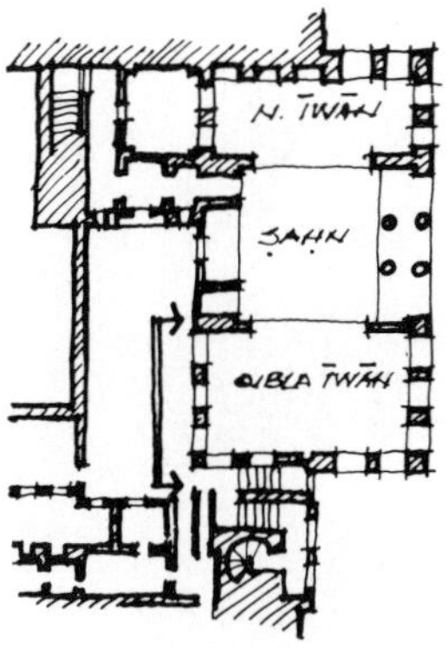

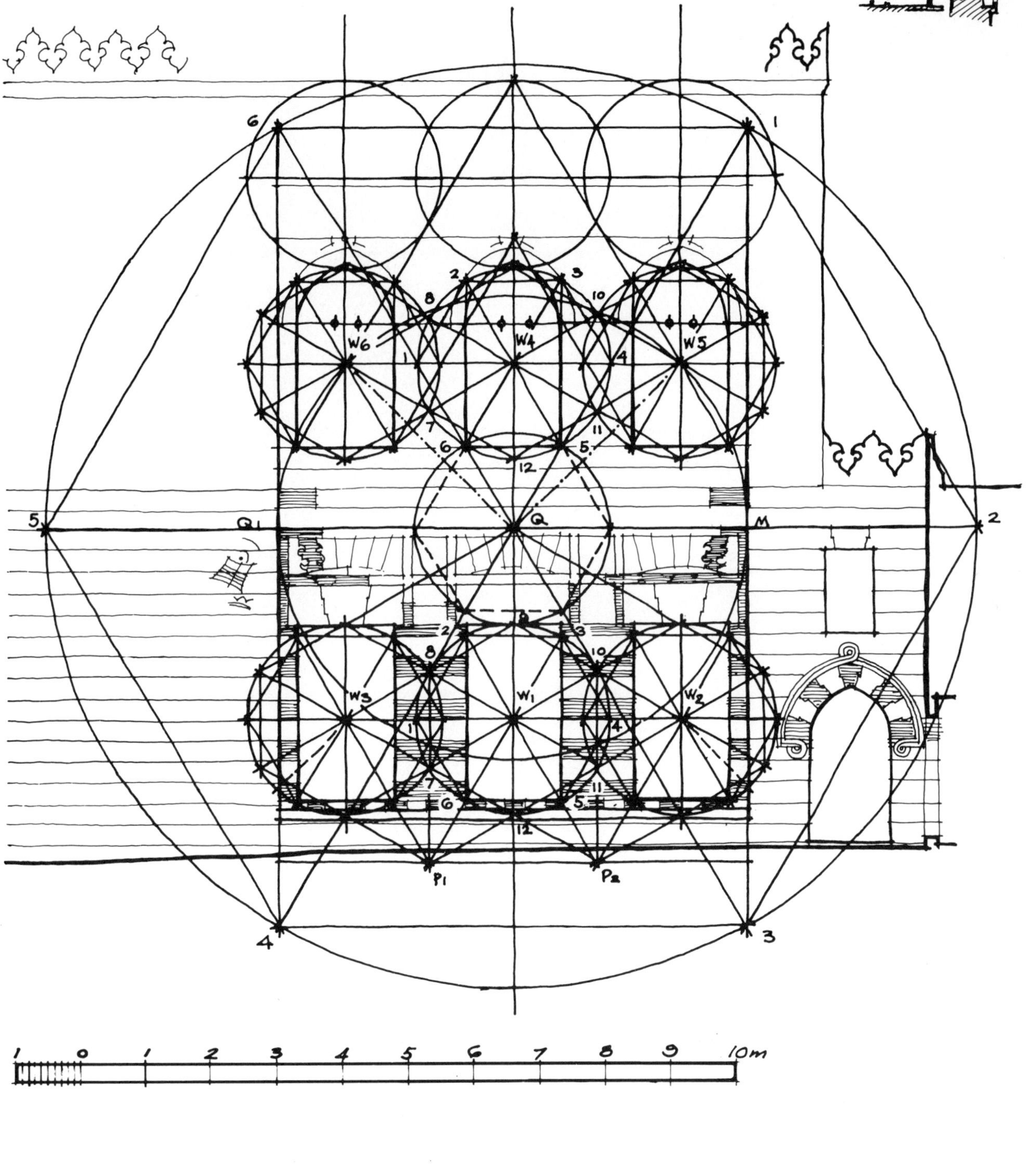

Fig. VII/25 The *qibla īwān*, the exterior of the side wall: the fundamental geometry rotated

Plate 14 Cairo, Mosque and Mausoleum of Qāytbāy. The cruciform mosque, with its lantern above the *ṣaḥn* and its characteristic fenestration, is seen flanked by the minaret on the left and by the domed tomb on the right. (Creswell Archives, Ashmolean Museum, Oxford)

Chapter VIII
THE LOGGIA

Van Berchem in his *Corpus* gives a detailed historical and architectural account of the Ashrafiyya, including the description by al-'Ulaymī written shortly after it was built. Al-'Ulaymī was struck by the originality of the eastern side *īwān* which formed a *tārima* rather like a pavilion, a belvedere or loggia opening out on to the Ḥaram through three arches supported by two marble columns. Van Berchem notes that it was rare to see such external features in religious monuments except around the Ḥaram in Jerusalem where there are several small loggias. However, he suggests that although these may have inspired the architect, as the loggia of the Ashrafiyya was so much larger than its neighbours, the model in fact used was more likely to have been a certain type of hall in Egypt which through arches opens on to a road or into an internal courtyard.

At the same time, van Berchem makes it clear that arcading inside cruciform planned mosques or madrasas in Cairo was not unknown. He cites several examples, the Mosque of al-Qāḍī Yaḥyā 856/1452, the Mosque of Sīdī Madyan c. 871/1460 and the Mosque of Abū Bakr Muzhir 884/1479-80 (plate 15), and in relation to the latter he goes further by including a plan showing arcading placed across both the *qibla īwān* and the *īwān* opposite, and perspective drawing of this arcading.[1]

Based on the observation of al-'Ulaymī that there were three arches and two marble columns, van Berchem correctly concludes that the architecture actually requires two arcades, one to separate the loggia from the *ṣaḥn* and the other to separate it from the Ḥaram. In his plan of the Madrasa[2] he shows a total of four circular columns, a proposal I do not entirely agree with. I am fully aware that his priorities lay with the inscriptions of Jerusalem and their details rather than with obscure details of its architecture. Unfortunately this cannot be said of Tamari whose aim was an architectural analysis of the Ashrafiyya. Tamari accepts the four column solution not only in plan, but he incorporates it into his restoration of the east elevation (see Appendix B).

Despite the presence of internal arcades in Cairo mosques, their proportions are incompatible with those which would fit the design of the Ashrafiyya. For example, although the height of the arcading of the Muzhiriyya is 32 stone courses, the arcades are 18 metres wide. Which means that if the arches were sealed down to fit the 9 metre width of the loggia, their height would drop proportionately to 16 courses. As a result they would become similar in size to the other loggias in the Ḥaram which are too small to comfortably fit into the east elevation of the Ashrafiyya.

These architectural features were recorded visually by Edward Reuwich of Utrecht in the drawing of Jerusalem published in 1486, and contemporary with the completion of the Ashrafiyya. Three tall arched openings are depicted therein, and their height can be estimated as being equal to the combined heights of the windows and clerestories of the *qibla īwān*, a fact which immediately identifies the loggia with the aesthetic traditions of Egypt. The drawing provides us with another proof: the loggias which existed at this time, and which still exist around the Ḥaram, are not exaggerated by Reuwich. Surely, if the Ashrafiyya had in any measure resembled the size of these loggias it would have been drawn accordingly.

In view of this, the investigation into the architectural form of the loggia is greatly helped by the existence in Cairo of a similar loggia in the House of Qāytbāy, a secular complex built by the sultan three years after the completion of the Ashrafiyya (plate 17). The house has on one side of the central courtyard a loggia with an arcade of three arches and two columns. It is a fine example of this feature, designed and built by the sultan's own craftsmen, possibly even under the direction of the same Christian architect.

The reconstruction of the somewhat elusive design of the loggia must begin with a careful study of the details surrounding the centre of the east elevation, which either belong to the destroyed loggia or to the features flanking it. The fundamental geometry will then be rotated against the elevation to

Plate 15 Cairo, Mosque of Abū Bakr Muzhir: the arcade separating the *qibla iwān* from the *ṣaḥn*. (*Survey of Egypt*, pl. 128)

Plate 16 The Ashrafiyya and the Minaret of the Gate of the Chain in 1486, from Bernhard of Breydenbach, *Peregrinationes in Terram Sanctam*, detail (Bodleian Library, Oxford)

enable comparison to be made with the restored features of the *ṣaḥn* and the *qibla īwān*, and to establish the architectural framework of the east elevation.

The same process will then take place inside the Madrasa, firstly in relation to the east wall of the *ṣaḥn* and then in the area linking the east elevation and the *ṣaḥn*. Each study will produce its own framework which, when combined with that of the east elevation, will create a three dimensional architectural framework which can accept the arcading and at the same time satisfy the structural practicalities.

The Loggia: its East Elevation

The minimal remains of the loggia are contained within an area defined by the remnants of a moulded frame close to the centre of the parapet of the east elevation. A joggled *ablaq* string course is set on the base of the frame with four courses of the *ablaq* jambs of the loggia abutting the truncated vertical mouldings at either end. The intervening distance is divided into three almost equal parts by two red rectangular stones set on edge. Other stones lie in between the jambs in a muddled fashion: the **fig. VIII/1**

Plate 17 Cairo, House of Qāytbāy: west elevation of courtyard with the loggia at its centre. (Tarchi, *L'Architettura e l'Arte Musulmane in Egitto e nella Palestina*, tav. 97 bottom)

precision of the original stone coursing has not been maintained, the placing is unmethodical and the red and white stones follow no pattern, suggesting that much of this area was rebuilt after the earthquake of 1545.

In order to make any sense out of these remains they must be set into the restored plan of the Madrasa, and seen against the details of the west *īwān* on the other side of the *ṣaḥn*. **fig. VIII/2**

This will help to clarify their position in relation to the main axes of the Madrasa, and as a first step it is useful to recap on the essential features of the plan which will have a bearing on the design of the loggia.

All the significant details so far established have been placed symmetrically about the two main axes. Consequently, when the great arches of the *ṣaḥn* were reconstructed, the position and size of their eastern abutments established the east side of the *ṣaḥn*. Also as a result of the symmetry, the existing windows in the west walls of the *qibla* and north *īwāns* were balanced by windows in the east walls. Indeed, if the lines of the north wall of the *qibla īwān* and the south wall of the north *īwān* are extended to meet the east elevation, they not only coincide with the vertical straight joints to either side of the moulded frame of the loggia, but also define the sides of the external recesses of these eastern windows.

When these essential features are combined with the existing details of the loggia seen in the east elevation, the following observations can be made. The *ablaq* jambs of the loggia are in line with the southern jamb of the cupboard and the northern jamb of the entry to the *ṣaḥn*. The pair of red stones appear unrelated to any established feature. In some ways the most interesting point is that the description of the arcading given by al-'Ulaymī was not full enough and so could be misconstrued as referring to only one arcade. However and despite this, van Berchem interpreted the description correctly, in that he took from the description the idea of two arcades. This has to be so if the loggia and the *ṣaḥn* are to be aesthetically satisfying and, more importantly, structurally feasible. They do require a second line of support along the east side of the *ṣaḥn* in addition to that provided by the arcade in the east elevation.

Some of the design problems can be solved by making certain assumptions on the basis of the importance of the symmetries. In the arcade between the *ṣaḥn* and the loggia it would be logical to assume that the intrados of its arches would be equal to the intrados of the arch in the west side of the *ṣaḥn*. Furthermore, the abutments at either end of this arcade would have been aligned not only with the *ablaq* jambs of the outer arcade, but also with the door jambs in the west side of the *ṣaḥn*. The forms of the existing door jambs differ, with the result that they provide a choice of form for the abutments of the two arcades: the north and south walls of the loggia could either run in a straight line or be recessed. Either could be correct, but in the drawings preference has been given to the recessed form, as this accentuates the position of the arcades. Finally, it can be assumed that the columns of the inner arcade followed the centring of the pair of red stones. Having thus completed the general outline of the plan of the loggia the question of the geometries can now be broached. **fig. VIII/3**

As soon as the geometries are rotated against the remains of the loggia in the east elevation, it becomes apparent that these features are aligned with those features in the west side of the *ṣaḥn* which have already been found to relate to the geometries. It is logical, therefore, to use the same figures here, starting with the circle centred on S with the radius SZ. In VI/11 it is apparent that the circumference of this circle coincided with the northern jamb of the entry and the southern jamb of the cupboard. It would therefore be expected that the circumference of the same circle rotated against the east elevation would coincide with the *ablaq* jambs of the loggia, since they are known to be aligned with the jambs on the west side of the *ṣaḥn*. Similarly, point Z on the circumference should define the height of the arches of the loggia, assuming that the zeniths of all the arches associated with *ṣaḥn* are on the same level. **fig. VIII/4**

Now that this simple geometry, copied from the west side of the *ṣaḥn*, has proved to have a relevance when applied to the east elevation, it can be extended to include further features, such as the pair of red stones, by the addition of the primary geometry with its double hexagon 1-12. The distance separating the centre lines of the stones is found by constructing a ½ BUG diameter circle centred on S, and inscribing a hexagon within it. The 45° axes intersect the circumference in the lower half of the circle at two points, and lines drawn from these points to the upper angle of the hexagon intersect the horizontal axis. These points of intersection lie $^{1}/_{5}$ BUG apart, and since they coincide with the centre **fig. VIII/5** **fig. VIII/6**

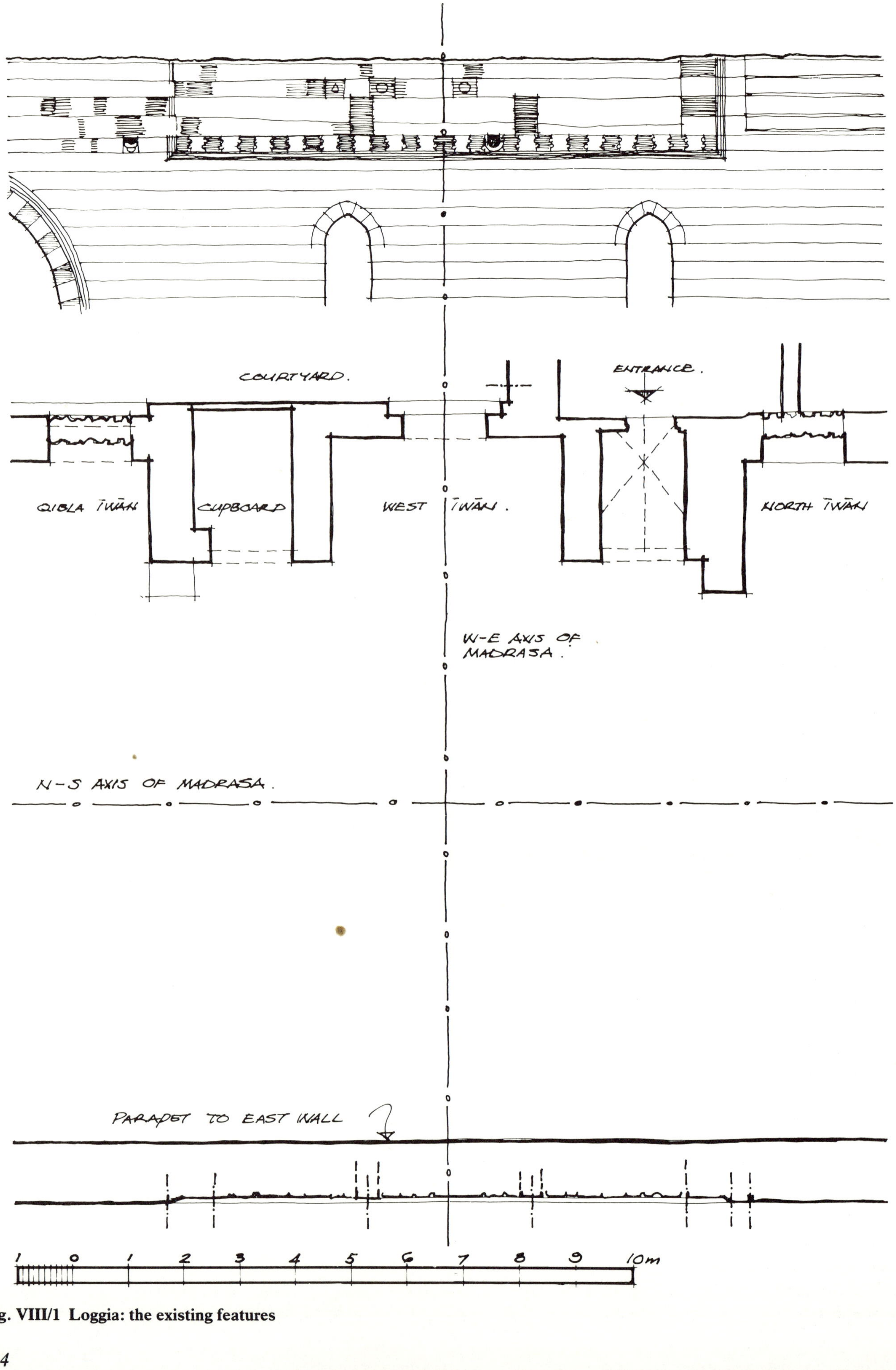

Fig. VIII/1 Loggia: the existing features

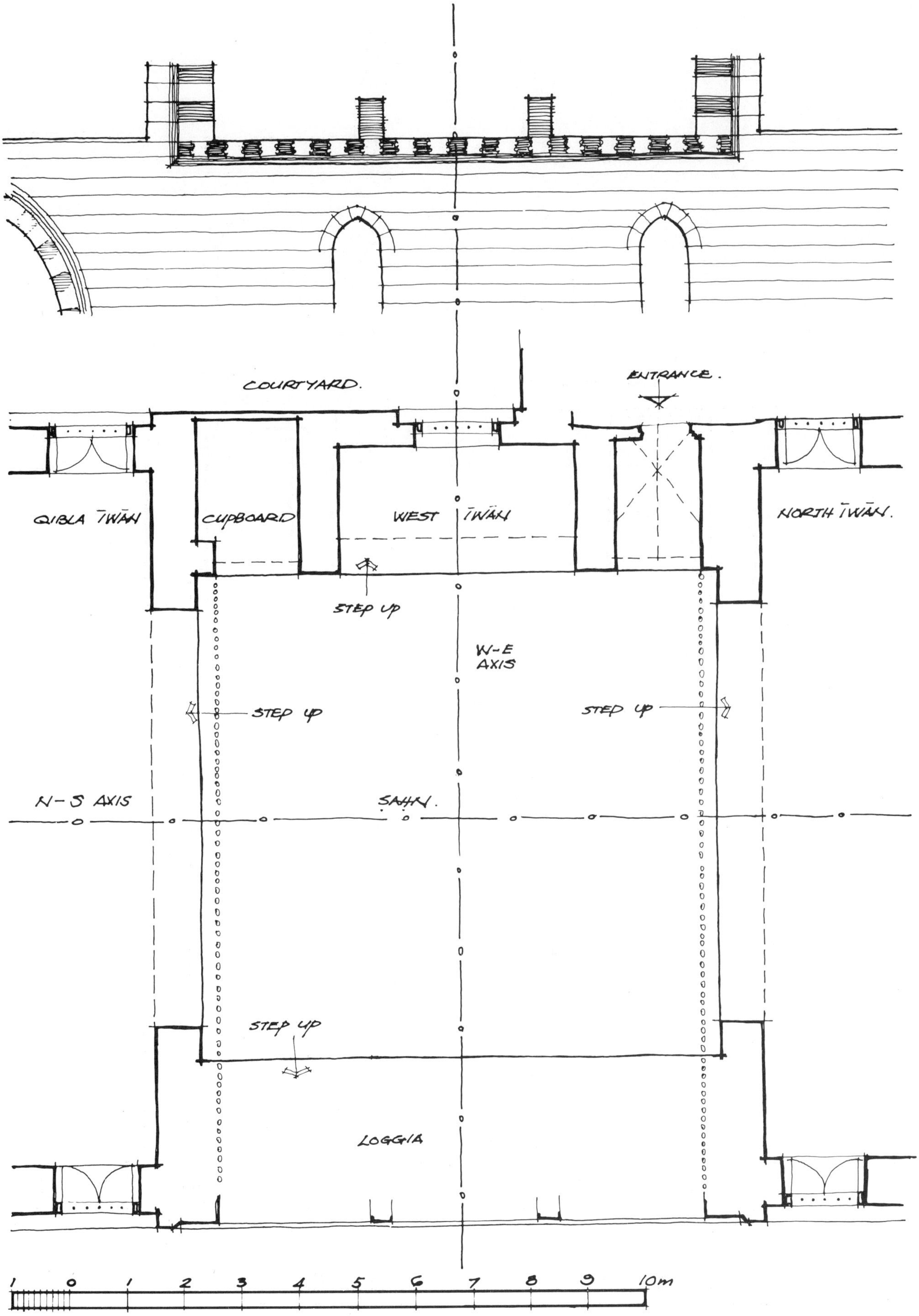

Fig. VIII/2 Loggia: the existing features considered

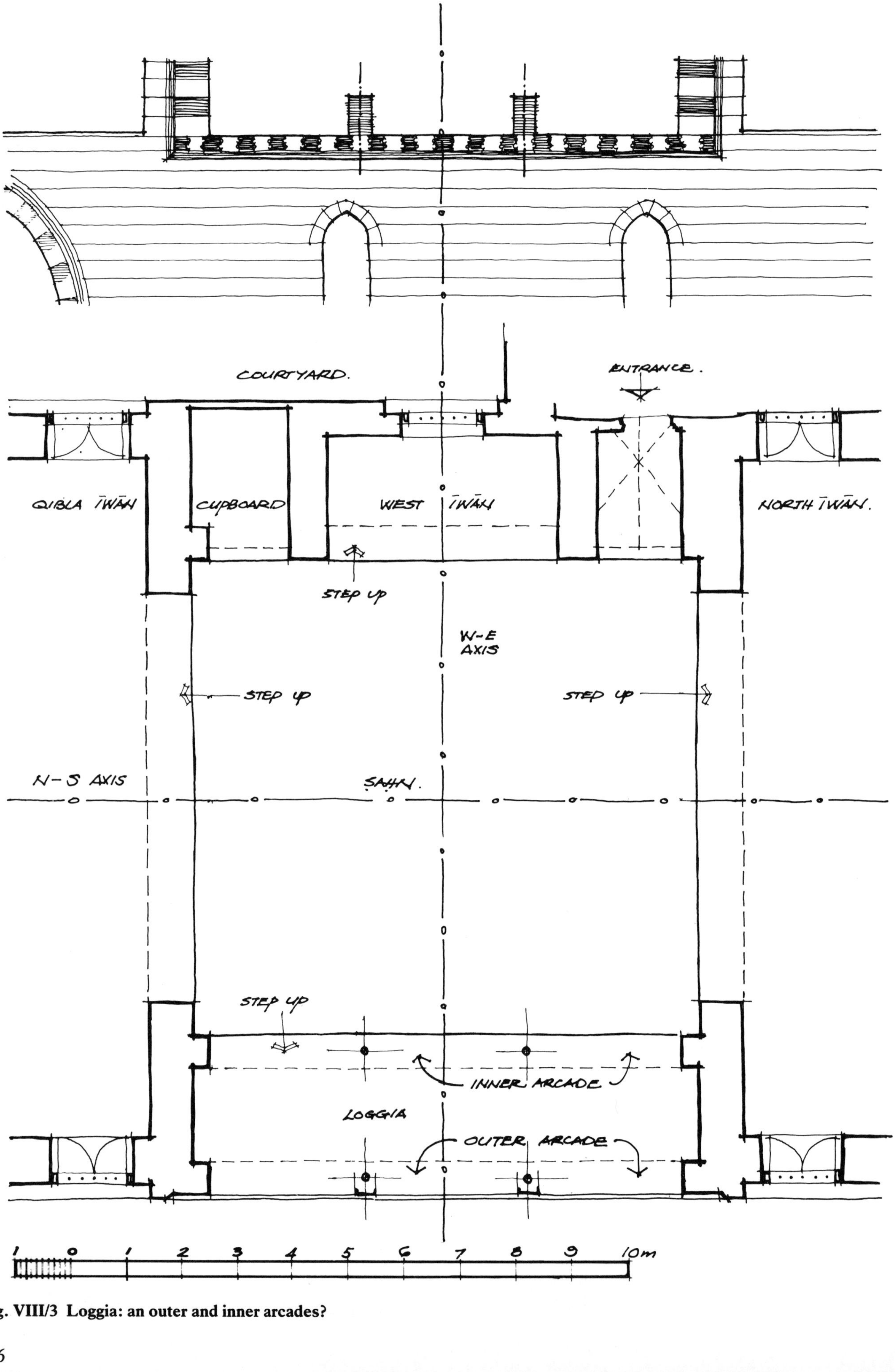

Fig. VIII/3 Loggia: an outer and inner arcades?

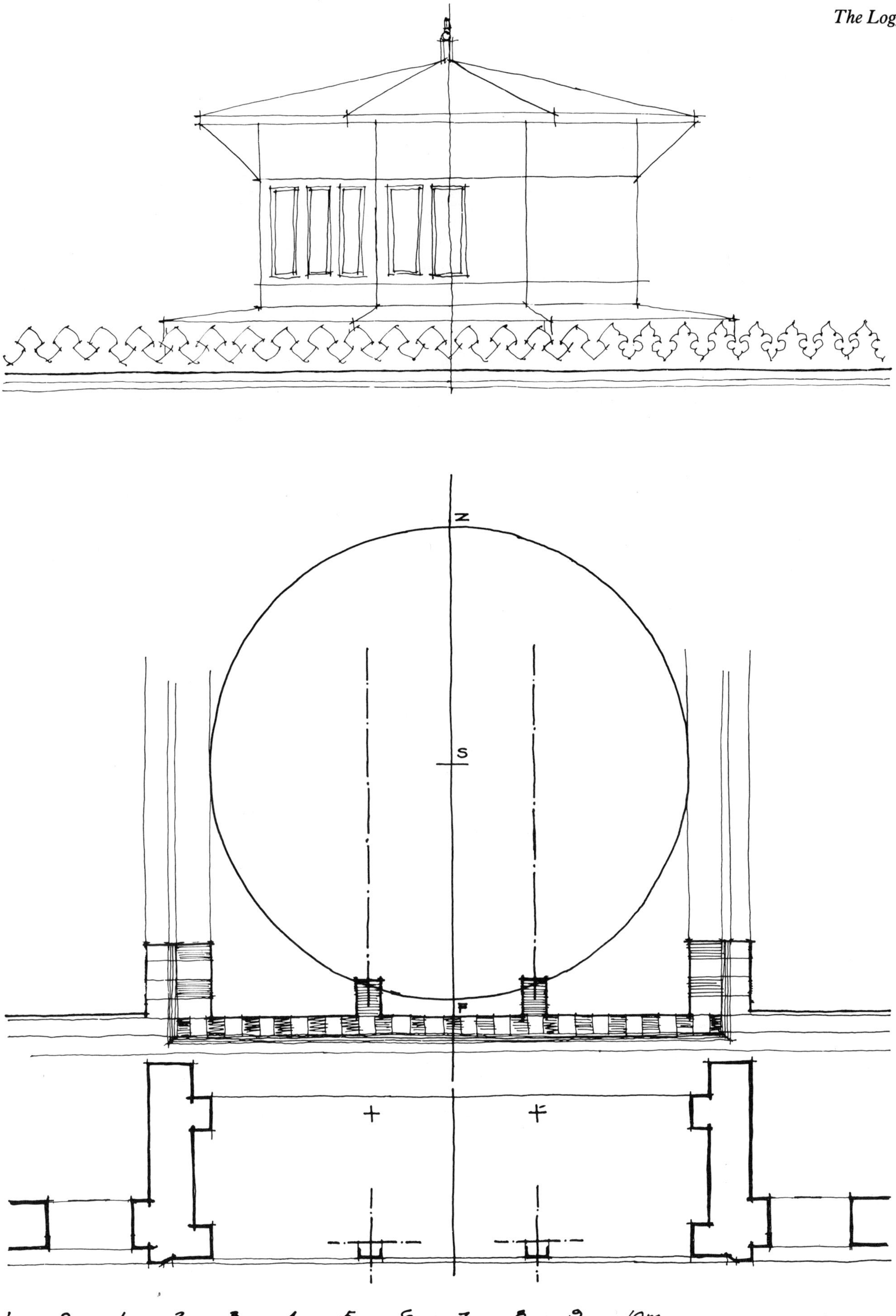

Fig. VIII/4 Loggia, its east elevation: the S-Z circle

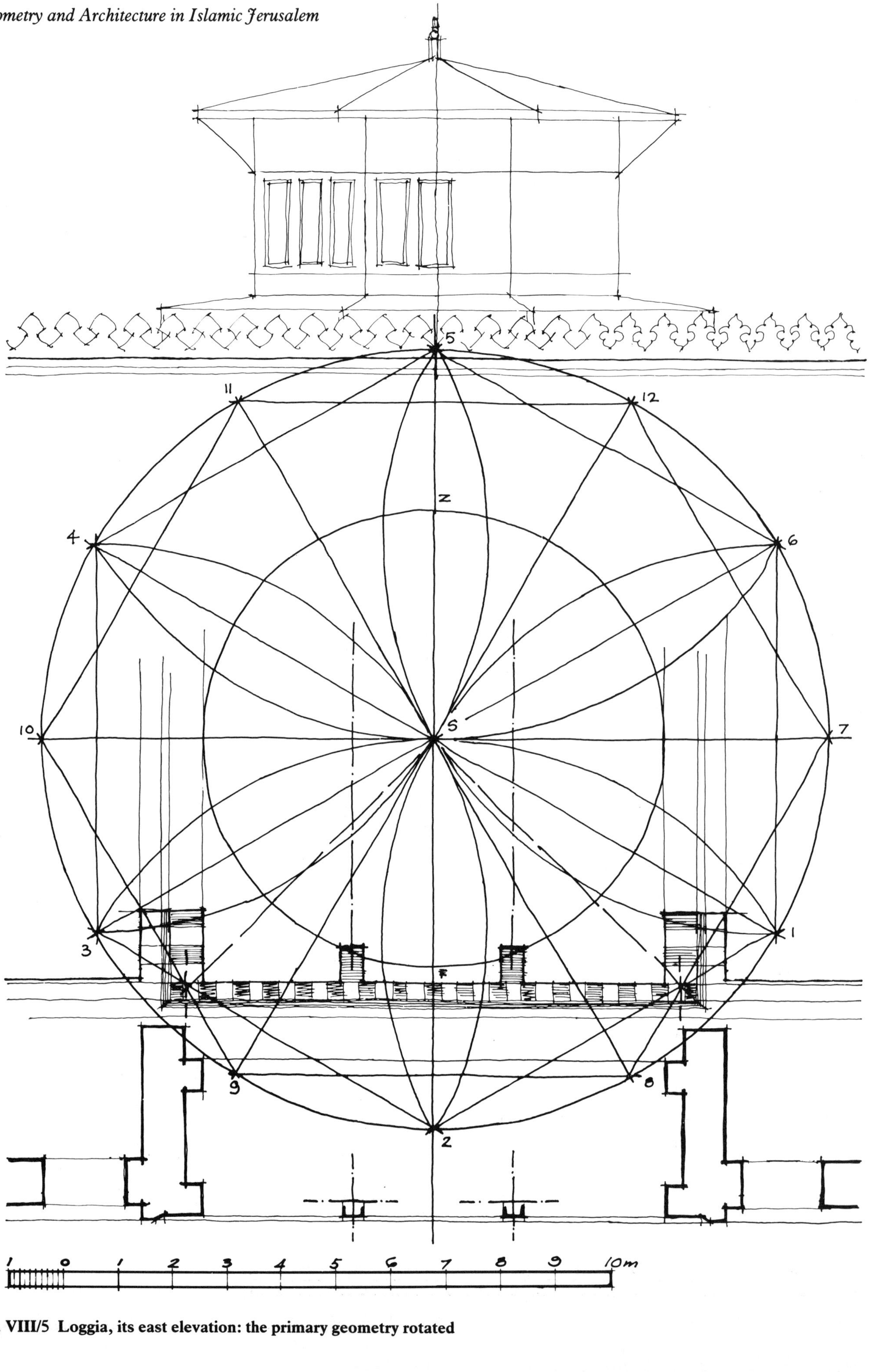

Fig. VIII/5 Loggia, its east elevation: the primary geometry rotated

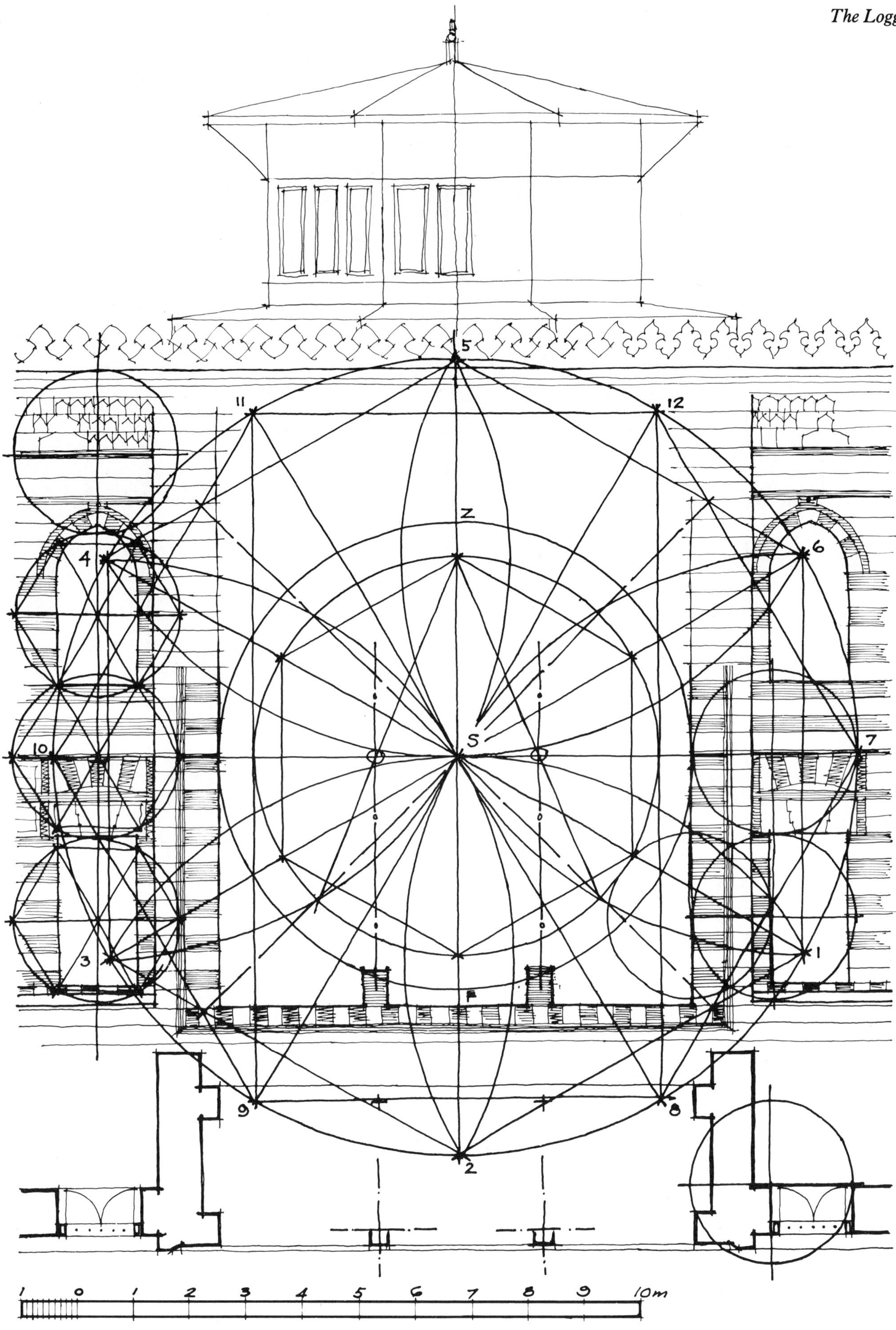

Fig. VIII/6 Loggia, its east elevation: the detailed geometries

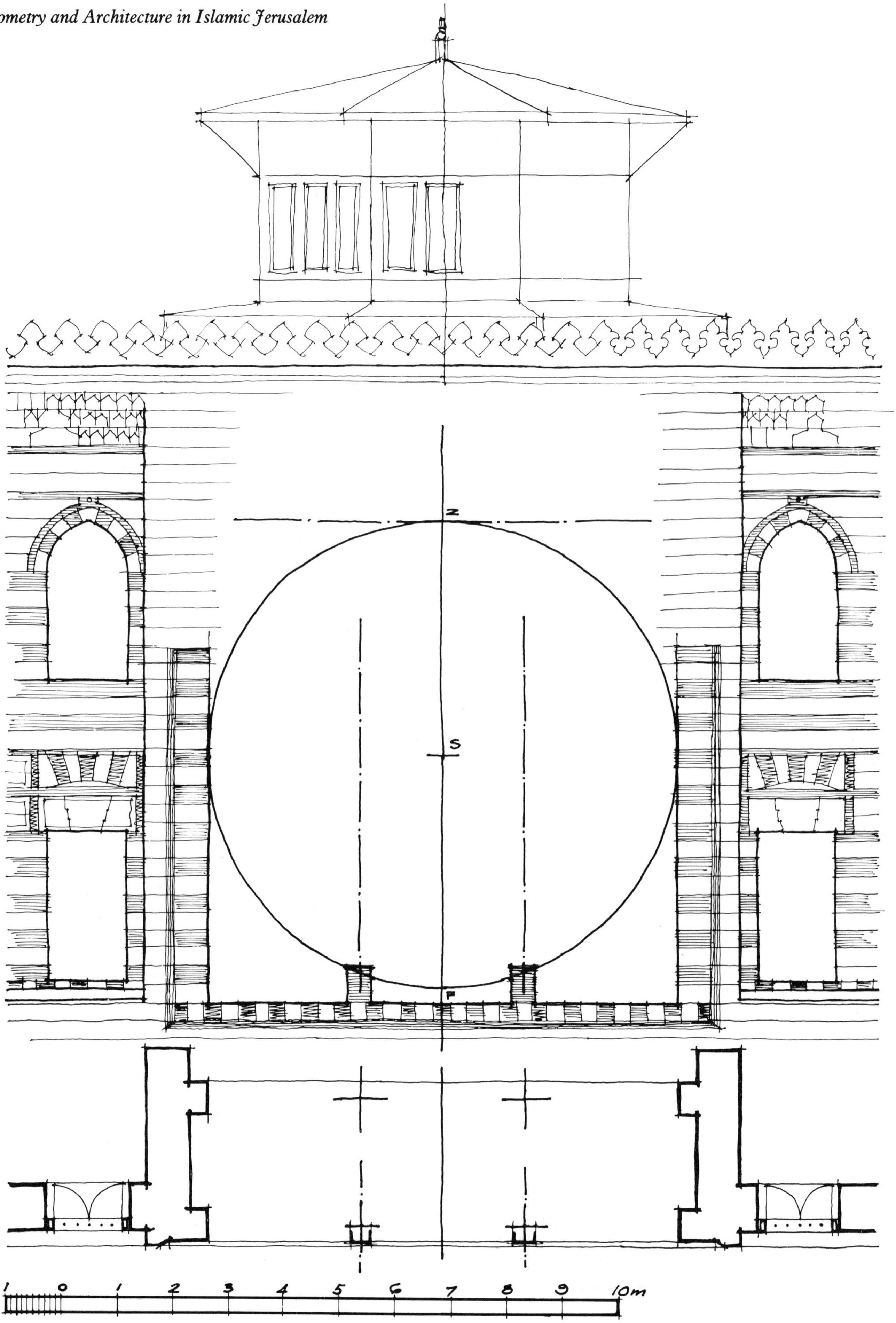

Fig. VIII/7 Loggia, its east elevation: the architectural framework

lines of the pair of red stones, the stones too are separated by a distance of 1/5 BUG.

The restored plan of the Madrasa has shown that recessed windows existed on either side of the loggia in the *qibla* and north *īwāns*, and since the loggia should not be considered in isolation but rather in the wider context of the east elevation, it is helpful to draw in these windows. Their restored design, established when studying the exterior wall of the *qibla īwān*, relied on 1/10 BUG radius circles which among other things defined their width as 1/10 BUG. These same circles can be used again here, and not only do they assist in the drawing of the windows, but they also highlight two other relationships: firstly, the distance between the ingo of the *ablaq* jambs and the ingo of the windows of the adjacent *īwān* is equal to 1/10 BUG, and secondly, the vertical moulded frame lies exactly halfway between these two points.

This completes the architectural framework surrounding the loggia in the east elevation. However, to assist its comparison with the other architectural frameworks of the loggia which will be needed, the rotated geometry can be reduced and simplified to the earlier figure of the circle centred on S with a radius equal to SZ. **fig. VIII/7**

The Loggia: its Interior

The second architectural framework of the loggia to be established is that which surrounds the inner arcade lying across the east side of the *ṣaḥn*. No physical evidence remains to support its existence, but as explained previously, a second arcade was required for the Madrasa to maintain its essential symmetries and for it to be structurally stable.

Since the essential symmetries are to be maintained, the design of this arcade will need to be consistent with the designs of the other walls of the interior of the Madrasa. Since these have relied on the rotated primary geometry with its double hexagon, the design of the framework for the inner arcade can also be assumed to be based on this same geometric theme. Before this can be verified, however, some parts of the design of the arcade must be anticipated so that there is base to which the geometry can be applied.

Of the original design two facts are known: the arcade had three arches and two columns. From this it can be deduced that at the extremities of the arcade the abutments did not incorporate either engaged or free standing columns, and that consequently some other means of support had been used. If the information gathered when the plan of the loggia was studied earlier is added to this, it becomes clear that the end abutments must have been in the form of masonry nibs which would have included impost blocks similar to those of the other arches of the *ṣaḥn*. This enables a mental image of the arcade to be made, but further details are required in order to translate this image into a more definite form.

For this the symmetries occurring in the *ṣaḥn* should be referred to, and these provide further points of reference from which the following details will emerge which can be related to the rotated primary geometry: the floor level of the *ṣaḥn*; the floor level of the loggia which coincides with that of the *īwāns*; the height of the impost blocks of the arcade (level with that of the side and great arches of the *ṣaḥn*); the springing level of the arches of the arcade (equal to that of the arch to the west *īwān* on the opposite side of the *ṣaḥn*). Furthermore, the zeniths of the arches of the arcade would be on a level with those of the other arches of the *ṣaḥn* and also with the zeniths of the outer arcading to the loggia. The level of the upper edge of the keystones, coinciding with the keystones over the other arches of the *ṣaḥn*, and finally the position of the inscription and moulding running below the cornice of the *ṣaḥn*, which must have encircled the *ṣaḥn*, can be established. **fig. VIII/8**

If the central axes of the two columns of this arcade are added to these points of reference, the surrounding framework of the inner arcade is nearly complete but for one point. Should the impost blocks at either end of the inner arcade be backed by vertical compartmentation, as are those in the west wall of the *ṣaḥn*?

Visually such compartmentation would destroy the imposts, reducing them in size so that they would appear as decorative elements rather than elements with a purpose, and shrinking the voussoirs to an unacceptable size when compared to those of the other arches of the *ṣaḥn*. It is, however, unnecessary, since when viewed from an angle the imposts are already bordered by the vertical compartmentation backing the imposts of the north and south great arches.

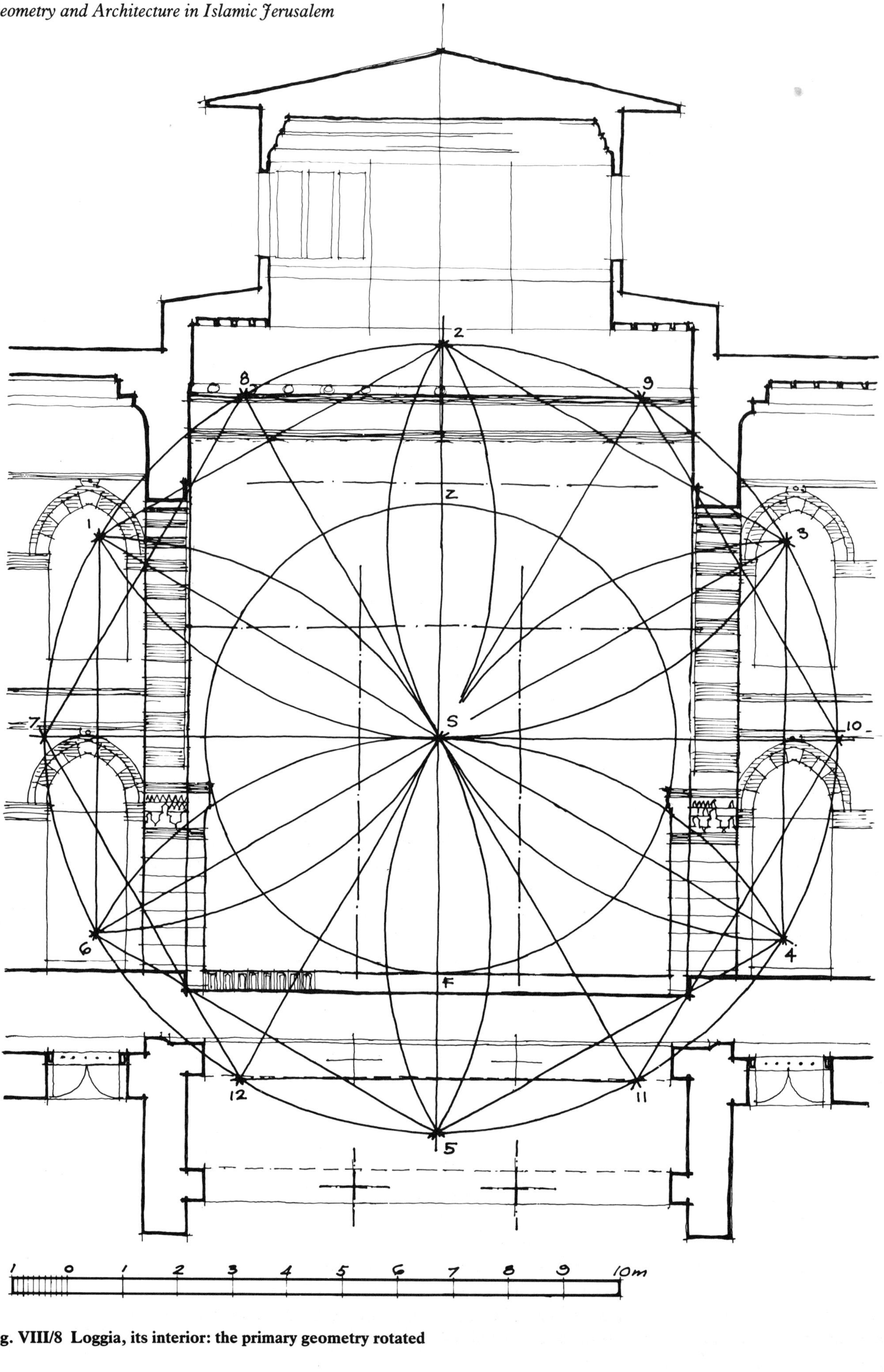

Fig. VIII/8 Loggia, its interior: the primary geometry rotated

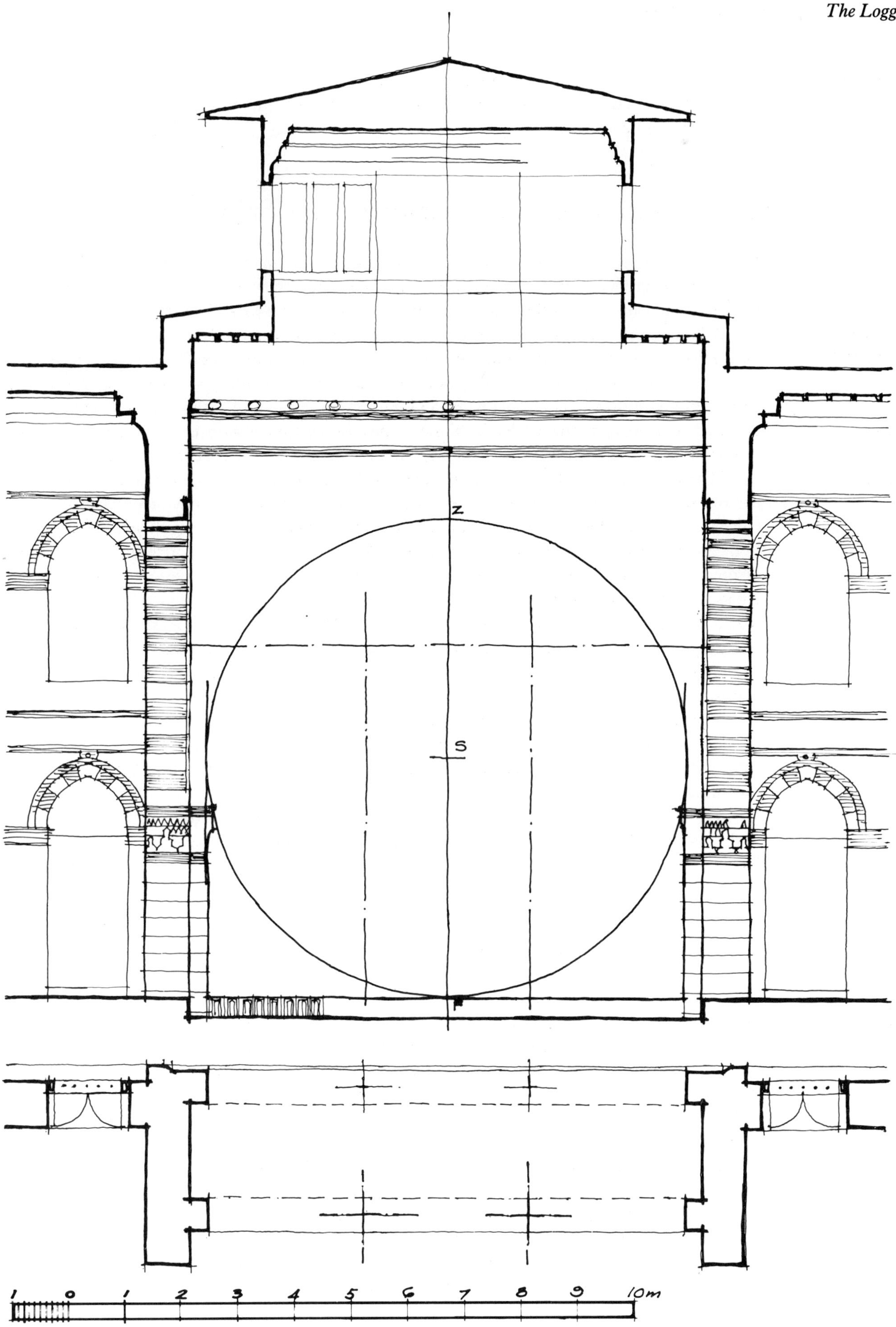

Fig. VIII/9 Loggia, its interior: the S-Z circle

fig. VIII/9 This completes the surrounding framework of the inner arcade, and again, to aid comparison with the other frameworks, the rotated geometry is simplified to the figure of the circle centred on S with a radius equal to SZ.

The Linking of the East Elevation to the Ṣaḥn

Naturally, these two architectural frameworks must now be linked together by the side walls of the loggia. However, before this is done, the details of the identical north and south walls of the west *īwān* must be established so that they can be modified when transposed to the loggia.

fig. VIII/10
fig. VIII/11
Although the north and south walls of the west *īwān* now rise only as far as the top of the grand inscription, as do the other existing walls of the Madrasa, they can be easily restored. The height, the number of stone courses and the depth of the cornice in this *īwān* must have been identical to the corresponding features in the *qibla īwān*, and the section through its exterior wall follows closely that of the *qibla īwān* except that here it is thinner. The cross section of the arch to the west *īwān* is equally simple to restore since the size of its intrados and the height of its zenith are both known. **fig. VII/23**

fig. VIII/12 When the section of the west *īwān* is transposed to the loggia only one change has to be made. The exterior wall of the west *īwān* with its recessed windows is replaced by the outer arcade of the loggia. Once this has been done certain relationships become apparent. The level of the lowest stone course in the *ṣaḥn* coincides with the top of the joggled *ablaq* string course (see dotted line). It also becomes obvious that the *ablaq* decoration, the alternating red and white stone courses, of the *ṣaḥn* and its arches is not synchronised with that of the east elevation. However, this interrupted *ablaq* pattern would not necessarily disturb the eye, for the transition is skilfully made, its success lying in the fact that the height of the impost of the inner arcade and its compartmentation is three courses, so enabling the middle course to be built of red stones which can be carried across to meet and fit in with the *ablaq* jambs of the outer arcade.

This transition should have been apparent from the outset as it occurs at all the external windows of the Madrasa. It may also have had important implications for the architect: as an architectural device, the transition in the *ablaq* courses separates the *ṣaḥn* from its surrounding *īwāns*, accentuating the different feelings they evoke.

This establishes the three dimensional framework linking together the two previous frameworks of the loggia. The outer arcade in the east elevation can now be studied again with a view to restoring its details.

The Outer Arcade Detailed

fig. VIII/13 It is fortunate that the pair of red stones survived the earthquakes since their axes and widths define the limits of the central arch. They must be viewed in conjunction with the *ablaq* jambs for they are linked by the rhythms of the joggled *ablaq* string course: joggled white stones lie directly below each of the red stones and both of the jambs, in contrast to the joggled red stones coinciding with the central axes of the arches. The architect's idea seems to have been to create a sense of tension or opposition within the joggled *ablaq* string course which could respond to the position of the supports of the arcade in one way, and to the centres of the arches in another.

The top of the sill of the arcade would have been on a level with that of the *īwān* windows, and it seems probable that it would have been constructed in a plain white stone in order to counter the exuberance of the joggled *ablaq* string course and the *ablaq* jambs.

Two final items can be added to the drawing before turning to the geometries: the level of the springing of the stilted arch of the west *īwān*, even though it is unlikely to coincide with the springing of the arcade as their spans differ, and the top of the keystone, which is on a level with those of the interior.

The geometries are now required to continue the restoration, and a construction must firstly be made on which the arches can be constructed. As before, a start is made with point S, and since the

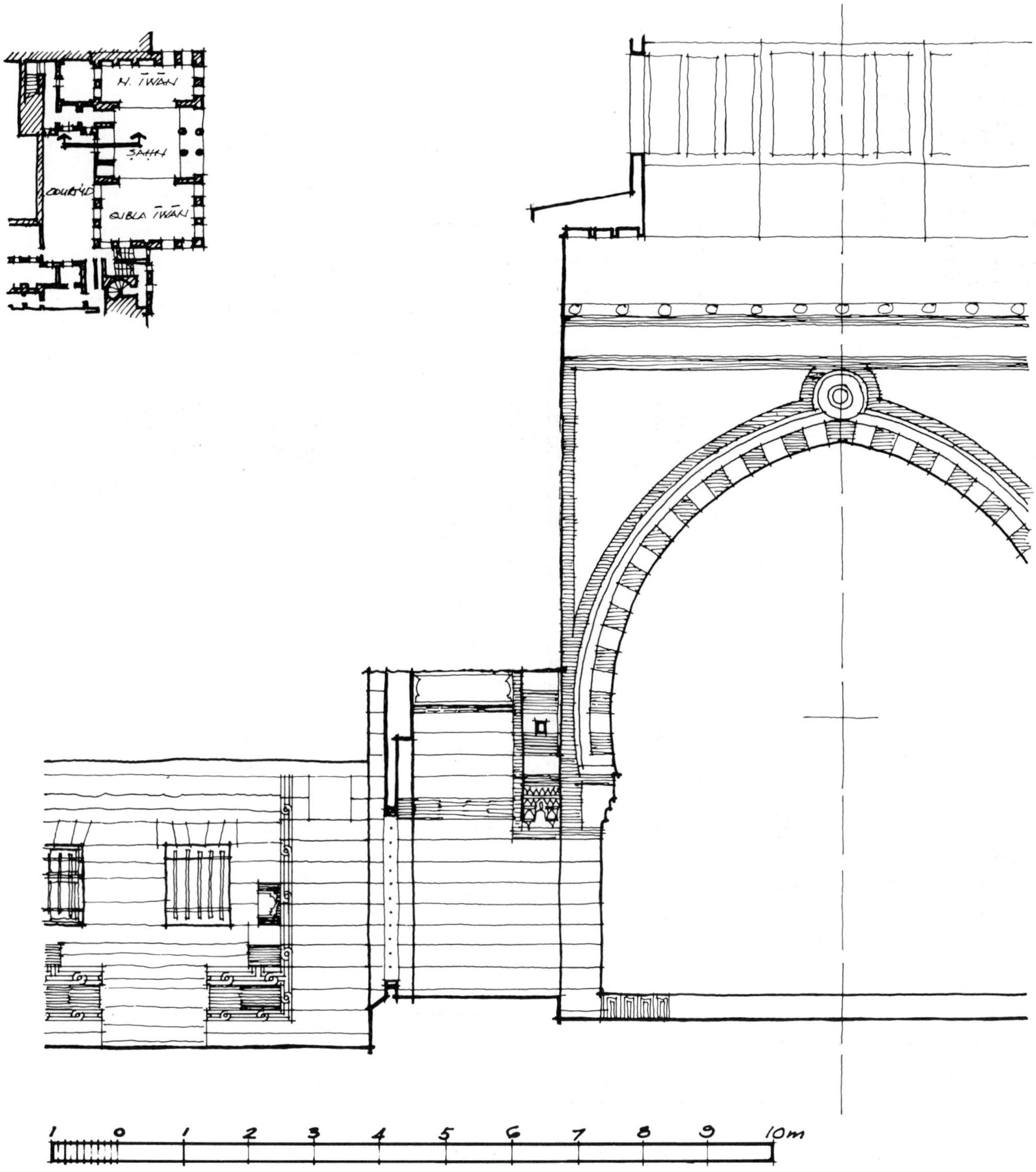

Fig. VIII/10 West *īwān*, north wall: the existing features with the restored *ṣaḥn* added

central axes of the pair of red stones are 1/5 BUG apart, the first construction must be a 1/10 BUG radius circle inscribing a hexagon (1-6). If a second hexagon centred on point A_1 is then drawn below the first with side 3-4 common to both, the lower side of this second hexagon is level with the tops of the red stones.

The sides of the red stones and the positions of the *ablaq* jambs are found by constructing a double hexagon (7-12) about point S. The sides 8-9 and 11-12 define the inner corners of the red stones, and by constructing similarly orientated hexagons about points A_2 and A_3, the positions of the other sides are found.

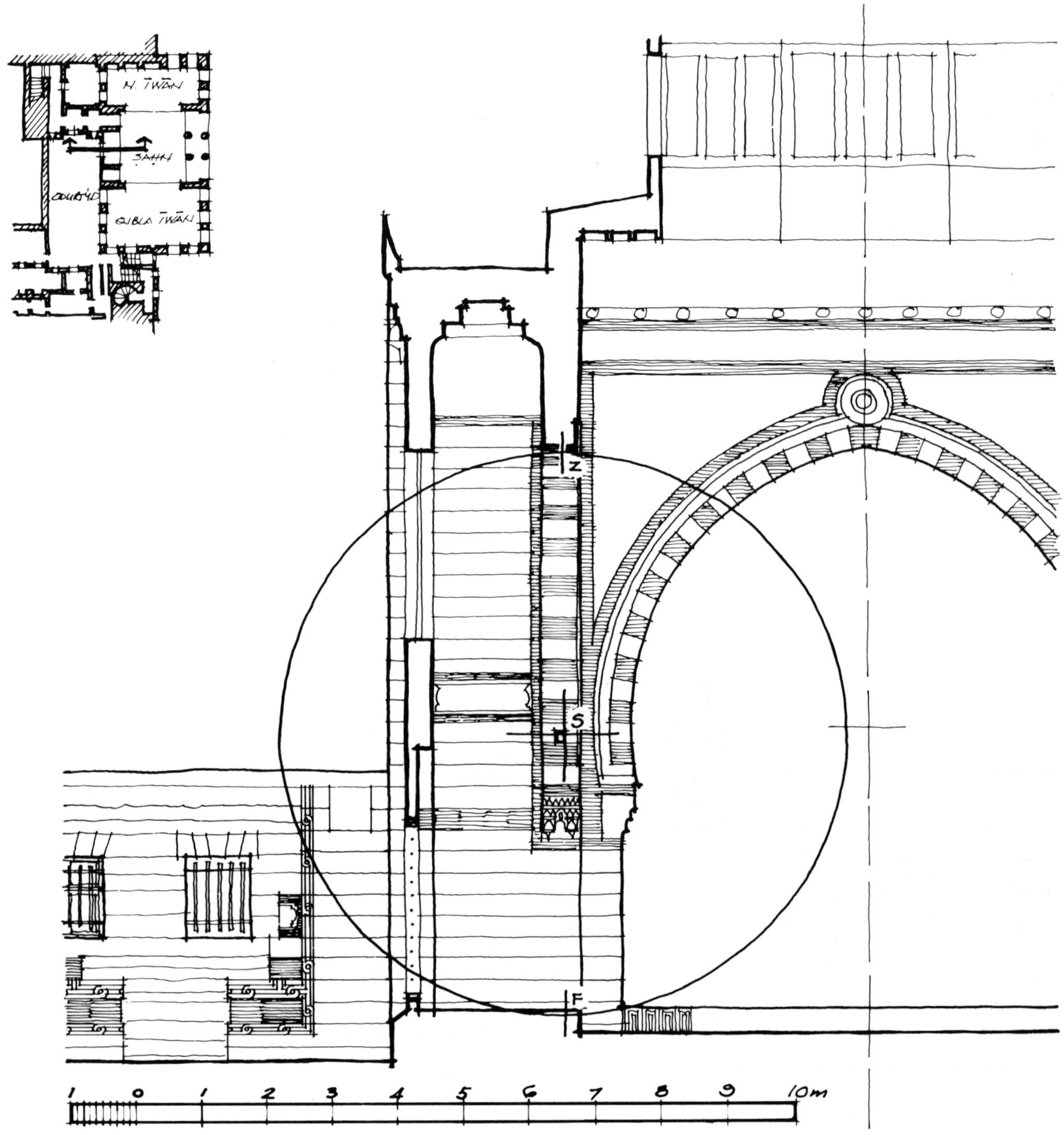

Fig. VIII/11 West *īwān*, north wall: the S-Z circle and the completed section

It will be remembered that the contemporary description given by al-ʻUlaymī specifically mentions two columns and three arches, and that this has since been interpreted to mean that there were two arcades each with two columns. However, I am convinced that al-ʻUlaymī was correct in so far as his description went. What he did not bother to mention was that the outer arcade had two piers rather than columns.

Furthermore, it was to the inner arcade that the attention of al-ʻUlaymī or any visitor would have been drawn initially, and subsequently when looking out from the loggia, the outer arcade would have been disregarded, the eye being drawn to the breathtaking views of the Dome of the Rock and the Ḥaram, with the Mount of Olives in the distance.

Accepting that these were piers and not columns in the outer arcade poses a new problem: what plan shape had they? They cannot have been square with sides equal to the known width of the red

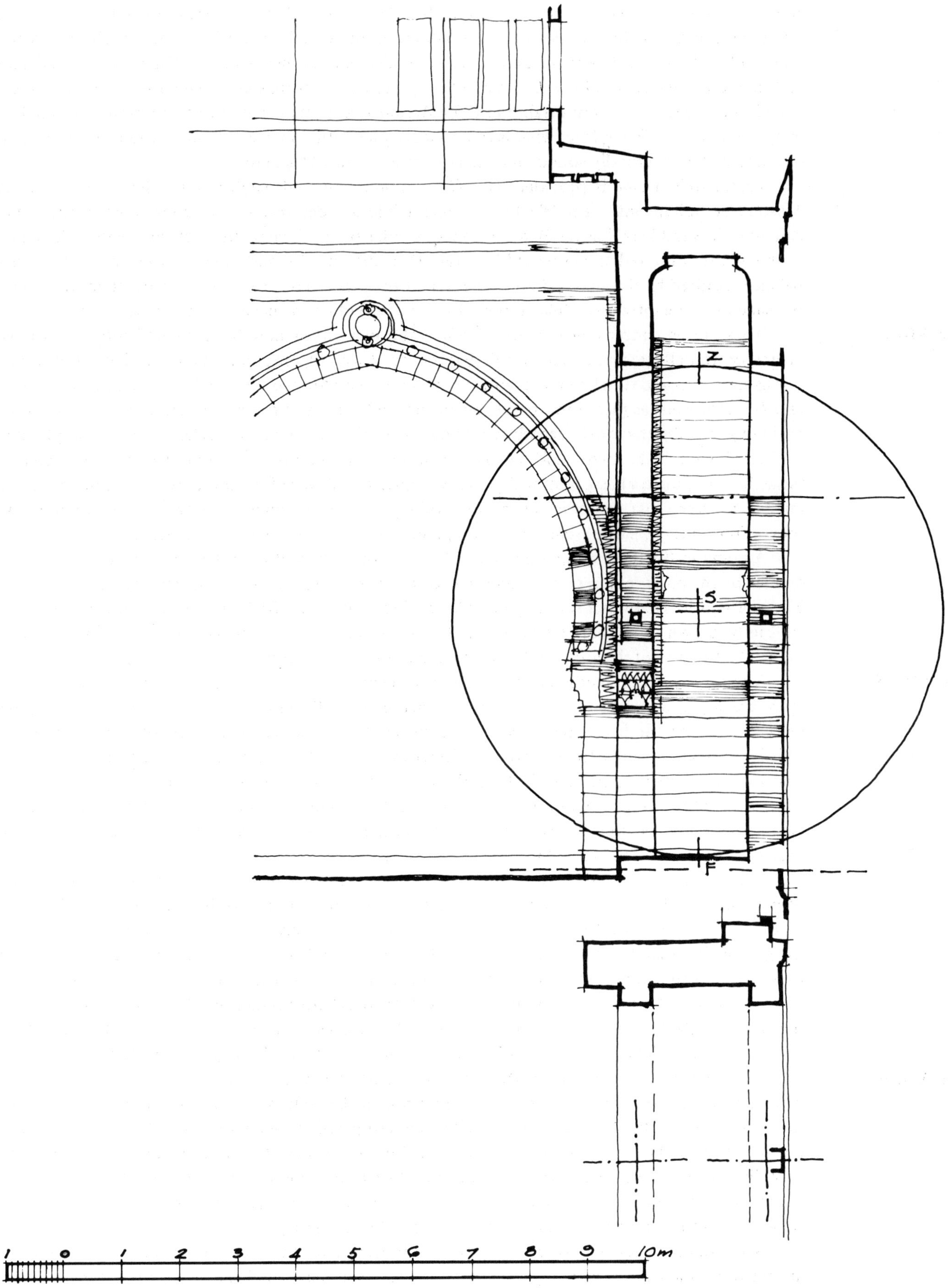

Fig. VIII/12 Loggia, north wall: some features transposed from the west *īwān*

stones, for this would have made them too small and slender, and their inner faces would have formed a line the middle of the intrados of the arcading, an impossible condition. They might have been rectangular. This would increase their cross sectional area, but they would still have been too slender and, in view of the spans of the arches and the size of the other masonry elements, rectangular piers would not be seen to fit comfortably into the Ashrafiyya, as they would certainly have projected an image of weakness. Therefore, what is required is a pier with dimensions which would suit the width of intrados, be structurally sound, and visually balance the *ablaq* jambs.

Fortunately a clue is provided by a Cairo monument built slightly after the Ashrafiyya, the Mosque of Sulṭān Shāh (pre-901/1496). Here triple arcades rest on octagonal piers rather than columns. It is unlikely that the Ashrafiyya had similar piers, since regular octagons with sides equal to the width of the red stones would be larger than the intrados and too large to provide the visual balance required by the *ablaq* jambs. However, if the piers were irregular octagons, then they could be made to fit the intrados, whilst at the same time providing the necessary aesthetic balance.

fig. VIII/14 These ideas concerning the plan form of the piers must now be translated into a workable geometry. Initially it would seem that all that is needed are suitable points of intersection in the double hexagons A_1, A_2 and A_3 (shown in plan), for example those formed by lines 12-9 and 2-3, and by 8-11 and 4-5. However, as these same points when elevated will affect the radii of the arcs, the level of the springing, etc, they have to be regarded as tentative until the design of the arches is nearer completion.

The height of the arches and the exact position of the zenith of the central arch are known and these therefore form a basis from which to investigate the details of the three arches. To begin with it must be assumed that the radius of the arcs will equal $^2/_3$ of the span of the arch, thus matching the proportions of the existing arched window openings in the west wall of the Madrasa.[3]

Automatically this assumption leads to the question of the widths of the piers, and if those widths defined by the points of intersection mentioned above are accepted, the puzzle starts to fall into place. The pier widths establish a span, two thirds of which equals $^1/_{10}$ BUG. By using this as a radius, an arc can be drawn from point Z which cuts the 'thirds' of the span at R_1 and R_2, and using the same radius the two arcs of the arch can be constructed from these points.

fig. VIII/15 A slightly different method is used to find the centres of the arcs in the side arches because their spans are larger, as can be seen from their plan geometries. Therefore, whilst retaining the springing level of the central arch and the $^1/_{10}$ BUG arcs, the centres of the side arches cannot coincide with the 'thirds'. Instead, to define these centres $^1/_{10}$ BUG arcs have to be described from the extremities of the spans to cut the springing line. Taking these cuts as centres, the arcs of the side arches can be completed, although centred on the span the zeniths do not coincide with the vertical axes of the geometries below. A similar variation between the spans of the central and side arches exists in the loggia belonging to the House of Qāytbāy in Cairo.

If, as outlined, the designs of the arches are to work in practice, then at some point the octagonal plan at the base of the piers has to be exchanged for a rectangular plan to allow the arches to sit easily. Also, it is possible for the final shape of the arches to follow closely these simple outlines suggested by the geometries, thereby maintaining a resemblance to the arched clerestories of the Madrasa. In fact if this arch shape were to be chosen it could be argued that perhaps it is the shape drawn in the illustration of 1486. But in spite of this 'evidence', there is better evidence to be found in the loggia of the House of Qāytbāy where there are three horseshoe arches. It seems likely that this same arch type and its associated details could with advantage be introduced into the loggia of the Ashrafiyya.

fig. VIII/16 This being the case, an appropriate level is required on which to reconstruct the horseshoe arches. The obvious line would be the level of the springing of the arch to the west *īwān*, and upon this the lower voussoirs of the arches can be set, with a curved profile to allow the lines of the arches to flow down and under the voussoirs before meeting the imposts. Above the arcade a number of mouldings, including the archivolts, subdivide the upper wall surfaces, following its tripartite divisions. At the crown of the arches the archivolts first form loops before continuing as horizontal mouldings at the same level as those in the *ṣaḥn* running below the wallhead inscription.

No evidence exists for decoration of the spandrels, but had they been decorated as was customary at that time, the central pair, if not all three pairs, could have held the shield of Sultan Qāytbāy. Alternatively, the spandrels of the side arches might, in the absence of the shield, have had a vegetal and ribbon design.

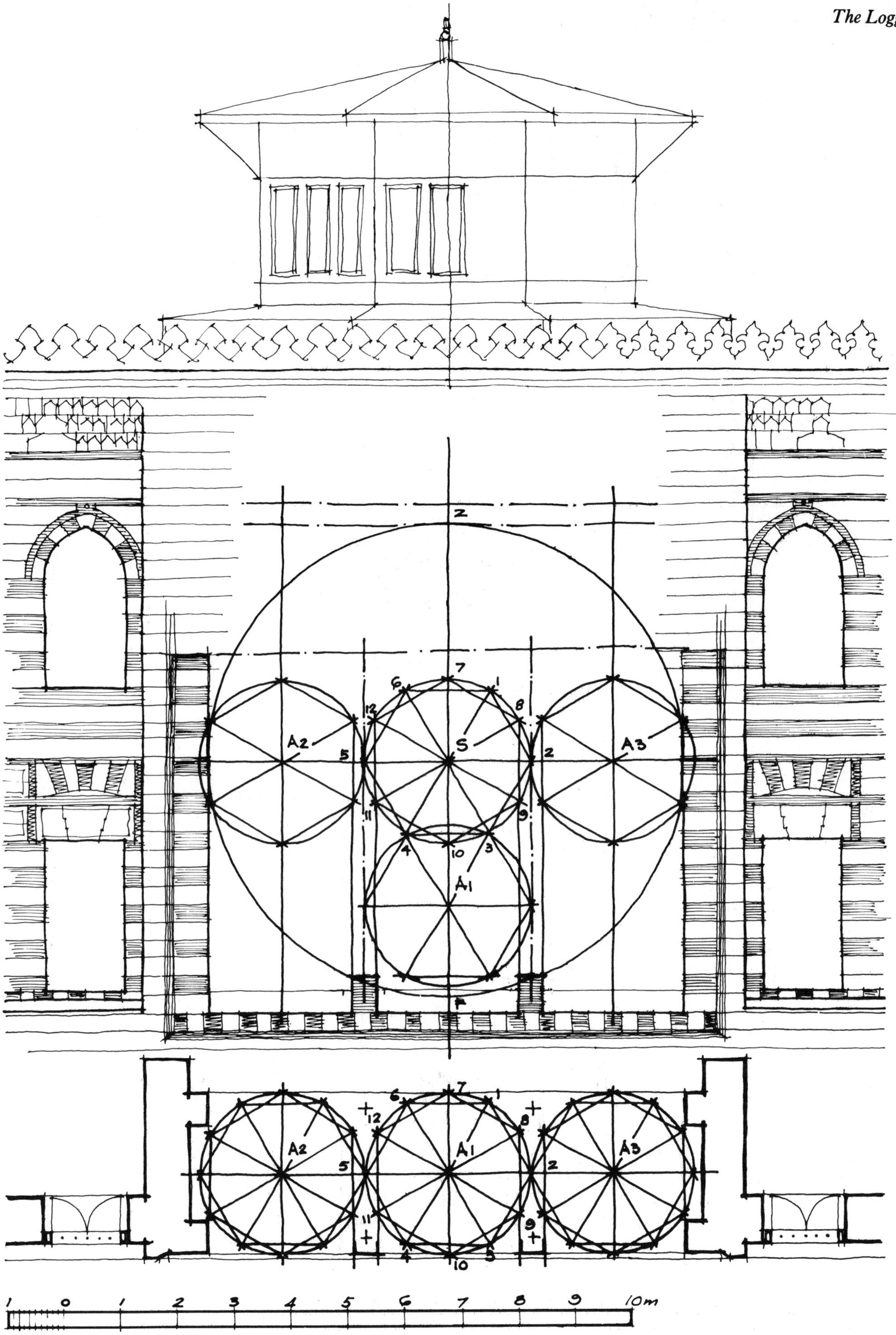

Fig. VIII/13 Loggia, its east elevation: the geometry underlying the three spans of the outer arcade

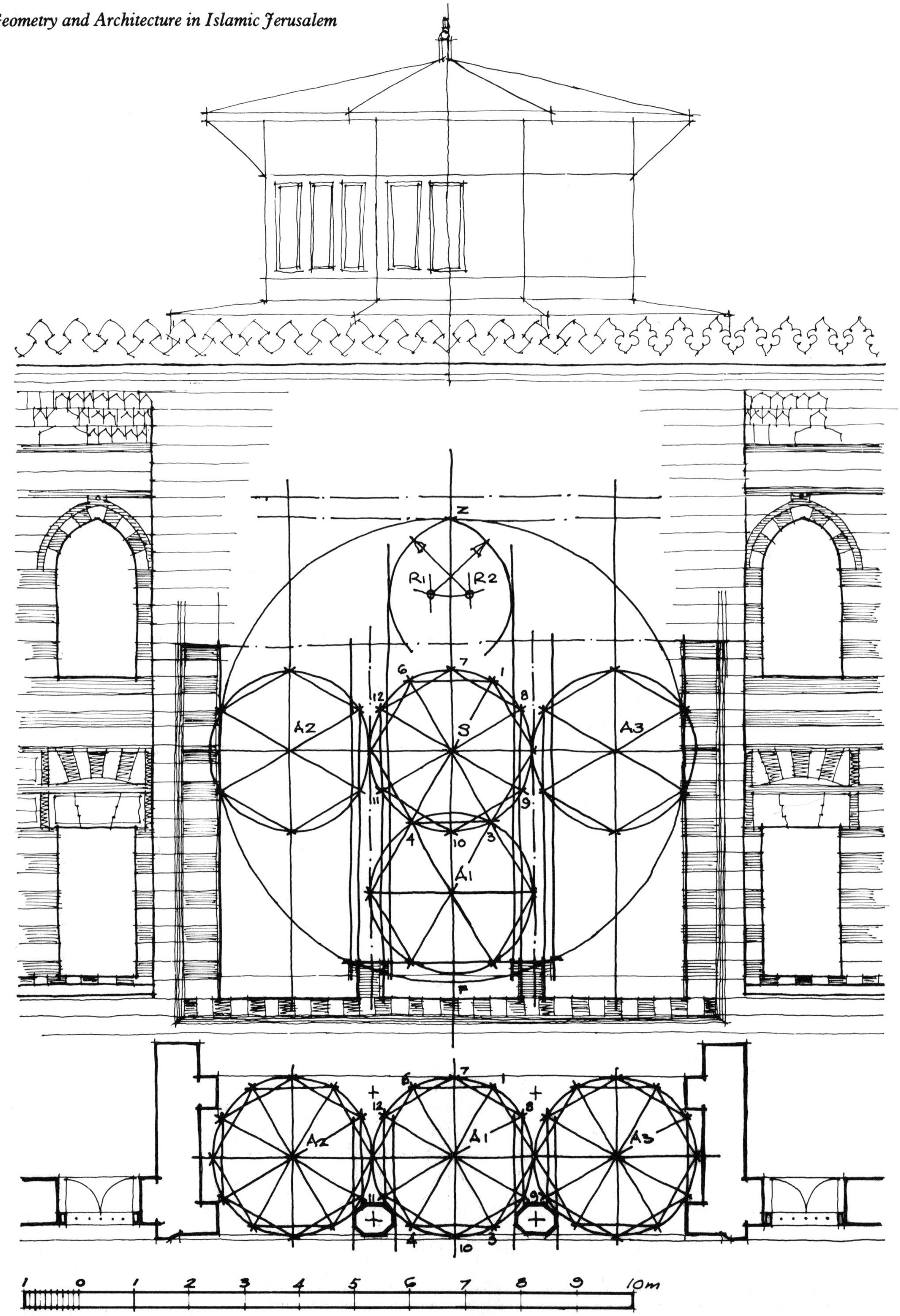

Fig. VIII/14 Loggia, its east elevation: the piers and central arch of the outer arcade.

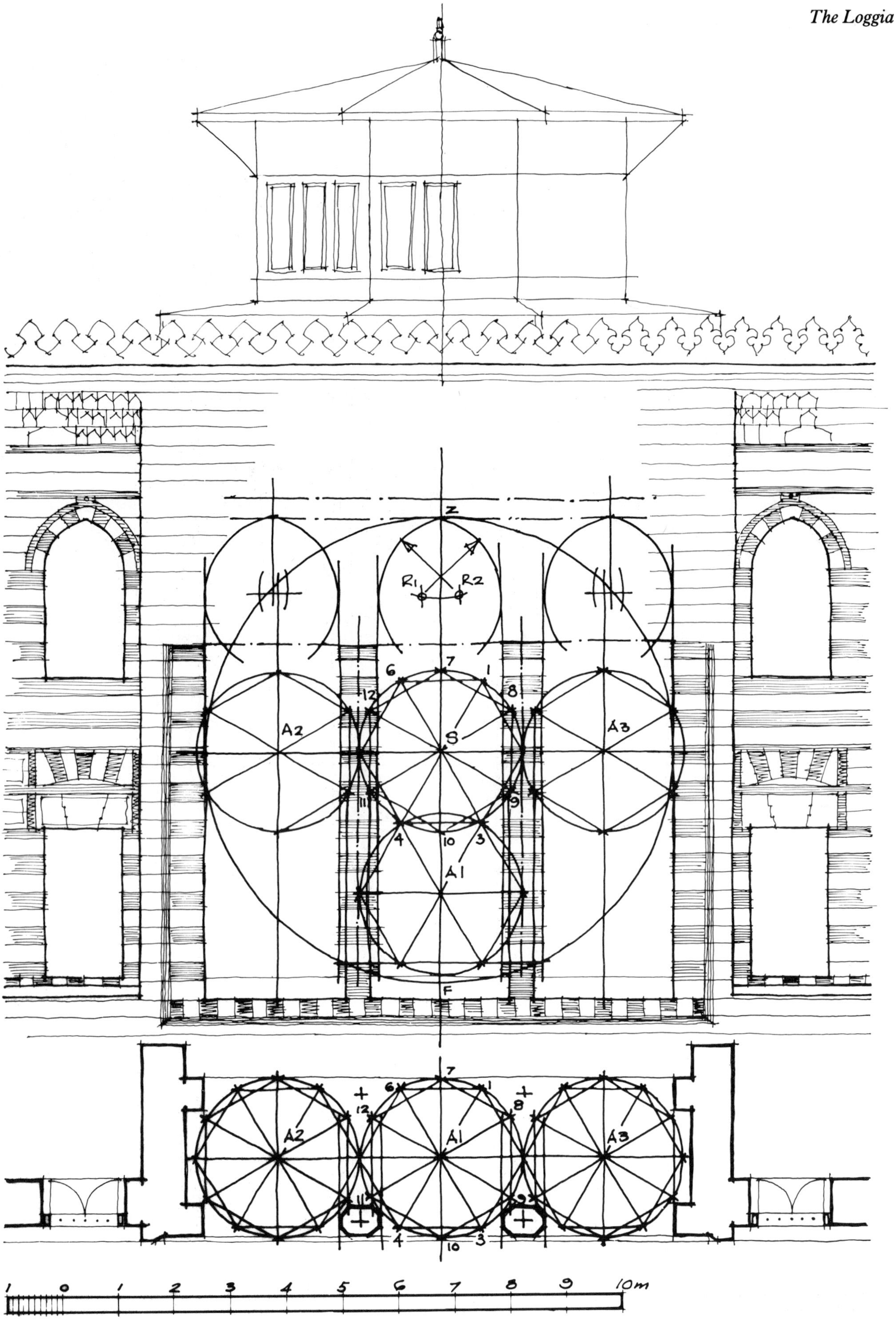

Fig. VIII/15 Loggia, its east elevation: the side arches of the outer arcade

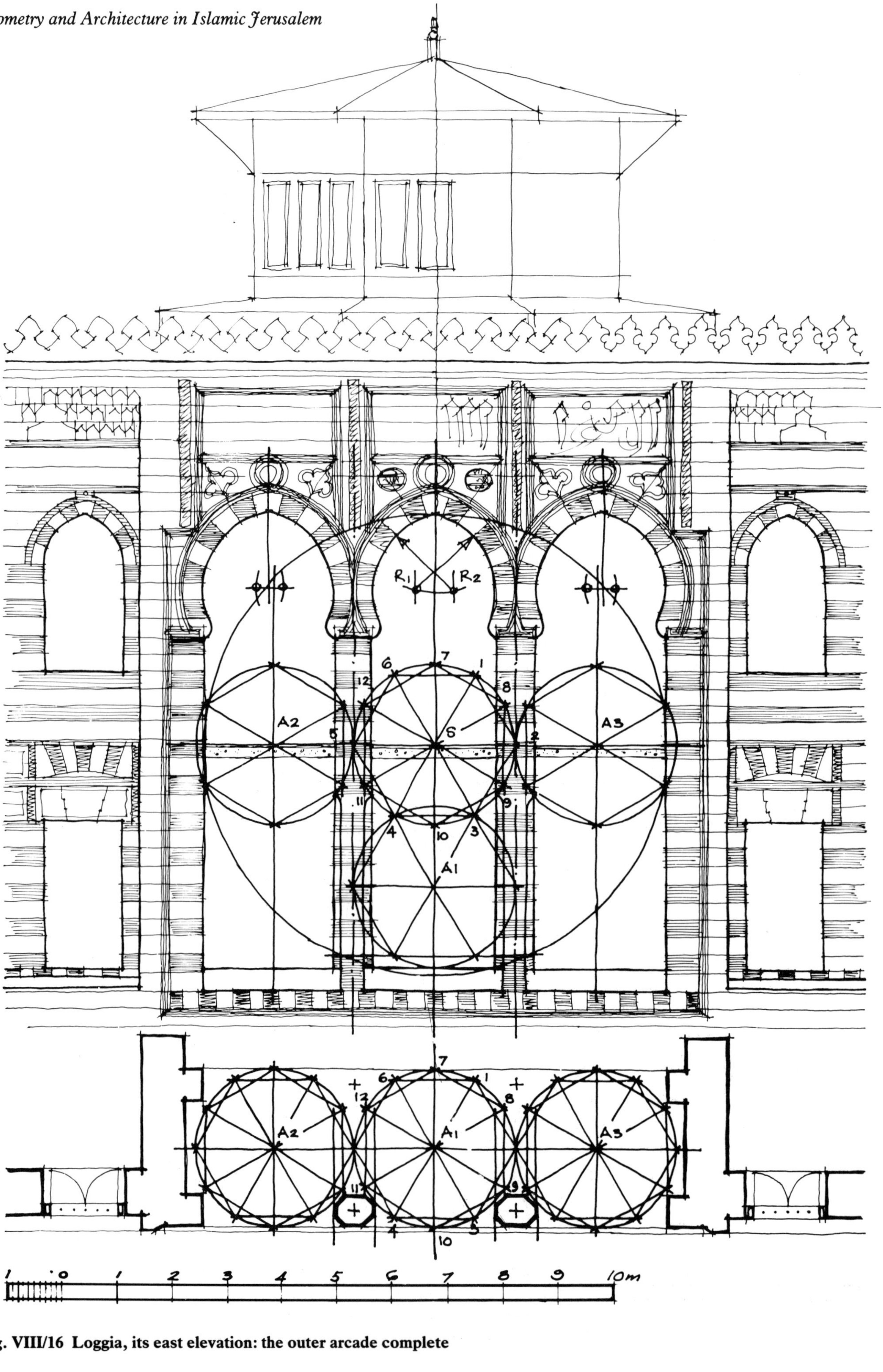

Fig. VIII/16 Loggia, its east elevation: the outer arcade complete

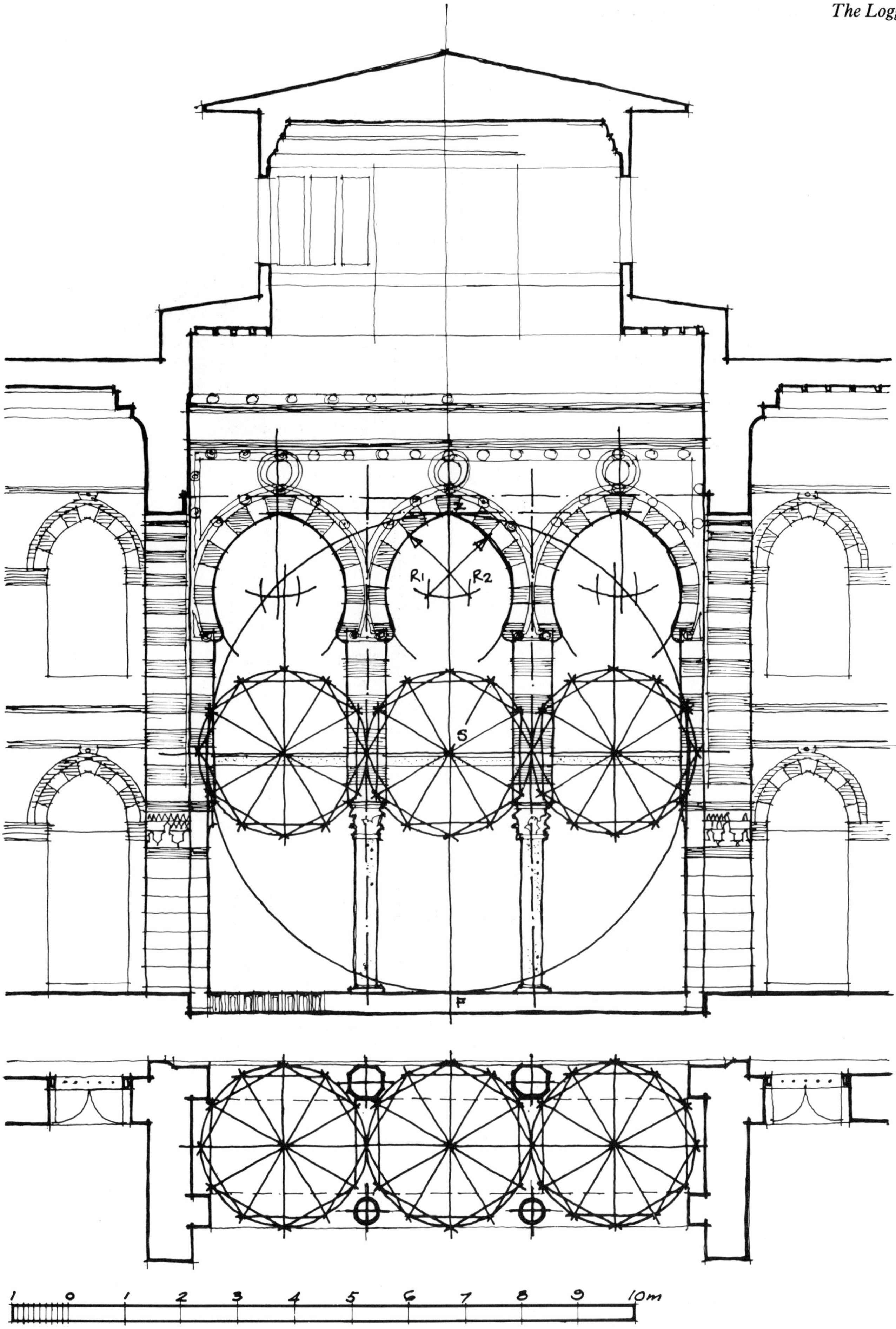

Fig. VIII/17 Loggia, its interior: the triple arched inner arcade complete

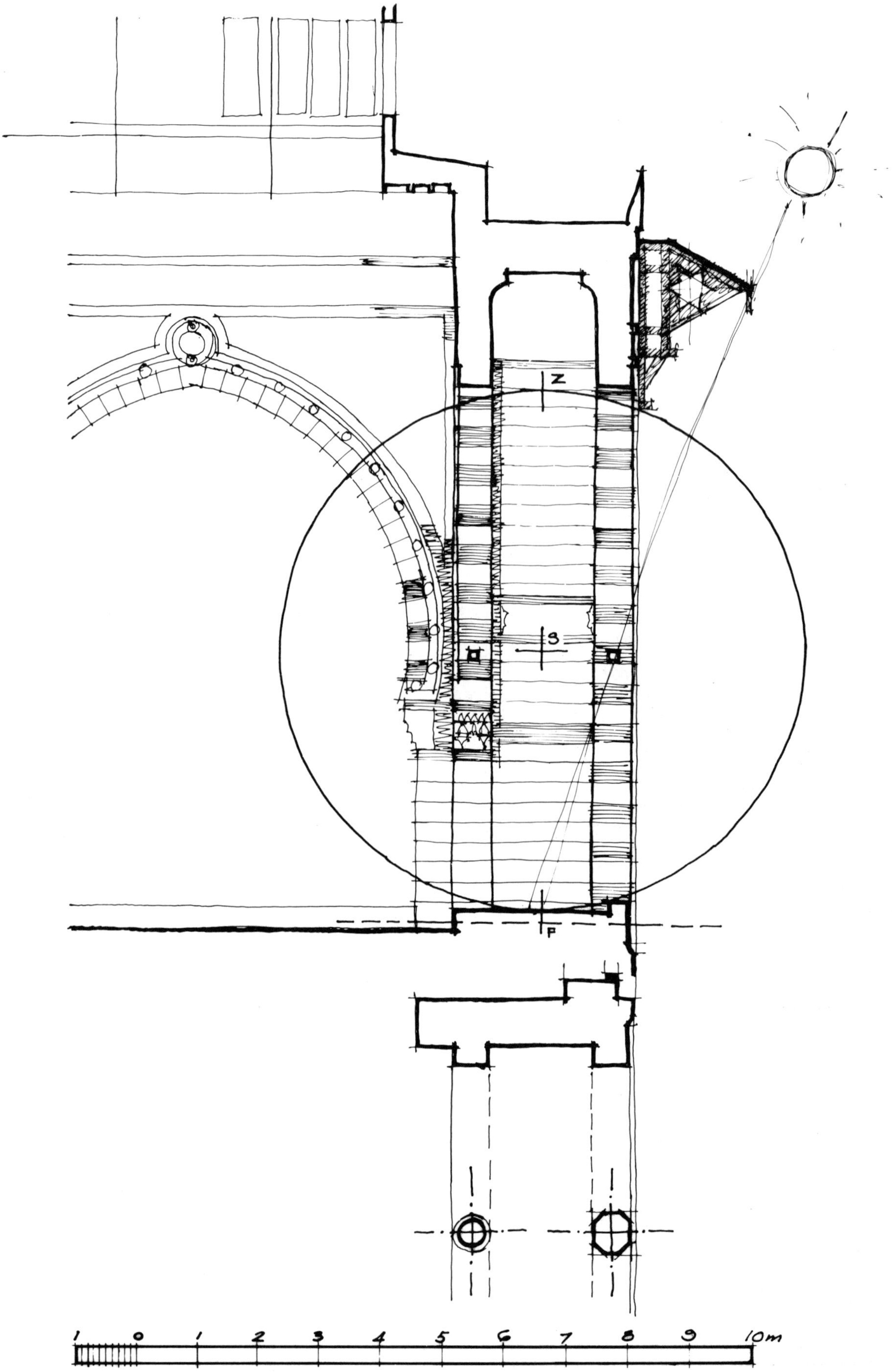

Fig. VIII/18 Loggia, north wall: the completed section

To complete the decoration of the upper wall surfaces, it is likely that the mouldings enclosed rectangular inscribed panels, and that four timber brackets supported a timber canopy to provide shade.

The Inner Arcade Detailed

Unlike the outer arcade, the spans of the interior arches are equal in size, for whilst small variations in the spans of the exterior arches might go unnoticed, the internal arches would have been under continuous scrutiny from close range. Consequently the internal arches have to equal the size of the central arch in the outer arcade, as it had the smaller span, and it is therefore the side arches which require to be reduced by making the necessary adjustments to the cantilever given to their imposts. **fig. VIII/17**

Nothing is known of the appearance of the two columns. They may have had *muqarnaṣāt* capitals or re-used Crusader ones, of which there are many examples in Jerusalem. But whatever their form, it is reasonable to assume, firstly, that the capitals of the marble columns were on approximately the same level as the impost blocks in order to retain the *ablaq* rhythms, and secondly, that the diameters of the bases and shafts suited the soffits of the arches.

Finally the inner and outer arcades are linked to complete the design of the loggia. This completed ensemble can now be combined with the other architectural units of the *ṣaḥn* and the three *īwāns*, to provide an overall architectural form for the Madrasa. Notwithstanding, one further element remains unresolved, the upper entrance, which though not essential to the general appreciation of the Madrasa nevertheless provides an attractive addition to it. **fig. VIII/18**

Notes
1. See van Berchem, *CIA 'Ville'*, figs. 63 and 64.
2. Op. cit., fig. 62.
3. The existing arched openings in the *qibla* wall and in the north wall of the Madrasa differ; they have arcs equal to 3/5 of the span, the proportion also used in the great arches and stilted western arch of the *ṣaḥn*.

Chapter IX
THE UPPER ENTRANCE

The Evidence

The restoration of the upper entrance leading to the Madrasa at the northern end of the courtyard must consider the evidence provided by three different sources: the existing features, two photographs taken by Creswell before the earthquake in 1927, and an inscription. Once gathered together the evidence can be consolidated to form a three dimensional framework which will determine the restored form of the upper entrance.

With the exception of the north wall of the courtyard where fragments of a portal remain, today it is difficult, in the area behind the north wall, to identify evidence which has any relevance to our study, for what little may remain is incorporated into a modern house.

fig. IX/1 In the north wall of the courtyard two vertical mouldings define the width of the portal, and horizontal mouldings define the width and height of the bench seats which flanked its doorway. Above these benches the width of the recess of the portal is provided by two red stones which abut the vertical mouldings. The remains of an inscription can be identified against the eastern moulding and, higher up and outside the line of this vertical moulding, there exist straight joints perhaps indicating the presence of an original window.

fig. IX/2 In one of his photographs, Creswell captures the eastern half of the north wall with considerably more of the portal than exists today, which allows the depth of the recess to be gauged. It also shows an inscription extending around half of the recess and into the door jamb. A *muqarnaṣ* bracket on the ingo of the jamb establishes the height of the door opening, and immediately above this a broken moulding framing a rectangular panel confirms the position of the sides and the height of the lost lintel. The shallow red course lying above is the remains of compartmentation.

The photograph shows the original window jambs as a pair of straight joints beginning at course number 9. The eastern jamb is four courses high giving the minimum height of the original window. At the level where course 15 would have been, a bonding hole exists in the wall of the Madrasa.

Despite the detail provided from this source, additional evidence is required to draw up an accurate plan.

fig. IX/3 Fortunately three of the stone blocks which made up the inscription have been identified in the Islamic Museum nearby, and through these not only can the dimensions of the portal recess be found, but the size of the vestibule and corridor leading to the Madrasa can be accurately assessed.[1]

The depth of the recess including its mouldings is found in the following manner: the combined length of two of the rediscovered blocks is 0.69m and when the 0.03m depth of the vertical moulding framing the portal is added it brings the total depth of the recess to 0.72mm, or $^1/_{20}$ BUG. The width of the recess can be calculated as follows: the length of the *in situ* block on the right hand side of the recess can be added to the constant thickness of the rediscovered blocks to give the distance from the vertical moulding to the beginning of the recess as 0.48m. This dimension when combined with the surveyed dimensions gives a recess width of 2.86m.

From the evidence offered by other Mamlūk entrance portals in Palestine, Egypt and Syria, it appears that there were a number of conventions which were generally followed in the construction of portals. One of these is that the door opening is equal to half the width of the recess. Applied here this 'rule' would produce an opening with a width of 1.43m—a difference of one centimetre from $^1/_{10}$ BUG.

Creswell's photograph of the exterior of the north wall shows parts of the recessed *ablaq* rear wall **fig. IX/4** of the vestibule and the springing of its vault. Another of his photographs gives a more detailed view of these internal features. In the jamb of the portal the end of the inscription and the *muqarnaṣ* brackets

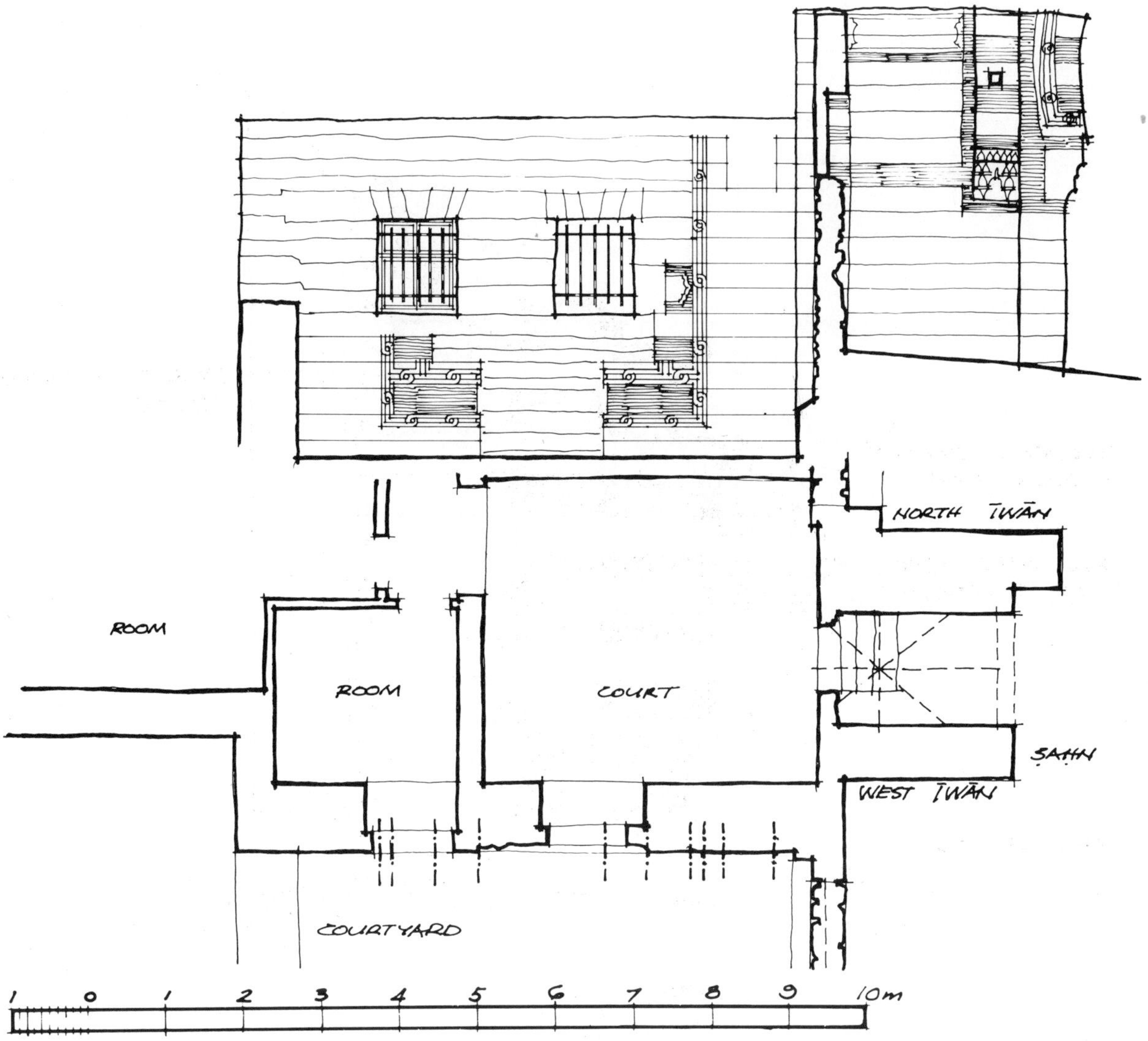

Fig. IX/1 Courtyard, north wall: the existing features

that once supported the lintel are visible. The inner reveals of the door continue to rise up and form an arch above it, and the springing of this arch coincides with that of the vault of the vestibule. In the east wall of the vestibule an arched opening with voussoirs and moulded archivolt leads towards the Madrasa. The voussoirs are unusual since they do not confirm to the strictly red-white-red *ablaq* sequence, but on one side appear as red-red-white-red-white, and on the other are separated by a red keystone from what appears to be three or four white stones, and one red stone. Above the opening an L-shaped stone can be seen which may have formed the lower left hand corner of a window.

It is clear from this photograph that the north wall of the vestibule was recessed, and it may even have had a bench set within it as did the recess in the vestibule on the ground floor. It is also possible to estimate from the photograph that the thickness of the stones in the wall at the rear of the recess was between one half and one third of their height.

The photograph confirms al-'Ulaymī's description of a vaulted room near the north *īwān* because the remains of a stone vault can be seen in the south east corner of the room behind the vestibule. Al-'Ulaymī mentions too that this room was entered by way of the vestibule and I have no doubt that this was so. However, the photograph shows that there was no direct connection between the vestibule immediately behind the entrance and the room, which means that the arrangement of the plan adhered to the general Islamic convention which requires the interior spaces of a building to be hidden from the public gaze. Thus a vestibule which could be regarded as a semi-public area would not be directly connected thereto. The foreground of the photograph shows the remains of a corridor or extension of the vestibule which may well have provided access to the vaulted room and to a stair leading to an upper corridor, although there is no extant evidence for such a stair.

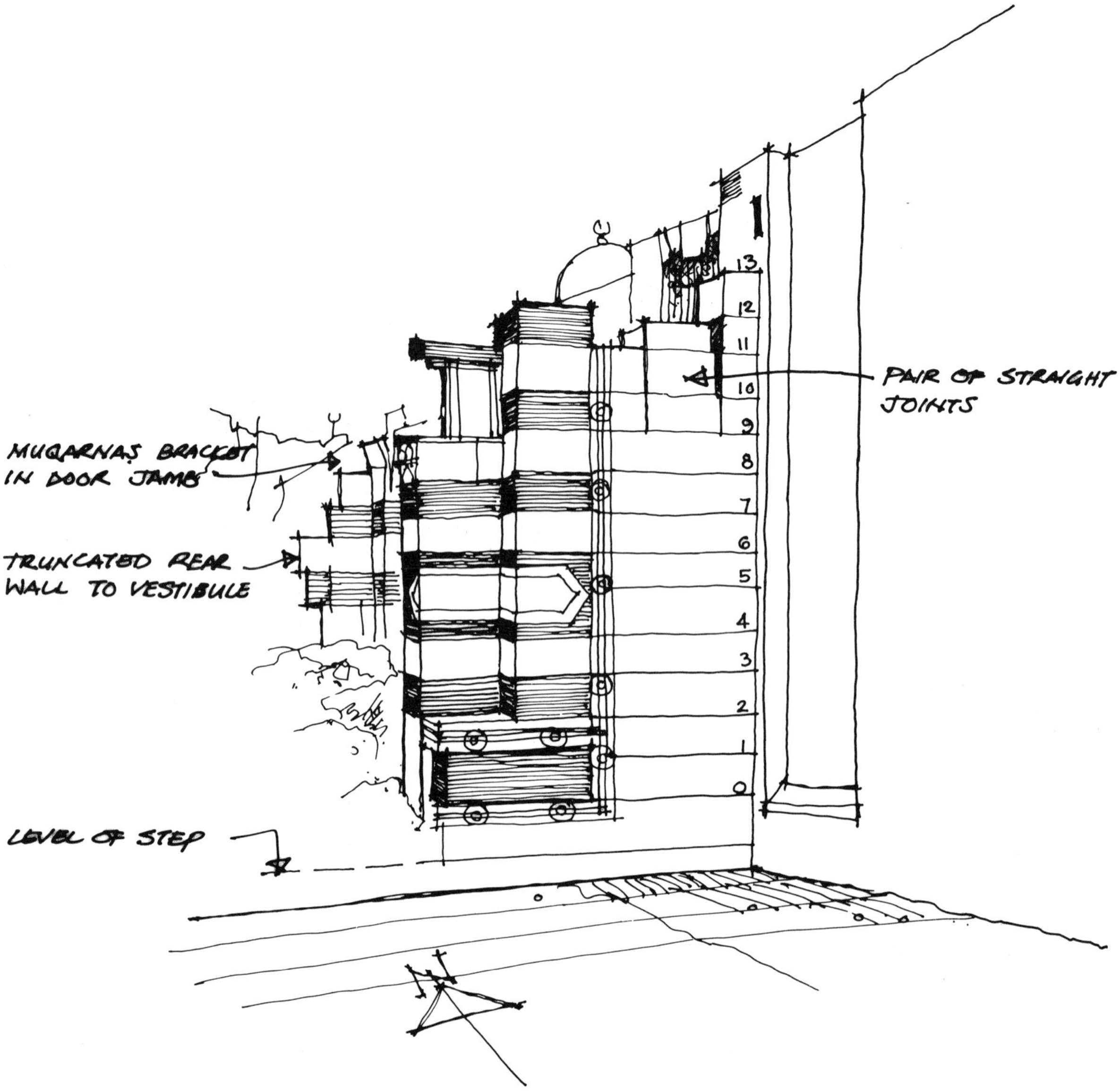

Fig. IX/2 Courtyard, north wall: after a photograph by Creswell showing remains of portal of upper entrance

It is more difficult to untangle and interpret the demolished vaults and masonry which lie beyond the arched doorway in the photograph. The space immediately beyond the arched doorway was spanned by a groin vault before narrowing to a width similar to that of the reveals of the arched doorway of the vestibule. Above this vaulted space, and represented by two straight joints in the upper courses of the wall of the Madrasa, there was a corridor that ended behind the recessed window, flanked by columns in the side wall of the *ṣaḥn*.

fig. IX/5 When this last photograph is compared to the grand entrance on the ground floor of the Ashrafiyya, a number of similarities can be seen which assist in the restoration of the details of the upper entrance.

The most obvious features common to both entrances are the arched doorways in the side walls of the vestibules. In the lower vestibule rectangular windows occur above the arches and these provide an answer to the question raised earlier by the cut stone above the arched opening in the upper vestibule. Undoubtedly, the cut stone is proof of a rectangular window here.

The jambs to both of the portal openings are similar. In each, two full *ablaq* courses separate the inscription and its compartmentation from the *muqarnaṣāt* brackets. An intricate fan vault spans the lower vestibule with distinctive springers in its four corners, and in Creswell's photograph a similarly distinctive springer is seen in the corner of the upper vestibule to provide certain evidence that here too an intricate fan vault had been built.

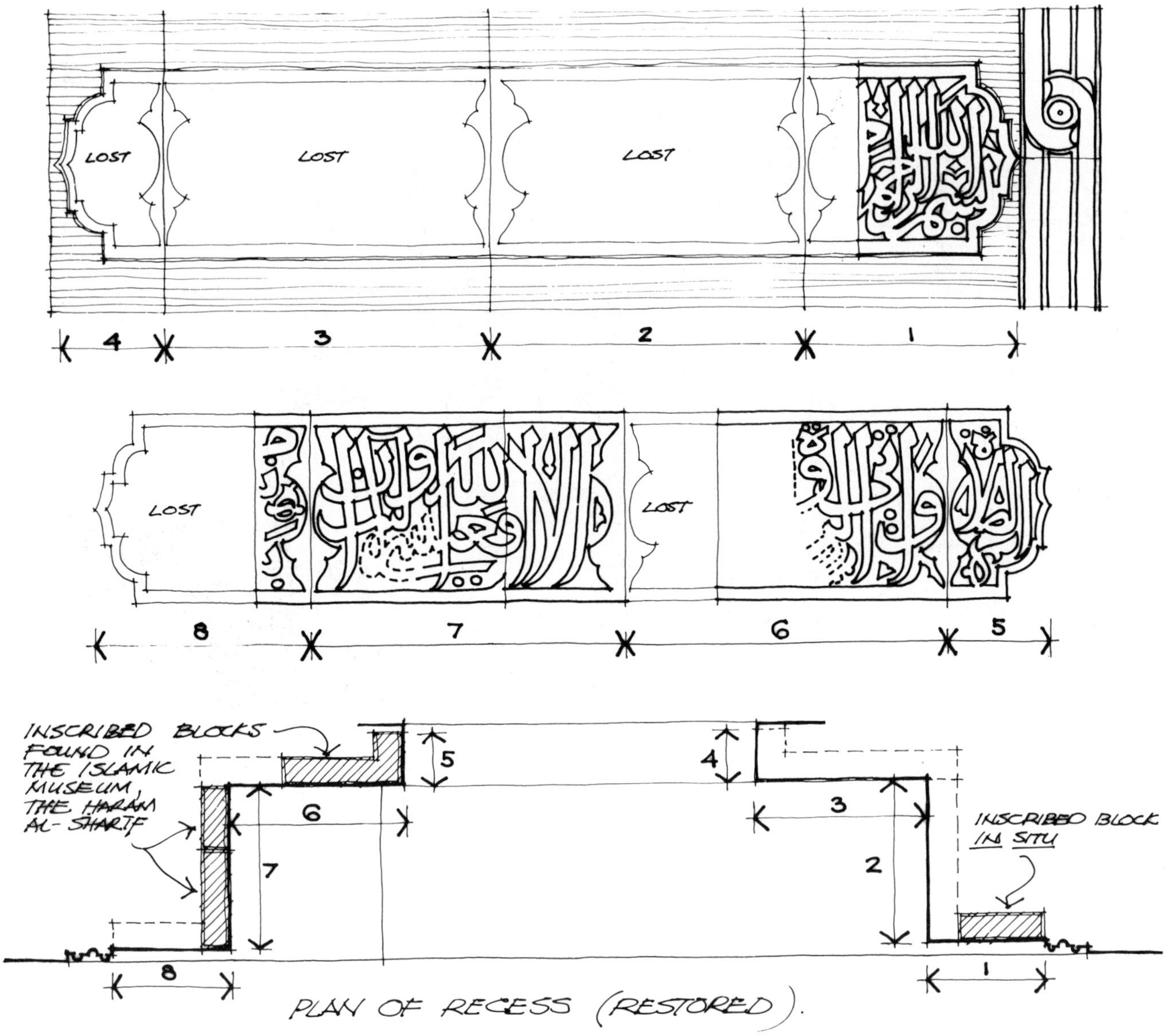

Fig. IX/3 Upper entrance: the inscription

Another similarity is found in the windows which flank the framed portals: on the ground floor they light the spaces adjacent to the vestibule, and it would therefore be expected that the space behind the arched doorway of the upper vestibule would likewise have been lit by two windows, now represented by the straight joints to the east of the moulded frame of the portal. The plans of the space behind the arched doorway and the ruined walls seen in the foreground of the photograph resemble those of the adjacent spaces on the ground floor, which is logical since their functions are similar.

Were it not for Creswell's second photograph, it would be almost impossible to unravel the essential features of the exterior of the Madrasa seen from the small court. Over the years various layers of plaster and cement and liberal coats of paint have been applied to the wall, but uşing the evidence provided by the photograph, a drawing can be made which adds these features to those still in existence. **fig. IX/6**

Valuable evidence is provided by the short stretch of the original corridor that now leads to the *ṣaḥn*. This establishes the following features: firstly, its width is equal to 1/10 BUG (also the width of the corridor on the ground floor); secondly, its main axis is precisely positioned; thirdly, its existing but truncated groin vault can be measured so as to locate the levels of its springing and its zenith, and despite the damage it sustained the drawing shows how the two lost springings can be easily retrieved by extending the groins. Finally, the coursing of the masonry in the corridor is contiguous with the coursing in the *ṣaḥn*. **fig. IX/7**

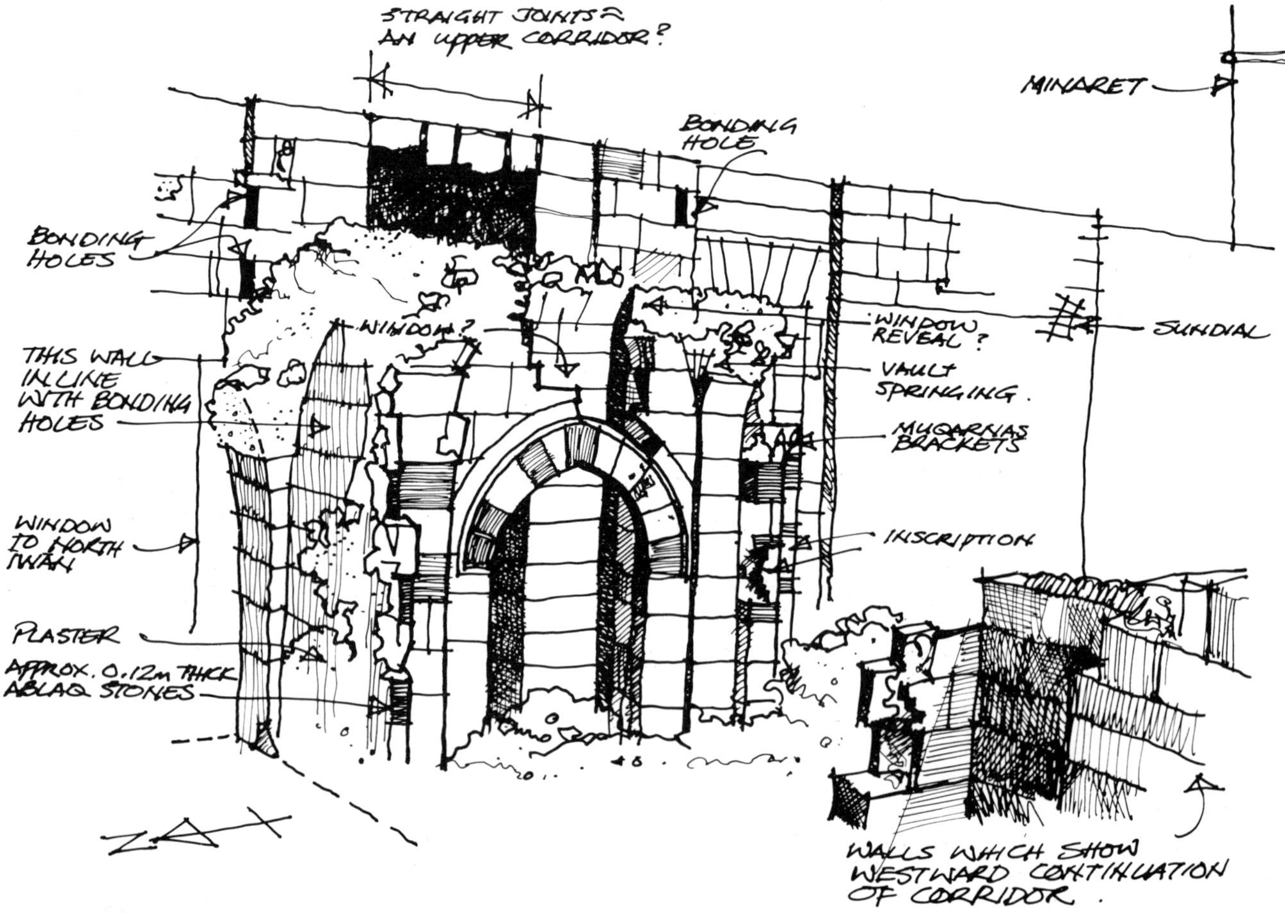

Fig. IX/4 Upper entrance: after a photograph by Creswell

The Architectural Framework

Having now assembled this evidence, the architectural features of the upper entrance are beginning to fall into place. At the same time the construction of the architectural framework, involving the arrangement of the material into a three-dimensional plan, has begun. The clearest way to portray this process and the images produced is in drawings which can be compared to each other and will gradually move towards a complete reconstruction.

fig. IX/8 The first drawing in the sequence shows in plan and elevation the original details, which still exist in the north wall of the courtyard, set alongside the restored external wall and west *īwān* of the Madrasa.

Only the lower components of the portal and two courses of the rectangular window remain. However, the drawing reconfirms previous statements concerning the contiguity of the external and internal stone courses, and the plan shows clearly the two main axes of the upper entrance and their point of intersection. Also, in the plan the springers of the completed groin vault coincide with the line joining the rear wall of the external window recess of the west *īwān* and the outer face of the wall of the north *īwān*.

fig. IX/9 By adding the evidence in Creswell's photographs and the dimensions provided by the inscribed blocks, the plan of the portal is established, including the width of the door opening and jambs. In addition a number of elevational details are confirmed. In the portal, the door threshold, the height of the door opening, the form of the lintel and its upper compartmentation have already been established. Outwith the framed area of the portal, the height of the rectangular window can now be seen to be four courses, as is the second rectangular window which is needed to give symmetry to this elevation.

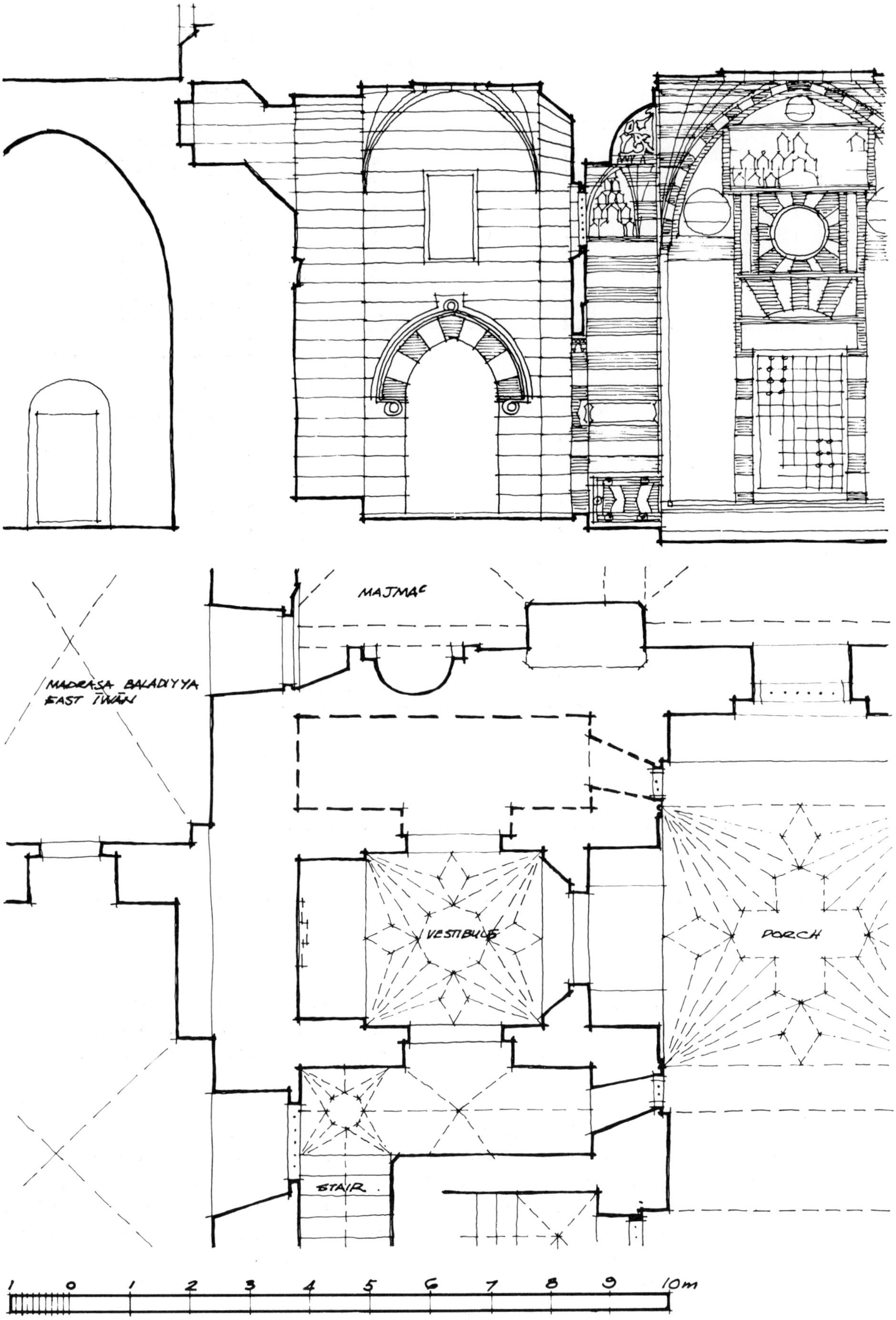

Fig. IX/5 The grand entrance coming from the Ḥaram into the Ashrafiyya

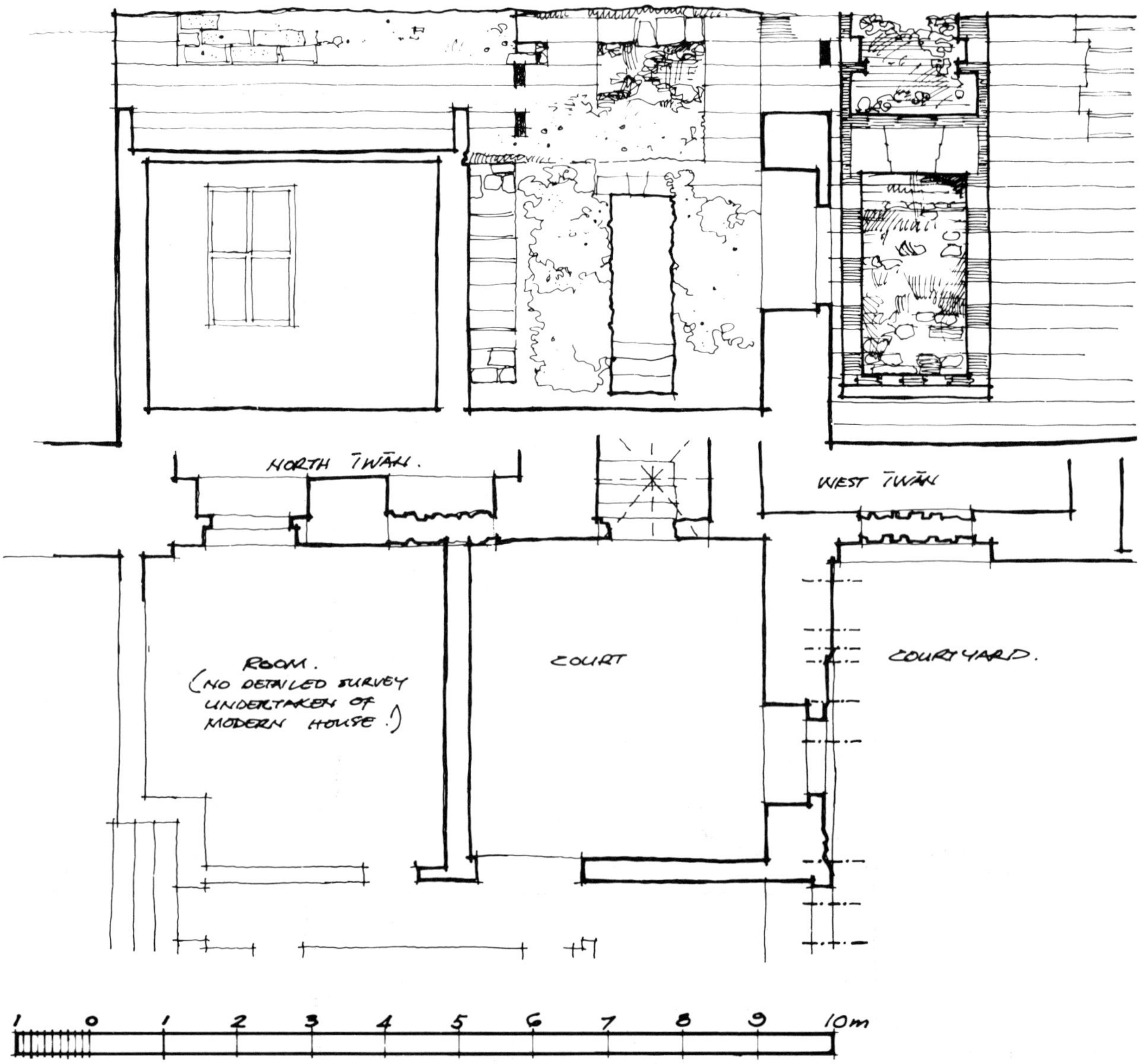

Fig. IX/6 Upper entrance: the existing features of the west wall of the Madrasa with the aid of the Creswell photographs

Internally the upper vestibule and its flanking corridors are arranged about the two main axes of the plan, and it would appear that their point of intersection is also the central point of the vestibule. The relative positions and sizes of the walls, estimated from the photographs, create a plan similar to that of the vestibule on the ground floor, albeit on a smaller scale.

fig. IX/10, 11 When sections incorporating all the known evidence are drawn along the main axes of the upper vestibule and entry to the *ṣaḥn*, the floors of the vestibule and the *ṣaḥn* are discovered to be level. These sections also define the heights of the arched doorways and associated rectangular windows in the side walls of the vestibule, and the heights and forms of the vaults spanning these internal spaces.

fig. IX/11 The section running parallel to the exterior wall of the Madrasa includes two rectangular window openings which connect the north *īwān* to the vaulted room. Since the west wall contains evidence of the corridor above the vestibule which was noted by al-'Ulaymī, it can be assumed that the arched clerestories opened into a room set above the vault which could be reached by way of this corridor. There may even have been two corridors, each lit by one of the rectangular windows set above the entry to the *ṣaḥn*. (Had two corridors been sandwiched between the vault over the vestibule and the roof they would have been cramped, cold, damp and rather dark—characteristics not unknown in the back stairs and corridors of its great contemporaries in Cairo.)

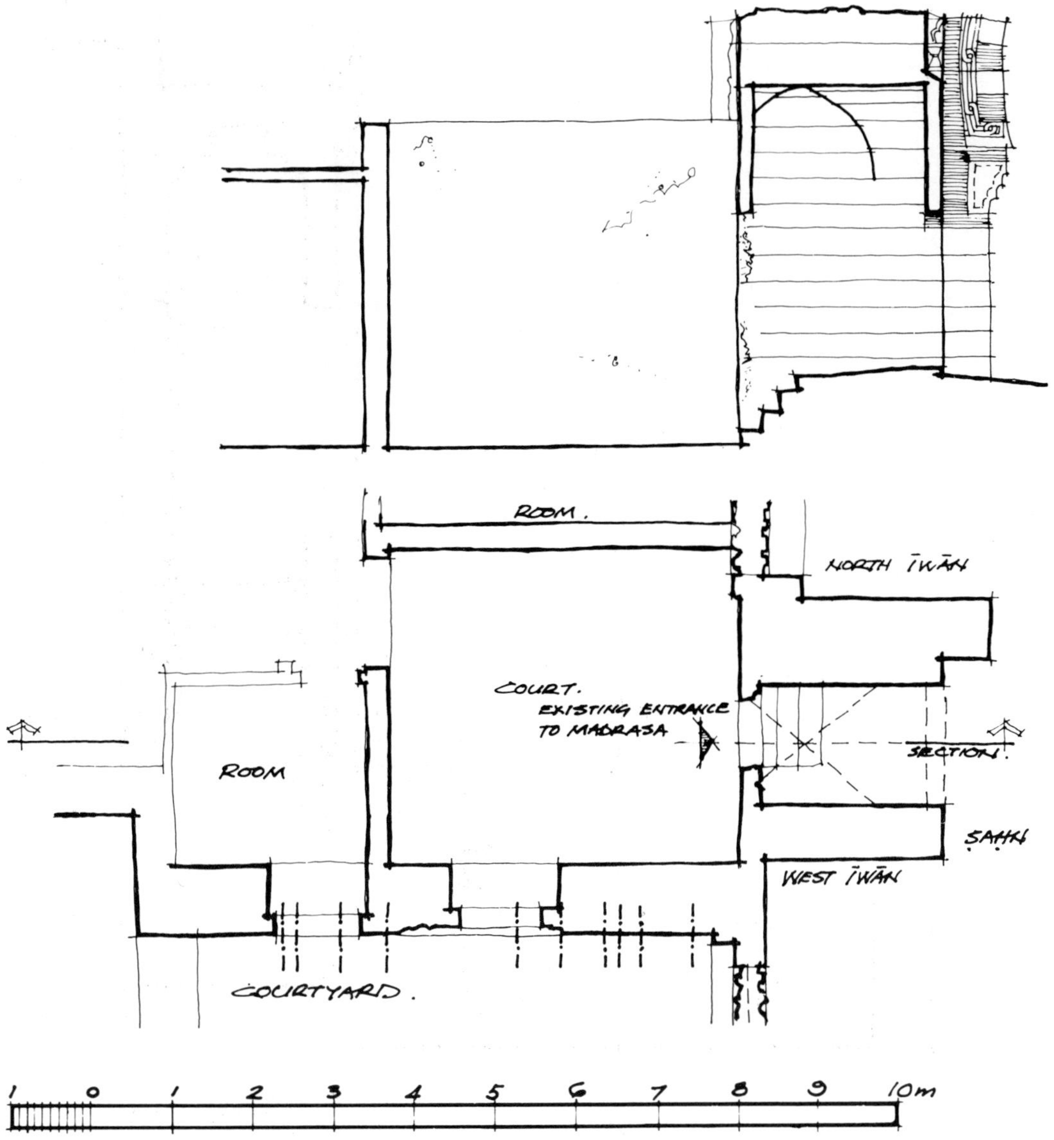

Fig. IX/7 Upper entrance, entry to the *ṣaḥn*: the existing features

The Geometries

Having used Creswell's photographs, together with the inscription and the existing evidence, to restore in part the upper entrance, it is now possible to verify the design through the geometries based on the BUG, despite slight variations in the dimensions of the recess and door opening. In the detailed geometries of the Madrasa $^1/_{10}$ BUG radius circles have been used successfully and it would therefore seem likely that these would apply here, especially since it has already been shown that the width of the recess is approximately $^1/_5$ BUG and its depth $^1/_{20}$ BUG.

Firstly, the $^1/_{10}$ BUG radius circle centred on point P is drawn in plan, point P coinciding with the central axis of the portal on the face of the north wall of the courtyard. Having done this, it becomes apparent that the circumference of this circle is tangential to the line separating the arched recess immediately inside the doorway from the south side of the vault of the vestibule. **fig. IX/12**

A hexagon (1-6) can now be inscribed within the circle in such a way that its diameter 5-2 lies along the external wall face. This places both points 5 and 2 in line with the west and east ingos of the portal recess.

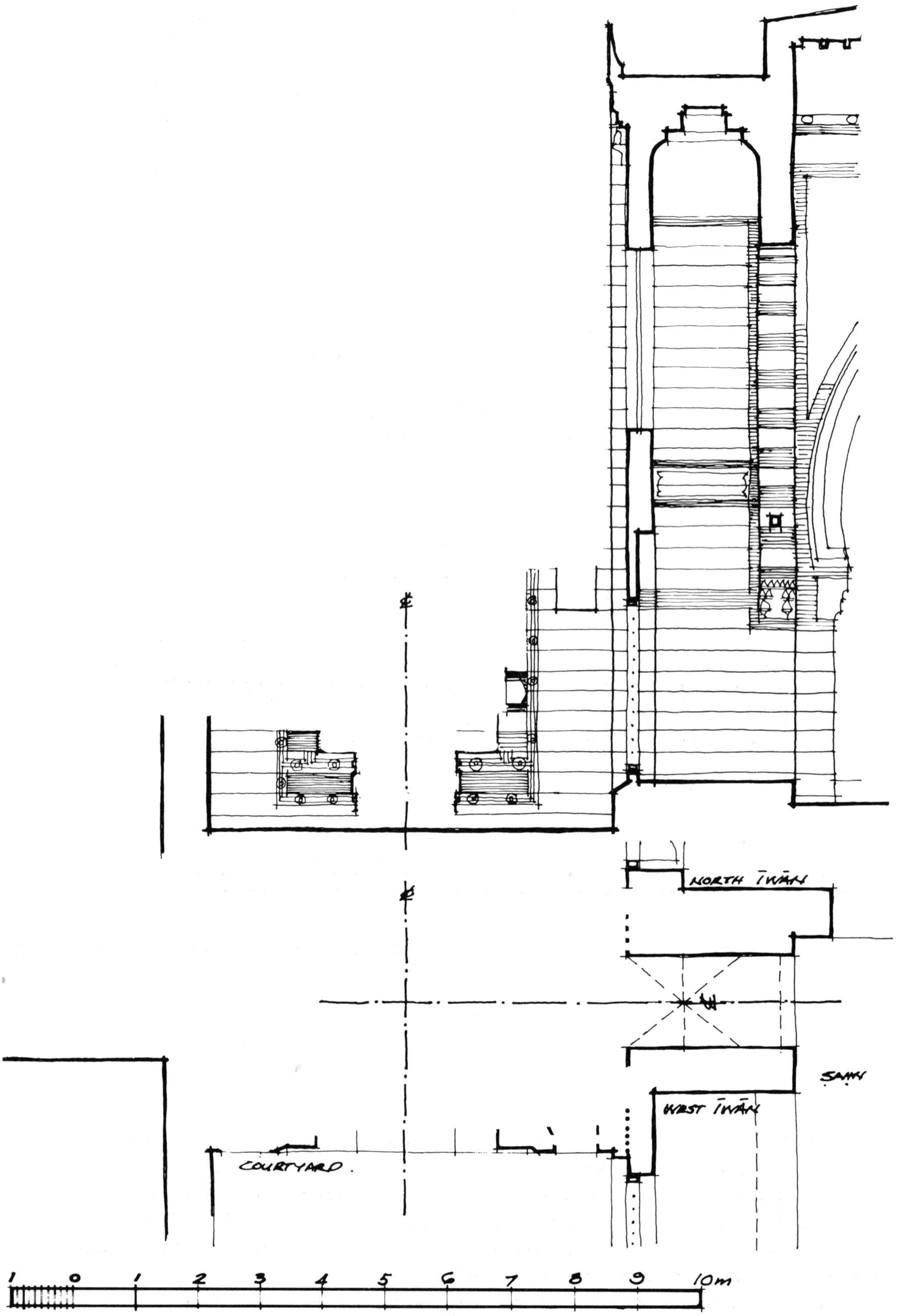

Fig. IX/8 Upper entrance, the portal: the existing features with the restored west *īwān* added

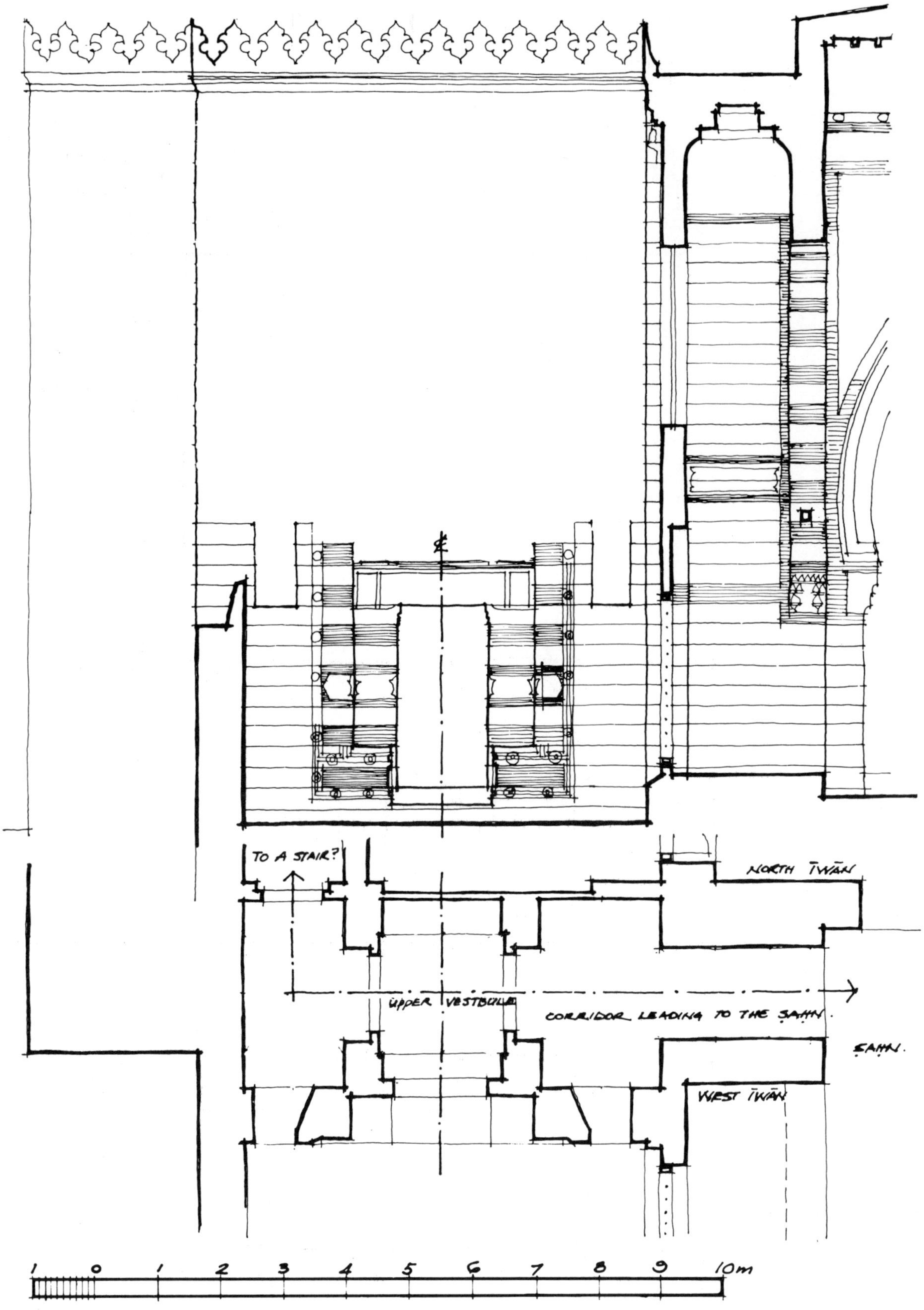

Fig. IX/9 Upper entrance, the portal: the evidence combined

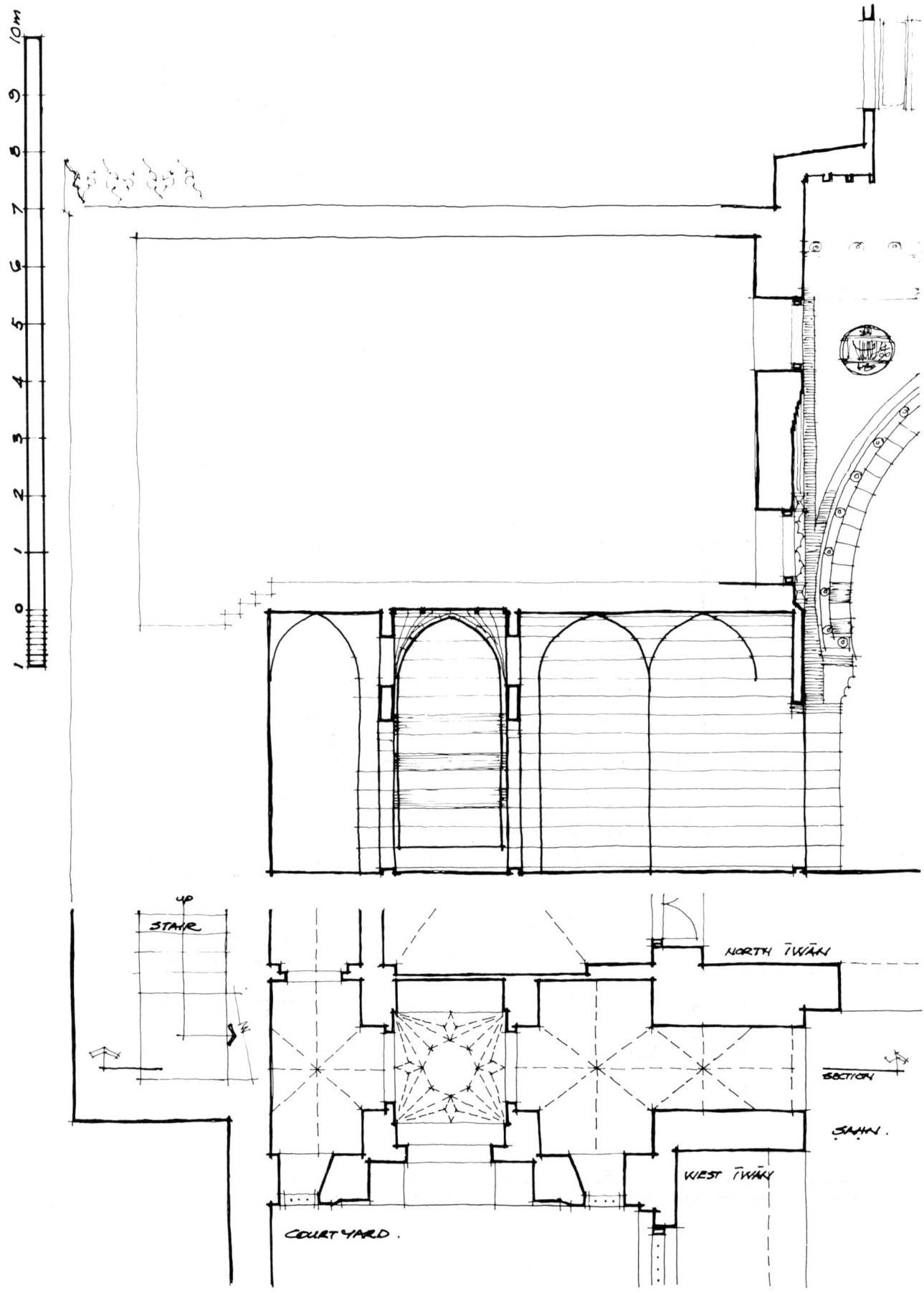

Fig. IX/10 Upper entrance, entry to the *ṣaḥn*: the evidence interpreted

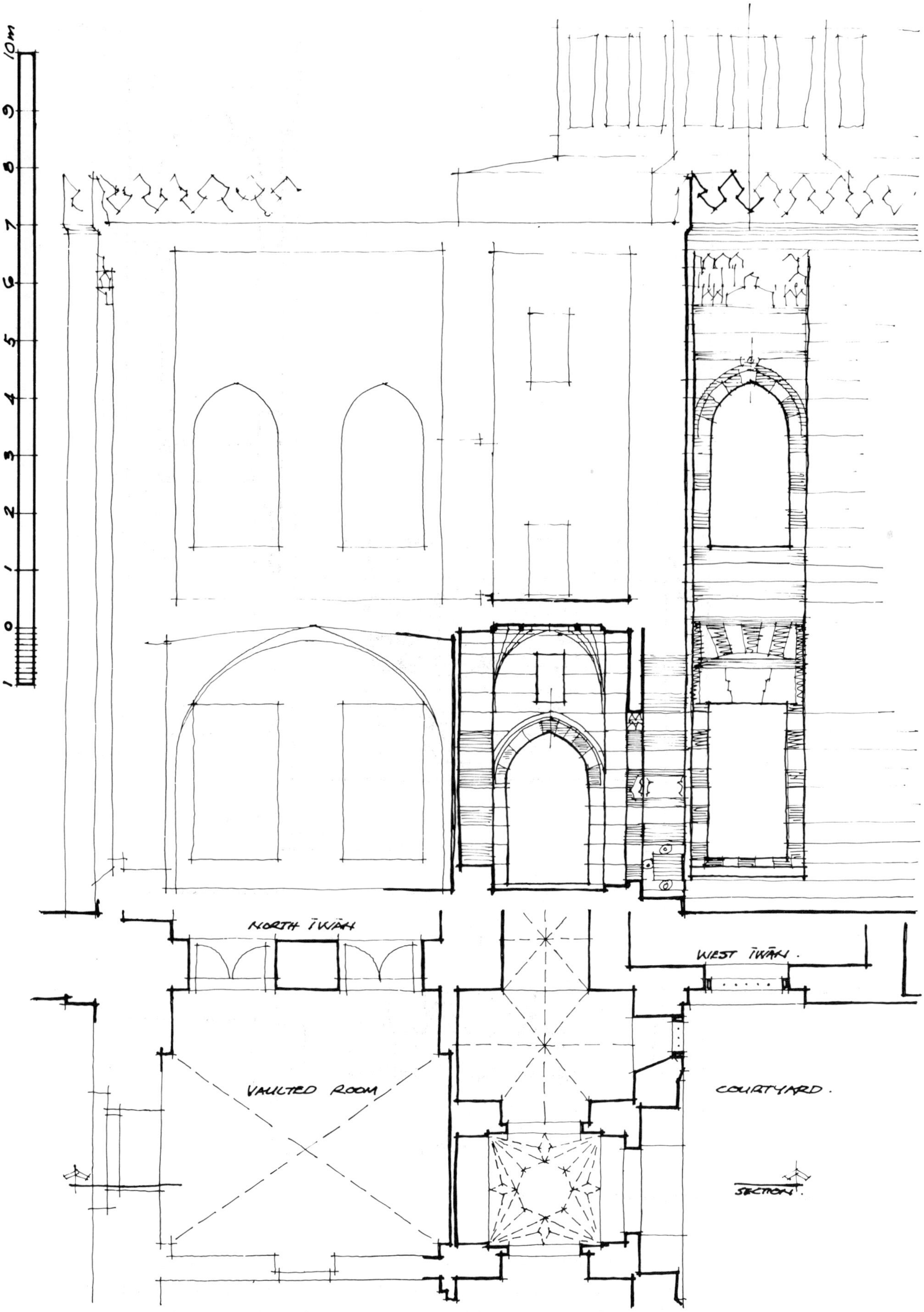

Fig. IX/11 Upper entrance, the portal and vestibule: the evidence interpreted

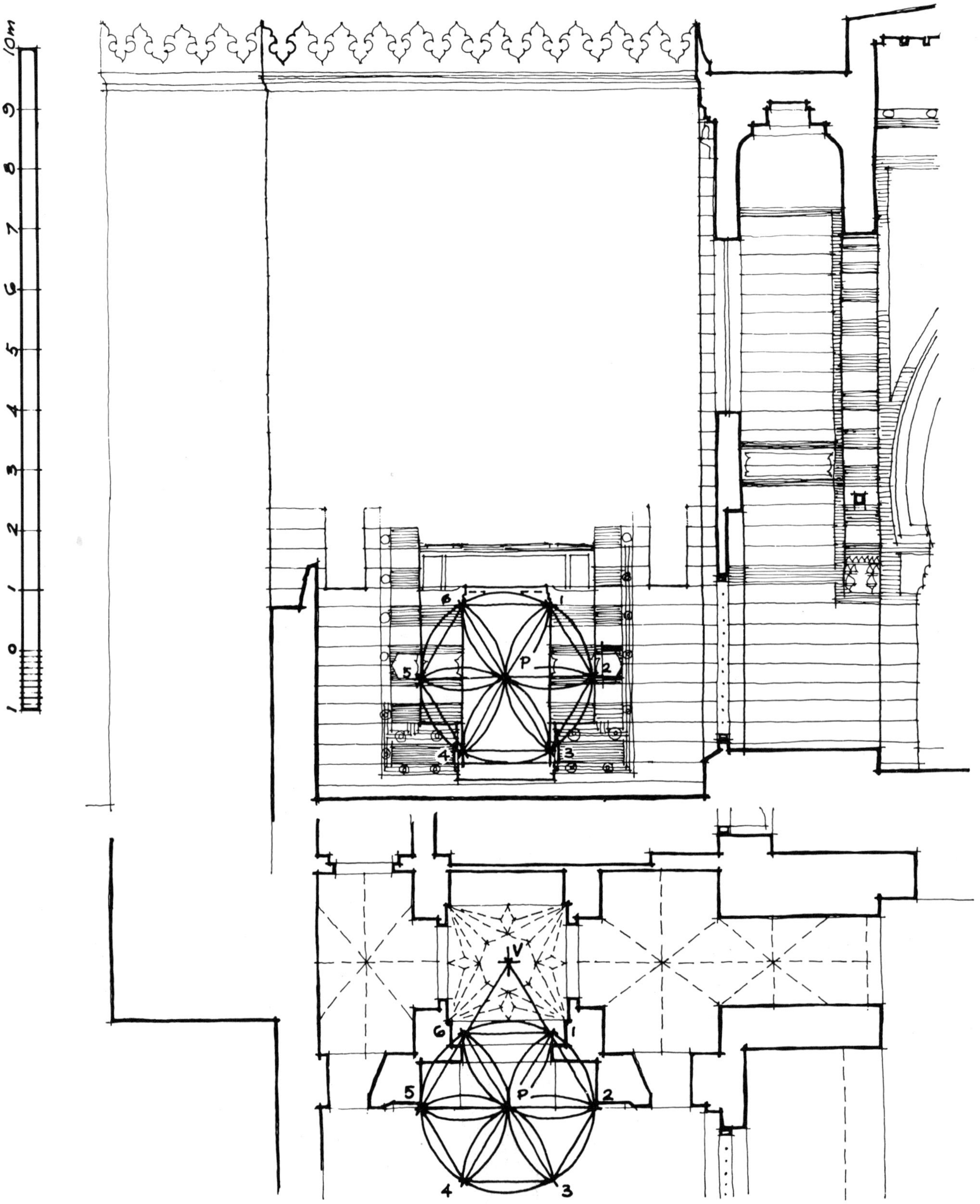

Fig. IX/12 Upper entrance, the portal: a fundamental geometry

The centre of the vestibule, point V, is also found through this figure. When sides 5-6 and 2-1 of the hexagon are produced they intersect each other at V to form an equilateral triangle (5-V-2) with sides equal to 1/5 BUG. This is an interesting geometrical relationship for it repeats, albeit at one fifth of the scale, the similar construction based on the fundamental geometry of the Madrasa which in plan defined the position of the *miḥrāb*.

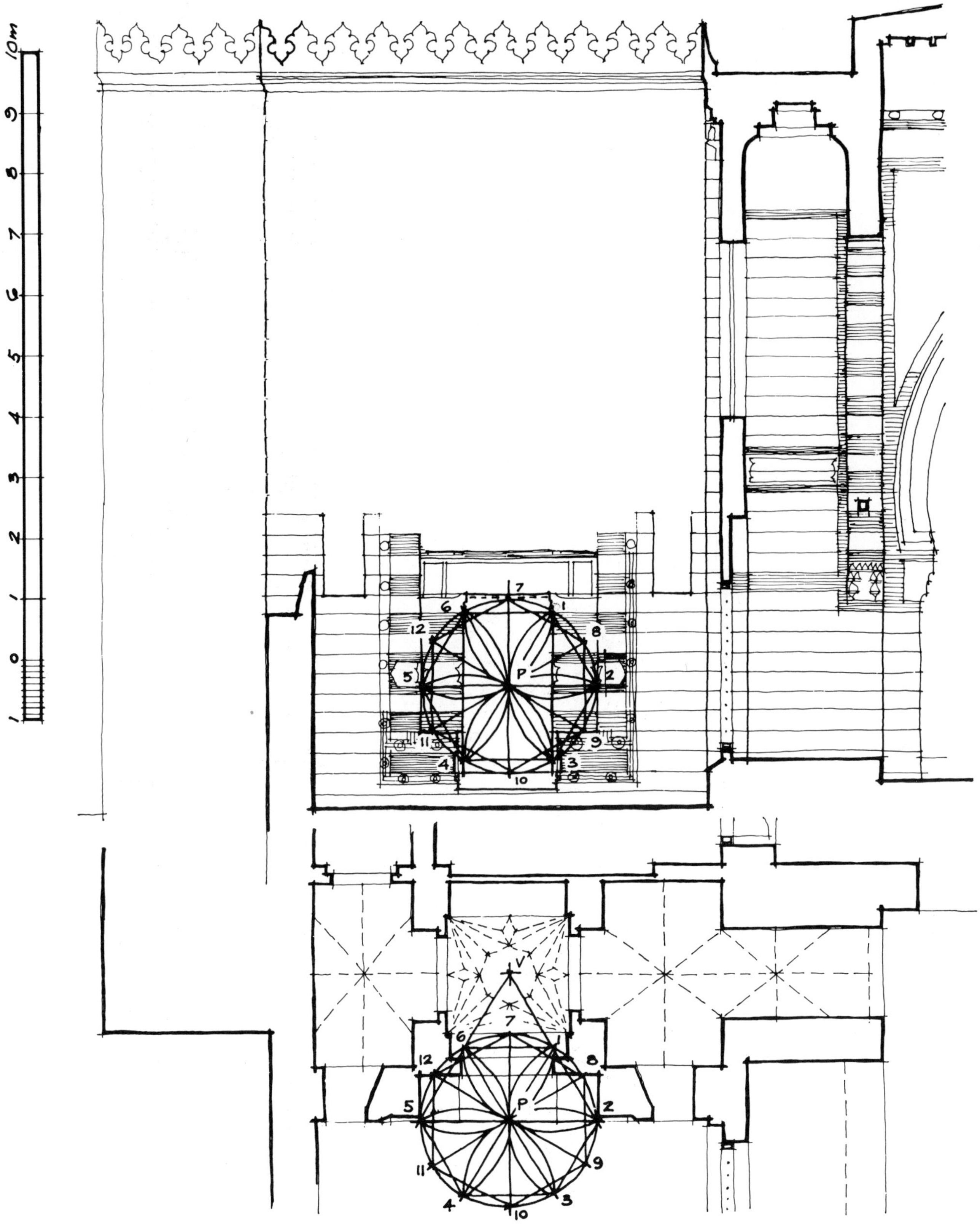

Fig. IX/13 Upper entrance, the portal: a primary geometry

When the 1/10 BUG radius circle is applied to the elevation of the north wall of the courtyard, with its centre P on a level with the base of the inscription running across the portal, it is found that the circumference is tangential to the threshold of the door opening. The threshold level also coincides with the top of the stone course in which is carved the lower side of the moulded frame surrounding the portal. This course also acts as the base line for all the external window recesses in the external wall

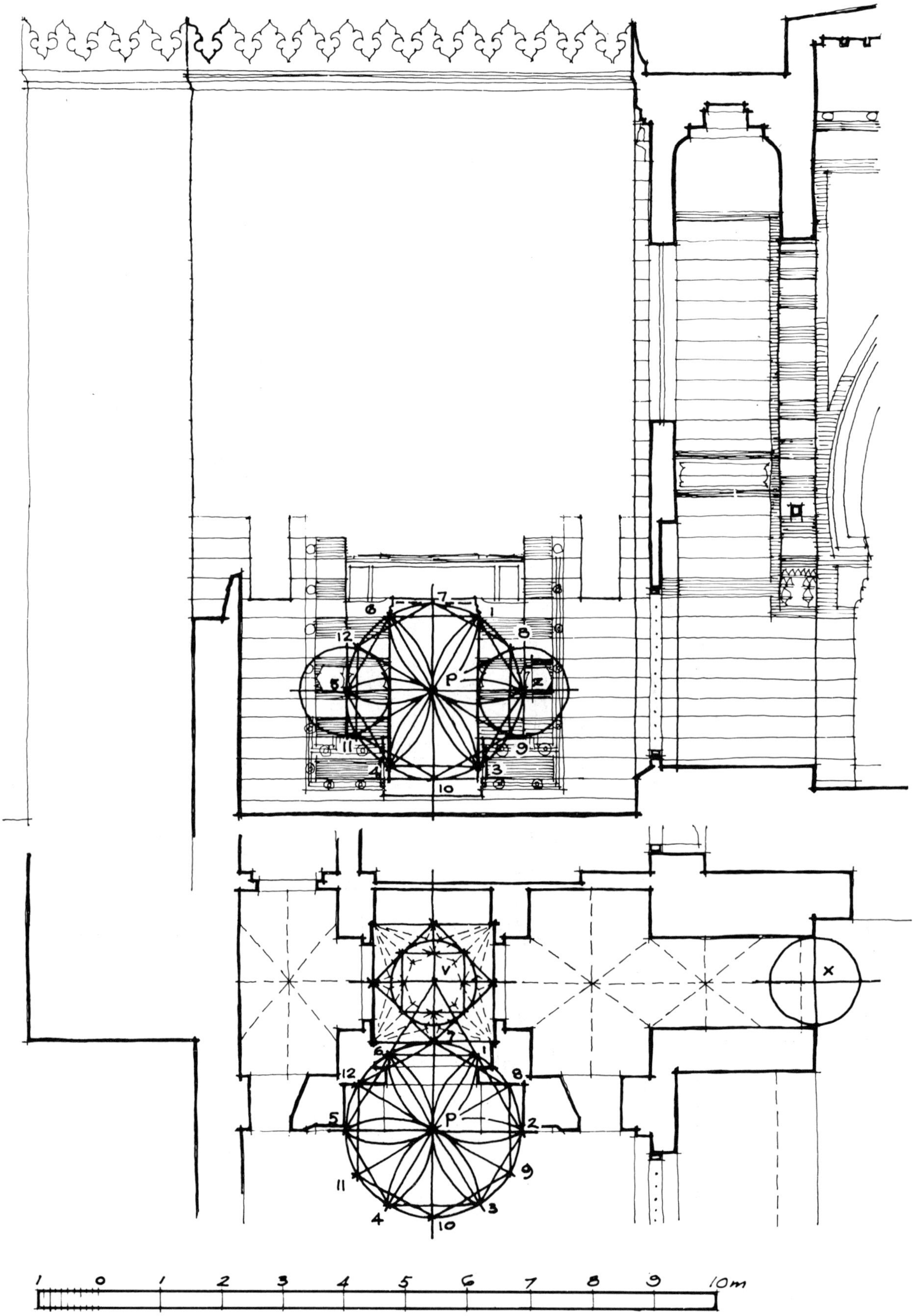

Fig. IX/14 Upper entrance, the portal and vestibule: detailed geometries

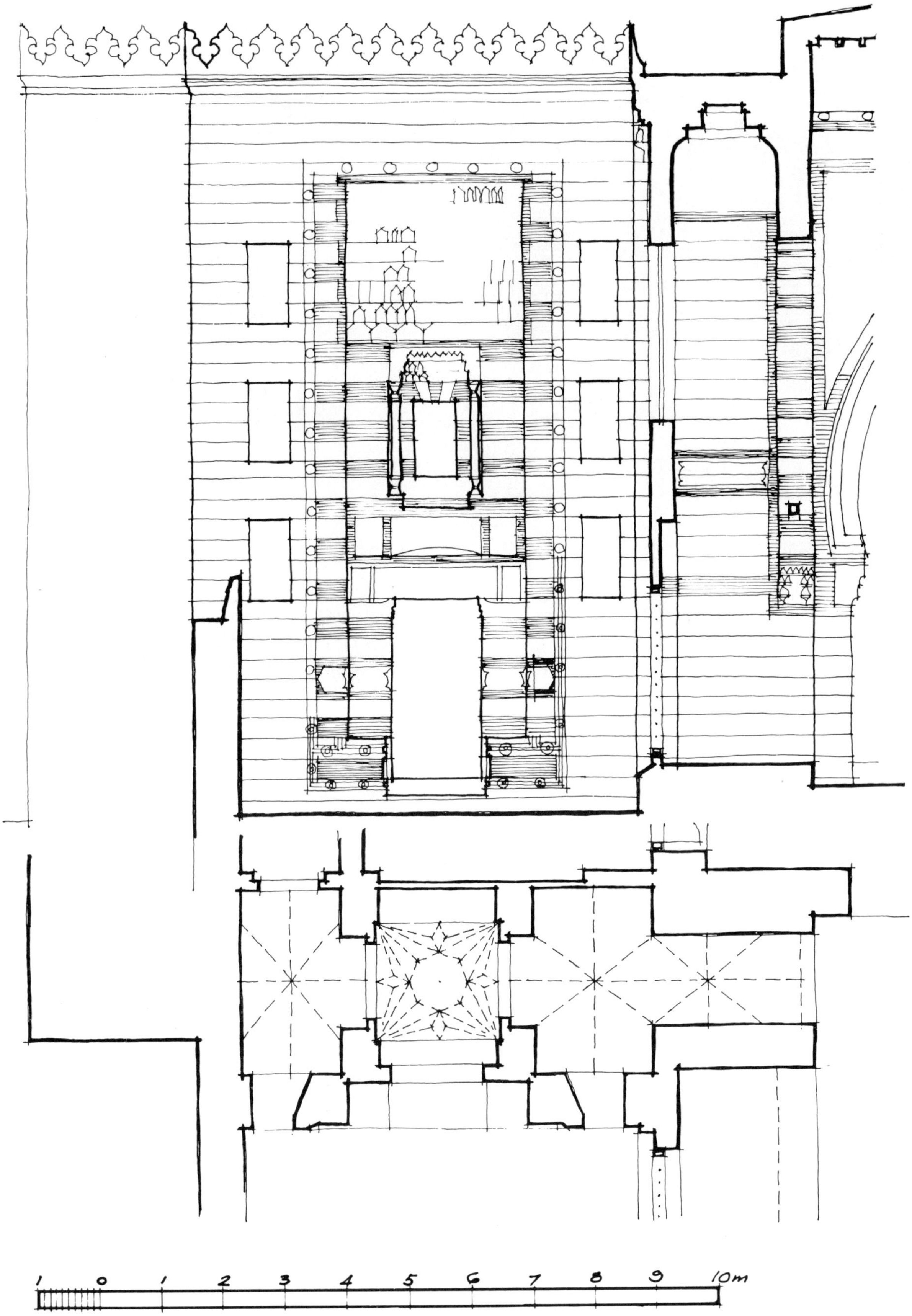

Fig. IX/15 Upper entrance, the portal: a possible design

Plate 18 Cairo, House of Qāytbāy: a portal recess spanned by rectilinear *muqarnaṣāt*. (Tarchi, *L'Architettura e l'Arte Musulmane in Egitto e nella Palestina*, tav. 98 top)

Plate 19 Cairo, House of Qāytbāy: a portal recess spanned by rectilinear *muqarnaṣāt*

of the Madrasa, and it continues into the Madrasa to become the lowest visible stone course in the *ṣaḥn*. Tracing this joint further across the Madrasa it appears on the east elevation where it defines the top of the joggled *ablaq* string course running across the loggia (see VIII/18). When taken together, these facts indicate the architect regarded this threshold level as one of significance in his overall design.

To return again to the vertical geometry and to the circle centred on P, it can be seen that on the top of its circumference is tangential to the line of the lower edge of the narrow moulding running below the door lintel (see dotted line). If then a hexagon (1-6) is inscribed therein, the side 6-1 is level with the top of the highest red stone course in the jambs of the door opening, and the jambs are themselves defined by lines 1-3 and 4-6.

fig. IX/13 If we regard the horizontal geometry as a miniature fundamental geometry, the next geometry in the sequence would be a miniature primary geometry formed by inscribing a double hexagon (1-12) in the 1/10 BUG radius circle centred on P.

Upon completing the double hexagon the points 12 and 8 coincide with the rear wall of the recess thus confirming a previously known relationship. If a double hexagon is centred on P, then in elevation points 9 and 11 are found to be level with the tops of the stone benches within the portal recess which flank the door opening.

fig. IX/14 Again, if this geometry is developed according to the sequence established on a larger scale in the Madrasa, a miniature detailed geometry evolves. The previous geometries have already defined the salient points in the plan of the portal recess. However, the detailed geometries can help to give a geometric structure to the plan of the vestibule.

With centre V a circle is drawn with a radius equal to 1/20 BUG, since the width of the entrance corridor has already been established as 1/10 BUG (this is confirmed by the 1/10 BUG diameter circle centred on point X). The circle with centre V is then described by a square with sides equal to 1/10 BUG which is set at 45° to the main axes of the entrance. One of its corners coincides with point 7, and the other three corners mark the midpoints along the sides of the fan vaulting. Additionally, two of these corners locate the centres of the doors in the side walls. A larger square enclosing the last square defines the boundaries of the fan vaulting.

Returning to the circle drawn about point V, if another square is constructed within it with sides parallel to the main axes, the points at which the square intersects with the axes coincide with the essential corners of the octagonal shaped centre of the vault.

Looking now at the detailed geometry in elevation, by drawing circles centred on points 5 and 2, with radii of 1/20 BUG, each can be seen to be approximately tangential to the sides of the frame to the portal, and also to coincide with the jambs of the door opening.

fig. IX/15 There is no further physical evidence available to allow us to extend further this restoration of the upper entrance. However, the *waqfiyya* does provide further details, it refers to a window flanked by a pair of marble columns and to the recess being spanned by a *muqarnaṣ* head. Is it coincidence that the details follow the pattern of an existing portal in the House of Qāytbāy in Cairo, the house which provided the model for the arcaded loggia? The only other details that can be assumed to have been included in the design of the portal are the two sets of windows lying outside the framed area, they would have been necessary to light the upper corridors.

Note

1. It is interesting that the left half of the inscription had disappeared when van Berchem visited the site in 1914. Since then the right half has disappeared whilst the left was rediscovered by Miss Abul-Hajj and identified by me in the Islamic Museum in the Ḥaram. The text is from Qur'ān IX:18 and reads: 'Bismallāh. He only shall tend Allāh's sanctuaries who believeth in Allāh and the Last Day and observeth proper worship and payeth the poor—due and feareth none save Allāh. For such only is it possible that they can be rightly guided.' The text is well chosen for it can be taken to refer to both the function and position of the Ashrafiyya.

Chapter X
THE RECONSTRUCTION

Eleven drawings have been chosen to illustrate the restored form of the Ashrafiyya. The architectural elements can be seen in the new light now that further relationships, both geometric and decorative, have been established.

The order of the drawings follows the steps taken by our investigation, beginning with the plan of the Madrasa. The subsequent drawings (sections or elevations) start with the *ṣaḥn* and gradually progress towards the conclusion—the east elevation, the facade which looks out on to the Ḥaram and beyond, and which established the unique reputation of the Ashrafiyya as the Third Jewel of the Third Shrine of Islam.

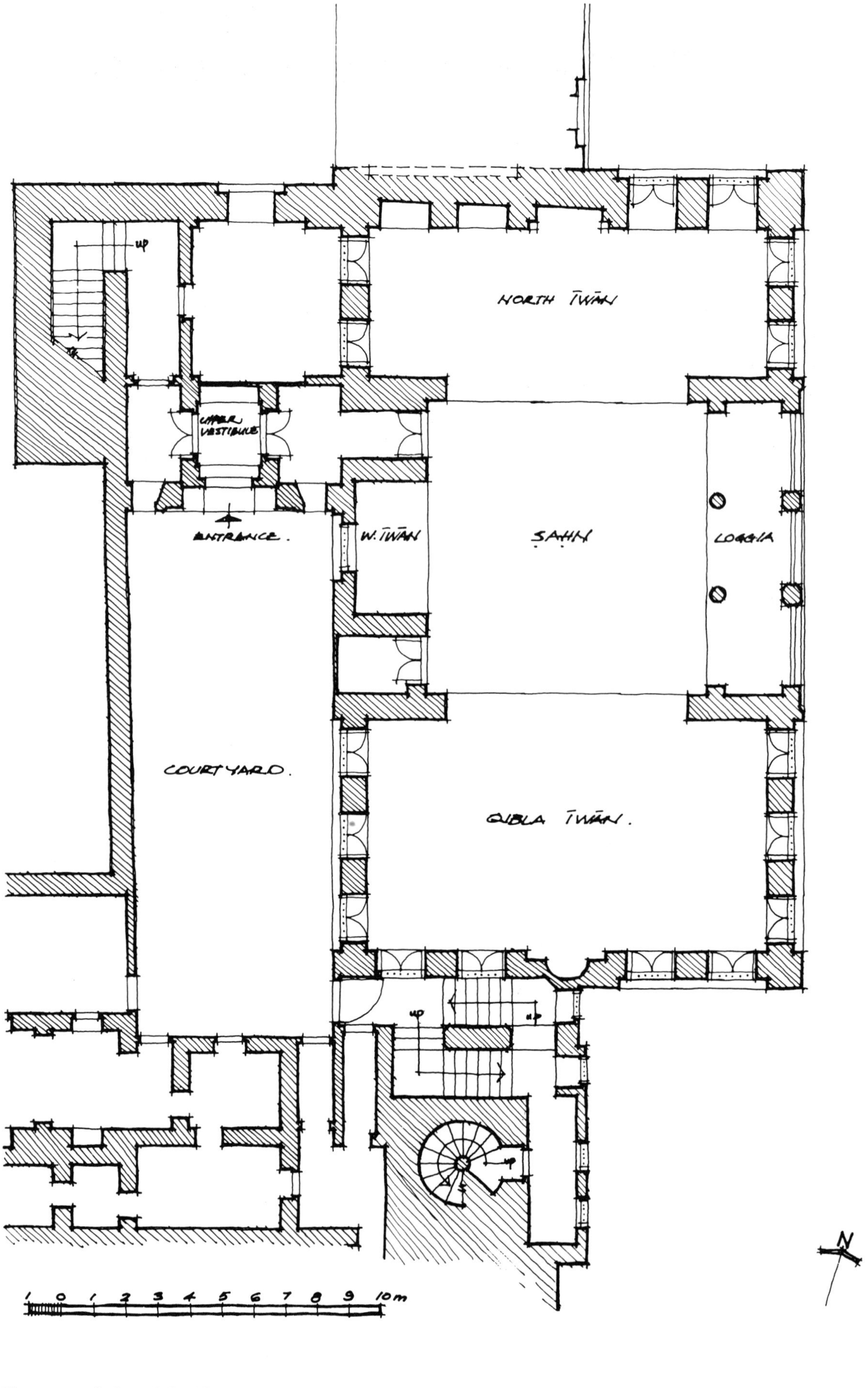

Fig. X/1 The restored plan of the Madrasa

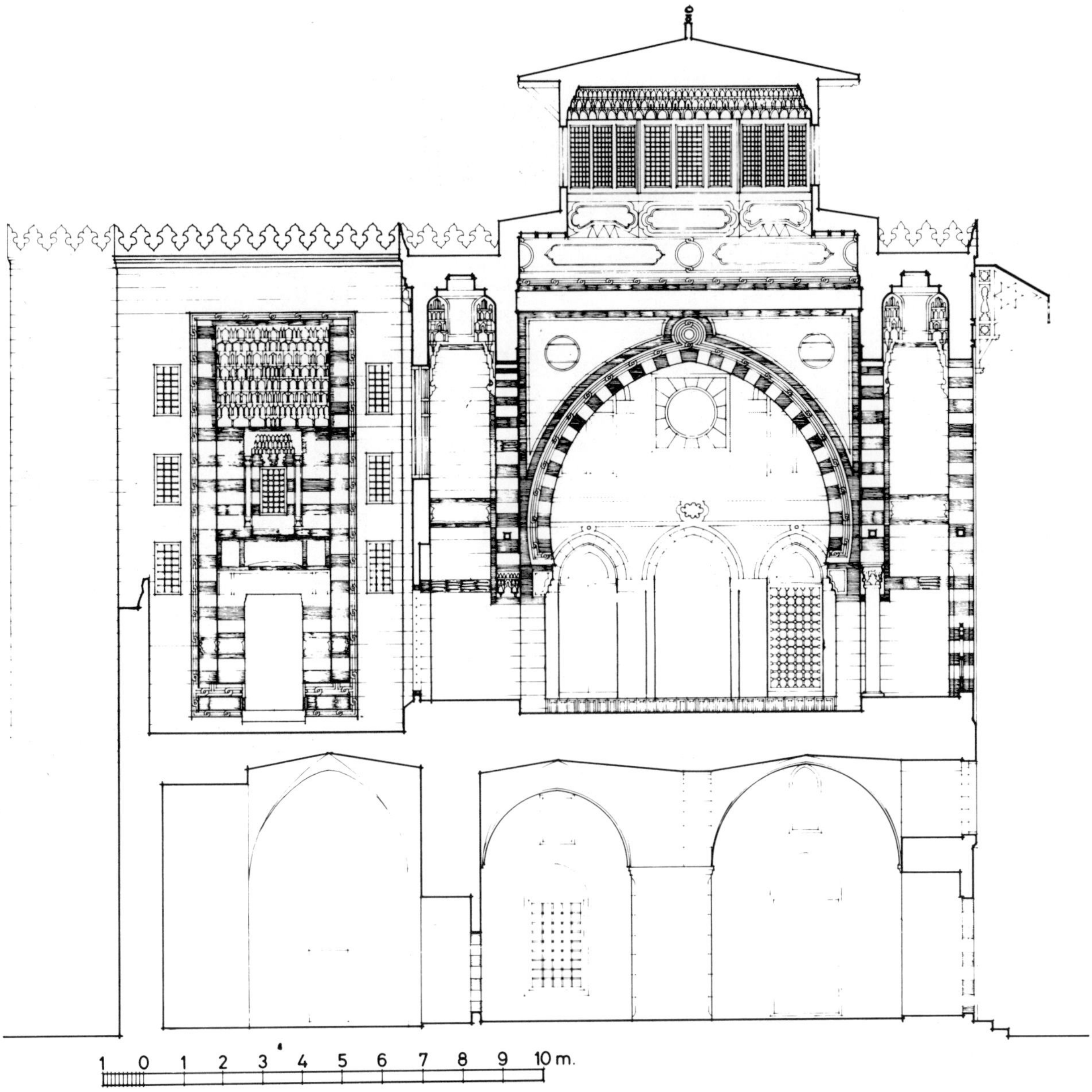

Fig. X/2 Section showing the great arch of the *ṣaḥn*, the loggia, the west *īwān* and the portal of the upper entrance

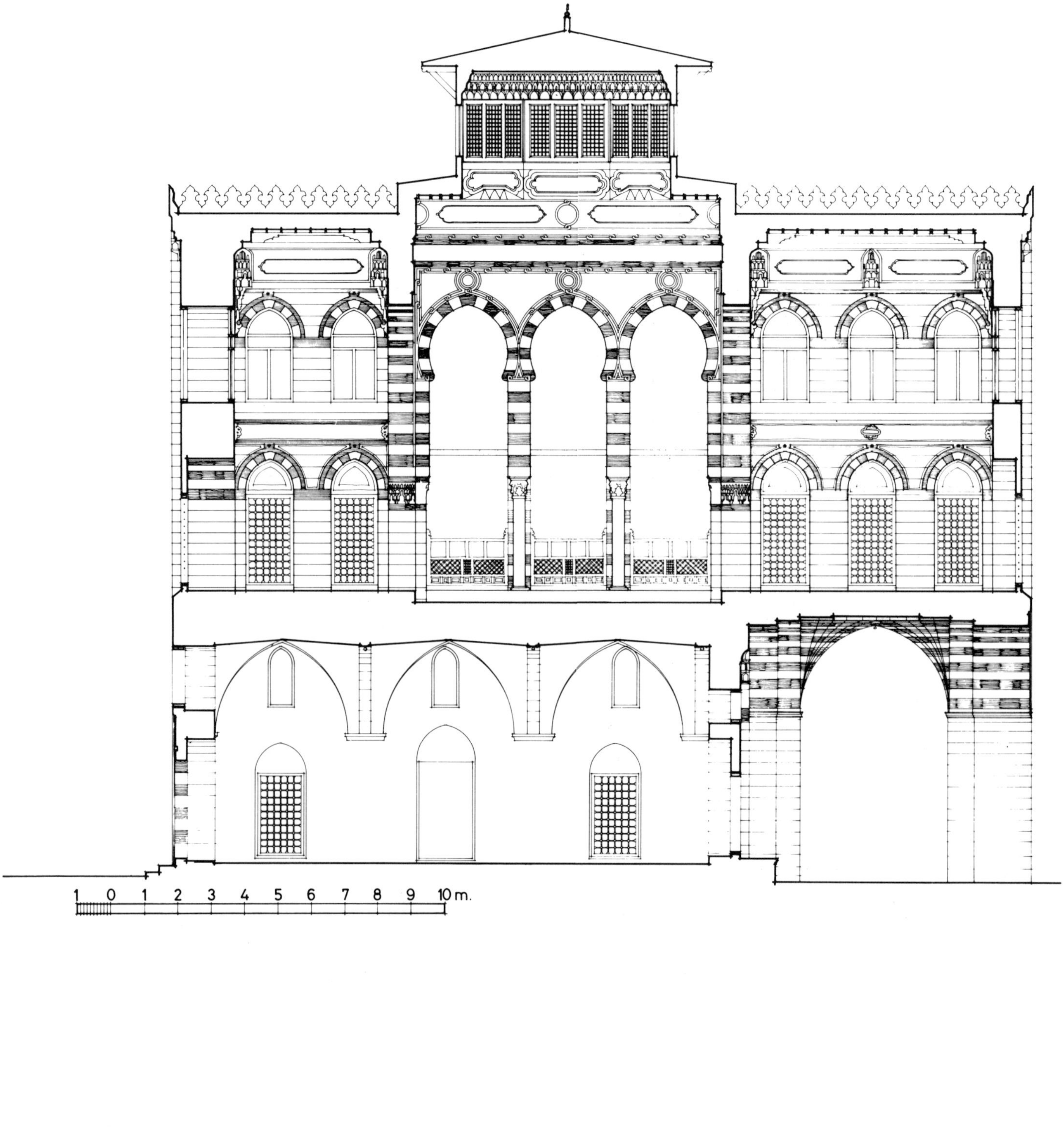

Fig. X/3 Section showing the interior of the loggia

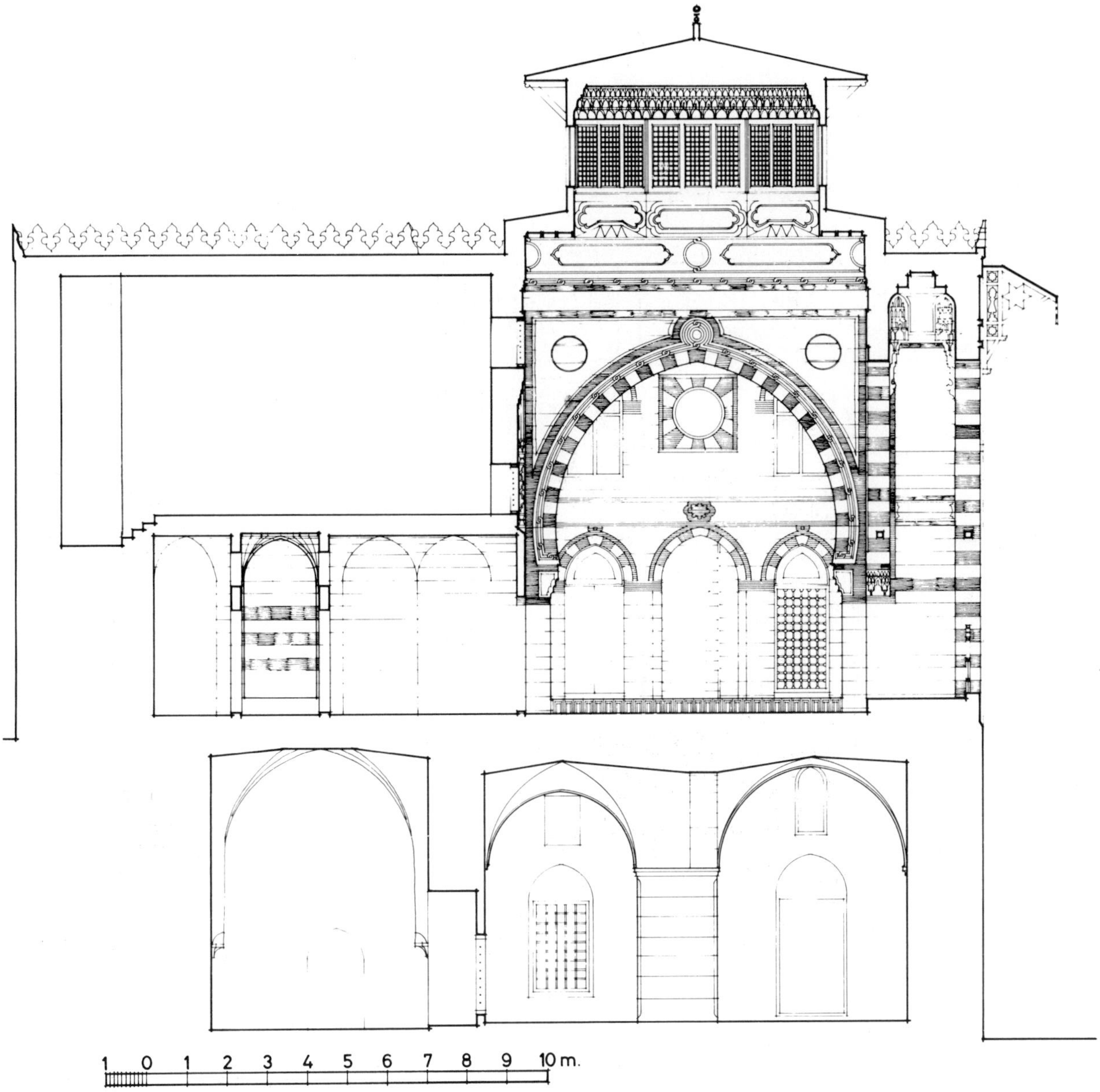

Fig. X/4 Section showing the upper vestibule and the entry to the *ṣaḥn*

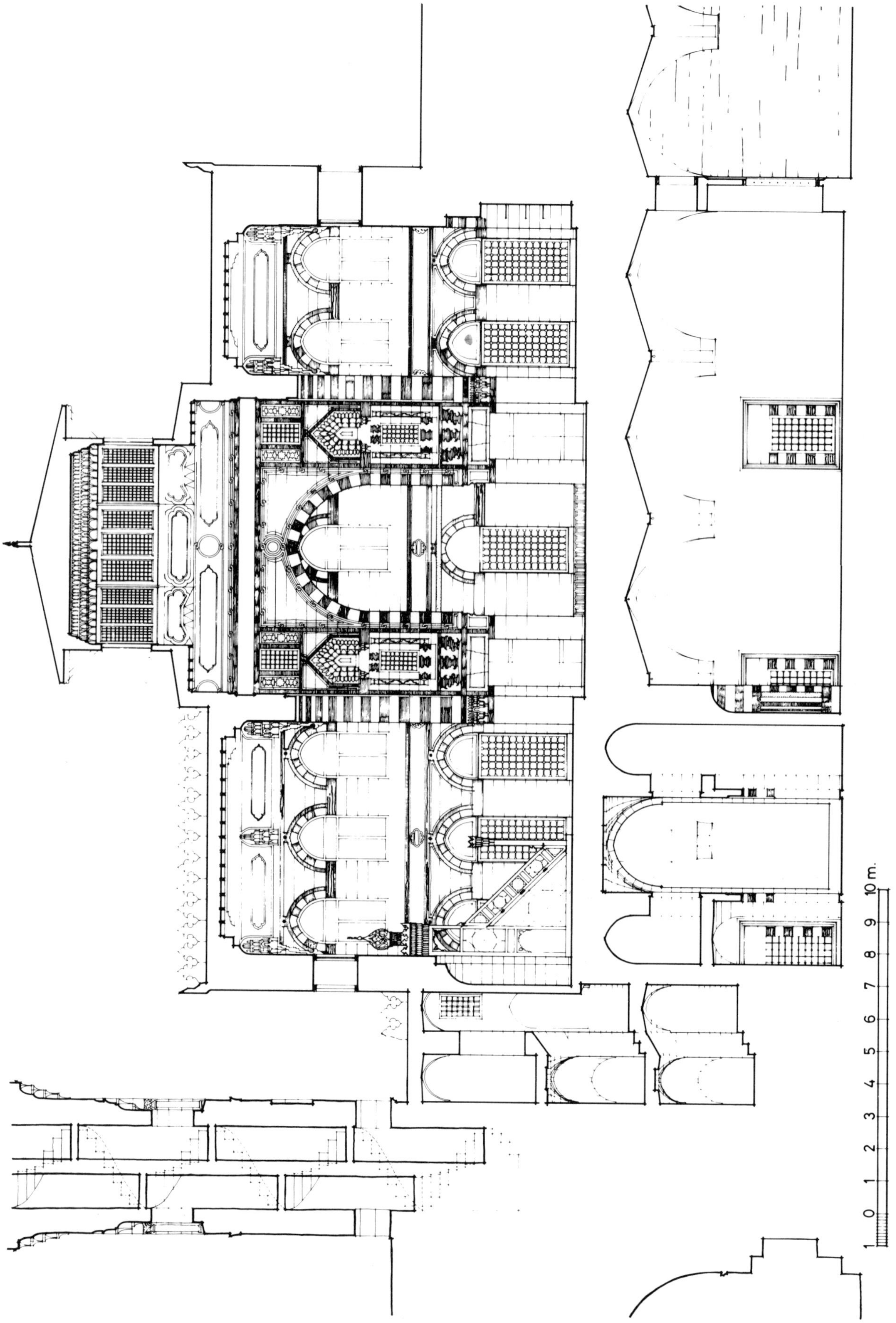

Fig. X/5 Section showing the side wall of the *ṣaḥn* and those of the *qibla* and north *īwāns*

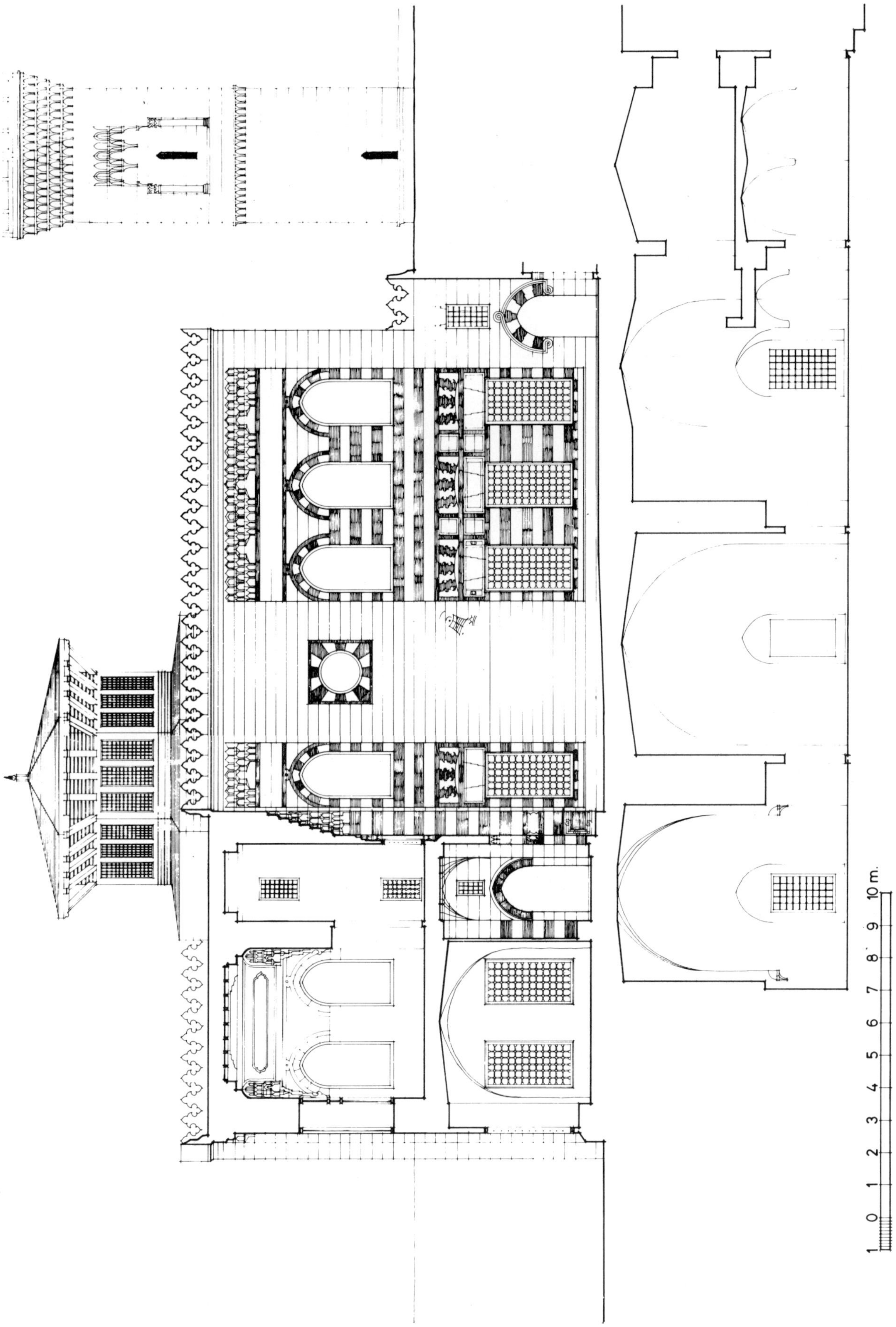

Fig. X/6 The west elevation

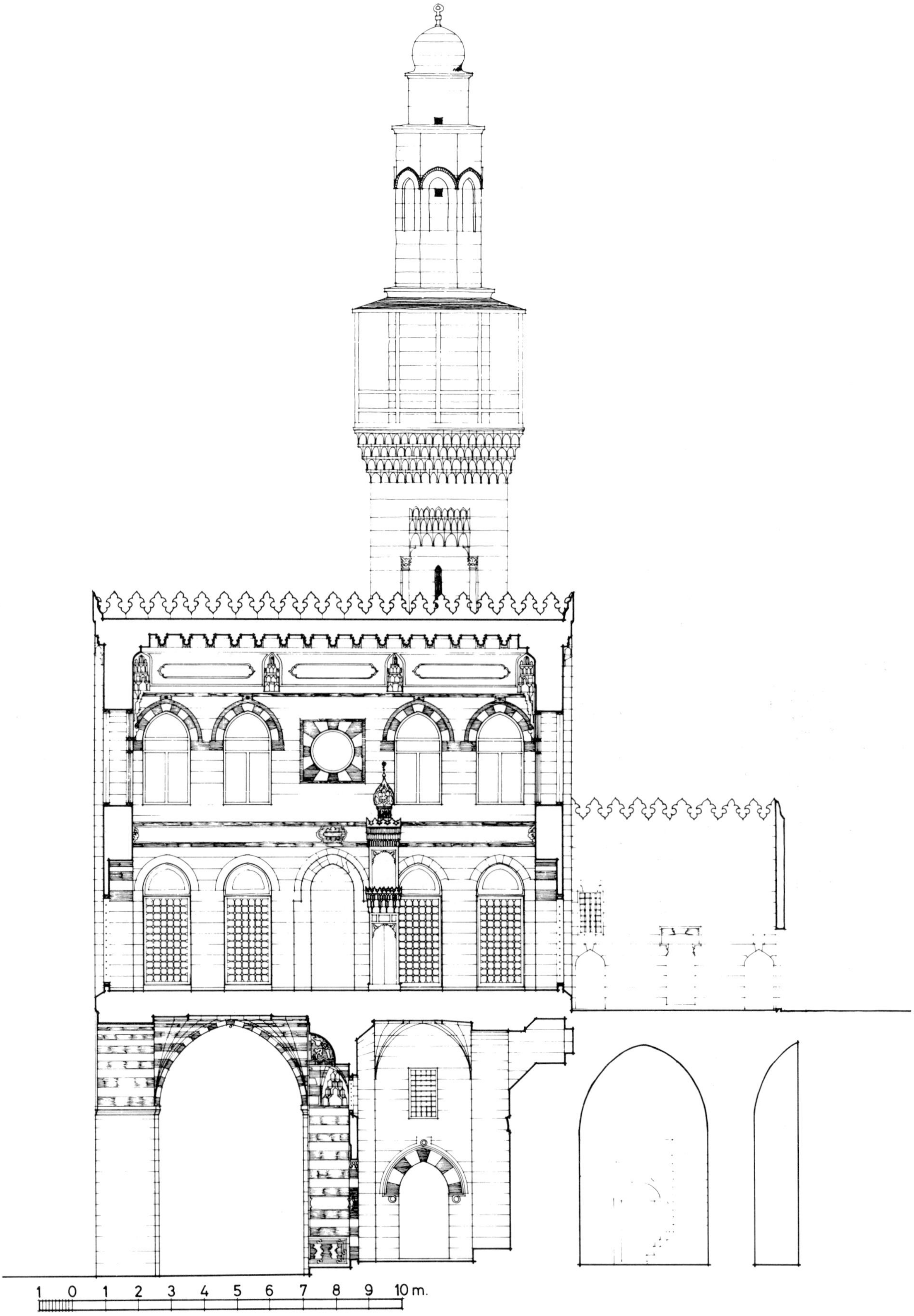

Fig. X/7 Section showing the *qibla* wall

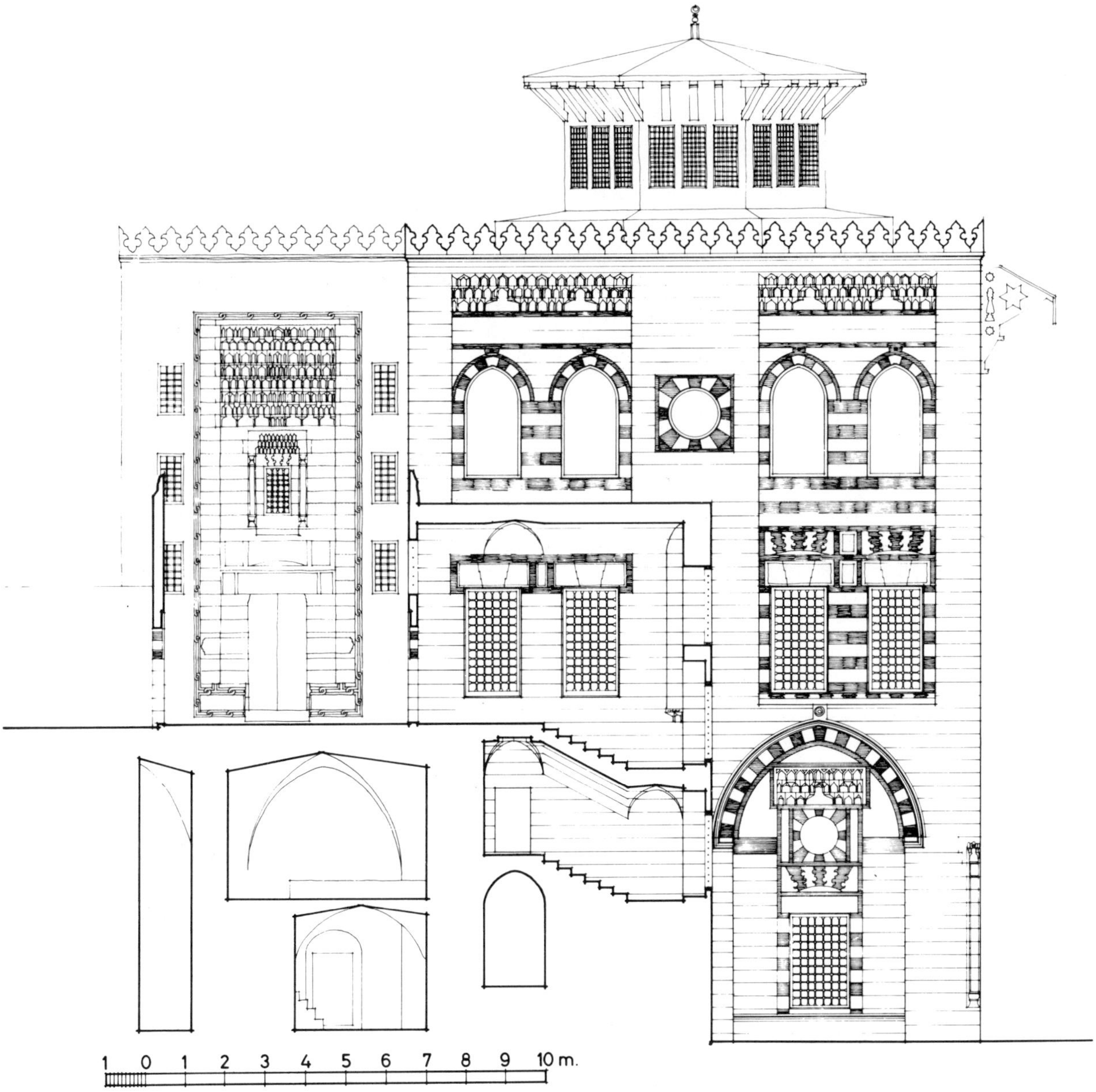

Fig. X/8 The south elevation

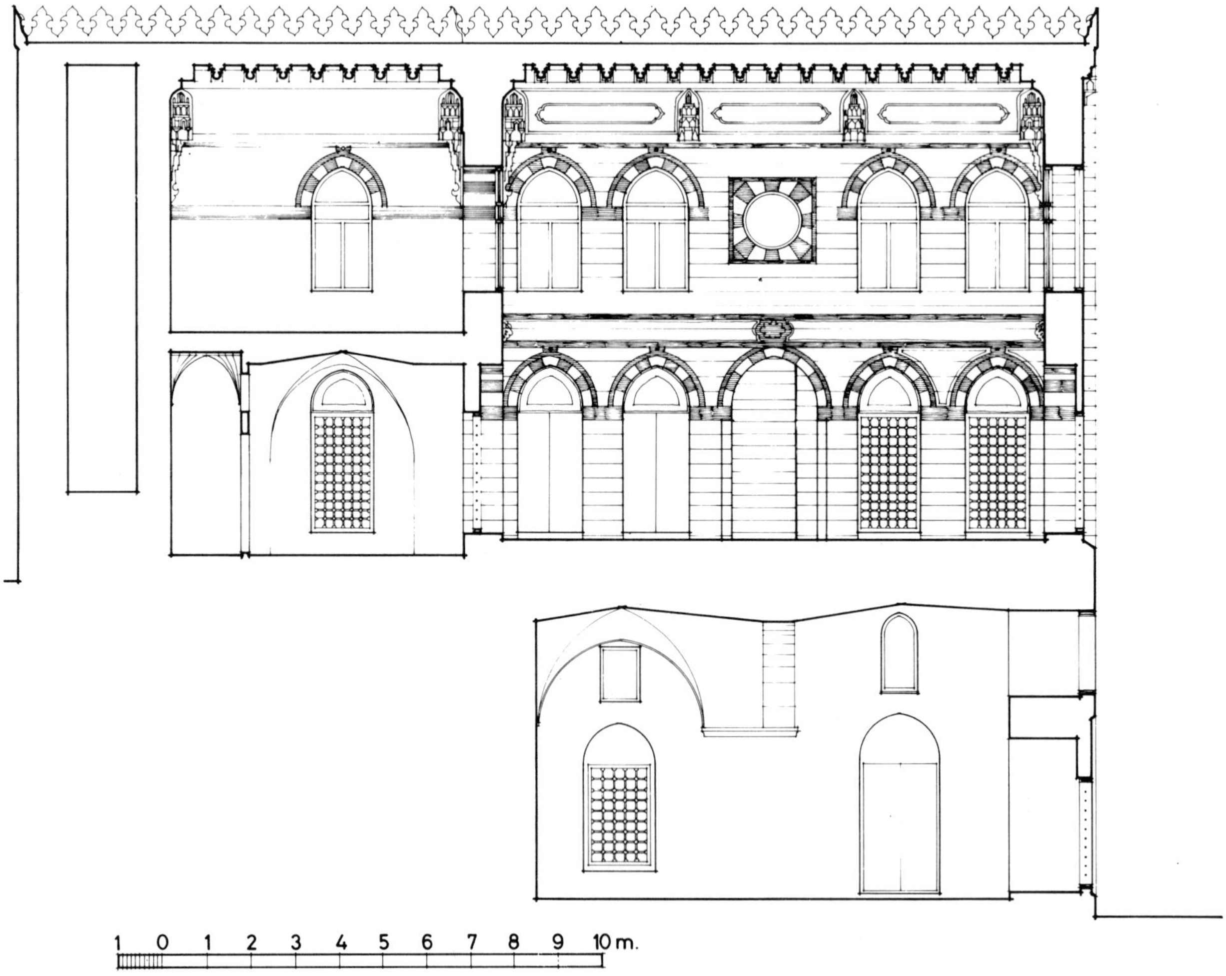

Fig. X/9 The north wall of the north *īwān*

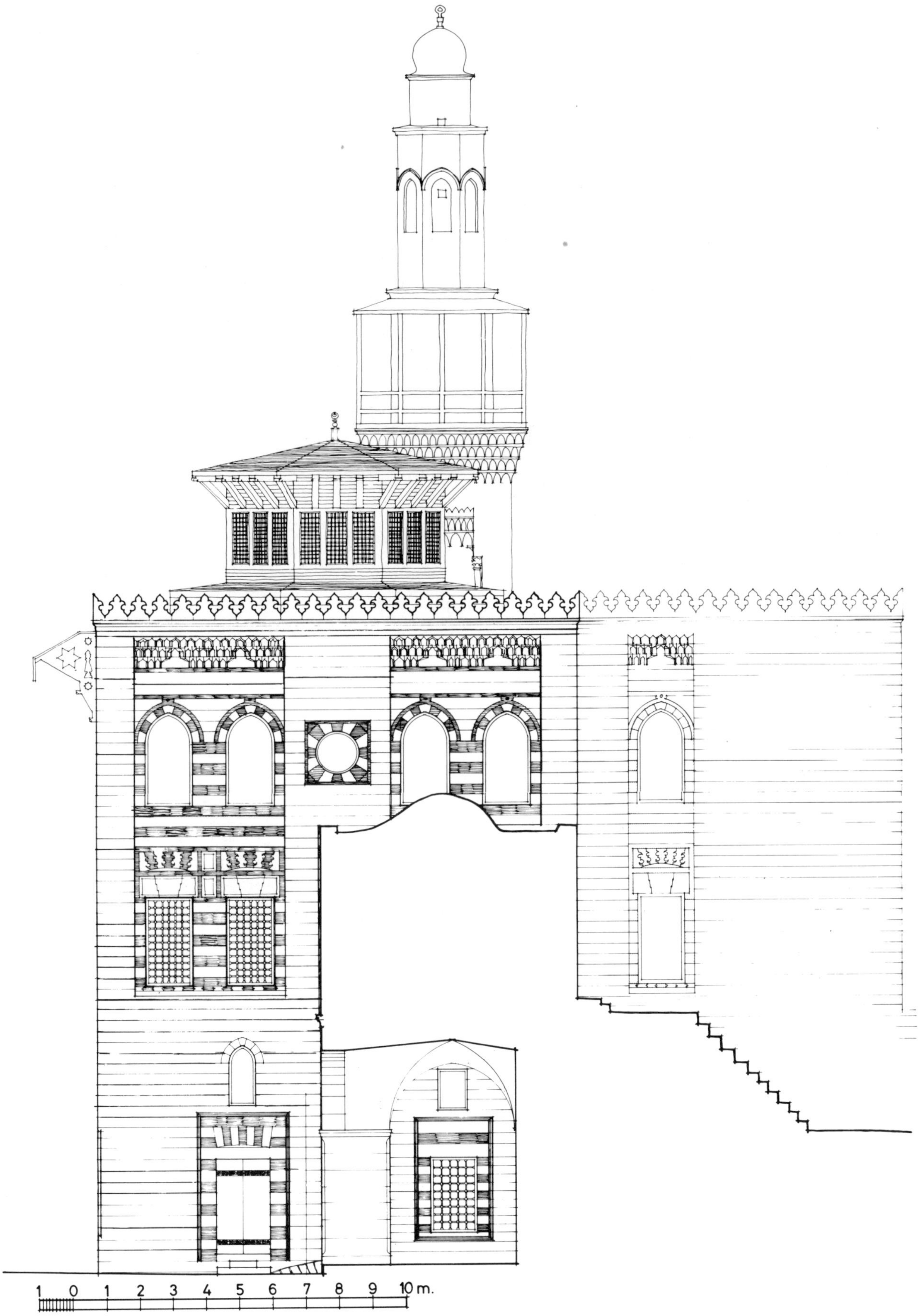

Fig. X/10 The north elevation

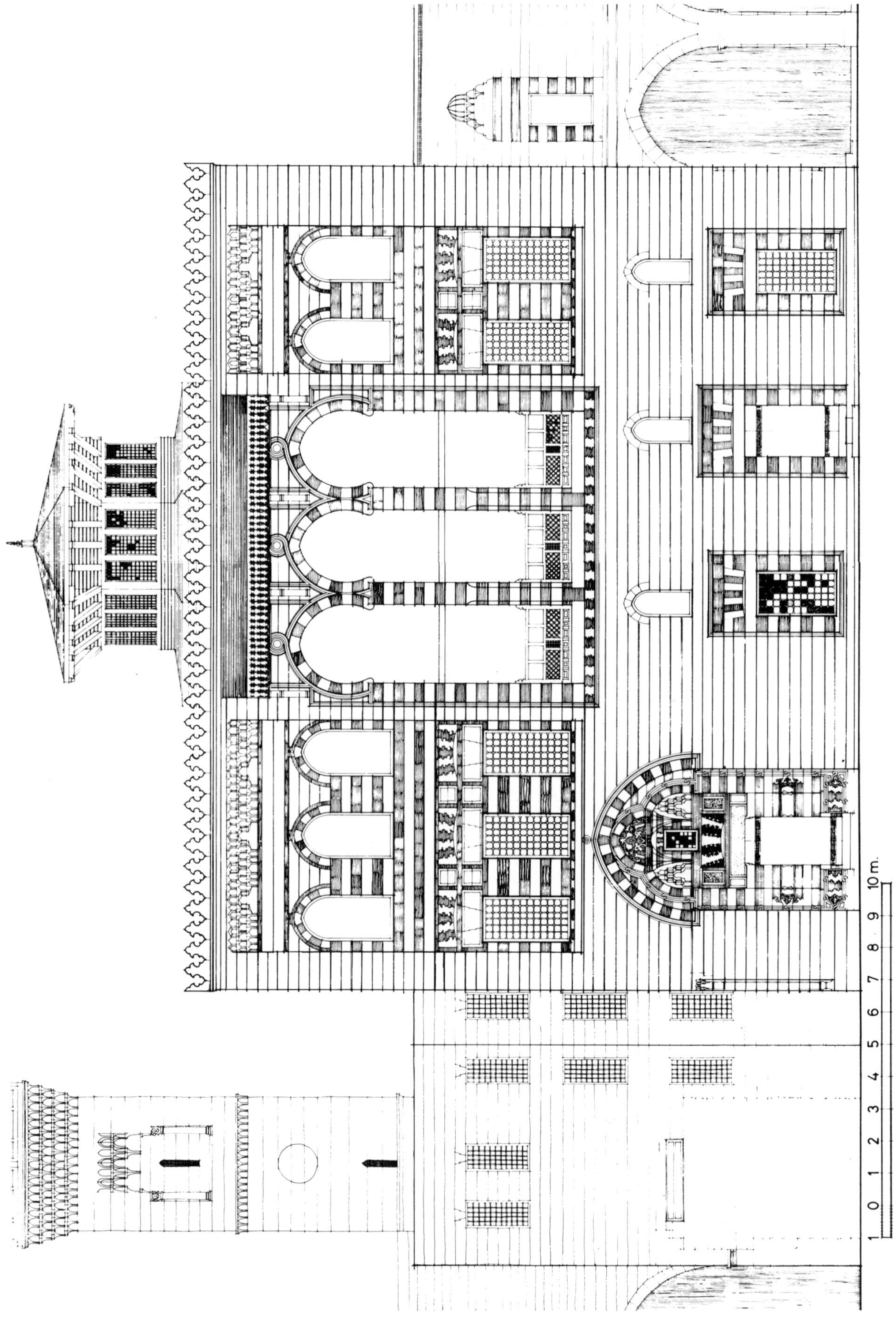

Fig. X/11 The east elevation

Chapter XI
THE IDEA

The form of the Ashrafiyya is a testament to the skills of the craftsmen employed by the imperial *dīwān* during the reign of Sultan Qāytbāy. They overcome the problems posed by the original size of the site and built a platform to suit their requirements, whilst in so doing introducing a new concept to the repertoire of Mamlūk architects.

When complete the Ashrafiyya must have exuded a sense of calm and tranquillity, feelings in keeping with its use as a religious school. It also had an image of grandeur appropriate to Sultan Qāytbāy.

These and other imperial qualities of the Ashrafiyya were recognised in its being referred to as the Third Jewel of the Ḥaram, putting it on a par with the two great architectural masterpieces in Jerusalem—the Dome of the Rock and the Aqṣā Mosque. If this accolade were appropriate in the context of Jerusalem monuments, the Ashrafiyya would certainly have been outstanding amongst Qāytbāy's own collection of architectural jewels.

As is the case with most artistic achievements, the process required to create the Ashrafiyya was gradual. In general a designer embarks on a project with one simple aim—in this case the building of a new madrasa for the sultan. The basic idea can then be extended, modified, divided and rearranged in order to produce a satisfying solution. Such a complicated design process is impossible to retrace precisely, even if all the relevant sketches and notes were available, since the unrecorded thoughts of an architect will always influence the design. It is, however, possible to try and reveal the basic progression by reversing the process and working backwards from the completed form to the fundamental image.

So far, the investigation into the Ashrafiyya has taken the ruined form, analysed it and gradually built it up again. Much of the analysis concerned the discovery and use of the ideas and geometrically inspired methods of the architect, which must help us to understand the original thoughts underlying the construction. However, in the main these affected the details rather than the ideas controlling the fundamental design of the building, the size and shape of which had to allow the inclusion of all the specifications of its imperial founder.

It would seem obvious that any search for the source of the idea which gave birth to the design of the Ashrafiyya would have to take into account the geometries which have been found to order the ideas of the architect throughout the investigation. The plan of the Madrasa was controlled by the fundamental and primary geometries centred on point S, and when these geometries were rotated against the external and internal elevations they likewise controlled their design. At the same time point S (or, in the case of the *qibla īwān*, point Q), the centre of the rotated geometries, maintained the same level throughout the Madrasa. Consequently the first step in this new search for the architectural idea is to review the combined primary geometries of the plan (see IV/12) and reduce them to a simpler and more easily understandable figure. **fig. XI/1**

The simplified version of the combined primary geometries can, as found previously, be rotated—in this instance against the east elevation. It will be seen that point S coincides with the central axis of the loggia, just as it did when that elusive architectural element was sought. **fig. XI/2**

The rotated geometry fits some of the general subdivisions of the elevation, but not others, as would be anticipated from previous analyses.

In the areas associated with the *qibla īwān* the following points of coincidence are seen: both ends of the external window recess; the chamfered sill of the recess; the red compartmentation above the joggled relieving arches (which coincides with a major axis of the geometry); and the blind loops over

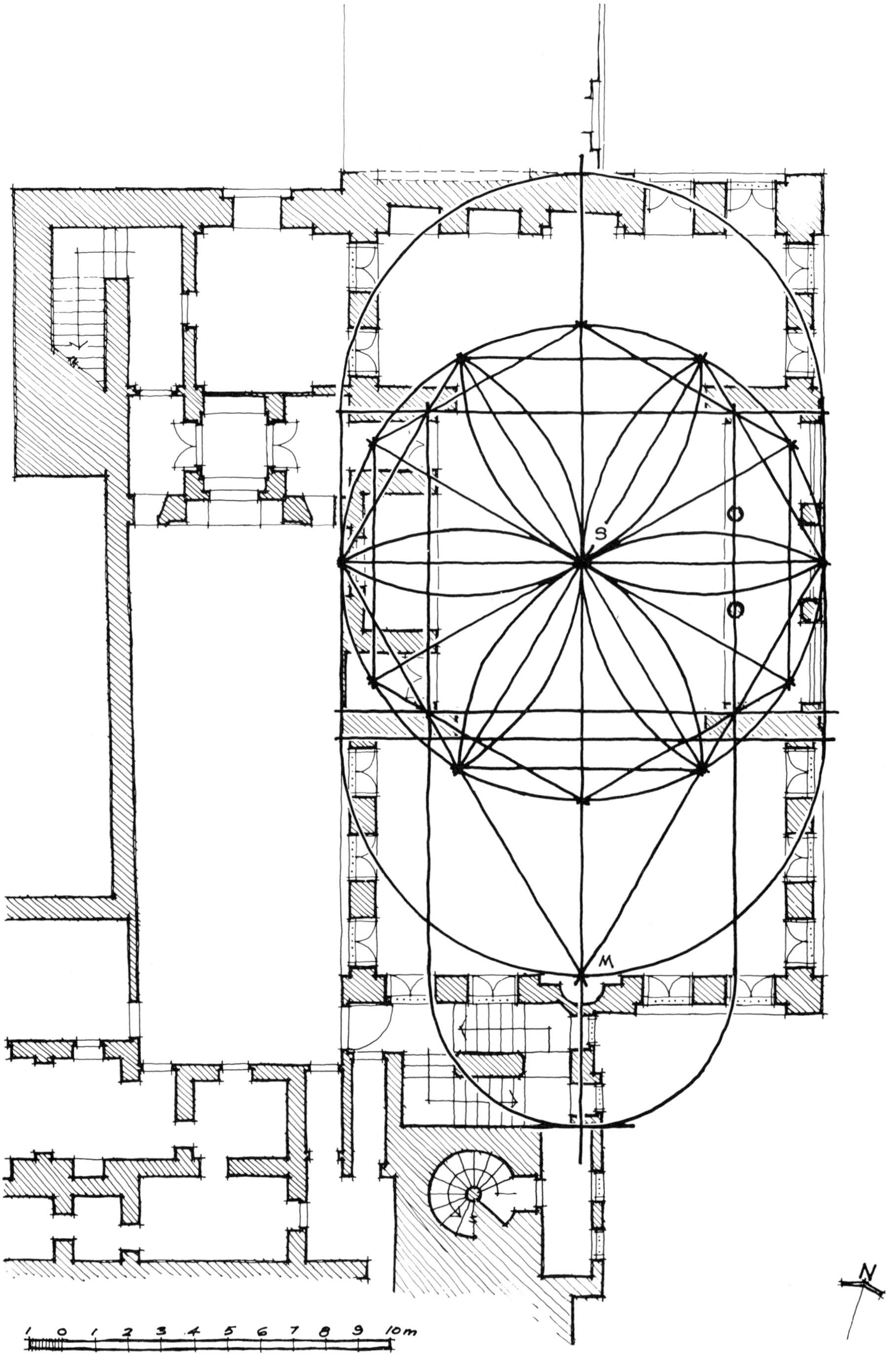

Fig. XI/1 The Madrasa plan: the primary geometries combined and simplified

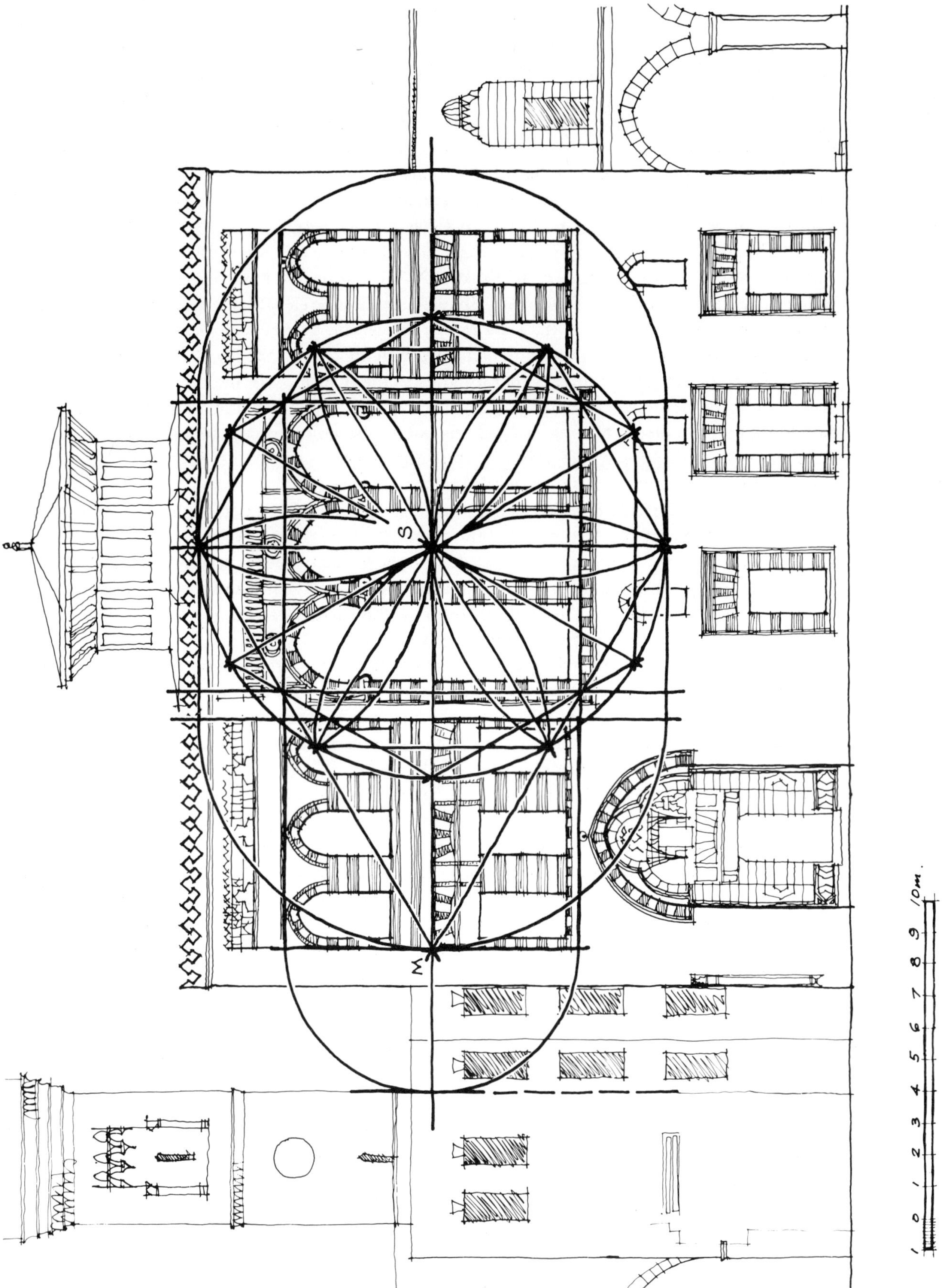

Fig. XI/2 The east elevation: the primary geometries rotated

the clerestories. Around the loggia the points include the central axis of the arcade (also a major axis of the geometry), the joggled *ablaq* string course and the tops of the keystones. A final point of coincidences is the external face of the north wall of the Madrasa.

fig. XI/3 Earlier in the *ṣaḥn* it was discovered that the apex of the roof of the lantern produced a 1 BUG equilateral triangle when combined with the horizontal axis with point S as the midpoint of the base line (see VI/23 and 25). This interesting relationship can be repeated in the rotated geometries of the east elevation by constructing a similar 1 BUG equilateral triangle above the horizontal axis. However, this addition disturbs the previously balanced geometry, and to correct this imbalance a further 1 BUG equilateral triangle may be constructed below the horizontal axis. **fig. XI/4**

Within these rotated geometries of the east elevation there are three 1 BUG equilateral triangles, each with point S as the midpoint of their base lines. They form an interesting group. The first of these triangles defines the position of the *miḥrāb* in plan, and now in elevation it defines the southern edge of the external window recess of the *qibla īwān*. The second triangle coincides with the apex of the lantern, and the lowest apex of the third coincides with the level of the floor of the *riwāq*.

The significance of the latter is that it indicates the floor level of the *riwāq* as being one of two crucial levels for the architect, the other being its roof. This apparently simple conclusion has not been easy to find, nor to prove. Having reached this point it becomes overwhelmingly obvious that these were the only two levels which existed before the construction of the Ashrafiyya that required consideration, for it was only to these levels that the building could be linked.

More relationships are revealed as the rotated geometries are studied further, including the fact that the step within the recessed portal of the main entrance is on a level with the floor of the *riwāq*. However, a disturbing feeling persists that despite the geometry being centred on the loggia arcade and thus the *ṣaḥn*—the architectural centre of the building—a balance and equilibrium has still to be found. The eye is disturbed by the combination of the three triangles: they are balanced vertically, but a fourth triangle is required to balance them horizontally.

fig. XI/5 If, after adding the fourth triangle, the complete geometric composition is moved across the east elevation until the outer apex of this fourth triangle is aligned with the north wall of the Ashrafiyya, it becomes clear that the essence of the rotated geometry is a square: the apexes of the four equilateral triangles mark the *riwāq* floor, the north and south walls and the top of the lantern.

fig. XI/6 These relationships must also have some relevance for the plan of the Madrasa and its general proportions. With the removal of the geometric centre from the centre of the *ṣaḥn*, the north and south facades of the Ashrafiyya are defined by the outer apexes of a pair of 1 BUG equilateral triangles placed back to back. The west and east facades are determined by the extremities of their common base line, **fig. XI/7** and these points enable a rectangle to be drawn around the outside of the Madrasa. As it has already been established that the width of the courtyard is ½ BUG, it is a simple matter to represent it by half of the fundamental geometry in order to complete the essential geometry of the plan.

fig. XI/8 To simplify these ideas further, if the architectural details are ignored the three dimensional image is of a box with dimensions and a volume equivalent to the Ashrafiyya. Two faces of the box are square and four are rectangular, but all are related, having been generated by the 1 BUG diameter circle with its inscribed double hexagons.

Knowing something about the way architects think about and design buildings, often on the back of envelopes, it is possible that from such a box the proportional geometries were developed to control the entire design of the Ashrafiyya.

From this box the general measurements of the building could have been worked out and the potential of the site considered by the architect and his design team while they were still in Cairo. They could have received Sultan Qāytbāy's agreement to the design before the construction team set out for Jerusalem. The site information required was minimal, the architect would surely have known the length and breadth of the original site on top of the roof and the height from the *riwāq* floor to the roof. Even if the site information had been slightly inaccurate, by having a design based on a system of proportions the architect could be confident that few design changes would be necessary once building started.

fig. XI/9 As a final indulgence we could flatten out the box and draw on it the plan, elevation and section of the Ashrafiyya as well as the essential geometries.

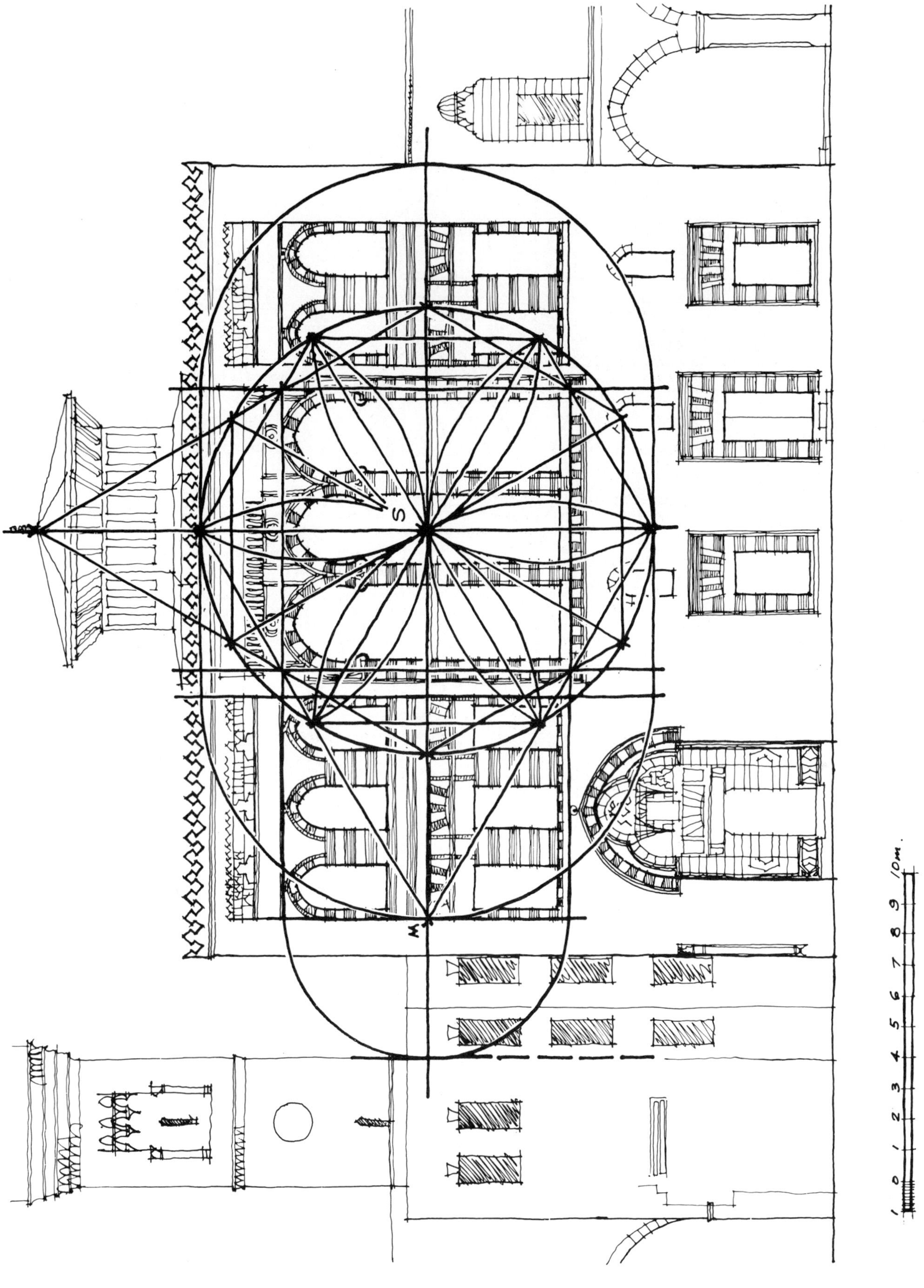

Fig. XI/3 The east elevation: the lantern triangle

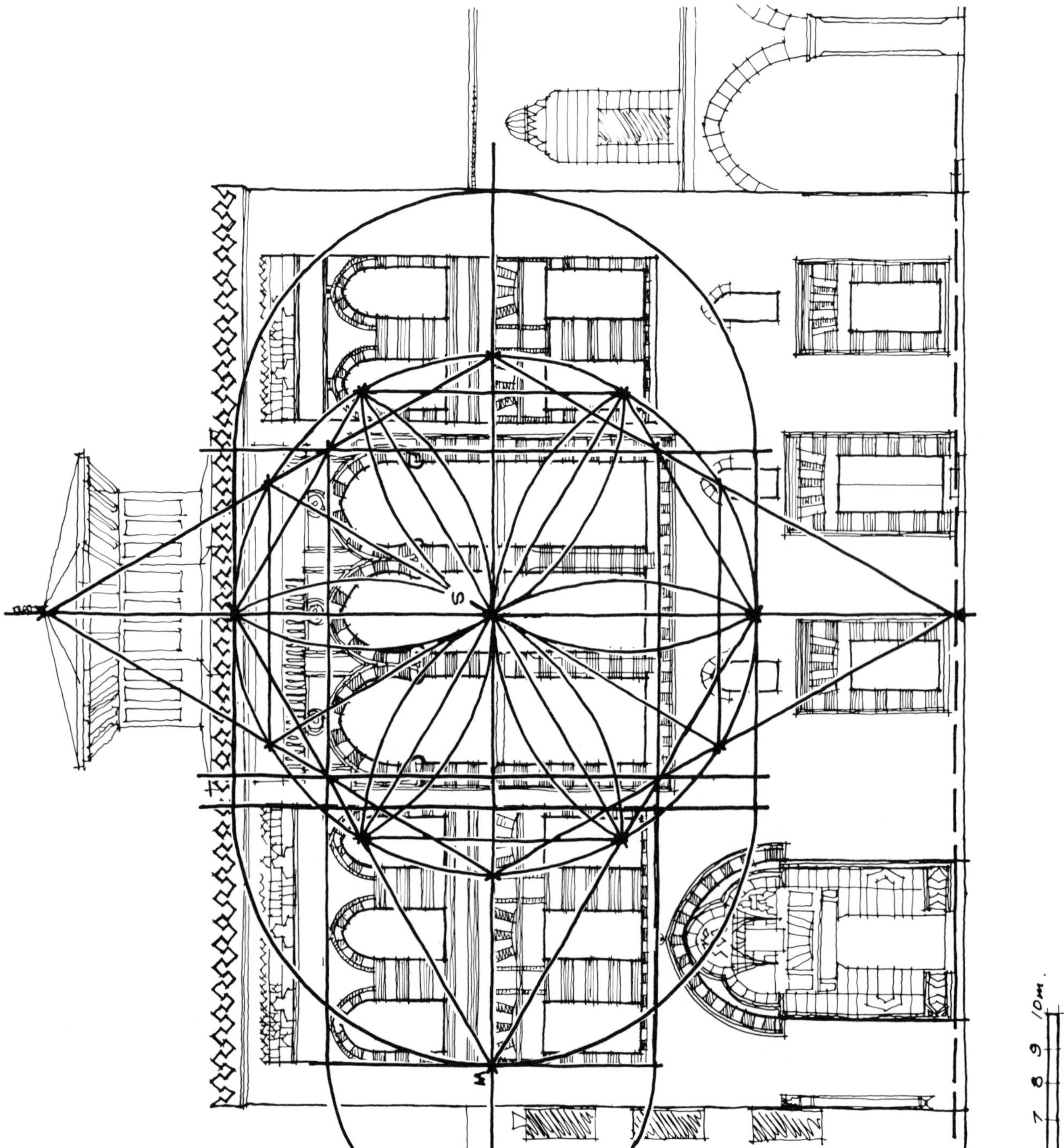

Fig. XI/4 The east elevation: the base triangle

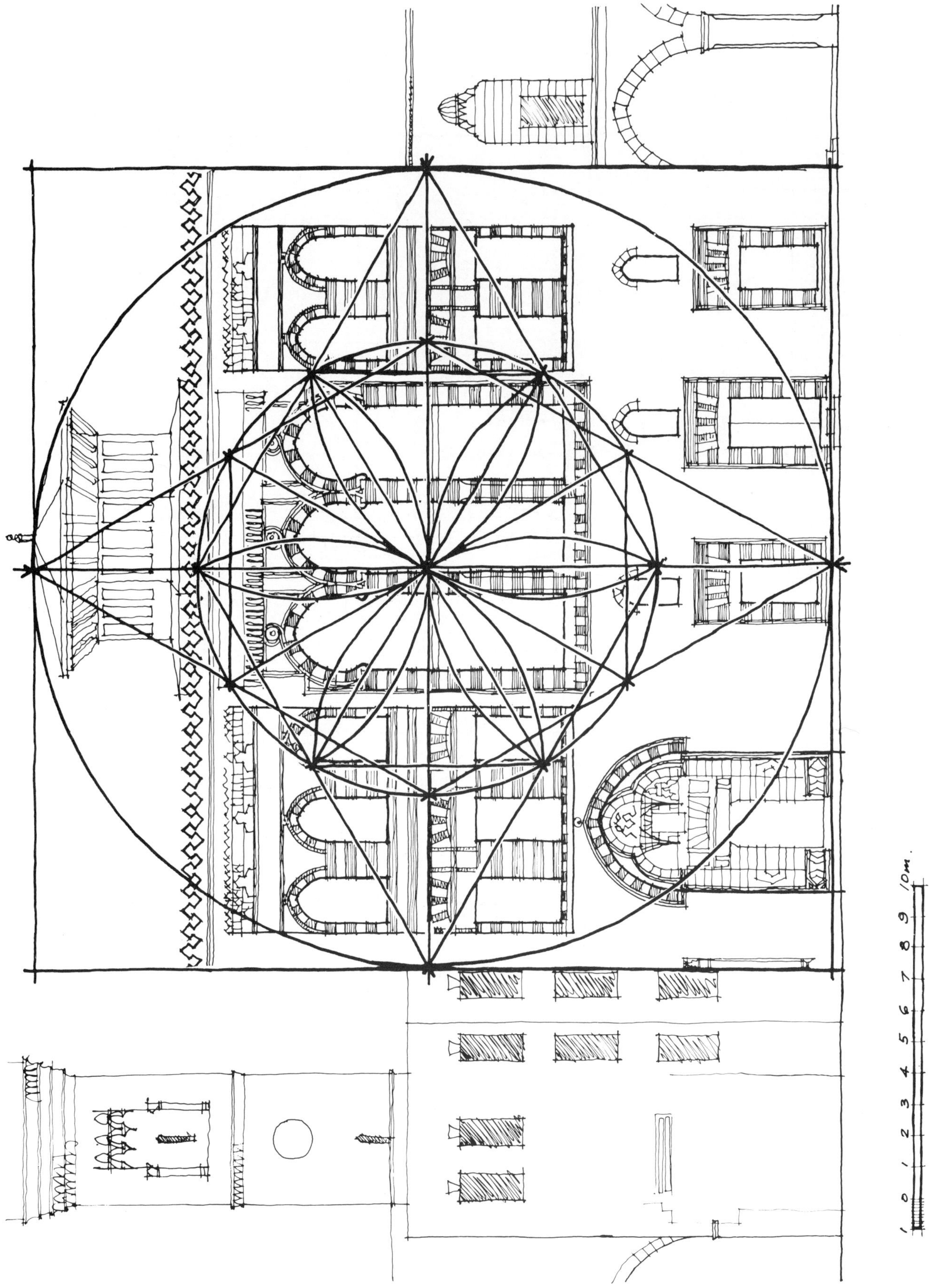

Fig. XI/5 The east elevation: four equilateral triangles and a square

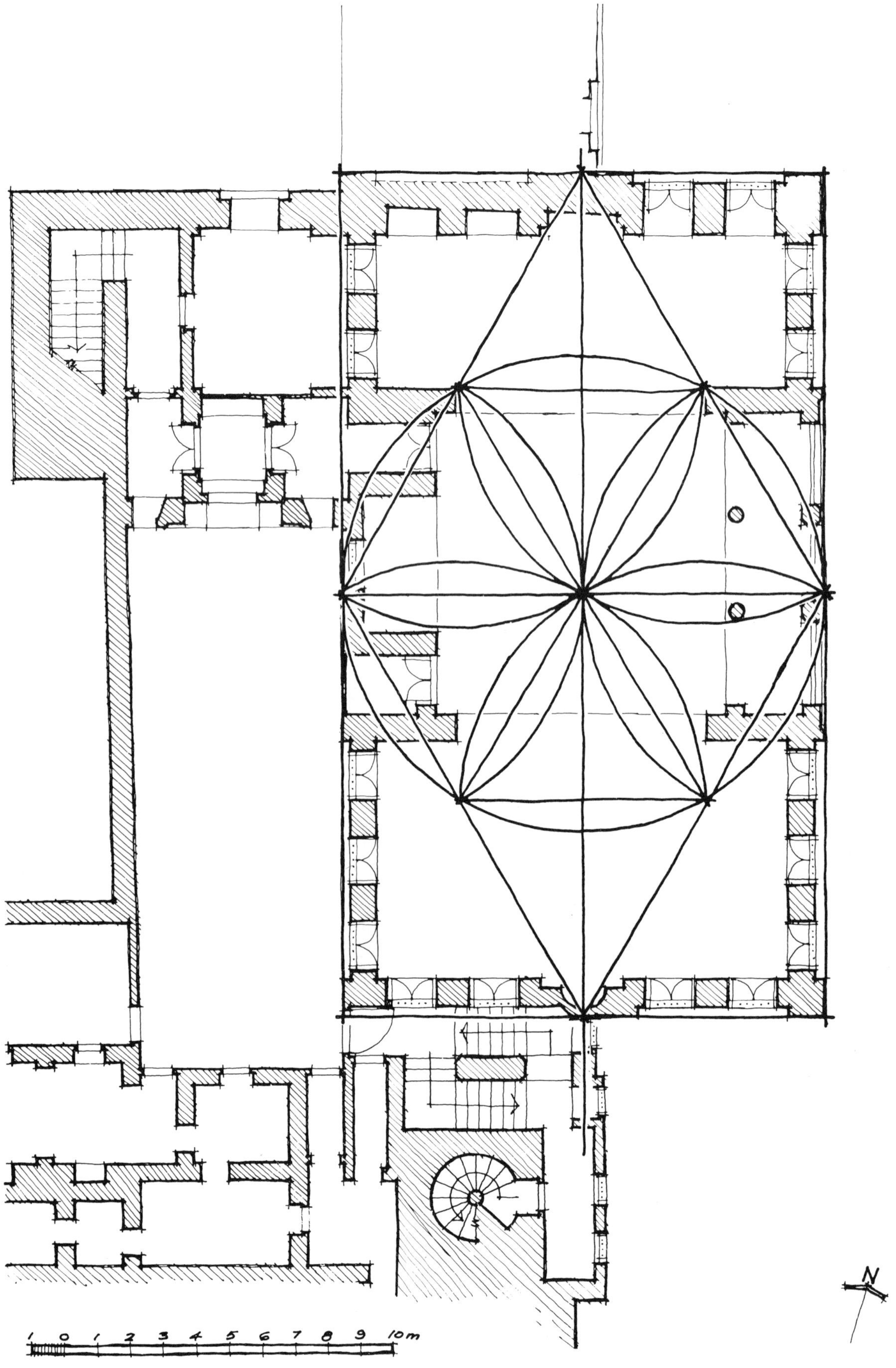

Fig. XI/6 The Madrasa plan: the essential geometry

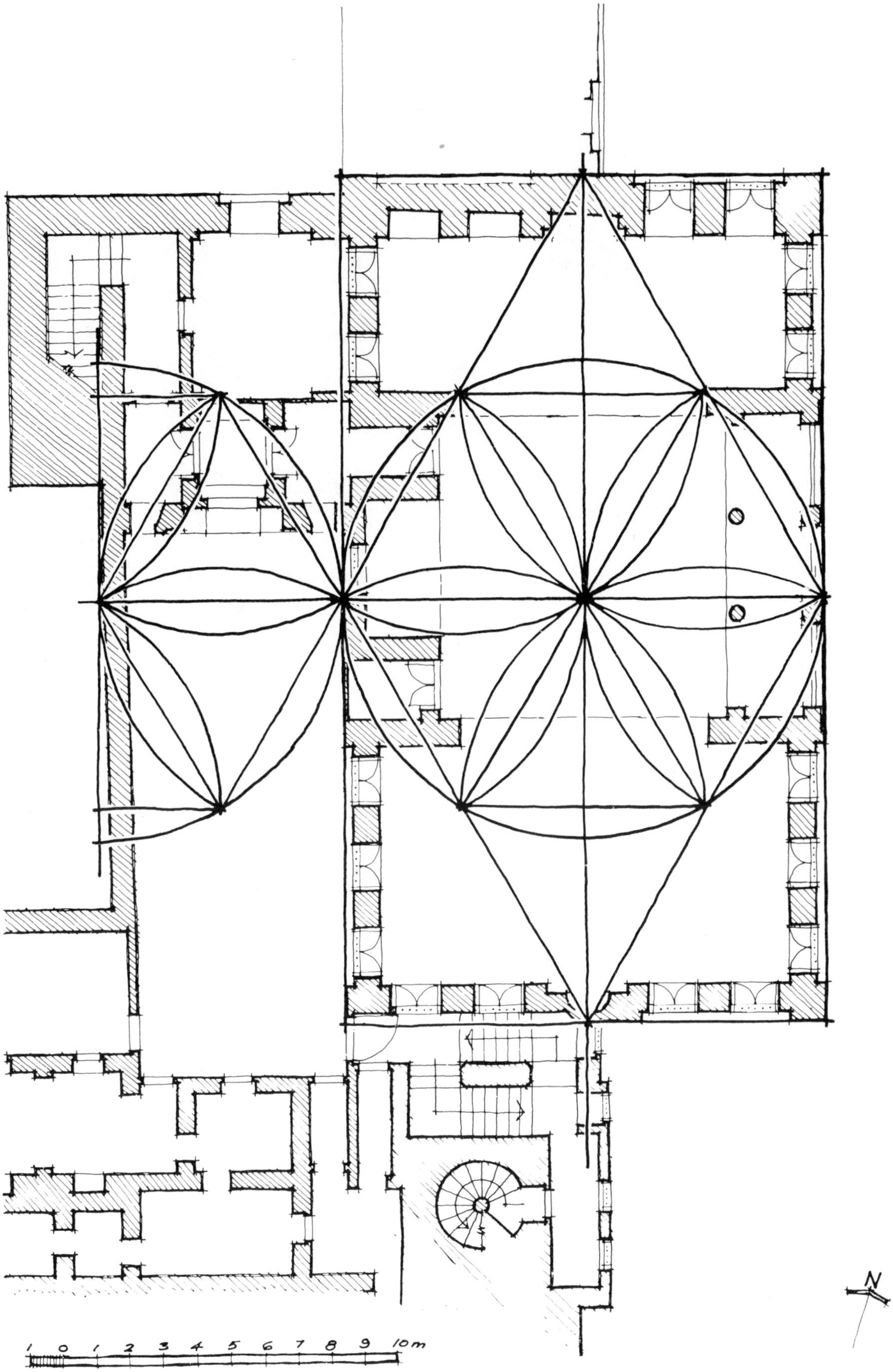

Fig. XI/7 The Ashrafiyya plan: the essential geometry complete

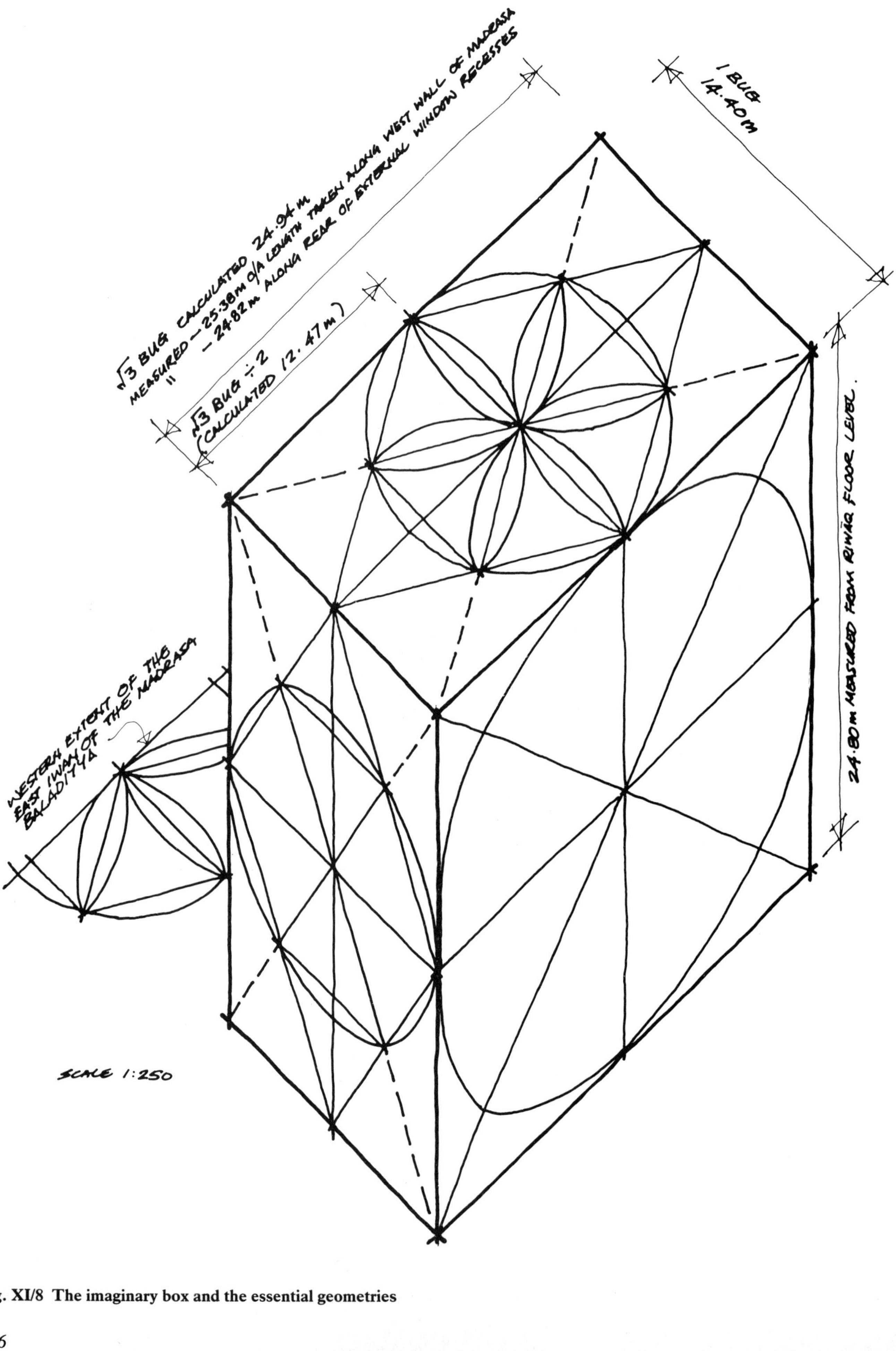

Fig. XI/8 The imaginary box and the essential geometries

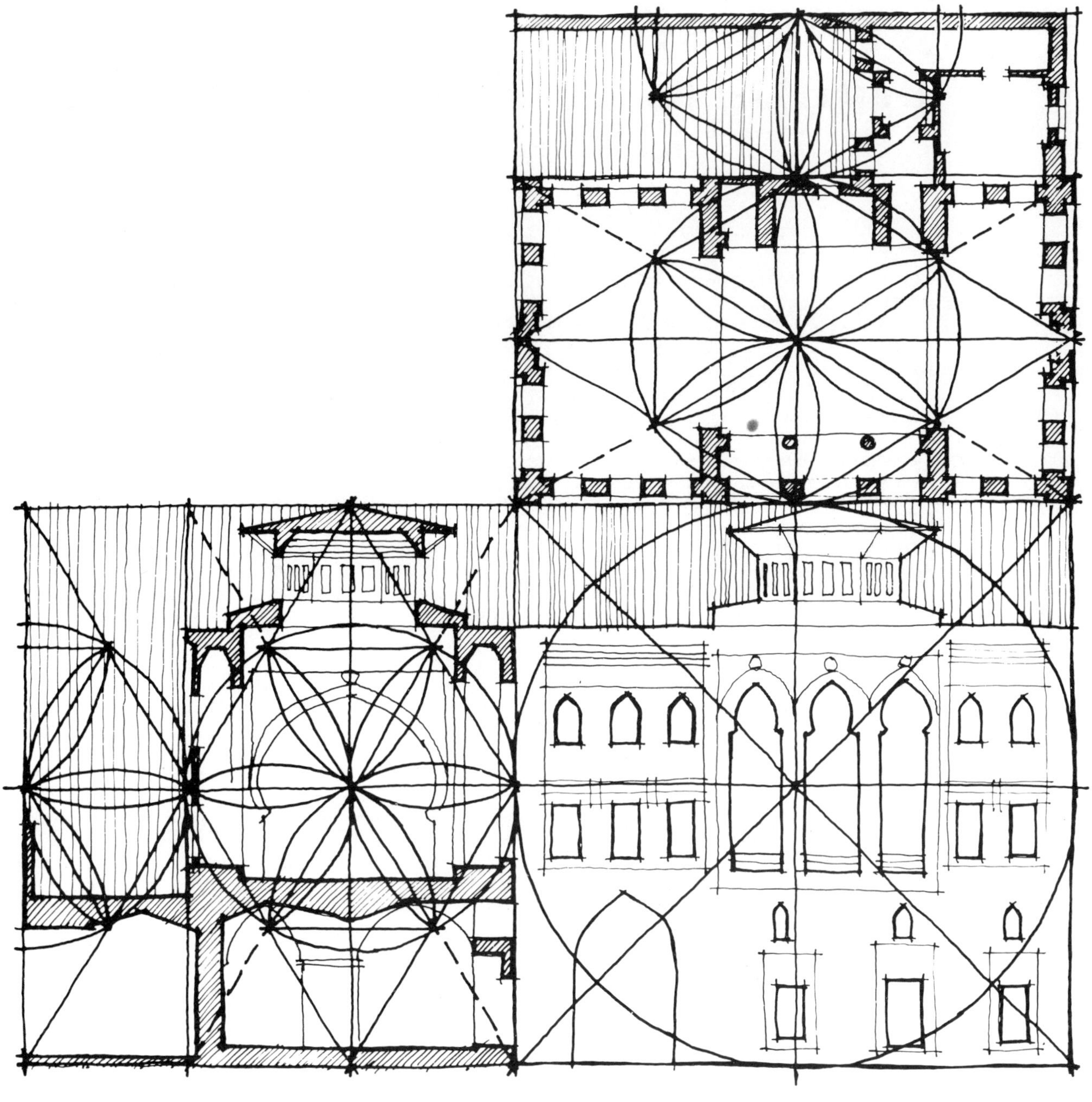

Fig. XI/9 The Ashrafiyya: plan, section and elevation

Appendix A
A CHRONOLOGY OF THE BUILDING OF THE ASHRAFIYYA

The chequered building process of the Ashrafiyya can be pieced together with the help of contemporary texts and subsequent commentaries.

Firstly, there is the sheikh, Khitāb al-Danhāwī, who wrote the *waqfiyya* or title deeds to the Ashrafiyya. Secondly there is the Qāḍī Mujīr al-Dīn al-'Ulaymī who wrote a guide to the monuments of Jerusalem and Hebron in 901/1496 and to whom a *Dhayl* or sequel is attributed.[1]

Within the last century a number of authors have written of the Ashrafiyya, notably the epigraphist Max van Berchem, who clarified the historical record in his exhaustive work: *Corpus Inscriptionum Arabicarum*.[2] There has also been the works of Shlomo Tamari (see Appendix B) and of the British School of Archaeology.[3]

Van Berchem discusses in great detail the textual evidence relating to the construction phases of the Ashrafiyya, which continued intermittently for 17 years from 869-887/1465-1482.[4]

The significant dates and events relating to the construction and eventual destruction of the Madrasa the Ashrafiyya are as follows:

870-872/1465-67
A small and simple madrasa, typical of those found in Jerusalem, was constructed for Sultan Khushqadam on top of the west *riwāq* of the Ḥaram al-Sharīf by the Amīr Ḥasan al-Sharīf, Superintendent of the Two Ḥarams in Jerusalem and Hebron.

872/1467
Following the death of Khushqadam two sultans briefly ruled before al-Sulṭān al-Malik al-Ashraf Sayf al-Dīn Abū Naṣr Qāytbāy ascended the throne.

873/1468
The Amīr Ḥasan travelled to Cairo to pay homage to the new sultan, and requested that the madrasa might be honoured with Qāytbāy's name, which, if he was agreeable, could be inscribed on the entrance of the Old Madrasa. The interior of the Old Madrasa (now named the Ashrafiyya) was completed by the Amīr Bardibak Tājī, the new Superintendent of the Two Ḥarams. We are told that it was entered by the same gate as that which lead to the Minaret of Bāb al-Silsila (Ma'dhanat al-Maḥkama) by a narrow and difficult stair. It had a meeting hall, a passageway and a separate room for the sheikh, all of which were on top of the *riwāq*. Opposite these, over the east *īwān* of the Madrasa Baladiyya, was a courtyard or terrace with further rooms.

875/1470
The construction text was placed over the entrance of the Old Madrasa, dated 1 Rabī' I of the year 875 (28 August 1470). It included the name of Nāṣir al-Dīn Muḥammad b. al-Nashāshībī, Qāytbāy's treasurer, who in Muḥarram 875 (July 1470) had been appointed Superintendent of the Two Ḥarams.

876/1471
Qāytbāy ordered the demolition of the Old Madrasa and the construction of a replacement.

877/1472
Qāytbāy attached 60 sufis, pupils and lawyers, to the Madrasa and also donated to it *waqf* property situated in the town of Gaza. The upper parts of the Old Madrasa were partially demolished.

880/1475
On Monday, 27 Rajab, Qāytbāy visited Jerusalem and attended mid-day prayers in his madrasa. He was far from impressed by the appearance of the Old Madrasa and ordered its demolition so that an edifice more in keeping with his royal stature could be built.

884/1479
A demolition order was sent from Cairo and arrived in Jerusalem on Wednesday, 3 Rabī' II.

885/1480:
The foundations of the new Ashrafiyya's first phase were cut on Sunday, 24 Sha'bān. The architects began with the construction of the *majma'* for the sufis below the *riwāq*, and at the same time began to demolish the Old Madrasa on top of the *riwāq*. The sheikh of the Madrasa went to Cairo to involve Qāytbāy more fully in the project, possibly because local workmen were being used and he felt their standards were not up to those required by the sultan.

886/1481
A team of masons, architects and sculptors under the leadership of a highly skilled and trusted Christian architect was dispatched from Cairo. The leader used his authority to demolish the recently started building because the work was unsatisfactory. He extended the demolition work further south to include three arches of the *riwāq*. So began the construction of the final Ashrafiyya.

887/1482
An inscription dated Rajab I of the year 887 (August/September 1482) commemorated the completion of the building of the Ashrafiyya. As was customary the marblers began their work once the structure had been completed.

952/1545
The Ashrafiyya was devastated by an earthquake.[5]

Notes

1. The *Dhayl* is discussed by L.A. Mayer in his paper 'A Sequel to Mujīr Ad-Dīn's Chronicle', *Journal of the Palestine Oriental Society*, XI/2, 1931, pp. 85-97 (pp. 1-13 in the separatum).
2. Max van Berchem, *Matériaux pour un Corpus Inscriptionum Arabicarum Deuxième Partie: Syrie du Sud. Jérusalem—Planches 1920; Jérusalem 'Ville'* (1922-23); *Jérusalem 'Ḥaram'* (1925-27). In this *Corpus* 300 Arabic inscriptions have been edited and are accompanied by translations into French, with commentaries containing information ranging from comparative epigraphic studies to historical background and associated architectural aspects.
3. BSAJ, *Mamlūk Jerusalem*, see especially no. 63, Al-Ashrafiyya, pp. 589-605.
4. *CIA 'Ville'*, pp. 352-73, 'Madrasa de Malik Ashraf Qāyt-Bāy (Ashrafiyya)'.
5. There are problems regarding the precise date of the earthquake and they concern principally the authorship of the *Dhayl* of al-'Ulaymī and these are discussed by Mayer in 'A Sequel to Mujīr ad-Din's Chronicle'. In the Leiden text of this work it is stated that the earthquake occurred on the afternoon of Thursday, the tenth of Dhu 'l-Qa'da of the year written ٩٤٢ . Mayer pointed out that ٤ stood for the number 5 in medieval Arabic script, but since the year 952 was 25 years after the death of al-'Ulaymī, Mayer preferred to conclude that the year 902 was intended. Using the tables given in Freeman-Grenville, G., *The Muslim and Christian Calendars*, 1963, Mayer's 10 Dhu 'l-Qa'da 902, was found to be 11 July 1497, a Sunday. In contrast, 10 Dhu 'l-Qa'da 952, was 24 January 1545, a Thursday. The latter date corresponds to the day of the week given in the text of the Leiden manuscript.

Thus there are two possible dates for the earthquake, either Mayer's 902/1497, only fourteen solar years after the completion of the Ashrafiyya, which is still within the life time of al-'Ulaymī and is still in the Mamlūk period; or the later date 952/1545, 63 years after the completion of the Ashrafiyya, after the death of al-'Ulaymī and in the Ottoman period.

The date of 952/1545 is supported by architectural evidence gather from two sources. In the Ashrafiyya a considerable part of the fan vaulting over the porch has been rebuilt, no doubt after the earthquake that devastated this monument. However, the rebuilt stone courses are irregular and have been disguised by bands of red and yellow paint mimicking the original *ablaq* coursing. Further the decorated cruciform shaped central panel which is composed of six stone slabs was replaced with the wrong stones touching each other. There is no way of dating this rebuilding, but from the amount of effort that had to be put into this work I consider it unlikely to have been undertaken in the declining years of the Mamlūk Empire, but rather in the early years of the Ottoman Empire. Also I have discovered in the porch traces of gold leaf laid on a red bole or clay which have been painted over by red paint. This suggests that the gold had time to be eroded by wind and dust and that the red bole was thought to be the original colour, the gold leaf having been forgotten. I think it unlikely that the eroding process could have been completed in 14 years. Surely it is more likely that the gold leaf would have vanished in the 63 years between completion and 952/1545.

The second source is the Khaṣṣakī Sulṭān completed in 959/1552 for Roxelana, wife of Sulayman the Magnificent, and lying about 300 metres from the Ashrafiyya. Fortunately in 1974 before various walls were plastered I was able to photograph and identify inscribed and decorated stones that had undoubtedly been taken from the ruined Ashrafiyya and re-used. Thus we have specific evidence proving that the Ashrafiyya was being quarried in 959/1552, and I propose that the removal of stones could only have happened over a limited period of a few years, and that the Ashrafiyya could certainly not have been quarried for 60 years.

Appendix B
AN IMPERIAL MADRASA IN JERUSALEM

Shlomo Tamari published, first in Hebrew in the *Bar-Ilan Departmental Researches* I (1973) and then in English in the *Atti Della Accademia Nazionale de Lincei* (1976), his study of the Ashrafiyya in which he attempts to comprehend and explain the architecture of this ruined but still beautiful and evocative Madrasa Ashrafiyya.

He begins by providing an authoritative and exhaustive list of the many articles, and publications in Arabic, English French and German which deal in some way with the Ashrafiyya, and he goes on to list Arabic manuscripts that are relevant. Under the heading 'Construction Stages' he gives a room by room description and provides dimensions of the rooms and their window and door openings whenever possible. He continues with a chapter on the 'Stylistic Design', features associated with Sultan Qāytbāy and his architectural projects generally, and he concludes with an 'Architectural Analysis'. In both publications he uses forty plates, four drawn plans and one elevation.

Despite all the effort that Tamari has obviously given to his work and acknowledging the importance of bringing together the diverse sources, it is unfortunate that his architectural analysis of the Ashrafiyya is suspect.

My misgivings concern the number of factual errors given in his plans, some so essential to the understanding of the Ashrafiyya that they require to be precisely recorded.

In his ground floor plan two errors are immediately apparent. The first concerns the pier at the south east corner of the entrance porch, its size and shape are drawn wrongly. The second is more serious, the chamfer in the north wall is completely ignored and the same wall thickness is maintained throughout. This chamfer is important, for by bringing the wall face of the *majma'* back into the line of the *riwāq* pier, it defines the boundary between two different building phases, and it raises the question why the north face is not straight. The answer has to be that the plan and especially the east elevation of the Madrasa required the extra length the chamfer provided.

fig. App. B/1

The first error in the first floor plan is in the side wall of the Madrasa where the wall section separating the triple window and single recesses is shown as a later blocking, which it is not; and the wall thickness is drawn at approximately one metre, not the actual thickness of fifteen centimetres. The second error is that the external and the internal south faces of the *qibla* wall are drawn in line, this is incorrect since behind the *miḥrāb* a chamfered corner is used to reduce the thickness of the wall. However, the most misleading of all of the errors are the dimensions given for the Madrasa. Those I have checked and rechecked to assure myself that my measurements were accurate whilst Tamari's are inaccurate, and although almost any of the series of measurements could be chosen the two series which follow were selected from the *qibla īwān* and are juxtaposed alongside my own results.

For the *qibla* wall:

Tamari	0.80m	0.55m	1.10m	0.55m	0.80m	1.30m	1.10m	1.30m	0.40m
Walls	0.70m	0.54m	1.26m	0.54m	0.71m	1.46m	1.00m	1.45m	0.31m

For the west wall:

Tamari	0.40m	(1.30)m	1.10m	1.30m	1.10m	1.30m	0.60m
Walls	0.30m	1.44m	1.14m	1.44m	1.14m	1.44m	0.30m

In his drawing of the east elevation it is surprising that the *ablaq* courses are not emphasised as they define and underline the architectural features. In addition it is noticeable that the arch to the entrance porch is a semicircle, whereas it is in fact pointed. The most disturbing items of his restoration are those which indicate that the notion a Cairo-sized madrasa appropriate to the imperial needs of Sultan Qāytbāy has just not been understood. The crenellations are too low, they appear to be about the same level as the existing wall heads which are the result of the 1545 earthquake. The shape of the arched windows (shown by dotted lines) in no way resembles the arches of the existing windows and indeed the existing ones when viewed from the exterior have rectangular openings not arched ones. Admittedly the triple arched loggia, being the element unique to this cruciform madrasa, is more difficult to portray, but the manner in which it is drawn here makes it the same size as the other triple arcades which exist along the west and north boundaries of the Ḥaram.

One final comment on this interpretation by Tamari is necessary. Although he has not given a cross section of the Madrasa imagine what shape the great arches of the *ṣaḥn* would have had if the height from the floor to the arch zenith followed Tamari's drawings; they would have been slightly over five metres high with a span of seven metres.

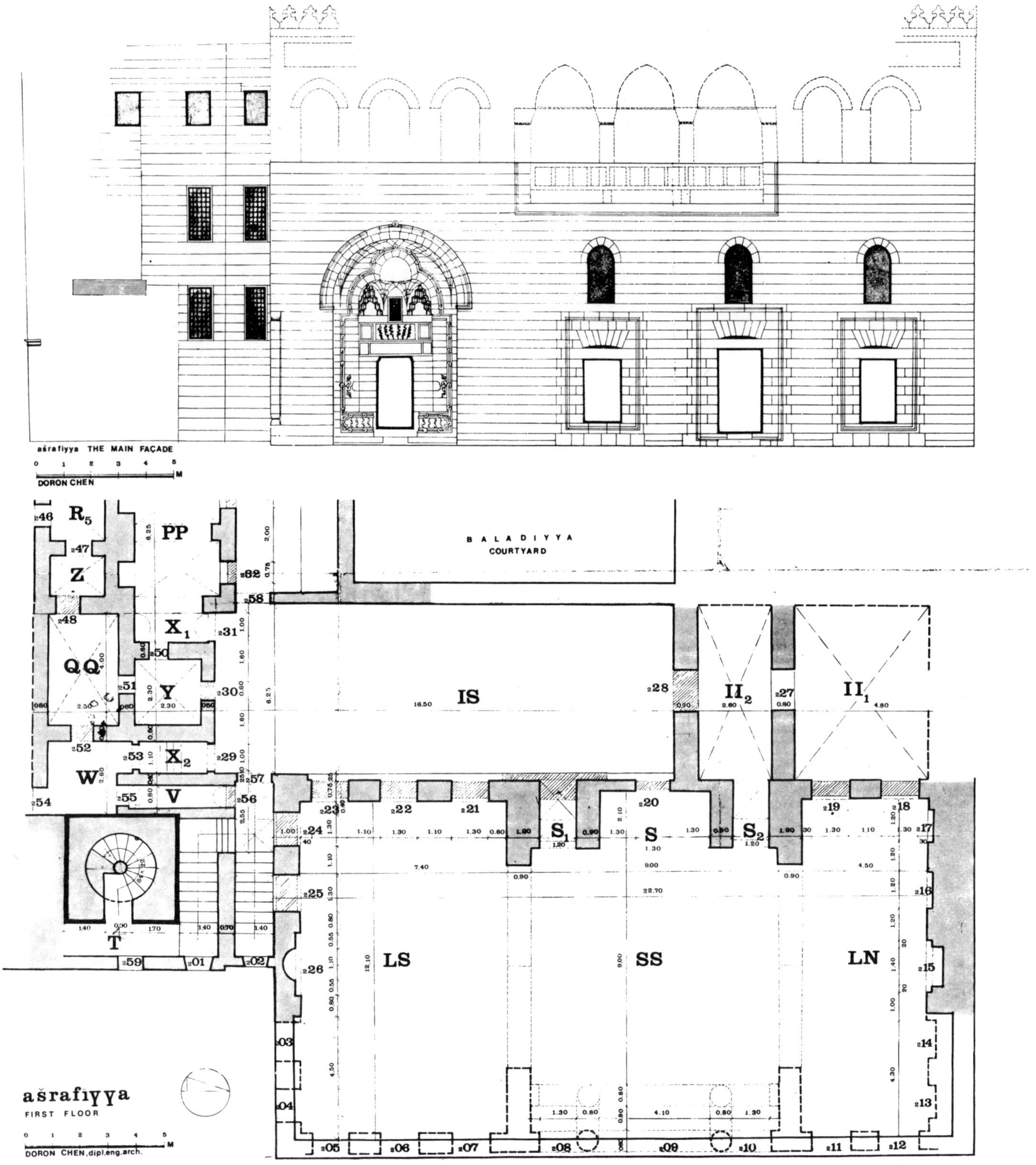

Fig. App. B/1 Tamari's reconstruction of the Ashrafiyya

Appendix C
THE MINARET OF BĀB AL-SILSILA (GATE OF THE CHAIN)

The structure of the minaret is considerably older than the Ashrafiyya and its predecessor the 'Old Madrasa'. Indeed, the site as the site of a minaret may have originated in the Umayyad period. But whatever its precise age, the minaret has generally maintained an independent existence in spite of it being incorporated into the Ashrafiyya. So this new foundation of Sultan Qāytbāy is placed in the tradition of Cairo madrasas which have their own minarets. Consequently the minaret does have an especial relationship with the Ashrafiyya and although I do not feel that its design is in anyway controlled by the same geometries as are present in the Madrasa, I do think that it was used as an anchor for these geometries.

We know the minaret was restored under Malik al-Nāṣir Muḥammad by the Amīr Tankiz in 730/1329-30[1] who had the previous year built his own Madrasa Tankiziyya[2] just outside the Gate of the Chain. Was this too an attempt to join the minaret to a madrasa, in an attempt to place the Tankiziyya within the Cairo tradition? Van Berchem considers that the main reason why the minaret and madrasa were not physically joined was out of respect for the historic sacredness of the Ḥaram and of the minaret. Three hundred years later, in 1059/1649 and 1071/1670-71, Evliya Chelebi visited Palestine. He recognised the independence of the minaret, it being neither part of the Madrasa Tankiziyya nor Madrasa Ashrafiyya but rather he saw it as being integral to the functions of the Ḥaram. He wrote:

> [The minaret of] the Madrasa Sultaniya [in other words the Ashrafiyya] at the Bāb al-Mutawaḍḍā' [Gate of the Ablution Place] is best, it has a minaret with three storeys which is one hundred and thirty feet high. The humble writer ascended it and enjoyed a complete view over the whole town . . .
>
> Besides these three [al-Ghawānima, Bāb al-Asbāṭ, Bāb al-Silsila] there are no other minarets in the Ḥaram area. Never have the mosques of al-Aqṣā and that of the Holy Rock any minarets. The Islamic call to prayer is recited from the heights of this latter minaret, as it is near the town.[3]

Today the call to prayer is still to be heard from the minaret's gallery, sadly the muezzin singing out the call from on high has been replaced by batteries of loudspeakers. Thus after many centuries the independent purpose of the minaret and its generations of muezzin have now bowed to electric equipment to provide exactly the same calling simultaneously from all of the minarets of the Ḥaram. At least we must be thankful that a muezzin is retained and that he has not been substituted by a recording.

fig. III/4, 5, 6

In the wall running between the Madrasa Ashrafiyya and the Gate of the Chain much is taken up by the base of the minaret. A straight vertical joint, approximately four metres high defines the junction between the lowest courses of the base from those of the Ashrafiyya; in fact, the stones belonging to the base prove to be quoins or corner stones and therefore are evidence of a true corner. The majority of the masonry to the north of the joint is that of Qāytbāy. There are a few exceptions showing surface textures and dressing techniques favoured in earlier periods, and these stone blocks could be reused from the demolished *riwāq* or from the Old Madrasa. Unquestionably in the slightly reused length of wall south of the porch there is a grouping of some six to eight stones: the remains of a demolished pier.

The vertical straight joint stops level with the stone course below the head of the window lighting the second landing of the grand staircase. It restarts where the long two line inscription[4] moves round it and along the upper edge for twenty centimetres before continuing its rise to about the window lighting the sixth landing; it then disappears.

To the south a pair of consoles or brackets suggest that there was a balcony or 'Jerusalem' window,[5] as the northern one occurs beside another straight joint, whose presence increases the probability of a balcony or window. Today this joint happens to be the most southerly extent of Qāytbāy's masonry. The semi-circular vault seen behind the adjacent area of rebuilding points to an Ottoman date. (This area was never inspected by me as it forms part of the complex extending to the south and over the Gate of the Chain; it is unfortunate for it is in one of the recessed windows belonging to this complex that the shield of Khushqadam inscribed on a marble or a white stone lies; see Chapter III above.) Inside the grand staircase more vertical joints can be seen associated with the base of the minaret and at the time of building the Ashrafiyya these were hidden by plaster.

fig. III/4, 13, 14

The first register of the minaret is introduced by a *cyma recta* moulded string course which acts as the sill to centrally placed ogival-headed lancet windows on the east, north and west faces. Over them, in the south, east and north, but not the west walls, are large chiselled-out circular areas which had some special purpose. When I considered them initially, I thought they might have held *ablaq* roundels similar to those seen on the minarets of the Khānaqāh Ṣalāḥiyya (820/1417) and the Mosque of Afḍal 'Alī (c. 870/1465-66),[6] but later I replaced them with the large golden cartouche of Sultan Qāytbāy, like that decorating the entrance porch. Then when I imagined the likely height of the completed Madrasa I realised that the northern circle would have been totally obscured and so I no longer looked to Qāytbāy for an answer: the circles had to be earlier. Sultan Khushqadam was the next likely candidate especially with the discovery of the small white stone with the inscribed shield of that sultan only

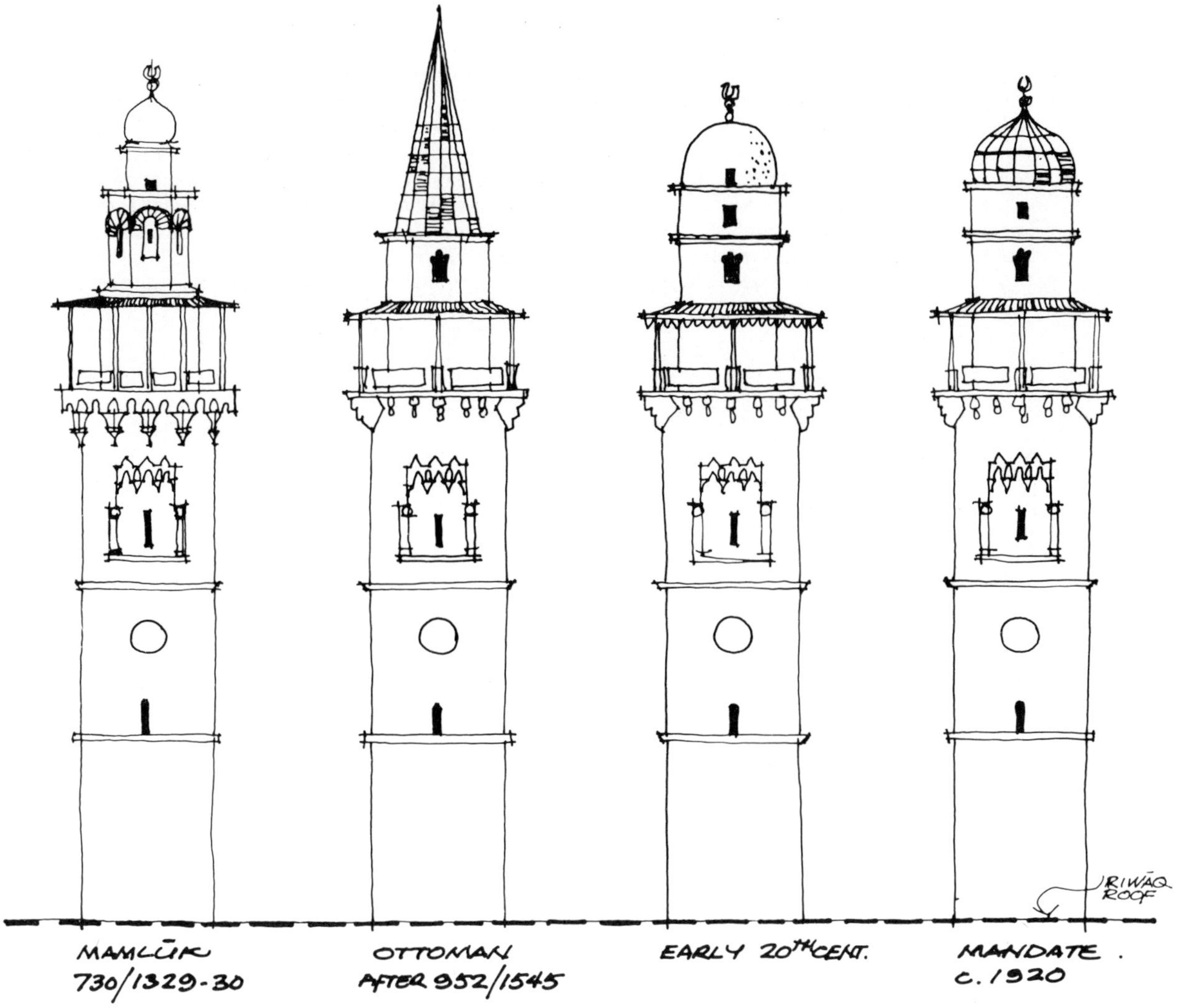

Fig. App. C/1 The Minarets of the Bāb al-Silsila

a few metres away.[7] Could not the circles on the minaret have belonged to him? The northern circle would have been visible from the courtyard of Khushqadam's madrasa (the Old Madrasa) built on the *riwāq* roof and in the shadow of the minaret. (Remember the Old Madrasa was only offered to Qāytbāy in 872/1467 after the death of Khushqadam.) The western circle would have proclaimed Khushqadam to the town and the eastern one to all those in the Ḥaram. But there is one objection to this: why were the shields of such grand proportions if, as we are led to believe, his madrasa was unimpressive?

If we can settle on Malik al-Nāṣir Muḥammad as the originator of the circular recesses during his restoration of 730/1329-30,[8] can we lay the blame for their demise on Qāytbāy? He was a man adept at finding some means of adding his name to earlier foundations and his vigilance in this matter would have demanded the removal of anyone else's heraldic device, since they would have detracted from, and certainly conflicted with, his own heroic and magnificent Ashrafiyya and its incorporation of the minaret.

The second register up the free standing shaft of the minaret begins with a *muqarnaṣ*-type string course, which is badly eroded on its north face. In each of the four faces of the minaret are recessed windows flanked by a variety of re-used Crusader marble columns and capitals. At the centres of the recesses are lancet windows with chamfered external reveals. The recess heads are decorated with curvilinear *muqarnaṣ*. There seem to be two varieties, one for the north and south faces and another for the east and west. At about this level the stonework changes in character, it becomes patchy, and the horizontal joints are dislocated and irregular. In these dislocated masonry areas there are one or two stone blocks with *muqarnaṣ* decoration and they may indicate that the gallery was corbelled out on *muqarnaṣ*, and not the inelegant and ugly consoles of the present gallery.

In the *Dhayl* of al-'Ulaymī it is noted the minaret was damaged by the 952/1545 earthquake[9] and from the architectural evidence it appears that the damage was restricted to the gallery and the upper registers above it. The existing gallery is Ottoman and it appears in early photographs taken in the 1880s.[10] I was only able on one occasion to climb up to the gallery and so I cannot be definite about the detailed chronology of the square shaft above the gallery, nor of the ultimate octagonal register with its blind trifoliate-headed windows. However, it is doubtful that the octagonal shaft dates from the Mamlūk period if the other accredited Mamlūk minarets in Jerusalem are looked at. The minaret of al-Ghawānima (c. 707/1307-08) has a square shaft[11] at the centre of its gallery, as do the pair of minarets belonging to the Khānaqāh Sallāmiyya 820/1417 and the Mosque of Afḍal 'Alī 870/1465-66 which appear to guard the Church of the Holy Sepulchre.

fig. App. C/1 Of course there is the contemporary drawing of Edward Reuwich of Utrecht which attains an uncommonly high standard of accuracy. From it the proportions of the minaret of the Gate of the Chain can be considered alongside the known proportions of the minarets either side of the church, and which are seen in sufficient detail to show that the octagonal shafts at the galleries rise up above the awnings, just as they do today. Notwithstanding these similarities, it is likely that on account of its size the construction of the gallery of the Gate of the Chain Minaret would have followed the pattern of al-Ghawānima rather than those of the smaller paired minarets.

Positive photographic proof exists to show that the present circular register and the lead covered dome must be 'early British Mandate' for Creswell photographed the minaret with a stone dome which along with its circular base replaced the Ottoman 'witch's hat' sometime after 1880.[12]

From the above it is possible to reproduce the four terminals that have adorned this minaret for six hundred years.

Notes

1. See van Berchem, *CIA 'Ḥaram'*, pp. 123-27, inscription No. 175.
2. See van Berchem, *CIA 'Ville'*, pp. 252-61, inscription No. 80, and Walls and Abul-Hajj, *Arabic Inscriptions in Jerusalem*.
3. Stephen, St. H., 'Evila Tschelebi's Travels in Palestine, VI', *Quarterly of the Department of Antiquities in Palestine*, vol. IX, 1942, p. 100; the text in the square brackets was added by Stephen.
4. The inscription commemorates the restoration of the minaret by the Amīr Tankiz under Malik Nāṣir Muḥammad in 730/1329-30, see van Berchem, *CIA 'Ḥaram'*, pp. 123-27, inscription No. 175.
5. For an example of this type of window supported by consoles, two or three stones courses high, see Walls, A. G., 'The Turbat Barakat Khan', *Levant* VI, 1974, pls. XV, A and B.
6. See Walls, A G, 'Two Minarets Flanking the Church of the Holy Sepulchre', *Levant* VIII, 1976, pp. 159-161, pls. XX A and B, also *Mamlūk Jerusalem*, pp. 517-518 and 568-569.
7. The significance of this inscribed white stone is discussed in Chapter III above, it was brought to my notice by M. H. Burgoyne sometime in 1973.
8. L. A. Mayer, *Saracenic Heraldry: A Survey*, Oxford, 1933, pp. 34-36. Referring to inscribed circular shields divided into three fields, Mayer states that, 'The first datable examples . . . are attributable to the later Baḥri Mamlūk sultans like Muḥammad, the son . . . of Qalāūn . . .'

   (a) *Muḥammad*
   (b) *'izz li-maulānā al-sulṭān al-malik al-nāṣir*
   (c) ornament

   Later Mayer informs us that, 'The fact that the three-field inscribed shield had originally only one, a middle line of text, to which at a later stage the first line containing the name was added, shows without need of further explanation that these rows of text must be read in the order b, a, c, and why they must be so read in most cases.'
9. See Appendix A, n. 5
10. My thanks are due to Dr K. Kessler for the reference to Wilson, Ch. W., *Jerusalem the Holy City*, 1889, pl. on p. 53. See also *Mamlūk Jerusalem*, pl. 63.13 after A. Salzmann (1854).
11. See *Mamlūk Jerusalem*, Ghawānima Minaret, pl. 10.1.
12. This photograph is reproduced in *Mamlūk Jerusalem*, pl. 63.14.

GLOSSARY

Ablaq: polychrome stonework generally alternating red and white, although occasionally black stone is used.

Bāb: gate.

BUG: basic unit of generation, 14.40m.

Ḥaram: a sanctuary or inviolable area.

Īwān: each of the four divisions of a cruciform mosque or *madrasa* surrounding the *ṣaḥn*.

Kufi: a square and often elaborately decorated Arabic script.

Kufesque: a word coined by the American numismatist George Miles as a synonym for pseudo-kufic.

Madrasa: a theological school or college teaching the Qur'ān, exegesis, the Traditions and canon law.

Mamlūks: literally 'owned'. Two dynasties of manumitted slaves reigning in Egypt and Syria from 1250-1517.

Majma': meeting hall for sufis.

Miḥrāb: niche indicating the *qibla* or direction to Mecca in a place of prayer.

Muqarnaṣ: an architectural element sometimes described as stalactites.

Qibla: the direction to Mecca to which a Muslim should turn when praying.

Riwāq: an arcaded ambulatory along the west and north sides of the Ḥaram.

Ṣaḥn: central court of a mosque or madrasa.

Sufi: member of mystical or ascetic order in Islam.

Tārima: a pavilion belvedere or loggia.

Waqf: land or other property endowed in perpetuity for the benefit of a pious foundation.

Waqfiyya: the signed legal document constituting a pious foundation which specifies the physical boundaries and the endowments of the foundation.

INDEX

Edward R. Hamilton
mail order ~ 12 Nov 1997
$7.95 + .30 post. & hand.